AROUND THE WORLD IN 80 TREASURES

DAN CRUICKSHANK

AROUND THE WORLD IN 80 TREASURES

DAN CRUICKSHANK

To Chris & Anne

Best Wishes

Dan Cruickshank

WEIDENFELD & NICOLSON

CONTENTS

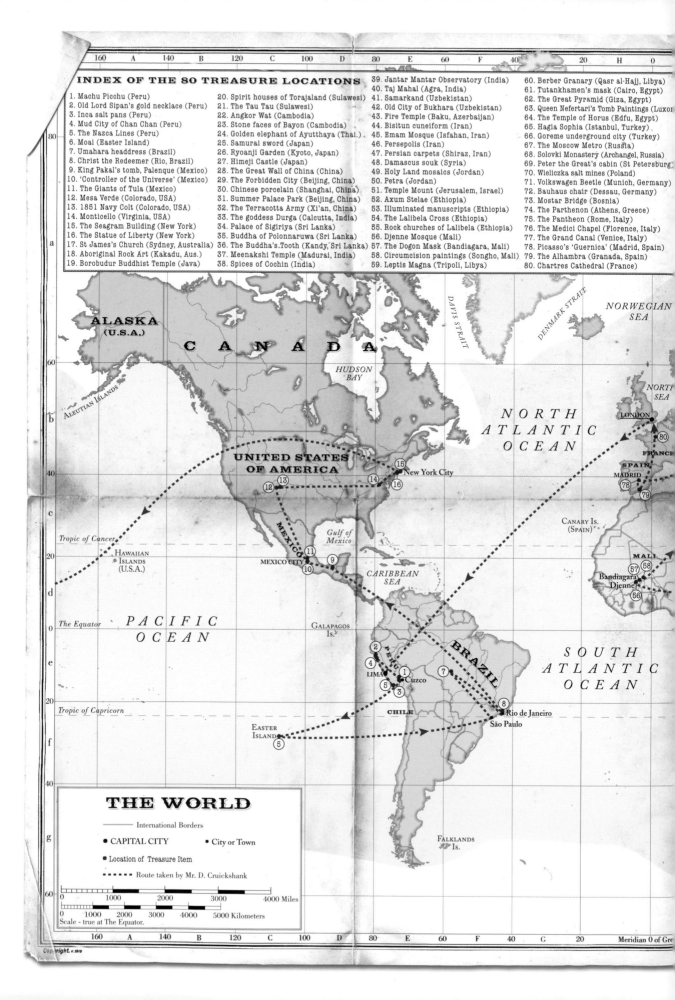

THE WORLD

—— International Borders

● CAPITAL CITY   ● City or Town

■ Location of Treasure Item

---- Route taken by Mr. D. Cruickshank

0 1000 2000 3000 4000 Miles

0 1000 2000 3000 4000 5000 Kilometers

Scale - true at The Equator.

Copyright

INTRODUCTION

As I write this introduction, a thrilling but far from certain future stretches before me. I am about to leave Britain on a quest that will take me around the world – to 40 countries! The aim of this journey – planned to last five months – is the production of a series of 10 television programmes for the BBC that will tell the story of civilisation through 80 man-made treasures – sacred and profane – ranging from exquisite individual objects to vast temples and cities. Some of the treasures will be familiar, others obscure, forgotten and under threat. All will help define human history, aspirations and endeavours. Each treasure must play its part in the telling of this story. So this book, and the television series it accompanies, is a quest. A journey of discovery to reveal the world that man has made.

The scale of the project and the speed with which it is undertaken must be unprecedented in BBC history. The first programme is to be broadcast in early 2005, and the book must be published by the same date. So this can be no conventional book. I do not have time to return, rest, read through my notes and then compose an elegant and considered account of the journey. I will have to write the book as I go along, then email the text and my digital photographs back to London whenever I reach a hotel with appropriate technology. The book will therefore be a journal, giving an account of events as and when they happen.

Britain has been excluded from this journey – its treasures are too well known – instead I plan to visit some of the most remote and politically volatile places on earth, including Afghanistan, a country I last visited just after the fall of the Taliban regime. I fear, though, that it will not be possible to return to Iraq, to visit the old Sumerian cities of Mesopotamia, Ur and Uruk, where technological civilisation – writing, the wheel, mathematics, planned urban communities – had its origin.

The world is daily becoming a more unsettling place. I am travelling with five other people – a team put together by the BBC – to remote and even dangerous regions, with the team swollen from time to time by the addition of translators, security personnel, fixers and extra equipment, raising its own logistical, and almost moral, problems. What will happen if one member of the team falls ill? Will the whole journey have to halt? A problem since speed is critical – we have deadlines and appointments to meet, and a budget. This is something of a worry. Of the old team with which I went to Afghanistan and Iraq I now only have Nick Reeks with me – the soundman and a tried and tested friend and colleague. The rest of my companions are new acquaintances, like production co-ordinator and second camera Tim Sutton, or old friends – Tim Dunn who is producer and director and Andrea Illescas, the researcher and assistant director – with whom I have only worked in the relative peace and tranquillity of Europe. The cameraman, Lee Curran, I have met only briefly, but Mike Garner – a cameraman standing by in England if needed – is a colleague, as is Jonty Claypole, the stand-by director. But we have all now successfully completed six-day courses designed for people who plan to work in hostile environments. These courses are packed with vital information, especially about first aid, but they are also tough, demanding and not a little frightening. All this will, I'm sure, have strengthened the resolve of the team and given it the necessary self-confidence and skill to confront and master the dangers we could face.

Opposite title page The colonnade in the Court of the Fountain of the Lions at Alhambra, Granada, Spain. Contents pages from left Inca salt pans, Peru; Moai of Easter Island; Mesa Verde, Colorado, USA; Djenne Mosque, Mali; Borobudur Buddhist Temple, Java; Persepolis, Iran; Leptis Magna, Libya; Palace of Sigiriya, Sri Lanka.

Sunday 20 June 2004 – The beginning

At last we are on our way to Lima, Peru. The journey will start with the great civilisation of the Incas and then look at some of the fascinating but lesser known cultures and peoples of South America. We will look at some of the world's most awe-inspiring and mysterious treasures. It will be the story of man's relationship with the natural world and with the cosmos.

We had an early start – meeting at Heathrow at 3.00 am – and then we had to enter into lengthy negotiations to get our heavy luggage accepted by the airline, which eventually charged a hefty excess baggage fee of £2500. A bit of a blow this. We have to board well over 70 flights and simply cannot afford the time, money and anxiety our baggage appears to demand. Perhaps we've just had an unfortunate start and other airlines will not be so demanding. We'll have to wait and see and come up with a radical plan if necessary. At least now the waiting is over. I've done the journey many times in my mind during the last few months, trying to work out what the problems will be – to anticipate them and avoid them. I've researched and written about the treasures we plan to see and now places like Persepolis and Machu Picchu inhabit my imagination. Very soon I will confront them in person. What will be the result of this continual collision between informed fantasy and stark reality? The oddest thing perhaps at this stage is the realisation that I am undertaking a journey that will change my life. For better or worse, I won't be the same man when I return. I will have seen more places, more great treasures, and met more people in five months than most people see and meet in a lifetime. It will be exhausting – mentally and physically – but incredibly stimulating. What happens when someone keeps going on adrenalin for months on end? I'll find out. What concerns me now is that I will become addicted to this hectic way of life. The extraordinary will become the ordinary while the ordinary will become intolerable. How will I settle back into ordinary life when I return? Will I want to return? This could turn out to be escapism of a very high and sustained order. It worries me more than a little. What I discover may be myself just as much as the great man-made treasures of the world. And I may want to change what I find. I may be forced to change. We will see.

By way of launching my journey I went to see a map of the world now housed in the British Museum. This is a map with a difference – it is tiny and one of the earliest manifestations of man's grasp of the larger world in which he lives. It dates from around 700 BC and was probably made in Sippar, in what is now southern Iraq but was then ancient Mesopotamia, the cradle of civilisation, and part of the Babylonian Empire. This map shows us the world as perceived by Nebuchadnezzar and the Jews he held captive in around 600 BC. Babylon is shown in the centre of the world with the region of Mesopotamia ringed by a circle labeled 'salt sea' with, beyond, the rest of the world – my destination.

One of the first maps of the world now housed in the British Museum. In cuneiform it shows the Babylonian world c.700 BC.

MYSTIC AMERICA

1 MACHU PICCHU, PERU

Monday 21 June

The railway is narrow gauge, diesel powered, and winds gradually up towards the looming peaks, through narrow valleys, hand-hewn passes and tunnels blasted through the mountains. One of the tunnel arches is emblazoned with the date 1928, so the railway arrived soon after Machu Picchu was rediscovered by the West in 1911 in the person of American archaeologist Hiram Bingham. From the start the potential of the place – cultural and commercial – has been fully realised. Machu Picchu is calculated to fulfil dreams and fantasies – a lost sacred city, perched high in the Andes, remote, well-built and harmoniously planned – an abode of the gods, a Shangri-La. It has an appeal that cannot be denied, a fantastic pulling power.

But, like so many of the world's great archaeological sites, Machu Picchu is on the edge of becoming a victim of its own appeal and power, of being killed by the crowds who flock to see it. The unbroken lines of visitors converging on this Inca mountain retreat make it only too clear that this is now primarily a tourist destination, one of the most popular in the world, rather than the destination of one's imagination. Its setting is still beautiful, but remote and secluded it is not. Somwhat ominously, the train on which I travel is packed with tourists, the carriages buzzing with the languages of the world. Human beings take on a certain persona when they become a tourist – determined, grim, humourless, aggressive, rude, and apparently miserable. I wonder if the magic of the place has been lost, if it will be possible to connect with what was, to contemplate the nature of the people who created this place and to experience the drama of the setting as they would have experienced it. I file up the last quarter of a mile, puffing through the thin atmosphere at 2350 metres above sea level, full of trepidation.

Machu Picchu is shrouded in mystery. Not only was it forgotten by all but local people for nearly 400 years, nobody is quite sure what its precise function was or exactly when or why it was abandoned.

What is agreed is that Machu Picchu was constructed by the Inca in the late 15th century during the golden age of their empire, and that it was not discovered by the Spaniards after they had crushed the Inca armies in the 1530s. The mystery now – for me – is what will I discover in the place? Will it be an arid, over-restored museum city or will Inca power still resonate?

I reach the top of the path, turn a corner and suddenly get my first view. There are the ruins, nestling on a natural shelf – extended by Inca engineering – between a series of peaks. The ruins are manicured, and the terraces form a geometrical kaleidoscope to reveal the Inca's skill at making the most of the little land available for housing and agriculture. No, the journey has not been in vain.

As I look down on the ruins I can read the place – it's a diagram of Inca urban ideals. It is stone-built and orderly but subtly integrated into the landscape, poised on its plateau and aligned between the snow-clad peaks that the Inca held to be sacred. Far below, winding in a lazy U-shape around the mountain on which Machu Picchu nestles, is the Urubamba – the river sacred to the Inca. And the highest point within Machu Picchu is very clearly occupied by a temple, the altar of which is visible and carved from the peak of the mountain on which the temple stands! This is clearly no ordinary city.

Entering the city remains a moving experience – akin to walking through the streets of Pompeii. Terraces of housing are linked by steep steps – many treads cut into the rock

I catch my first glimpse of Machu Picchu, sacred city of the Inca, high in the mountains of Peru. Tourists stream through the ruins, but they are breathtaking.

Left *Looking down I can see the residential zones of Machu Picchu rising up to the perimeters of the city, which is thought to have housed as many as 1000 people in its heyday.*
Right *Everywhere I see examples of superb 15th-century Inca stonework. Precisely crafted with no mortar, these walls were built to resist earthquakes.*

on which the city sits – and the houses are virtually intact but for their timber and thatched roofs. I enter one single-room house and it is easy to see how the Inca lived here 500 years ago. They used little furniture and into the thick stone walls are niches – acting as cupboards – to store a few household goods. There is no fireplace for heating or cooking but, probably, a communal kitchen for each street. Water was brought from adjoining high land and channelled through the city to feed fountains and stone tanks and then used to flush out the drainage system. This sophisticated water system – along with Inca masonry construction and a road network consisting of thousands of miles of trails that by 1500 linked the vast empire of 12 million people – is Roman in its quality and scale.

But the architectural glories of Machu Picchu are its temples. The Temple of the Sun is a truly extraordinary structure. It is a single-storey, open-roofed building that sits on a rocky outcrop. In its western wall is a tapering rectangular window that at dawn on the winter solstice allows a ray of sunlight to fall across an altar, cut from the rock on which the temple stands. The wall wrapped around the altar is curved, like an uncoiling spiral, but perhaps most impressive is the manner of the construction. The walls are made of blocks of hard stone, each hammered into perfect rectangles with edges so straight that joints between the blocks are infinitesimal. This would have taken much skill and effort. But that's the point – the temple, in its laborious construction as well as in its design and arrangement, was an act of homage to the Sun.

I climb to the temple on the highest peak within the city. Its central altar is carved from the mountain peak itself. As I stand contemplating this strangely formed stone a rainbow suddenly appears, arching from one side of Machu Picchu to the other – in fact, one end disappearing into the ground on the very terrace from which I gained my first view of the city a few hours before. For the Inca the rainbow – a fusion of sunlight and water that forms in the air and sweeps to earth – was very special. They saw it as the son of the Sun and a personification of the divine Inca king. For a moment I think I can see things from this temple through the eyes of the Inca. Many religions hold stones as sacred. For them this altar was the Axis Mundi – the axis around which the world turned – the very centre of their universe.

Tuesday 22 June

We spend the night at a remote hotel perched on the banks of the Urubamba at Huaran, within the Sacred Valley of the Incas. The focus of the day is flight, by paraglider, and my target the Sacred Valley. Being a novice to this exciting sport I am to be the passenger of an experienced 'pilot'. Richard Pethigal is a laid-back, LA beach boy who has decided to surf the thermals rather than the waves. But a skein of small scars across his face brings vividly to mind the perils of a botched take-off or a bad landing.

We ascend to 3800 metres, I am squeezed into a harness, told the principles of a good take-off and then shackled to Richard. All I have to remember are three instructions – 'run', 'stop' and 'sit'.

Then a brief ritual. To deal with high altitude, to get your blood loaded with oxygen and to help it circulate readily around the body, the locals chew coca leaves. These leaves are the basic ingredients of cocaine and they are a controlled drug in most countries, but not Peru. Here they are part of the high Andes culture and so easily available and much used. Richard suggests we scatter a few leaves as an offering to the wind god and then chew the rest. At this point, I feel I need all the support I can get. I whisper a few prayers and stuff a handful of leaves into my mouth and start chewing. They taste pretty awful, well, just like chewing leaves really. To delay the frightful moment I cheerily ask Richard if there are legends about Inca flying. He says yes, and tells me a brief tale that goes straight out of my head about condors and how the majestic bird still cruises over the Sacred Valley.

Suddenly I feel my spirits rise. I will see the Sacred Valley through the eyes of the Inca's sacred bird – I will be the condor. 'I am the condor' is my battle cry as we thunder to the mountain's edge. But I discover that my body has a mind of its own. It simply thinks no, when it perceives I am hurtling to a mountain's edge. My body shuts down and refuses to jump. Richard almost catapults over me, and we end in a frightful heap, draped in the shrouds of the collapsed parachute and its ropes and tottering on the edge of oblivion. I don't want to think about what would have happened had the whole event taken place a few yards further forward. 'My worst take-off ever,' Richard mutters good humouredly.

My battle cry the next time is 'Run, run, run…' And I do. My will overrides my body and I am airborne, feet pounding in space. We glide, we spin, we find a thermal and shoot up, we level out – and I am over the Sacred Valley. I am the condor. I see the Inca-made landscape – trails, fields, towns and terraces – as they dreamt to see it. We touch down, then collapse and I skid along on my bottom. 'Great,' says Richard. 'Well done. Were you nervous?' I shrug, and smile weakly. God, what liars we are. A great experience? Yes. To be repeated? Not in a hurry.

Then we fly on to Lima. Another flight. At the airport Paul Cripps, our fixer, presents

A closer view of the residential zone at Machu Picchu showing rows of small houses running along the stepped terraces. Niches in the walls stored household goods.

me with a farewell present – a freshly baked guinea pig, a Peruvian delicacy and a favoured food of the Inca. It looks like a cooked rat – its face burnt into a grimace. I taste it – not bad at all. Rich, gamey, a bit like rabbit. I notice my colleagues recoiling in disgust and, more alarming, fellow passengers backing away. Never mind. I munch on. Not every day do you chew coca in the morning and dine on guinea pig in the afternoon.

We fly to Chiclaya in the coastal Lambayeque Valley. We are here to see gold from the 1st century AD royal tombs of once-powerful warrior princes – the Lords of Sipan. Low mountains appear and, in front of them, a pair of mighty gnarled hummocks that look organic, almost natural, but not quite. They are the two great flat-topped pyramids at Sipan.

2 GOLD NECKLACE OF THE OLD LORD OF SIPAN

Wednesday 23 June

For me these pyramids and tombs are haunting. They remind me of the larger and far older stepped pyramids or ziggurats of Mesopotamia, created between 6000 and 2600 years ago by the Sumerian and Assyrian empires. Like those in Mesopotamia – now known as Iraq – these at Sipan have cores constructed of sun-dried clay brick, here called adobe. As I approach the Sipan pyramids local children appear. They want to sell me postcards and trinkets. But they are not aggressive, rather charming, smiling and delighted to see us there. They have powerful, strong-featured handsome faces – one young girl being particularly striking. Looking into their eyes was to look into the eyes of the once all-powerful Moche people – the rulers of this land who disappeared in mysterious circumstances around 1200 years ago.

The site in Peru of the tombs of the great pre-Inca warrior princes, the Lords of Sipan. In ancient religions high lands were considered the domains of the gods, and the pyramids were man's sacred offerings to their deities.

The tombs tell a vivid and recent story – a story of looting organised on an almost industrial scale and the sordid story of the voracious appetite of the international black market for stolen pre-Columbian art. In fact Lord Sipan's tomb, which dates from around AD 300, was only discovered in 1987 when the archaeological authorities in Lima noticed a number of high quality artefacts suddenly flooding onto the black market. The source was discovered and gun-fights took place between police, looters and

poor local villagers who believe the wealth buried in their homeland to be their birthright. An extraordinary Peruvian archaeologist – Walter Alva – realised that gun battles were not the way forward. He set about winning the hearts and minds of the locals by explaining the historic and cultural importance of the finds. The tombs were, he stressed, worth more preserved, as a focus for tourism that would fuel the local economy. This policy seems to have worked. A good amount of looted treasure was returned or reclaimed and during Alva's exploration of the looted site Lord Sipan's spectacular tomb was unearthed. This contained the body of the lord, flanked by seven other people, a dog and a llama. All appear to have been killed – sacrificed – after the death of the lord. But astonishing to the archaeologists who made the discovery were the quantity and quality of the artefacts placed in the tomb. There were hundreds of clay pots and daily and ornamental artefacts – including armour and weapons – made of solid gold

One of the richest mausoleums to be discovered in the Americas, the treasure in the tomb of the Lord of Sipan contained the bodies of seven sacrificed companions as well as exquisitely wrought solid gold, silver and gilded copper jewellery and artefacts.

and copper coated with gold. These are treasures that are not only intrinsically beautiful and valuable but also tell so much about the beliefs and customs of the mysterious Moche culture. What was immediately obvious was that they had a strong belief in an afterlife – that you could take your power, prestige and possessions with you, not only objects but people, or at least the power those people represented. Also confirmed was the Moche use of the ritual of human sacrifice. Evidence suggests the poor wretches were bound, decapitated, arms and feet cut off or – alternatively – their throats cut to provide a gory feast for the triumphant Moche. These rituals are not only suggested by archaeological discoveries but – more convincingly and chillingly – by the Moche's own beautiful art and artefacts. Soon further tombs were discovered within the mausoleum, including what, for me, is the most spectacular of all – what is now called the tomb of the Old Lord of Sipan, that dates from around AD 100. Together these are, arguably, the most important ancient tombs found intact since that of Tutankhamen in Egypt and are certainly the richest mausoleum found in the Americas. To see these objects I go to a new museum in Lambeyeque entitled the Museum of the Royal Tombs of Sipan.

One of these treasures is a necklace formed by ten large, bulging golden discs, each about 5 centimetres in diameter. Each disc shows a spider, in the form of a fierce-visaged decapitated human head, sitting on a golden web. This is the image of the spider god who was a god of healing – the spider's web possesses properties to staunch bleeding – but also a god of human sacrifice. The Old Lord's tomb also contained a crab god that seems to have been the deity of decapitation and an octopus god whose eight encircling tentacles may show how the Moche bound their victims before dismembering them.

All this suggests that the Moche believed they could assume the power of their enemies by devouring their blood, mutilating their bodies and – in particular – by removing their heads in a specific, ritualistic manner. I must say, as the museum emptied and I found myself alone in the darkened upper gallery with these beautiful but deeply sinister objects, I had a most unpleasant feeling. These things are worrying – disturbing, but also provoking. They speak of a lack of restraint, a crumbling of boundaries when it comes to the satisfaction of dark desires.

The erotic ceramics, for which the Moche are famous and which command such a high price on the black market, complete the picture – a culture seemingly dedicated to violence and sex. As I view the collection I am alone apart from an occasional stalwart tourist making their discomfort apparent by the tone and content of their somewhat strangled jocular remarks. Yes, these pots do have the power to shock and the Moche people are communicating a message to us, across the centuries, of sex and violence. Our society is just as cruel – but in a subtle and dishonest way. The Moche expressed their passions, we just dissemble.

The solid gold necklace of the Old Lord of Sipan is made of ten discs showing an image of the spider god, a god of healing but also of human sacrifice. Though the Moche were artistically advanced, they were also chillingly savage.

By way of contrast – to escape the memory of the steely gaze of the lord – we take ourselves off to taste some Peruvian food that carries with it a taste of the old civilisations of the region. For all the old coastal cultures, the fruits of the sea were as important as the fruits of agriculture – both were gifts that could be won from the gods through skill and devotion. So fish is almost a sacred dish – like wafer and communion wine. Most famous are delicate, sole-like white fish called tiradito and ceviche. We were served tiradito – sliced thin, marinated in lime and hardly warmed – a kind of sushi really, that melts in the mouth and is delicious. Then to follow – not quite so subtle – fried goat and yucca, duck with peas and coriander rice and beans cooked in pork juice. Then, a four-hour drive and we arrive at the urban oasis of Trujillo, second city of Peru. We meet in the bar to discuss lessons to learn and apply.

3 INCA SALT PANS

Thursday 24 June

We arrive at our next destination – the Inca salt pans near the village of Maras. In a small valley tier upon tier of basins – about 3000 of them – rise up the Qaqwray mountain to create a weird cubist landscape with the edges and sides of each stone-built basin crusted white, strongly defined with dried salt. The Inca discovered that a stream running out of the bowels of a nearby mountain contains a high level of salt. The river runs at a high level and was directed to cascade down the pans, filling one after the other. When filled, the pan was dammed and the water left to evaporate in the sun so that only salt was left behind. This salt works is still in use today. Looking down at the salt pans, rising in neat terraces far below me, I grasp the extraordinary nature of the Inca empire. We take salt for granted now, but humble salt is one of the cornerstones of civilisation. When man is released from the constant battle for survival – for the quest for food – he gains leisure to develop the arts, architecture and all those things we perceive as the hallmarks of civilisation. To achieve plenty it is necessary not only to grow adequate supplies of food but also to store it when the season of harvest is over or against bad years. Salt was one of

The Inca were the first to develop these amazing salt pans which are still in use today.

the answers – it not only sustains the body but preserves meat and fish, allowing a population to ride out the ups and downs of nature.

The Inca concern for the preservation of food is suggested by another site nearby. At a place called Mori are curving terraces – including a huge terraced circle like an amphitheatre – cut within a shallow valley. Some think the terraces enjoyed a microclimate that allowed the Inca to experiment with the ideal conditions for the growth of various crops within their large empire. Others, including the local people, believe that the terraces were used for freeze-drying potatoes – a surprisingly modern activity that the Inca achieved, so the champions of this theory argue, by the balance of cold nights with hot days. If correct this is yet further evidence of the highly advanced civilisation of the Inca. Freeze-drying meant preservation – so that bumper crops of potatoes could be retained in edible condition during the cold winter months.

4 THE MUD CITY OF CHAN CHAN

Then on to a very different place – Chan Chan, the great city of the Chimu people, on the coast 5 kilometres from Trujillo. This is the largest mud-built or adobe city in the world – indeed, when in its prime in about 1400, Chan Chan was huge, covering nearly 20 square kilometres and with a population of up to 100,000 people. It attracted people from surrounding valleys and – in certain ways – was a pioneer in the modern phenomenon of urban life. But it's not just the scale of Chan Chan or its material of construction that makes it so fascinating – it's also the design of its buildings, its plan, urban organisation and functions.

There were no other cities like this. It was divided into ten massive citadels each covering the equivalent of 26 football fields (142,000 square metres), each defined by tall walls up to 10 metres high, built with hard abobe brick. So essentially Chan Chan was a series of individual but adjoining walled towns, with each citadel containing its own mix of temples, public buildings, palaces and modest housing. Within each were even canchones – fields in which intensive agriculture was pursued and in which the soil level had been lowered to reach groundwater so as to create what were effectively paddy fields in a potentially barren land.

The thick mud walls around the citadels and of the individual houses within each citadel had a fascinating series of functions. They were, it seems, not so much defensive, or even to define territory, but primarily intended to control the sand, protect against wind and to act as solar collectors, insulating in the day and releasing the heat collected at night.

The founder of the Chimu Dynasty was, according to myth and legend, Tancanaymo. The tradition is that he arrived on the coast of the region by small boat, was clad in

The ruins of Chan Chan, the world's largest mud-built city which fell to the Inca around 1460. I am impressed by the sophisticated method of construction and the thoughtful urban design, both ideally suited to the climate and conditions.

cotton and possessed a yellow powder that he used in various magic ceremonies. He was greeted with respect and devotion by the natives because all that came from the sea was sacred and divine – a popular conception that was to repeatedly prove fatal to South American empires as waves of European conquistadores were welcomed, or at least initially tolerated, as they arrived by sea. Indeed the sea was the driving force in Chimu life. They venerated it – along with the Sun, and fresh water, as the givers of life. They saw water as a great creative force – from the sea came fish and from fresh water the fruits were won through irrigation and agriculture. Indeed, the Chimu became agricultural experts and were the only ancient American culture that depended so heavily on irrigation.

The importance of water is everywhere apparent in Chan Chan, particularly in the processional corridor leading from the great square of the city to the temples near the coast. In this corridor the walls are decorated with moulded mud images of fish, fish-eating pelicans, large stylised fishing nets and horizontal banding representing the deity of water. Although of similar date to the Moche, the Chimu people couldn't have been more different. They venerated the benign creative forces of nature rather than the dark precedents found in nature to justify human cruelty. The Moche looked to the sea and saw crabs with vicious claws that cut their prey to pieces and octopus that enveloped and crushed with their tentacles. The Chimu looked to the sea and saw its bounty and the life-giving force of nature.

Setting out to see my fifth treasure, the Nazca Lines, in the Peruvian desert, an hour's flight from Lima.

Wandering around the ruins of this great city is an uplifting experience, with an atmosphere so different from that of Sipan. All the team feel the difference. And we keep finding fascinating details. In one citadel virtually all the buildings have walls in the form

of large-scale fishing nets, perforated to allow air to flow into, and through, the buildings. An elegant system of cross ventilation well calculated to deal with the hot summer months.

The social structure of the Chimus was, like their capital, fascinating. There was a strict class system and they believed that nobility and commoners had been created separately – the nobility from one pair of stars, and commoners from another pair. By the 1450s the Chimus ruled over 60,000 people and commanded nearly 1000 square kilometres of terrain. Then in about 1460 Chan Chan fell to the Inca empire which, in its usual manner with defeated rivals, systematically dismantled it. Now the battle is on to save what remains and the main enemy is the elemental El Niño – as a recurring cycle of exceptionally heavy regional storms, the lethal enemy of all mud building, threatens what is left.

5 THE NAZCA LINES

Friday 25 June

Today we plan to fly south from Lima to view the famed Nazca Lines – massive images marked out in the Pampas Colorades between 1900 and 1400 years ago by the enigmatic Nazca people. These images, some of creatures, others of geometric forms measuring up to 280 metres in size, can be seen only from the air. Unless the Nazca could fly, they would never have seen their works – but I suppose they were made for their all-seeing gods, not for man. Not being divine, we have had to charter two small planes from Nazca airport to fly us over the lines but, as is the way with human affairs, fog hovers over Nazca on the day we plan to fly and we are now waiting patiently at Lima airport for the sun to burn off the fog so we can land in Nazca.

Two hours later we squeeze into the twin-engined, propeller-driven Beechmaster and take off into a thick veil of cloud, which turns out to be fishy-smelling Lima pollution. At cruising height we quickly break through into bright sun and blue sky. An hour later we land at Nazca airport – a quaint place with thatch roofed airport buildings but a very efficient and snappily dressed staff. This is all down to Bobby who greets us as we land. Bobby would be almost too gay for LA, let alone Nazca. He wears an incredibly smart pilot's uniform of Aero Condor Airlines with sharp creases where tradition demands and a discreet display of flyer's jewellery – wings and rank badges in tasteful old gold.

A view which for centuries was the preserve of the gods. From the window of the plane I can see the amazing Nazca Lines – carefully crafted giant images of birds, animals and geometric forms etched into the Pampas thousands of years ago – which can only be seen from above.

Elegantly attired and pretty Nazca girls with clipboards stride around checking things while, posted in a sentry box by the Pan-American Highway that skirts the dusty drome, is a young lady dressed in tight uniform jacket, mini-skirt and thigh-high leather boots. She is a sight to see – a hallucination in the barren landscape and no doubt a constant joy for the truckers who thunder along the highway. It's as if we have flown into a scene from 'Priscilla, Queen of the Desert'. We decide to first experience the lines from the ground, load into buses and head off into the desert landscape, along the straight-as-a-die Pan-Am Highway, cut through the Nazca Lines in the 1930s, before anyone in authority had noticed they were there.

I get out of our vehicle and contemplate the stone strewn landscape, virtually barren of vegetation. This is a strange place. The ground is covered with a dense

The Spanish conquerors of South America were quick to replace Inca buildings with their own. On the site of the old Inca Palace in the pretty city of Cuzco in Peru is the baroque Cuzco Cathedral, started in 1559. It sits on the Plaza des Armes along with the Presidential Palace, a church and a convent.

layer of small boulders, reddish brown in colour and many rounded in form. Below these stones – if you kick them aside – is a darker-coloured gypsum earth. And this, incredibly, is how the lines were made by the Nazca people. They simply removed the stones, banked them on one side and revealed the darker gypsum below. Astonishingly, this subtle etching of the landscape has – due to the dry and remote nature of the site – survived for nearly 2000 years. Nothing of the lines is to be seen. They are invisible. Suddenly I realise that this is the entire point. It's not just that the images and straight lines that cut across this landscape can only be appreciated from several hundred feet up but, equally important, they cannot be seen by man walking across the landscape.

Only by flying – by assuming the attribute of a god – will I be able to read, or at least see, the message in the stones. We return to the airport. Our small single-engined plane is waiting, we pack ourselves inside and hurtle upwards. Nothing could have prepared me for what I see. We bank violently, twisting and turning above an extraordinary and barren terrain. Arid, reddy brown, scored by thousands of old watercourses and suddenly erupting into rugged hills, it seems lunar in its bleakness. Then the images and lines spin into view. They are breathtaking – suddenly this dead landscape comes to life. The first thing I see are the straight lines, hundreds and hundreds of them, stretching for mile upon mile into the distance, as far as the eye can see, in all directions, criss-crossing but each one seemingly pursuing a goal, aligned on something, perhaps hundreds of miles away. All dead true. How could they have been etched so straight? For what earthly purpose? And then the figures start to appear. There is a spider, perfectly formed and measuring 46 metres in depth. This puts me in mind instantly of the Moche and their sinister spider god. The Nazca people and the Moche were contemporary. Does this overlap of imagery mean these two peoples had connections, or is it evidence that, anciently, there was a universal religion, long forgotten, and of which we now see only isolated fragments?

What the lines and images mean remains a complete mystery. Suggestions are many, but none really stands up to detailed objective scrutiny. We do not know – and that perhaps is as it should be. It is the mystery of the Nazca Lines that attracts and stimulates – their message to the modern world is a reminder that we cannot know everything. Some secrets must remain veiled.

We make the journey back to Lima and the day ends with the team going for a quick drink in the old city. We have our drink – pisco sour, a cocktail made from brandy, sugar, egg white and lime – at the Bar Cordano, a rare survivor of a 1920s interior complete with cracked terrazzo-marble table tops, gently faded orange and porphyry-coloured plaster walls and once luxurious but now rather forlorn bars. I'm told that presidents often creep across the road to this bar for a quick drink. They'd be insane not to.

A little news about the team. There is, it seems, general misery over so many early starts, long working hours, irregular days off and potential planning confusion that close study of the schedule has revealed. I don't see how we can complete the series as planned without having to suffer early starts and long flights. The work will be hard but the reward is to see the most wonderful places and man-made treasures in the world. But today, filming over the Nazca Lines went very well and we were all uplifted by the experience. So things are looking better this evening.

Saturday 26 June – Cuzco Festival

As if to confirm the justice of last night's complaints we are to leave our hotel at 4.15 in the morning for yet another flight – this time to Cuzco. But spirits are buoyant. The frank discussion at dinner seems to have cleared the air, decisions were made, actions taken, emails sent off and the schedule problems are being resolved. So the somewhat negative reaction to the schedule has produced immediate and positive benefits. Good. We will proceed as planned – but with some of the really painful moments ironed out.

Cuzco, secreted in a valley at an altitude of 3250 metres, is the old Inca capital and today a curious Inca festival called the Inti Raymi, the Festival of the Sun celebrated at the time of the winter solstice, takes place. Cuzco is a magical little city. Seized by the Spanish in 1532, it passed to the Dominican order, which rapidly set about eradicating the old religion, replacing Inca religious institutions with Catholic ones. The Inca had no written language so there was no literature or records to hand down to posterity, and their precious artefacts, full of beauty and power, were destroyed or – if gold or silver – melted down to form ingots that were shipped back to the treasuries of Spain.

The Inti Raymi, the most important of the Inca religious celebrations, was quickly suppressed by the Spanish conquerors. It took place three days after the winter solstice and was to celebrate the rebirth of the Sun. Offerings were made to ensure the Sun, giver of life and plenty, would return annually. The festival lasted 30 days – a little longer than a lunar month and, curiously, exactly the same length as an ancient Egyptian month.

Inti Raymi was revived in 1944, with actors playing the role of the Inca, nobles, priests, chosen women and soldiers. It is now just a piece of popular theatre. But it has a serious aspect. It is an expression of identity, of growing pride in the past, in the achievements of the many indigenous civilisations of Peru. Contemplating the mighty works left by the Inca in and around Cuzco it is clear that – in the end – the conquerors did not win entirely. They obliterated much of the past, gradually introduced the European ideal of technological civilisation, and planted Roman Catholicism firmly in the land. But the Inca spirit – the Inca identity – lives on. The empire is not dead in the hearts, minds and imagination of its people.

The day ends with a journey through the heart of the Inca homeland to their Sacred Valley, through which runs their sacred river, the Urubamba, a tributary of the mighty River Amazon. The valley is incredibly beautiful. Mountains rise steeply on either side of the river valley and, beyond the first range, a second and a third, getting progressively higher until they end in snow-capped peaks.

The Inti Raymi was the most important of the Inca religious celebrations. It is now celebrated by the Quechuas, descendants of the Inca. I was lucky to be there to see it. This group of women and children caught my eye with their brightly coloured skirts and curious hats.

6 MOAI OF EASTER ISLAND

Sunday 27 – Monday 28 June

After nineteen hours of travelling, from Lima via Santiago in Chile, we arrive in Easter Island, or Rapa Nui as it is known to its Polynesian inhabitants – a 22.5 by 11-kilometre speck in the Pacific Ocean, 3540 kilometres from the South American mainland. The airport is in the island's only town, Hanga Roa, and it is an amazingly pleasant place in which to arrive. The evening air is warm, the airport buildings tiny and the atmosphere relaxed. Locals loll around, talking, drinking – watching a game of football on a brightly illuminated beach-side pitch. And there I catch my first glimpse of a Moai – a giant stylised representation of the human figure. This is the treasure I have come all this way to see and, to my mind, one of the most powerful works of sacred art ever made by man.

Rapa Nui is a volcanic atoll that erupted from the ocean bed millions of years ago. Polynesians – the masters of the sea – are thought to have arrived on this island, after a 3000-kilometre or so journey from the west, in about AD 500. Soon something strange happened. These Polynesians, who were eventually to peak at a population of about 10,000, developed a theology – or at least an expression of a theology – that was unique. They took it into their heads to carve huge figures – over 880 have so far been identified on the island – over a period of centuries, to place along their coastline. These Moai have an elemental and spiritual power that astonished the Western world when reports of their existence percolated to Europe in the 18th century. Who made them, when, how and for what exact purpose were the questions asked then, and these questions are, to a degree, still asked now. One of my earliest visual experiences – one of my earliest memories – is of the Moai that is displayed in the British Museum. I was very young, but the image of it – the strong face, the stylised yet individual features that seemed to carry a message in code and the solemn, faraway gaze – burnt itself into my imagination. I wanted to come to Easter Island to see if I could discover more about the Moai by viewing them in their native landscape – in their homeland.

Tuesday 29 – Wednesday 30 June

At dawn, which comes late near the equator at the time of the winter solstice, we leave for our first destination – the fifteen standing Moai at Ahu Tongariki. This is my first confrontation with a full array of these extraordinary creatures. They stand on an Ahu – a sacred platform – all face inland and all once had pukaos on their heads, which some say are round hats and others say are stylised hair. Strikingly, the pukaos are made of reddish tuff while the bodies are of brown tuff. All have solemn expressions – perhaps gloomy – and seem to be contemplating an event taking place some distance inland. They have long noses, generally slightly concave, pouting, straight-lipped mouths, beetling brows, prominent chins, elongated ears and their hands crossed in front, over their navels. As has often been observed, they look little like Polynesians now and presumably little like Polynesians a thousand years ago. So who is being portrayed and to what end? No one knows for sure but the current view – supported by most archaeologists and by the Polynesians I spoke to on the island – is that these figures represent ancestors, who were set up as protective spirits – as deities to guard and guide their people. Each Ahu represents a clan base and the figures look inland because they watched over the clan village that would have stood nearby, beneath the Moai's gaze. Some believe the Moai are stylised portraits of individual chiefs – made after their deaths – so that the figures on an Ahu could have been assembled gradually, over several hundred years.

A few hundred yards inland a large Moai lies on its back – it must weigh many tonnes. It tells a story about the sudden and dramatic end of the ritual and tradition of Moai veneration. It seems clear that this mighty Moai was being painstakingly moved towards

the Ahu but was abandoned en route – left, a thing of no purpose. The quarry from which it and virtually all the Moai come rises in front of me, a spectacular volcanic eruption with a jagged rim that, I know, conceals a vast crater. This particular volcano that produced the ideal tuff for Moai construction is known as Rano Raraku and is an astonishing place. On the grassy slopes leading up to the steep rock face are nearly 100 Moai, standing in pits, some buried up to their necks, some at crazy angles and looking in all directions, but most out to sea. Some are compressed of feature like those at nearby Tongariki, others are of a more elegant and elongated form. What on earth are these Moai doing loitering here? Without doubt the volcano became a factory for virtually mass producing Moai and this slope appears to have been the storage depot. The cliff face, just below the rim of the crater, is more amazing still. There are just over 300 Moai in course of construction, some nearly complete and ready to be launched down the slope but still attached to the rock face by a few slender fingers of stone, others just emerging out of the tuff – weird petrified giants latent in the rocky, undulating and volcanic landscape. What is clear, from the many Moai on the cliff face or in storage pits on the slopes below, is that the production of these ancestors was in full swing – had perhaps reached a desperate peak of production – when it all suddenly stopped. Looking down from the quarry I can make out in the distance many Moai abandoned along the ancient tracks leading from the quarry in different directions to the sea. Whatever happened took place with incredible speed, and an entire way of life, of religion and veneration, had suddenly ended.

There is one last surprise. When I reach the top of the volcano I have an extraordinary view of a crater, framed by clopping banks and full of glassy water and reeds. A secret – sacred – world. And looking down into the water of the crater I can see a group of Moai. For all the world the Moai appear to be watching the crater – waiting for something to emerge or looking at the spot where something submerged.

A rational explanation is now offered to make sense of what appears to have been irrational, bizarre behaviour. Why did they suddenly abandon and turn on their ancestor

Easter Island is a story of Paradise Lost. A heaven became a hell because the natural resources of the island were exploited faster than they could be replaced. I have come to see the Moai, of which there are hundreds on the island, each figure essentially similar, but subtly different.

My next treasure is the fifteen standing Moai at Ahu Tongariki on Easter Island. These extra-ordinary creatures are made of the local tuff and stand on an Ahu or platform. They all face inland with their backs to the sea. They are said to represent ancestors who looked over the clan villages nearby.

gods? The current opinion is that as the population of the island increased, its natural resources decreased. Trees were cut – for moving Moai, for house and boat building – more quickly than they grew. And with no trees, there were finally no boats, and with no boats, little fishing and not enough food to eat. And it got worse. With no trees to hold down the soil, the wind eroded the surface of the island and crops were increasingly difficult to grow. So the island became the scene of a ruthless battle for survival between the different clans, each attempting to secure the dwindling resources for its own use. Gradually a heaven became a hell. This period – perhaps 500 or 600 years ago – is still referred to by the Polynesian islanders as the civil war. It is possible that, during the internecine fighting, rival clans attacked each other's Ahus, toppling Moai, breaking their necks and tearing out eyes. It seems that the old gods – the long-venerated ancestors – were repudiated, that people lost faith in the old religion in their desperate battle for survival. I go to see an Ahu at Hunga Te'e where the gods had been toppled and where they still lie with their faces in the sand, necks or heads broken, pukaos scattered and eyes ripped out. It is still a shocking sight. For people to murder their ancient gods something must have gone terribly wrong. Perhaps the prospect of gradual starvation was enough to trigger this reaction, for clan to try to obliterate clan by destroying that which was held most sacred – the protection and memory of the ancestors.

What is more certain is that a new theology emerged. Probably some time in the 18th century came the Birdman, the representative on earth of the creator god Makemake. This god seems to have been a somewhat malevolent spirit for it presided over war, perhaps even cannibalism, and over the relentless and brutal battle for resources.

Some few Moai seem to have been standing when various Europeans visited Easter Island in the 18th century – including Captain Cook in the 1770s – but all had been toppled by the 19th century, suggesting a second phase of their rejection by the islanders. If this is the case, then the reason is not hard to find because the experiences the islanders suffered after their discovery by the 'civilised' world confirmed that the Moai had little or no protective power. Many islanders were seized by Yankee and Peruvian slavers with, in the 1860s, 2000 kidnapped in one raid – with many destined to die rapidly from working Peruvian guano mines. By the end of the 1880s when Easter Island was annexed by Chile, the Polynesian population of the island was down to just a few hundred. Equilibrium has now been restored. The population now stands at nearly 3000, with 70 per cent being Polynesians, the rest mainly from Chile.

Ironically, the repudiated Moai have been the island's salvation. They have put Easter Island on the cultural map of the world, created a unique identity for this tiny island, attract many visitors and are the cornerstone of the island's economy. So, in the end, the ancestors have looked after their people.

Thursday 1 July

We gather early at the airport for our flight back to Santiago. The plane is going to be full – including thirty or so members of the Manatau band and its entourage flying out to give a concert in Madrid. Music – a blend of traditional Polynesian, rock and blues –

is the one genuinely creative artistic act of the current islanders. Otherwise it's the endless carving of miniature Moai to sell to tourists. The male band members wear feathers, standing erect in their tightly bound long hair. They look like magnificent if slightly self-conscious manifestations of the Birdman. They all wear black shirts and trousers edged with a yellow pattern. I look closely – it's a hieroglyphic text. It provokes me to reflect upon the one last, great mystery of the island, the solution to which could explain much. The people who created the Moai and the Birdman may have had a written language. It's called Rongo Rongo and certainly it looks like a language – one expert has seen similarities with ancient texts from the Indus Valley in India. But no one has been able to decipher it – partly because many samples, written on wood, were destroyed during the mid-19th century by Roman Catholic missionaries in the battle to save the souls of the islanders. Another piece of the white man's legacy – not only slavery, occupation and the imposition of an alien religion but the destruction of ancestral records.

I feel angry at the arrogance and ignorance of the whites. But, as the flight drones on, the band starts to play – ad hoc, disconnected but harmonious. People clap. Nick Reeks, a man of great spirit and conviviality, joins in. He becomes the lead singer in a weird version of the Beatles' 'Yellow Submarine'. Manatau, delighted by the effort, clap Nick. The white man – in the person of our sound recordist – is forgiven, or so it seems to me at the moment as I slip off into one of those strange, dream-like waking sleeps induced by long plane journeys.

7 UMAHARA HEADDRESS OF THE HIKBATSA TRIBE

Friday 2 July
From Santiago to São Paulo, Brazil. Here the team splits. Tim Sutton and Andrea Illescas fly direct to Rio de Janeiro, the location of one of our treasures. They are to start filming the city and making arrangements. The remainder of the team flies to the city of Cuiabá, in the western Brazilian state of Mato Grosso. Tim Dunn and I go to a bar with our fixer Jim to check the schedule for the next couple of days. We each have a beer – served, explains Jim, 'ridiculously' cold as all Brazilians like it – taste a little local food (beef dripping with melted cheese), look at the people parading the streets and overnight in a simple, clean hotel. We get up at 4.00 am for our journey – by light plane, vehicle and boat – 750 kilometres into the rainforests of the Amazon basin, into a region from which most visitors are firmly excluded. Here we hope to find our treasure, our living treasure – the indigenous Hikbatsa tribal people and their emblematic Umahara headdress made of parrot feathers and human hair. As the sun rises above the runway

we board our six-seater, 1970s-made, twin-engined, propeller-driven plane. We are all feeling a trifle desperate. We have had to abandon much of our luggage at the airport because, we were told, it was too heavy for the small aircraft. So I am going into the Amazon basin – into the rainforest to meet these primitive, once bellicose people – with just a camera, pen, notebook, hat, a change of shirt, a few essential pills and a toothbrush.

We land on a tiny airstrip at Juina – a frontier town that, we quickly perceive, has a lively Wild West character. We load

The Umahara feathered headdress is the symbol of the Hikbatsa tribe who live deep in the Brazilian rainforest and fight for the right to retain their traditional hunter-gatherer way of life. Originally worn in war, the spectacularly coloured headdress is now worn on ceremonial occasions and for tribal dances.

our vehicle and start on our four-hour drive to the river that will lead us to the Hikbatsa. Immediately we leave the airport compound we come upon the local whorehouse – marked by a jaunty red-painted tower and called the Red House. Then along the main street, lined with innumerable garages, showrooms selling vehicles, others selling agricultural machinery and – of course – bars. But the place is neat and obviously under control for, as we speed past a little arid park marking the town centre, I notice a number of monuments. One for the local Rotary Club, another – formed by a set square and compass – is obviously for the local lodge of Freemasons. Strange. Then, after a quarter of a mile, the blacktop stops and we hit the bumpy, dusty red earth road that is to carry us west. Eventually we reach a fence with a gate. The difference between each side of the fence is shocking. On one side – the side through which we have travelled – is rolling prairie, with a few clumps of trees, the odd farm building, towering termite nests and wandering cattle. On the other side of the fence is dense, primeval rainforest. The contrast between two worlds, the modern and the ancient, could not have been more dramatically expressed. We put the key in the padlock, open the gate, and pass into another world, another age.

Suddenly the river is in front of us. We have reached the Juarema, a tributary of the River Amazon that gives its name to this region. Our guide lets off firecrackers – they are to warn the Hikbatsa that we have arrived and will be with them soon. Nick says it is to warn them to hide their mobile telephones and change out of their jeans and tee shirts into something more ethnic. We all laugh – I wonder. The Hikbatsa are out of the modern world, but they are of course also in it – it's a mighty presence that cannot be escaped, it is a crude reality that devours any finer, gentler sentiments or histories. Their awareness of the benefits of modern technology is revealed by the 'fee' they have requested in return for allowing us to film them – an outboard motor.

The Hikbatsa were only identified as a specific people as late as the 1940s, and then followed two decades of strife as rubber planters and gatherers, loggers, cattle ranchers and farmers struggled to possess the Hikbatsa lands. Jesuit missionaries set about the conversion of the Hikbatsa to Catholicism and, as part of this process, carried off young Hikbatsa children to missionary schools, often miles from their families. And the beleaguered Hikbatsa were also stricken by diseases previously unknown to them – influenza, chickenpox and smallpox – and their population of around 1300 was cut by

around 75 per cent. But from the late 1960s things started to improve. The Brazilian government – latterly under pressure from organisations like FUNAI, Brazil's National Indigenous Bureau – moved to safeguard the Hikbatsa homeland, and in 1968 80,000 hectares were demarcated at Evikbakta, increased by a further 152,500 hectares in 1986. The missionaries changed their policies to support Hikbatsa autonomy, children were returned to their families and the population of the tribe has now returned to around 1100. This is the world – fragile, fought over and seemingly secure – that we have been allowed to enter. But safeguarding such a world has brought new problems. The species within the demarcated areas are protected, which sounds sensible, except the Hikbatsa need to hunt and kill some of these species – certain monkeys and parrots – if their traditional way of life is to continue. So, ironically, the very laws and attitudes that have evolved to protect the Hikbatsa could, if imposed without flexibility, lead to the eventual demise of their culture.

In due course a number of modern, flat-bottomed skiffs appear – all powered by outboard motors and driven by smiling men in jeans and tee shirts! Our gear loaded on the boats, we head along the Juarema. Three extraordinary figures are waiting to receive us, all naked to the waist, with chests and legs ornamented with abstract patterns rendered in an indelible blue dye. One carries a club, another a bow and a handful of long arrows. I am the first ashore – I smile, wave, bow and shout a greeting. The men stare back – unmoved, unsmiling – aggressive it would seem. It occurs to me that this is a quintessential 19th-century moment. I, the intrepid explorer, land with nothing other than a bottle of water to face the disdain and steely gaze of the painted savage. The warriors motion me forward and we enter the village – Indian file – and then I realise that the warrior in front of me is wearing on his head the object of my quest – the Umahara feathered headdress! We are led into a village formed by a collection of long huts, mostly constructed of vertical timber planks with pitched roofs covered with timber shingles or thatched with leaves. Most of the village is gathered in the shade, men in one group, women in another. They are waiting for us, and as we appear they all start to smile and gesticulate. The message is clear – we are welcome

The appearance of the Hikbatsa men and women is I realise as I survey the scene, really quite extraordinary. The faces and bodies of both men and women are ornamented with blue dye – mostly arranged as vertical bands, although many have curved bands

The Juarema river, a tributary of the Amazon, is majestic in its width, the forest tumbling down to the water's edge. We head along it, further into the rainforest, towards the fragile world of the Hikbatsa tribe, deep in the Brazilian rainforest.

following and framing the curves of the mouth. And many have dabs of red, or red bands instead of blue. This makes them look wondrously barbaric. But, somewhat incongruously, most of the men wear rather natty sports shorts while the women – with only a very few exceptions – wear bikini tops or bras and roomy pants. And then I notice the football pitch with goalposts and, standing next to a newly built hut on a concrete plinth, a huge satellite dish surrounded by a wire fence. Clearly, all is not quite what it first seemed.

I am then led to the ceremonial hut. It's overwhelming. I expected to see one or two Umahara headdresses, but the hut is full of them and other bright feathered headdresses, hanging from hooks on the wall and from the timber beams that support the roof. The Hikbatsa have put their treasures on display. I gasp and gawk, smile, congratulate and thank them – they beam back, nod, shake my hand. First we are to see the headdress in a dance, then, I am told, we can discuss how it is made and its meaning. The dance takes place every day for 90 days after 1 June and is to do with 'celebrating new things'. I suppose that means it relates to harvests and crops but, since the Hikbatsa venerate the moon, I wonder if the 90-day period has to do with a series of new moons. Then the dance starts. Four ranks of men, each four men wide, all wearing large palm leaves strapped to their backs, blow instruments made from hollowed bamboo stalks and thump, to one side of the football pitch and back again, the tingle from the bells on their ankles mixing with the deep moans from the bamboo pipes to make a very distinct sound. Up and down they go, hypnotic in their music and their movements. All wear feather headdresses, but only a select few the Umahara. After a number of turns across the pitch the dancers make their way into the ceremonial hall and continue, moving from one side to the other, still puffing on their pipes.

After the dance I talk to one of the celebrants, a splendid looking fellow with a Umahara on his head and feathers stuck horizontally through his nose. His name is Juarez Paymy. He explains, in a most articulate manner, the meaning of the Umahara. It used to be worn in war but is now worn in peace, in dances such as we have just seen. It represents continuity with the past, a powerful memory, and ensures the continuing identity of the tribe – in the present and in the future. It is the symbol of the tribe, the emblem of its pride.

A Hikbatsa tribesman wearing the feathered headdress and carrying a monkey hunting knife. All the Hikbatsa hunting implements – arrowheads, bows and knives – are carved from wood and are deceptively strong.

Before bed there is dinner, and another dance. We gather around a fire – made by twirling a wooden stick to create friction. Do the Hikbatsa always light their fires like this, or is it just being done for our benefit? I'm now getting slightly suspicious. I sit around the fire with my new Hikbatsa friends, we beam at each other. Then the dancers appear – it's the same routine but this time women carry on after the men have finished. In the flickering light the chant-like rhythm and tone of the bamboo and bell music is even more hypnotic.

When cocooned in our hammocks, hanging all in a row from the walls of our hut, something odd happens. Thumping dance music starts to echo across the village – the Hikbatsa are having a disco! I am surprised, but drift off to sleep to the sounds of Latin American pop music. Quite pleasant really.

Sunday 4 – Monday 5 July

In the morning, before sunrise, we are up and packing. We have a long journey. The villagers – our savage painted and feathered friends of the previous day – drift towards our hut. Now they are attired in jeans, tee shirts and baseball caps. The show is over –

The Hikbatsa tribal dance, one of the occasions when the Umahara headdress is worn. The dance is performed in front of the ceremonial heart of the village, a structure clad entirely in maize fronds.

they come to say goodbye, and to trade. Much of what they offer we would not be allowed to keep – jewellery made from the feathers or teeth of protected birds or animals. They escort us to our craft and look at us wistfully and with curiosity as they wave us goodbye. What can they make of us, I wonder? We whisk in from another world, rush around in a frantic manner, ask simplistic questions, they give us the answers we want, dress as we expect them to dress and then we rush off again. Nick says sardonically, as our craft speeds away, that they're now climbing back into costume and waiting for the next tour group to arrive. They're not, of course, but there is some truth in what Nick says. The Hikbatsa are being drawn into the modern world – like it or not. The authorities must know this and realise that, if things continue, the Hikbatsa will be a thing of the past, dispersed into the nearby towns and cities, their culture and traditions just a memory – and their lands available for development. Is it really just a matter of time before all this is gone?

As we make our way back from Juina, our little six-seater offers us the big view with chilling accuracy – farming and cattle land wrenched from the rainforest. The sad little clumps of forest, marooned among huge fields and pasture, are poignant indeed. As we approach Cuiabá I notice a complex of tower blocks rising out of what looks like rainforest. What an image. It seems to me, as I fly towards it – like a moth into a flame – that Brazil has been developed with almost unseemly haste. It has the sixth largest economy in the world, but this seems to be fuelled by the exploitation of resources that, in many cases, are not being renewed. It wants to be one of the world's great nations – and no doubt will be but, I fear, at a daunting price. The evidence of the country's ruthless rush to material prosperity is now part of its history, and the indigenous people are not the only losers. Brazil has a population of over 178 million. Over a third lives on less than a dollar a day. It's a beautiful country but troubling – and now we are going to see its other side, a place that could hardly be more different from the rainforest of the Hikbatsa – the great hedonistic dream city of Rio de Janeiro.

We arrive at Rio late at night, the plane landing at the water's edge, and we drive through the bustle of a great metropolis to our hotel just next to Ipanema Beach. People are strolling in the hot evening air along the seafront and in the busy streets behind. One thing is immediately striking: many people – both men and women – have very little on. Rio is one of the few great cities of the world where a chap can go for a stroll in his underpants, no matter how brief or how late or early the hour, and no one blinks an eye.

Despite the late hour I have a drink with Jim, a passionate advocate for Rio and for Brazil in general. Jim recommends cachaça, a cocktail made from sugar cane and rum, and caipirinha, made from cachaça plus green limes, sugar and lots of ice. He talks of what the Brazilians call 'jingu' – the joyful, fun-loving, easy-going spirit of Brazil – of the passion of the place and of the creative and positive way the different people of the land have fused, coalesced, to create a nation with the virtues of many diverse races. I am intrigued by this, but wonder what survives of the different cultures that, according to Jim, now lead such an ideal life.

8 CHRIST THE REDEEMER, RIO DE JANEIRO

Tuesday 6 July

We wake up to discover a mist hanging over Rio. We cannot see our treasure! We have to wait – and hope that the weather lifts to reveal the statue of Christ the Redeemer that hovers, open-armed, on a mountain top 710 metres above the centre of the city.

The statue was conceived in 1921 to celebrate both the Roman Catholic faith of Brazil and the country's independence from Portuguese rule a hundred years earlier. Carlos Oswald designed the figure – Christ with the cross, amended to the familiar figure of Christ with open, welcoming arms. The revised project was taken up by engineers Hector de Silva Costa and Pedro Viana to work out how to actually build the mighty statue on its narrow mountain peak. They decided that it was to be built of concrete reinforced with steel, with the concrete given beauty – and protection from the salty sea air – by being clad in a mosaic-like veneer of shiny, pale cream soapstone. Finally the French sculptor Paul Landowski modelled and manufactured the 45-tonne, 4-metre-high head in France and sent over moulds for the outstretched hands. When finally assembled the figure stood 30 metres high, on an 8-metre plinth.

By the afternoon, the clouds have burnt off, but only a little. I can now just make Christ out, breaking through the gloom. We decide to ascend the mountain for a closer look. But, as we arrive, the clouds return and I see Christ only as a shadowy form with wide outstretched arms, through an almost mystic mist. It is strangely moving. But I have not chosen Christ the Redeemer as a treasure because of its majestic scale or because of its artistic quality – rather because it was, from the moment of its completion, such a powerful symbol. In its scale it seemed to capture the great aspirations of these lands, in its open arms it celebrated the mix of peoples making up these nations and – of course – in its Roman Catholic imagery it made the statement that this part of the globe was to be the new Catholic heartland and that the old religions of the displaced civilisations were finally dead. Seventy years on it is possible, with hindsight, to take a different view. The statue has great spiritual power and it has become the image of Rio and of Brazil. But it presides over a curious and troubling world – the city of beautiful beaches and people, luxury apartments and style also contains the largest slums in Brazil and streets in which beggar children are still killed by vigilantes as if they were rats. Here is poverty and inequality that is almost incomprehensible. As I wrestle with these terrible thoughts the mist finally descends and veils the prospect of Rio – this heaven and Hades combined, this wondrous but flawed creation that seems such an accurate reflection of humanity – from the view of the windmill-armed Christ.

The statue of Christ the Redeemer, a symbol of the aspirations not only of Rio de Janeiro and Brazil, but also of all South America. Though it stands 30 metres high, when I view it from nearby, it looks relatively intimate and not the giant it appears from below.

PROMISED LANDS

Wednesday 7 July

From Rio de Janeiro we fly north to Mexico City, and on to the modern and prosperous town of Villahermosa in the south of Mexico. We overnight in an anonymous international hotel – a place without character or soul, but rather expensive. This, and the long days and early starts, has rather knocked the spirit out of the team. It is, shall we say, languid. Tempers are short, energy low, people are starting to seriously get on each other's nerves, and anger erupts over trivial matters. I wonder how long this will go on before something serious happens. Tomorrow is another early start. We visit the great 7th-century AD Mayan city of Palenque. I hope this experience perks spirits up.

9 THE TOMB OF KING PAKAL, PALENQUE, MEXICO

Thursday 8 July

The imagery on the huge stone sarcophagus of King Pakal at Palenque shows his death and rebirth – it reminds me of similar scenes on tombs in Egypt. These hieroglyphs are as fresh as when they were cut, preserved by being buried for 1300 years.

Palenque was built during the late, golden period of Mayan culture, during the hundred years after AD 650, by King Hanab Pakal and his sons. It grew to a great size, incorporated architecture of highly sophisticated design and engineered construction, and then, between AD 850 and 900, was abandoned. So this great city – when at the height of its glory – was left to rot in the rainforest that quietly but remorselessly engulfed it. The treasure is Pakal's own tomb that lies in the heart of Palenque's greatest structure – a burial pyramid now called the Temple of the Inscriptions. When this tomb was discovered in 1952 it was immediately recognised as one of the richest and most important pyramid burials yet found in the Americas.

Unlike many Central and South American civilisations, the Maya evolved writing – hieroglyphs with a phonetic value that expressed their rituals, traditions and history – and even books with pages made of bark or vellum. From this writing and other sources much has been learned about Pakal and the Maya of Palenque.

Pakal died in AD 683 and before his death organised the creation of his sarcophagus

and burial pyramid. The pyramid has nine levels or steps, generally believed to symbolise the nine levels of the Mayan underworld. Cutting through and up these nine levels is a steep staircase that must represent the journey of the deceased. It leads to a temple on the top level, and from within this temple another staircase snakes down to the core of the pyramid – the burial chamber and sarcophagus of Pakal. It was down this inner staircase that I travelled, into the bowels of the pyramid, into the Mayan underworld. On the day I made the journey, the air inside the pyramid was hot and humid, with moisture running treacherously off the steep and slippery steps – and very soon off my body in salty torrents. The staircase is an extraordinary feat of engineering. Its roof, as the stairs descend, has to support the increasingly heavy load of the masonry above. To achieve this a structural device evolved by the Maya is used – a corbel vault. It's a splendid thing. At the top of the vertical walls on each staircase stone slabs project horizontally. From these corbels rise flat but inclined stone walling, connected at the top by another horizontal stone slab, to create a massively strong V-shaped roof or vault above the staircase. This vault transfers the massive load to the thick walls on each side of it – a really simple but elegant engineering solution to a demanding structural problem. Certainly the immense structural strength of the staircase suggests it was built to last, to allow Pakal a chance to be reborn – to ascend – no matter how long it might take.

I reach the bottom of the staircase, the lowest level of the Mayan underworld, and see a great triangular stone slab, the massive door that sealed the king's tomb – and it's standing open. When this tomb was discovered in 1952 five human skeletons were found on this spot. It is believed they were people who had been sacrificed when the king was interred.

The Temple of the Sun, the best preserved of the Palenque temples, with a honeycomb roof crest – a hallmark of late Mayan architecture that was both ornamental and practical – was built around AD 700.

And then I see my prize. I peer into the vaulted tomb chamber – dripping with condensation – and am confronted by an extraordinary sight. There is a huge stone sarcophagus, so big that it is obvious the chamber, indeed the pyramid, was built around it. In the centre is cut a recess to receive the body of the king, in the shape of a uterus. In death the Maya believed there was new life. They observed the cycles in nature – the seasons, stars and planets, and human life. There was no such thing as death, only change, transformation, and rebirth. Pakal had his body placed in a womb of stone – a sign of his certainty of this rebirth.

The scene of his death and rebirth is shown on the massive stone slab that lay on the top of the womb-shaped recess. In the centre is Pakal, falling almost ecstatically into the maw of the jaguar god – the god of death and of the underworld. From Pakal's stomach, or behind him, grows the cross-shaped Tree of Life, the axis of the earth. On the ends of the cross are stylised dragon heads which symbolise blood, the sacred element of the Maya. It was the thing of greatest value man had to offer his gods to ensure that the cycle of creation continued. To obtain human blood for sacrifice the Maya would, it seems, arrange battles with their enemies and a key objective was to take prisoner men of noble birth. They would be decapitated or have their heart removed which, while still pumping, would spurt blood over the images of gods.

Pakal's sarcophagus slab with its images of snakes, dragons, a jaguar and men carved on it, puts me in mind of the creatures combined in the Sphinx of Egypt – the lion, the snake, the human – and the four beasts of the Apocalypse – the lion, the bull, man and the flying eagle. Visual similarities between different civilisations often seem to be too overwhelming to be mere coincidence. Civilisations, we are told by academics, evolved similar theologies and building forms independently, as if humans – no matter how different – are programmed to come up with matching ideas in matching circumstances. But the circumstances – certainly the terrain and climate – were not matching. I really don't know.

On the walls of the tomb chamber are yet further images. I jump down into the puddle of water lying around the sarcophagus to approach these more closely. They are carved out of stucco – a fine plaster – and show nine figures, now believed to be the gods of the nine levels of the underworld.

Pakal's body has now been removed from the sarcophagus and it, along with the grave goods, is in a museum in Mexico City. He was buried dressed as Ah Mun, the maize god, one of the Maya's highest deities. In his human manifestation the maize god was the epitome of male beauty and excellence – at least in the eyes of the Maya. The Maya's concept of beauty was individual – they liked foreheads that sloped back (achieved by putting children in head boards) to form a continuous straight and sloping line with a high bridged Grecian nose. Nothing particularly extraordinary here, but they also favoured the cross-eyed look – to such an extent that mothers would dangle beads in front of their babies' faces to make them boss-eyed!

A narrow shaft snakes up through the bulk of the pyramid from the tomb to daylight. This suggests that Pakal wanted to keep in touch with the world from his tomb, that he required air to continue living – that he was, in fact, not dead. I climb the staircase and emerge into the light. I see all before me with different eyes – I'm beginning to understand the long-forgotten world of the Maya.

The ruins of numerous buildings – including a series of small, exquisite temples – lie below me, each with its story to tell and secrets to reveal. Immediately in front is the palace that Pakal started in about AD 650 and that his sons altered and

extended. It is a curious structure, sitting on a small hill – a minor acropolis, the residence of a divine king. The upper level is approached by wide, steep steps. The palace itself is asymmetrical in form, its most striking external feature a squat, square tower, placed off-centre. This puzzles archaeologists. Some think it was an observation post. Others think it sacred – a place from which the king and his priests could, on the dawn of the winter solstice, watch the rays of the rising sun fall symmetrically across the adjoining Temple of Inscriptions. Pakal's name means Lord Sun Shield.

The centre of Palenque is what most tourists see. But Palenque was a huge place in its prime, its population living in adobe and timber structures that have long since perished. As I venture into the surrounding rainforest I stumble on mounds of rubble entwined by mighty roots and then chance upon a new excavation site, simply called Temple XIX. The day is drawing to an end, the light is fading and then suddenly I have a vision. On a square column, rising from floor to ceiling, is a brightly coloured, life-size figure – a Maya, in full regalia. I stare in amazement. This figure has only recently been discovered, an image as clear as when it was made around 1200 years ago. This is a Maya as a Maya saw himself. I take my leave of this extraordinary city with this image in my head, pursuing me as I feel my way through the twilight of the rainforest.

One of the most striking things about Palenque is the scale and design of Pakal's burial pyramid (left) and its relation to the landscape, the other temples and the palace (the tall building at right).

10 RIVERA'S 'MAN, CONTROLLER OF THE UNIVERSE'

Friday 9 July

We fly to Mexico City and drive to the Palace of Fine Arts in the centre of town, a government building and so guarded by mounted police, complete with short blue coats and huge white sombreros. The palace is a beautiful, and beautifully maintained, Art Deco building of Classical design that was completed in March 1934. We enter and make our way to our goal – the huge mural painted in the same year by Diego Rivera. I have chosen this as a treasure because it says so much about the age in which it was created – and about the man who painted it. Rivera was born in 1886 at Guanajuato, Mexico, and developed into something of a child prodigy, at the age of 20 winning a government stipend to study art in Europe. Here he met Picasso and Braque and immersed himself in the Cubist movement. But even the limited abstraction of Cubism proved inappropriate for Rivera's particular artistic ambitions. In 1921 he returned to Mexico, a fortuitous time to return to his native land as the 1920s were to be Mexico's 'belle époque'. Rivera expanded with the decade – in every sense. Corpulent, huge-headed, with frog-like bulging eyes, he was a larger than life character with big ideas, boldly expressed. While his politics were radical his life was exotic. He played a leading role in Mexico's Communist Party, but he was also a self-obsessed womaniser and socialite, choosing the company of the rich, the famous, the beautiful. He fathered a string of children in Europe, in 1922 married Lupe Marin in Mexico and divorced her in 1928 to marry the bisexual and strange artist Frida Kahlo.

In the early 1930s Franklin Delano Roosevelt's 'New Deal' was providing funds for artists to create public works in the United States, and in this atmosphere of patronage Rivera found himself offered a major commission. As he puts it in his autobiography: 'When Nelson Rockefeller decided to decorate the main floor of his new R.C.A. Building in Radio City [New York] with murals, he also decided to get the best artists for the job.' Rivera came up with a subject entitled 'Man at the Crossroads', client and architect approved, and the work was commenced. But patron and artist were an unlikely pair. Rockefeller was an adamant supporter of the capitalist system while Rivera supported the benefits of communism. This divergence of view was revealed in the most dramatic manner when Rivera chose to make the mural a piece of propaganda attacking capitalism and promoting communism – a deeply provocative act. This boldness was to have fatal consequences for the painting.

Rivera described the mural thus: 'In the centre [was] a worker at the controls of a large machine. In front of him, emerging from space, was a large hand holding a globe on which the dynamics of chemistry and biology, the recombination of atoms, and the division of a cell, were represented schematically. Two elongated ellipses crossed and met in the figure of the worker: one showing the wonders of the telescope and its revelations of bodies in space; the other showing the microscope and its discoveries – cells, germs, bacteria, and delicate tissues. Above the germinating soil at the bottom, I projected two visions of civilization. On the left of the crossed ellipses, I showed night-club scenes of the debauched rich, a battlefield with men in the holocaust of war, and unemployed workers in a demonstration being clubbed by police. On the right, I painted corresponding scenes of life in a socialist country; a May Day demonstration of marching, singing workers; an athletic stadium filled with girls exercising their bodies.'

As if to cause maximum offence to his patron and his fellow New York businessmen, Rivera included an idealised portrait of Lenin, 'symbolically clasping the hands of a black American and a white Russian soldier and worker, as allies of the future'. Such imagery was bound to lead to an explosion.

Rockefeller wrote Rivera a letter asking him to paint out the face of Lenin and substitute the face of an unknown man. Rivera thought this a reasonable request but

worried that one request might lead to others and '…hadn't every artist the right to use whatever he wished in his painting?' He brooded for a few days and then replied that 'rather than mutilate the conception, I should prefer the physical destruction of the conception in its entirety, but preserving, at least, its integrity'. He was to get his wish. In the second week of May Rockefeller made his move. The security force of Radio City swooped and Rivera and his assistants were escorted out of the building. The mural was covered with canvas sheeting and a new battle started. The confrontation had become a public issue. Some nationalistic Americans supported Rockefeller for his direct action while others – intellectuals and artists – tried to persuade him to reconsider. These protests probably delayed the inevitable. In February 1934, after Rivera had returned to Mexico, the mural and the plaster on which it was painted were smashed.

But this was not the end for Rivera's conception. Less than a year later he was invited to contribute a mural for the newly completed Palace of Fine Arts in Mexico City. This was the opportunity to recreate the mural – but in a significantly revised form: 'I added a few figures…the most important of the additions was a portrait of John D. Rockefeller, Jr, which I inserted into the night-club scene, his head but a short distance away from the venereal disease germs pictured in the ellipse of the microscope.'

Much of the mural is as Rivera described the New York version. In the seventy years since the mural's completion the world – its aspirations and its experiences – have changed enormously. As a work of social and political art it has dated painfully – not least because Rivera painted in a time-bound version of Social Realism that appears sadly hollow and clichéd. It is now virtually impossible to view the jolly marching workers and the stylised exercising girls without smirking. But despite its superficial absurdity, the mural is more than just a joke. View it with some compassion and it still has the power to move. It captures a moment when communism seemed the hope of the world. It is a vision of a better world, a promised land, a Utopia that turned to dust. Far from becoming a socialist realm – as Rivera hoped and prophesied – the Americas has become more deeply enmeshed in the coils of capitalism.

'Man, Controller of the Universe' stretches along one wall of the Palace of Fine Arts in Mexico City. It's a splendid space, and the mural has a particular power when you know about its first manifestation in New York. In the centre is man controlling technology – around him are figures of (from top left) men at war, happy workers, exercising girls, germinating soil and unemployed workers. Centre right is the portrait of Lenin, and, opposite him, Rockfeller shown in a bar next to venereal disease germs.

The idealised portrait of Lenin, symbolically surrounded by workers of different races, was recreated and revised in Rivera's Mexican version of his New York mural.

In the evening we drive through this city of 23 million people to witness one of its curious and characteristic events – the serenade of the Mariachi. It's a Friday evening and the traffic is dense and the air thick but as we approach Plaza Garibaldi something odd happens. Men appear at the side of the road – some sortie out into the traffic – dressed not as beggars or bandits but as operatic singers, refugees from a production of Carmen. They are mariachi looking for work, hoping to secure a commission for a song from a passing driver en route to a restaurant. A couple of mariachi stand in front of our van. We drive slowly at them. They don't move but wave and shout, our driver perseveres, and they jump aside at the last moment – but then pursue us. It's an extraordinary scene – I'm being chased by a picturesque figure in Spanish attire, waving and gesticulating, banging on the side of the van, demanding that we let him serenade us. Andrea is worried, and suggests we lock our doors in case they climb inside and strike up a tune. We turn a corner and are confronted by an even more bizarre scene – literally hundreds of mariachi milling around the plaza, singly and in groups, some playing instruments, others tuning them or carrying them purposefully. All are dressed exquisitely, most favour short Spanish jackets and button-embellished trousers – some wear huge, curving high-crowned sombreros and a few pack six-guns in fine leather holsters. I suppose these guns are replicas, part of the exotic Mexican bandit look, but I'm not sure.

We hurry to our destination – a restaurant called Tenampa. The genial host leaps upon us. The establishment is 80 years old, he boasts, and he sweeps his hand in a gesture that invites our gaze and approbation. On the walls are huge murals of mustachioed men in sombreros and portraits of dated beauties, no doubt Mexican starlets of years past. We sit and within minutes a mariachi group gathers around neighbouring diners and starts work. Before they are halfway through their song another band starts up, and then a third. The consequence is chaos – cacophony. One band is small, a harp and guitar, while its rival is large – four trumpets, four violins and at least two guitars. The small band doesn't stand a chance, but they don't appear to mind, nor do the diners whom they serenade. They smile and simper appreciatively. At one table a couple makes a brave attempt to tango between the closely packed tables and chairs. Extraordinary. Our turn comes. The mariachi close in around us and the blast when it comes is intense but not unpleasant. One chap hovers right over my head, violin next to my ear, and sings his heart out.

When they leave I sneak out for some air. I ask one wandering mariachi how long this goes on. Until four or five in the morning, he says. Another interrupts and says, with a smile, 'All night'. I go back to Tenampa, but this time I am frisked as I enter. As the hour gets later the chance of trouble must increase. Maybe those weren't fake revolvers I saw earlier on the hips of some of the mariachi. We slip away.

11 THE GIANTS OF TULA

The Giants of Tula – four great imperious carved figures – stand on top of a low pyramid at Tollan Tula. They were discovered in the 1940s and only recently restored to their original position.

Saturday 10 July

We get up early and grind our way through the Mexico City traffic towards what was – before the coming of the Europeans – the largest city in the Americas: Teotihuacán. It dates back to around 200 BC and was greatly enlarged by the Toltec civilisation that thrived from around AD 750 until the 12th century. Teotihuacán was taken up by the Aztecs who, from the 15th century, were the power in the land, having absorbed other civilisations and cultures such as the Toltecs. But the Aztecs were inclusive – adopting and adapting the gods and traditions of other peoples – and for them Teotihuacán, with its mighty ancient structures and huge scale, became a sacred city. The place still retains an overwhelming presence. The city was built to heroic proportions and is thought to

At the base of the pyramid that supports the Giants of Tula are the fragmentary remains of the sacred buildings that surrounded it. These stucco friezes show scenes of fierce snakes, animals and sacrificed prisoners.

have housed up to 60,000 people in its prime. Two mighty pyramids now remain; one – the Pyramid of the Sun – being the third largest pyramid in the world, with a base measuring 215 metres square and reaching a height of nearly 70 metres. This stepped pyramid – virtually rebuilt in the early 20th century, with an incorrect number of steps – is awe-inspiring in its bulk. But, for me, far more impressive is the Pyramid of the Moon. Rising behind the man-made sacred mountain is a real mountain – an extinct volcano. The avenue appears to lead to – or from – the volcano, the source of natural power. In plan and in the form of its building Teotihuacán merges with, and reinforces, the sacred meaning of the landscape. I want to know more about the Toltecs – but to do this I will have to look elsewhere. Teotihuacán is too restored and the crowds of tourists from Mexico City begin to obscure the place. It's time to move on.

We drive to the remains of the city that the Toltecs built in the 10th century when they decided to move the centre of their power away from Teotihuacán. Tollan Tula was built from around AD 900 as a virtual replica of Teotihuacán, but the city remains a relatively obscure and desolate ruin with little yet excavated. I approach the bleak landscape – it's hot but a strong wind is blowing. Among the rocky outcrops I see what I am looking for: a squat, flat-topped pyramid with a series of huge carved figures aligned along its windswept platform – the Giants of Tula.

Little survives of this once great city of 40,000 people. I look around and see just a few buildings with a mix of square and round section columns – the remains of once great palaces and temples. But the pyramid with its population of colossal figures looks, in a way, complete. The four great figures, each 5 metres high, were only discovered in the 1940s, buried face down in a nearby ditch. So their resurrection on the platform is relatively recent – although it is believed to have been their original location when carved in around AD 900. It is thought they functioned as columns, helping to support the roof of a temple that once stood on the platform, but their exact meaning remains obscure. As I confront the giants for the first time I find myself at last in direct and dramatic contact with an image that the Toltecs would have held in awe. I contemplate the four giant figures standing rigidly in a row against the dark blue of the afternoon sky. Each is made of four blocks of stone, each is virtually identical and all show signs of colour. They would have looked splendid, like great totem poles. I single one out for close inspection. The features of its face are strong and it stares ahead, over the land where the city once stood, with a stern and searching gaze. They wear feathered headdresses and in their hands they carry what could be weapons unlike any I've seen before on an ancient statue. Some say the figures carry bows, arrows and spears and this may be the case, but it looks to me, well, more like some sort of gun. Two fingers are wrapped around a trigger and there is a barrel of sorts. Most odd. More revealing is the item suspended on the chest of each figure: a huge stylised butterfly, the emblem of the great god Quetzalcoatl who was represented in the image of a plumed serpent, a butterfly or a pale-faced man with a white beard.

So little that is tangible remains of this once mighty power: the great giants – Toltec heroes turned to stone. But Toltec myth and memory lived on in the civilisation of the Aztecs. One myth is particularly poignant. One of the last Toltec kings – perceived as divine and a manifestation of Quetzalcoatl – was forced into exile but his people always expected him to return. The Aztecs adopted this myth and accepted the form in which it was ordained Quetzalcoatl would return – as a pale man, with a beard, who would come from the east – and the date, which was predicted by the 52-year cycle of the

Mesoamerican calendar. In 1519 it seemed to the Aztecs that this ancient prophecy was fulfilled. A pale-faced man with a beard did come from the east at the time predicted. But it was not Quetzalcoatl returning to his people. It was the Spanish conquistador Hernán Cortez who brought not a return of the great days but doom for the Aztecs and, ultimately, for all the civilisations of Central and South America.

12 MESA VERDE, COLORADO, USA

Sunday 11 July
We fly from Mexico City to the United States – the promised land of the white nations – landing at Denver and then flying on to Durango, Colorado. During this last leg of our journey a powerful landscape unfolds. In the distance I fancy I can see places that live in the imagination – Arizona and New Mexico, scenes of definitive and terminal conflict between whites and Indians, between the new forces of law and order and the anarchic freedoms of the old frontier. We soon leave the great plains behind and head into the foothills of the mighty and sprawling ranges of the Rocky Mountains. I am going to see the enigmatic remains of an indigenous urban culture that thrived in this mountainous land – that constructed sophisticated houses and sacred structures – centuries before conquering Europeans set foot in North America.

Created nearly 1000 years ago, the cave-like buildings of Mesa Verde are made of sandstone and harder rock from a nearby river bed. The neat stonework was rendered over and colour-washed in yellow and red ochre – it must have looked spectacular.

Durango is a charming but intensely provincial little town. It calls itself 'historic' because it was founded way back in 1881 as a mining and railway town. We don't linger but drive down the main street and on into the undulating landscape. Outcrops of flat-topped rock rear up majestically – what the pioneering Spanish explorers called mesas or table tops. And between these are great canyons or gulches, scooped out millennia ago by remorseless glacial movement. Within this landscape is the treasure I seek – stone-built houses and villages created between 700 and 1000 years ago and located within the very clefts of the cliffs below the mesa tops. This is human habitation and natural landscape combined in a sublime and creative manner. Collectively these dispersed habitations are called Mesa Verde.

The people who built these cliff-hugging houses are a secret people. They seem to have been part of a culture that moved into New Mexico, Arizona and Colorado from the south around 1500 years ago and so were contemporary with the Toltecs. Then, in around AD 1300, they disappeared. They left no written language and few artefacts beyond their architecture and their pottery. As for their fate – no one knows. Some say they moved back to Central America, others that the people split into smaller tribes and became the nation called by the Spanish the Pueblo – or house-building – Indians. By the time the Navajo moved into the region in the 15th century the house-building people were long gone – a thing of myth and awe. The Navajo referred to them as the Anasazi or 'ancient ones' – and so they have been called by the whites who discovered the remains at Mesa Verde in the 1880s. Now a new name has been invented for these talented but enigmatic people and the National Park Rangers who protect and display the site refer to them solemnly by the tongue-twisting name of the Ancestral Puebloans.

These people organised themselves into urban communities in which they evolved a series of building types including apartment blocks, houses, storage structures and round, semi-subterranean, cave-like sacred buildings in which clan and family members would gather for various ceremonies and rituals. These buildings form a haunting and elemental image of organic architecture.

The Anasazi had, as far as it is now possible to determine, venerated the earth – the great mother goddess – from which they believed mankind was born. Knowing this, it is

As I stand on the top of the mesa peering over the canyon where the cliff-side buildings of Mesa Verde lie beneath, I reflect on the fact that the Anasazi travelled nimbly between home and mesa top by specially cut hand and foot holds in the cliff that now appear impossibly difficult and dangerous to negotiate.

easy to believe that they sited their homes and sacred buildings in these great clefts not only because they offered shelter but because they represented the great nurturing womb of nature – places of power connected with their origin. The Anasazi's sacred structures, now called kivas – a Hopi word – seem to support this speculation. They are one of the most gripping and revealing fragments of the long-lost Anasazi culture. All the surviving collections of houses incorporate a number of kivas, seemingly one for each small cluster. Kivas, round in plan and semi- or entirely excavated, were originally roofed with layers of stone laid on stout timbers, the top of the roof level with the surrounding ground level. So they were man-made caves, earth wombs and symbols of the birthplace of man. The kiva was generally entered from above, through a square hole in the centre of the roof. This opening also served as a chimney, for within the kiva was a hearth and while hot air and smoke escaped through the roof-door fresh air was pulled in via a duct that opened outside the kiva. An altogether ingenious arrangement. This was a matrilineal society, so whatever happened in a kiva, it almost certainly happened under the control of the women of the family. A key clue to the nature of the religious ceremonies is a small circular hole in the floor. This is called a sipapu and it is thought to be a 'spirit hole' and to represent an opening into the bowels of the earth, into the underworld or 'spirit world' – to the great womb from which the Anasazi believed they had issued in primordial times.

The most striking of these rock dwellings is now called Cliff Palace. Current thinking is that this complex of buildings – it is no palace but a small town – was made up of a number of individual houses and structures containing, in all, about 150 rooms. The population of this small urban community is hard to estimate but it is thought to have been between 150 and 200 people. It was probably built, or rebuilt, around AD 1200–1250 when the culture was in its prime and its people achieving an agricultural surplus and enriching themselves through trade. The end of the Anasazi culture was evidently dramatic and rapid. Exactly what happened or why no one knows.

The structures at the Cliff Palace are impressive if – in some instances – somewhat over-restored. The buildings are made using blocks of sandstone with carefully tool-marked surfaces to give texture and improve weathering. Window and door openings are framed by larger stones and often taper slightly from bottom to top. To finish off the exteriors the neat stonework was rendered over and colour-washed. These little towns must have looked stunning and sophisticated with neat and regular window openings, yellow and red ochre colour-washed facades and the paved flat tops of the kivas forming little squares or courts around which buildings cluster. It must all have looked uncannily like a medieval Tuscan hill town.

Within, the buildings had slender wooden beams supporting floors and, amazingly, many of these beams survive. Fragments of interior decoration also survive to offer a

Left *The kiva, where family members would gather for ceremonies and sit on the built-in benches lining the wall. The sipapu, or spirit hole, in the centre is said to represent an opening into the underworld from which the Anasazi believed they had come.*
Right *Original floor structure and wall paintings survive in the Tower House at the Cliff Palace. The colours mirror the red ochre of the surrounding mountains at sunset. I think of the extraordinary similiarity to the Roman tradition of exterior/ interior relationships.*

glimpse of the domestic world these people inhabited. Most enthralling is the first-floor room in the diminutive Tower House at the Cliff Palace. The lower portion of the wall is painted Pompeiian red ochre and the upper part an off-white. The line between the colours veers up and down with geometric precision – the red invades the white to create a silhouette of pyramid shapes. The faceted, serrated profile is a stylised representation of the distant mountainous landscape that frames the Mesa Verde site. Colorado was given that name by the Spaniards for a good reason – the landscape is red, in certain lights intensely so. The Anasazi took the distant mountains that defined the horizon of their world as the inspiration for the ornamentation of the walls of their rooms – their private worlds. Again, there is a connection to European tradition for this type of interior/exterior relationship is a common theme in Roman interiors.

While the Cliff Palace is the most extensive and majestic Anasazi ruin, what is called Balcony House is the most dramatic and inspiring. It is difficult to reach, its buildings crammed into crevices in a high gorge, some of them only reached by climbing high, almost vertical ladders, seeming to totter above infinity. Strong nerves are needed and, I must admit, not all of my colleagues were prepared to make the pilgrimage. This was a grave error, for they missed something wonderful. This is the one Anasazi community of buildings that it is possible to walk, climb and crawl through – to inhabit spaces much as they would have known them – and to see views much as they would have seen them around one thousand years ago. In the distance is a range of mountain peaks, pyramid-like in form and red in hue as the sun sets. This view, and views like it, must have been the inspiration for the wall paintings.

From the palace watch room, reached by a curious tunnel, I reflect on the cultures and civilisations of Central and South America – civilisations that are often misunderstood and which are now only gradually being properly appreciated. They had their dark side – a tradition of human sacrifice and a belief in blood as a medium for venerating and appeasing their gods. But what's also clear is that these civilisations were sophisticated and, in many respects, pioneering in their skills and perceptions. Although diverse, they shared a remarkable knowledge of astronomy that gave focus to their complex religious beliefs. They also shared an advanced understanding of the forces of nature – a force they worked with, in empathy, rather than against. These regions of South and Central America were – in a sense – the spiritual heart of the world. Beautiful, brittle, mysterious, contradictory, these civilisations stood not a chance when confronted by the technology, prowess, greed and ruthless material ambition of the European adventurers who flooded into the land from the 16th century onwards. The loss of these civilisations – sudden and almost total – has been one of the greatest losses for humanity. Had they survived – and evolved organically – I can't help but believe the world would now be a better place.

13 THE 1851 PATTERN NAVY COLT

Monday 12 July
After the power of nature apparent at Mesa Verde, I contemplate the stark and brutal power of man. This is my dark treasure – the 1851 pattern Navy Colt revolver. I include this because the gun has become a central part of US culture and almost mystic in its significance. Many US citizens see the gun as a symbol of freedom, of independence, of the rights of the individual – almost as if it was the Bill of Rights and US Constitution made manifest. The message is enshrined in the Second Amendment, ratified in 1791, which states that: '…the right of the people to keep and bear arms shall not be infringed…being necessary to the security of a free state.'

Thus the gun became – as if by law – the symbol of the new nation, for it was the means by which freedom had been won and was, in the early days, the means by which freedom was maintained. Since the gun was granted this legal and moral authority it is not surprising that it became the means by which an ethically dubious 19th-century theory about the 'manifest destiny' of the white man to eclipse the native American was made reality. The gun became a symbol of pride and authority to compare with the Japanese samurai sword.

The 1851 pattern Colt revolver, known as the Navy. Its pioneering design and mass production technology were influential in permitting the 'white man' to win the West.

I want to reflect on this strange situation – and to do this I go to a gun club in Durango to see the handgun that started it all, and to talk to a set of people who still live by the gun – or at least by the symbolic values they believe it possesses. The gun I have in mind was invented by Samuel Colt who, in the 1830s, dreamed up the six-shot cylinder revolver and used pioneering methods of mass production to make repeating revolvers that were reliable, efficient and readily available. Armed with this formidable weapon – which could fire six shots in rapid succession before reloading was necessary, rather than the then usual one – a single man became a veritable army. As Captain Samuel Walker, a great champion of the new weapon, wrote to Colt: '…in the summer of 1844, Col. J.C. Hayes with fifteen men, fought about 80 Comanche. Without your pistols we should not have had the confidence to undertake such daring adventures.' Colt perfected his design in the 1851 pattern .36 calibre revolver that became known as the Navy because the standard version had a naval scene engraved on its cylinder. It is an elegant and functional if distinctly menacing design, made of interchangeable, mass-produced components that slip together and can be easily exchanged. With a mere push, the wedge can be removed and so allow the gun to be broken down into three main parts – barrel, cylinder and, all in one, hammer, trigger and grip – so that a component can be quickly exchanged or replaced.

At the gun club – really more a shooting range behind some stables at the end of a plot off the main street – I meet William D. Foote, known as Dale. He is the local authority on the Colt revolver. He wears a brace on his hip – hung in the Hickok draw, with butts facing forward. Apparently with this arrangement each gun can be drawn with either hand. It makes sense if you think about it – but I was thinking about Dale in the wild streets of Durango. Is it legal to walk around the streets with this pair of antique Colts loaded with soft lead balls that could tear your arm off? Yes, of course it's legal, smiles Dale, and reminds me that 37 states in the US allow their citizens to carry guns. Is a licence needed, I ask? Dale smiles again. Yes. But these are mostly issued on request to residents of the state with only the barking mad or convicted psychopaths having a little trouble obtaining them. It seems that no licence at all is necessary to possess antique weapons like these 1851 pattern Colts although they remain as lethal now as the day they were made. Dale is a great supporter of the US citizen's right to bear arms and a die-hard defender of the Second Amendment.

As we pore over and load one of his 1851 pattern Colts we talk about the ethics and social implications of the mass ownership of lethal weapons. He extols his Colt's virtues as a machine – as a tool. It's so efficient. That, of course, is just the point. Do they not make it easier for one person to hurt another – by mistake or in the heat of the moment? No, he says, it's the man that kills, not the gun. What does the gun mean to him? The answer is direct – it means freedom. Or as Dale puts it, 'A man with a gun is a free man, and a man without a gun is a slave.' We smile at each other – the gulf between us without measure. So we concentrate on his weapon as a piece of pioneering industrial design.

The time has come to fire the piece. We walk over to the firing butts and Dale slips the copper percussion caps onto the nipple behind each chamber. I fire the first chamber. There is minimal kick, a billow of sulphurous gunpowder smoke that smells like bad eggs, and the target topples. Strangely satisfying. Oh dear. And so I empty the piece at the targets, with a swirl of pungent smoke gradually enveloping the scene. There are no misfires – the Colt is indeed a fine machine.

All this revolutionary and reliable weapon needed to make it – and Samuel Colt – famous was a war. The American Civil War, starting in 1861, was what Colt had been waiting for. The mass-production technology used by Colt allowed nearly 100,000 Colt revolvers – mostly 1851 Navy pattern – to be produced in the first years of the war. By the end of the war the total made was touching 200,000. By then the Navy Colt, available in vast numbers, and the later improved six-guns that were its progeny, were probably the single most important piece of technology that permitted the white man to 'win' the West. Without a doubt the Navy Colt helped to make history and, in the process, became a national icon. The cult of the gun in the US – which the Colt did much to establish and the 3-million-strong and influential National Rifle Association now does so much to protect – and the consequent ease with which guns can be acquired have cast a terrible shadow over the nation. It has been estimated by one authority that since President Kennedy died from a bullet in 1963 more Americans have died from gunshot wounds than died in all the wars of the 20th century.

But such facts and figures wash over Dale. He knows that he is right and believes that his views represent America. He is defending what he perceives to be the national way of life and is being true to his view of history. As I leave the range I see the bumper stickers on the pick-up trucks driven by these champions of freedom. The slogans they carry are just as articulate as their owners, perhaps more so. One reads: 'Give me the Second Amendment and I'll protect the rest', while another declaims, 'If you outlaw guns then only outlaws will have guns'. When people have such inflexible and simplistic views about life it's hard to discuss the subtleties of cause and effect. Maybe that's the point. People who promote guns don't want to argue or discuss, they simply want their view – flawed as it might prove under scrutiny – to prevail. That, I suppose, is why they admire the gun – it's the supreme symbol of the ruthless, no compromise solution. When the gun speaks you're dead or alive, victor or loser, right or wrong – the argument's over, solved with extreme violence, with little room for dialectics.

That night we brood over the day's experience at the range. Firing the guns was exhilarating. Lee and Nick especially enjoyed themselves – popping away with Winchester 73s, and Colt 45s. We all enjoyed it – what's wrong with us? We worry, but I console myself. We weren't shooting people, only lumps of metal. To continue the Wild West fantasy for dinner I eat buffalo steak at our lodge. It is delicious.

The next morning we have a nasty surprise at Durango airport. We turn up with our mountain of luggage and discover that – for reasons that remain mysterious – we have been selected for special security. As we check-in, Tim Sutton's name appears on the FBI's list of wanted men. Glee all round, but a date-of-birth check rapidly reveals that it is another Tim Sutton who is the subject of a nation-wide man hunt. However this slows the flight down and we are 45 minutes late taking off. The result is that we miss the connection from Denver to Washington, DC and have to wait three hours for the next flight. The consequences of this delay are nearly disastrous.

14 MONTICELLO, THOMAS JEFFERSON'S HOUSE

Tuesday 13–Wednesday 14 July
We arrive in Washington, DC to find that, despite telephone calls ahead, the transport we have hired for the estimated two-hour drive to Charlottesville, Virginia, has gone. Eventually two vehicles are acquired at about 2.30 am – we have an appointment at 6.00 am to meet the museum staff at Thomas Jefferson's house at Monticello, Virginia. We hope that we can get a couple of hours' sleep before the meeting – but no luck. The drive is slow, but we help keep ourselves awake by spotting Civil War battlefields. We get to our hotel at around 5.15 am. All are exhausted and tempers short. There is a move to abandon the shoot. This is impossible. People have risen early to meet us at Monticello. Tim Dunn points out that the reputation of the BBC is at stake. We hatch a plan. Tim and I will make the 6.00 am meeting and film the interior of Monticello before the crowds of tourists arrive from 8.00, while the rest of the team grab some sleep and meet us mid-morning. I have a quick shower and 20 minutes after arriving at the hotel Tim and I are off – driving into a Virginia dawn in search of the peculiar world of Thomas Jefferson.

Monticello – the house Jefferson built for himself between the early 1770s and 1809 – is in many ways a microcosm of the United States, its origins, its strengths and its weaknesses. It says so much about the man who designed and built it – and consequently about the nation that he also played a key role in building. Jefferson drafted the Declaration of Independence and in 1801 became the fledgling nation's third President. In 1874 James Parton, Jefferson's biographer, observed, 'If Jefferson was wrong, America is wrong. If America is right, Jefferson was right.' Parton could have added – if you understand Jefferson, you will understand America.

As I walk through Jefferson's house I begin to understand him a little more. I start in the entrance hall, created in about 1793. Its architectural detail and inspiration are European – Italian Renaissance combined with late 18th-century French neo-Classicism. This is a reminder that Jefferson, although an instrumental force in the creation of a new nation in the New World, still looked to the Old World of Europe for artistic and political inspiration and imagery. Classicism at the time had a very precise political meaning. It was the architecture of freedom and it was largely associated with the egalitarian French Revolution. Obviously for the republic of the United States – which had just won its independence from Britain – such symbolism seemed highly appropriate.

But there is, in the hall, ornamentation that tells another story about the character of the new nation. Jefferson had dispatched Lewis and Clark to explore the north-west

Monticello is the most important building erected in the early decades of the United States' existence. Here Thomas Jefferson wanted to establish an architectural style for the new nation.

portions of the great land of which the United States was part. They sent a number of acquisitions back to Jefferson and so the hall is hung with regalia from various indigenous tribes. Jefferson called this his 'Indian Hall', and it makes a clear point: the best of the Old World and the best of the New are combined in the United States. Pondering this heady and ambitious message, this marker for posterity, provoked me to reflect on the subsequent history of this new nation. Has it lived up to this dream – has it realised the promise made by its founding fathers?

One of the cornerstones on which the United States bases its claim to be the champion of freedom are those ringing words now attributed to Jefferson: 'We hold these truths to be self-evident, that all men are created equal; that they are endowed by the Creator with inherent and inalienable rights; that among these, are life, liberty, and the pursuit of happiness.'

There is no reason to doubt that the powerful opening words of the Declaration reflect what Jefferson earnestly believed. Also important to Jefferson was religious tolerance and he helped establish the United States as a secular nation, with complete separation between church and state. He was an enthusiastic naturalist and ambitious amateur architect as well as being a gentleman revolutionary and politician. But, despite his obvious achievements, Jefferson had a dark side characterised by accusations of hypocrisy and racism. Like many late 18th-century utopians and idealists, Jefferson loved the common man – but at a distance. And, like other Virginia gentlemen at the time, he kept slaves. In 1822 – four years before his death – he owned 267 slaves.

Jefferson appears to have had a degree of racial contempt for his slaves, but he also treated them in a humane manner. Certainly there is evidence that his slaves had a deep regard for him. Jefferson's disturbing thought about what he described as the evils of the 'amalgamation of whites with blacks' is strange indeed when his own domestic arrangements at Monticello are considered. Jefferson's wife died after ten years of marriage and it was long alleged by his political enemies that he had a sexual relationship with at least one of his slaves – Sally Hemings. But this is just one more of the mysteries that surround this contradictory man.

The first phase of Monticello, from 1772, was as the ornamental home of a rich landed gentleman in a prosperous British colony. But as Jefferson changed his allegiances and as America moved from colony to revolutionary state to independent nation, so the design of Monticello changed. What started as an English-style ornamental cottage evolved into a French-inspired neo-Classical villa, and finally to a semi-public building that Jefferson imagined, by the time Monticello was complete in 1809, would act as a model for new architecture in the new nation.

Jefferson was clearly trying to create a house that was functional as well as ornamental. He designed a set of double doors between hall and parlour that both opened simultaneously when one door was opened; and his bedroom apartment is located on the ground floor and is entered directly off the entrance hall. Presumably, in the 18th-century tradition, he received favoured or intimate guests in his bedroom apartment. This is a curious room. The bed itself is placed within an open arch. So, of an evening, Jefferson would climb into bed from his bedroom but in the morning – by getting out of the other side of the bed – he would be in his study. The study forms part of an enfilade of three small rooms, all linked by wide arches. Both main rooms contain book shelves and together formed Jefferson's library. By placing 'public' rooms on the ground floor, Jefferson avoided the need for a grand staircase. Indeed he regarded the ornamental staircase as a waste of space and at Monticello installed two small, functional staircases – an idea taken from Palladio, the great source of English Palladian architecture, whose villas usually contained a symmetrical pair of small staircases.

Another consequence of Jefferson's determination to create a convenient, virtually single-storey building, was the idea of linking the main house by an underground passage (inspired by the Roman 'cryptoporticus') to a remote range of rooms – kitchen, brewhouse and the like, but also including rooms for some of Jefferson's slaves, with further houses for slaves nearby. And so this elegant villa – its architecture speaking of freedom won from British rule – surrounded itself with quarters for those who were not free. A shadow was cast over this paradise – and that shadow remains.

Left Jefferson's 'Indian Hall' at Monticello reflected his desire to include the best of the old and the new worlds in his design.
Right Jefferson's unusual bedroom apartment in an archway between the entrance hall and his study.

15 THE SEAGRAM BUILDING, NEW YORK

Thursday 15–Friday 16 July

In architectural terms, what is the essence of this promised land? Jefferson's vision of a classical America, in which freedom and democracy were to be expressed in columns and pediments, took root but was not exclusive. Gradually the potential of the New World cities and the opportunities afforded by pioneering technology coalesced to produce an architecture that was distinct and different. In Chicago and New York in the late 1880s the iron-framed high-rise building – the skyscraper – was born.

These early high-rise buildings, all making use of the newly invented elevator, were relatively modest in scale, and often not entirely free-standing – they still rose from traditional urban plots. But they were – and remain – spectacular. New materials were used – wrought iron initially, but soon steel and fireproof terracotta for cladding and internal partitions – and they had flexible, open-plan interiors since loads were carried not by internal walls but by the columns of the metal frame.

What is the golden age of the high rise? When did it reach its optimum – both technically and artistically – before becoming tainted as a standardised, industrialised expression of mass-produced commercial building and soulless urban renewal? When was it pushing back the boundaries of construction, and creatively questioning preconceptions about living and working in the city? New York offers outstanding examples of high-rise buildings from different periods so I set myself the task of finding what, for me, is the best of the breed.

First I look at the Flatiron Building. Completed in 1902 to the designs of D.H. Burnham, it has become famous because of its peculiar shape, after which it is named. Constructed on a narrow, tapering site, the chameleon-like Flatiron can look stunning from certain angles – walking around it, in changing light, is a compelling experience. Seen straight on from the north it looks like an unbelievable sliver of a skyscraper, a huge, rounded, pencil-thin tower. From a different perspective it's a different building, a great cliff-face of windows. However, the Flatiron is a standard product of its age. It is of steel-frame construction, but it is ornamented with Classical detail which makes the building look like an over-extended Renaissance palazzo. It does not for me express the full artistic potential and power of the skyscraper.

So I move on to the late 1920s when the skyscraper started to bravely display an aesthetic that expressed its revolutionary methods and materials of construction. There is the Chrysler Building, designed by William Van Alen and started in 1928, that develops the skyscraper compositional form in a truly memorable manner. Its spire is Art Deco married to a weird Hollywood version of Gothic. It has great charm but also does not realise the full potential of the new building type. So what about its great contemporary and rival, the Empire State Building? This was started in 1929 to designs by Shreve, Lamb and Harmon and is more tempting. Its steel frame – the components of which were mass-produced and delivered to the site in construction sequence – arose at incredible speed and it has a sheer functional form that, despite its restrained Deco detailing, is still almost shocking. But my imagination is gripped by two buildings that really mark the end of the golden era of the skyscraper, when this great architectural adventure was coming to a close. These are, it seems, what the earlier skyscrapers were leading to.

Both buildings are in Park Avenue and both are in appearance almost ruthless expressions of their function, materials and construction. They are Lever House, started in 1951 and designed by Gordon Bunshaft, and the Seagram Building, designed by Mies van der Rohe and completed in 1958. The Seagram Building is a development of some of the ideas found in Lever House and is, more importantly, virtually the last word in skyscraper design. Mies had been in the forefront of high-rise architecture, evolving

In my search for the finest example of the skyscraper I first consider the Flatiron Building, but its decorative veneer of history is charming rather than ground-breaking.

radical ideas for sheer towers of steel and glass while working in Germany before World War II. In the United States he developed and realised these ideas and in the Seagram the aim of the urban high rise for commercial use – a conceit born in American cities – reaches near perfection. The steel and glass tower has breathtaking elegance, its details a direct result of the demands of the material and construction techniques used. The building is set back in its own small square, free-standing like a massive piece of sculpture. In this way Mies liberated his design from the tyranny of the traditional urban plot that makes many early skyscrapers rise, somewhat absurdly, from low-rise neighbours. Long, straight avenues, lined by rows of towers, are one of the great images of New York. But functionally this arrangement is a compromise. Standing in dark, canyon-like streets, the skyscraper cannot achieve its true potential as a transparent finger pointing to the skies, offering unlimited views and enjoying maximum light.

The minimal columns of the steel frame and the fully glazed curtain walling that encloses it have an amazing sophistication and sleekness that speak of the maturity of the designer and, in a way, of the confidence of the age. Like most architects of his generation Mies had a deep regard for history, but he wanted to get to the essence of things, to reinterpret, not copy directly. He admired the rational structural systems of Greek and Roman architecture and so the ground floor of the Seagram is framed by simple column-like steels. He also saw that the essence of Classical architecture lay in the relationships between its various parts, in the systems of proportion that defined and united its different elements. So, if you look, you will see that the detail and form of the Seagram reflect ancient harmonies – the golden section, Root 2, the two-to-three proportion.

Inside, the functional and artistic advantages of Mies's structural and proportional systems are immediately apparent. The interior is open, with no structural walls beyond those enclosing the central core. Light floods in and the space can be used in the most efficient and flexible way with partitions placed and moved as required. Although minimal in detail, the interior has dignity and beauty. In the entrance hall Mies achieved elegance in the most simple manner – the fully glazed walls offer views out and let maximum light in and the space has a generous proportion. As Mies said, 'less is more'. The forms, the details, the proportions had a huge influence, and during the following decades were imitated in many cities around the world – often with dismal consequences. None has the power of the original, one of the ground-breaking buildings of the world. It is an expression of an ideal, of a modern architecture liberated from the dependence on history or superficial style, with its appearance – its aesthetic – being derived from its function and the techniques and technology of its use and construction. Love it or hate it, you've got to respect it.

The Seagram Building, designed by Mies van der Rohe and completed in 1958, for me combines all the functional, technical and artistic ideals of modern architecture.

16 THE STATUE OF LIBERTY, NEW YORK

Saturday 17 July

This is our last day in the United States and we plan to leave by looking at what was, for tens of thousands of people, their first hopeful glimpse of this promised land: the Statue of Liberty. To many people the statue is now more a kitsch icon than a world treasure. We all take it for granted, but I want to look at it afresh, to see it for the extraordinary creation it is.

A gift from the Old World to the New, it was conceived in France in 1865 when that country was descending into despotic authoritarianism under Napoleon III. It was intended to celebrate liberty, enlightenment and the belated end of slavery in the United States. It was inspired by one of the wonders of the ancient world – the Colossus at Rhodes – yet it was fabricated and constructed during the 1880s using modern technology under the supervision of the French engineering genius Gustave Eiffel. The statue is a distinguished member of an international family of super-scale human figures, many of which I plan to visit during this journey – but clearly its real power and significance lies in its meaning and symbolism.

The statue was born out of a paradox. Not only was freedom being eroded in France as it was being built, but also the very nature of the United States itself changed significantly during the time that elapsed between the statue's conception and its completion. In 1883 Emma Lazarus wrote a sonnet entitled 'The New Colossus' in which she created the timeless romantic meaning of the statue: 'Give me your tired, your poor,/Your huddled masses yearning to breathe free,/The wretched refuse of your teeming shore./Send these, the homeless, tempest-tossed to me./I lift my lamp beside the golden door.' Sadly the world had already changed. The previous year the United States had brought in the first broad federal immigration law excluding convicts, lunatics, idiots and paupers. Many of the world's oppressed who now crossed the 'seven seas' to enter New York were vetted and either interned or deported.

By the time it was unveiled in October 1886, relatively open entry to the United States had ceased. Liberty's bold message of welcome and offer of freedom and justice had been compromised, her radical symbolism had been undermined. The statue has something uncomfortably in common with Thomas Jefferson. He was able to write majestically that 'all men are created equal' and continue to own slaves. The statue celebrated a liberty that was rapidly eroding.

But the statue did move many and continues to move many. And, like the Eiffel Tower in Paris, it has become the symbol of a city, even of a country. At a time when the United States is becoming more defensive and closed, when its reputation as a champion of the oppressed and of liberty is being challenged, I wonder what the future holds for this great symbolic statue. Will it take on a new meaning or will it become a memorial to a vision that has been lost, a victim of an ever more dangerous and divided world?

The 47-metre-high Statue of Liberty holds a torch of truth and freedom which was to welcome the oppressed of the world who came to the United States.

THE SPIRIT OF THE NATIONS

Sunday 18 – Monday 19 July

As we take the long flight to Sydney, Australia, we're glad to leave New York. Its frantic pace is intoxicating and we need our energy for the mission. A couple of members of the team leave New York looking decidedly more ragged than when they arrived. Sydney could prove to be more of the same. We eventually arrive at our hotel in the Rocks district and experience a somewhat shocking climate change. We have moved back into the southern hemisphere so have flown into a relatively chilly mid-winter from a sweltering mid-summer in New York.

The Rocks – the old residential part of Sydney, perched right above the bay – has been massively overhauled since I was last here almost ten years ago. Its 1830s terrace houses and warehouses were threatened with mass oblivion in the 1970s, lay abandoned, became the focus of an epoch-making conservation battle and have mostly been preserved, but at a price. It is now the tourist heart of the city, bursting with restaurants and perplexing shops selling items that few people can really need. Emblematic is the bar/restaurant a few doors down from the hotel: its unique selling point is that it is the only (I hope) Bavarian beer cellar in Sydney in which the hapless staff are forced to don lederhosen, blouses and – I swear – speak in false German accents. That evening I meet my daughter Isabel – who happens to be passing through Sydney on a grand tour of the region. She has just left university and is having one last blast of freedom before settling into a career. We have supper with Amy, her travelling companion, in a harbour side fish restaurant, and make a point of not talking about her plans when her extended post-university holiday is over.

What characterises this next collection of treasures? I suppose each in some way, consciously or unconsciously, defines or catches the spirit of a nation. Certainly all the potential treasures I plan to examine in Sydney represent, in their different ways, the country, its origins and aspirations. So I set myself a challenge: to look at three iconic structures in Sydney, to hold a competition between them, and decide which says most about the city and the nation.

17 SYDNEY HARBOUR BRIDGE, SYDNEY OPERA HOUSE OR ST JAMES'S CHURCH

Tuesday 20 July

Early in the morning – before the rest of the team are up – Tim Dunn and I climb to the top of Sydney Harbour Bridge. The bridge is of ruthlessly utilitarian design, made of steel and takes the form of a huge arch – spanning 503 metres and rising to a maximum height of 134 metres between gigantic Egyptian-looking abutment towers – from which the carriageway is suspended.

Tim and I get kitted up – skintight windproof clothing, harnesses, cables and with all our filming equipment shackled to our bodies – and then scramble along a narrow walkway below the approach viaduct, wriggle through tight openings, climb a staircase, penetrate to the core of the structure and suddenly burst into the sunlight. We then mount to the top surface of the great arch and – slowly, carefully, tied to the steelwork – begin our gradually curving, upward ascent. The wind is sharp but the views magnificent. Way below traffic hurtles across the bridge and, below that, boats slice through the choppy waters of the harbour. We toil on to the top and stand below the snapping Australian flag, surveying the view.

The bridge linking each side of the bay, with its approach viaducts snaking through the city, for decades defined Sydney. Then, in the early 1960s, a challenger appeared on the scene.

In 1957 the Danish engineer Joern Utzon won the competition to design an opera house for Sydney. Opera houses have, it seems, the curious power to transform a city or a nation – to mark its cultural coming of age. The design was striking, with its main feature being a series of strangely but daringly poised vaults of complex design. These meant much – or nothing – depending on the eye of the

beholder, but they gave the design a very different and distinctly modern look. Some thought the shapes looked like shells – the opera house was to be built on Benelong Point, a sacred Aboriginal site that European observers had noted was covered with shells. Others thought the shapes were inspired by the sails of yachts in Sydney Harbour. Utzon himself was not explicit about his inspiration. He regarded the shells as the 'fifth facade' of the building, as something that would be seen from all angles, close and afar, a potentially living thing reflecting or being seen in profile with or against the sun, water and clouds. The play of light was to be all-important. However, he did explain that one major influence – not specifically for the shells but for the composition as a whole – were Mayan temples he had seen while touring Mexico in 1949. Knowing this, the design of the opera house does have a weirdly Mayan look – the shells rise from a Mayan-style platform, the top of which is reached by a wide flight of stairs – again a Mayan feature.

The foundations were laid in 1959. After that, nothing went right with the project. Utzon's complex shell structures appeared to be unbuildable, the construction costs rose alarmingly and as power shifted in the country the project became a political football.

Early on Utzon accepted that the original design was too complex, involving the manufacture of too many components with too many different curves. He rethought their structural nature and simplified them. Each shell, no matter its scale, was to be formed from a sphere, which should make manufacture easier. Recognising that shells with water-stained concrete outer surfaces would be far from attractive, Utzon specified that the shells should be covered with tiles glazed an off-white to reflect light and water and laid in a fan-ribbed pattern 'like a palm leaf'.

This change in design came as a shock to the champions of the scheme and still did not make the opera house much cheaper or easier to build. And there were unfortunate consequences, including the demolition of some recently completed work that was not suitable for the revised design. Politicians, clients and architects got locked into a never-ending cycle of blame and recrimination. Eventually problems over money coupled with what Utzon perceived as lack of respect made the existing arrangement untenable. In February 1966 Utzon resigned and suffered the heartbreak of abandoning his masterpiece, incomplete and with its future uncertain. Other architects were appointed and finally in 1973 the opera house was officially opened.

The day I see the opera house the sun is shining and clouds bustle across the blue sky. The shells sparkle, the water flashes – this is how it was conceived to be seen, and it looks magnificent. From near and far, from different vantage points on land and boat, the shells of the opera house compose, decompose and then recompose themselves in a startling, powerfully abstract manner. But what about the interior? I remember that,

Officially opened in 1932 the Sydney Harbour Bridge is of striking design. Its arch spans 503 metres and is 134 metres above sea level at its highest point. I climb to the top – the view is magnificent.

The stunning vaults of the Sydney Opera House were conceived as a living sculpture, reflecting or being seen in profile with or against the sun, water and clouds. The play of light is all-important.

after my first visit, I was disappointed. But that was ten years ago and I know that the place has been revamped recently. This time building works prevent me from penetrating too far into the opera house. This is a a disappointment. I point out that, as far as I know, I have been granted permission to go inside. Eventually I am granted limited access. I get inside – and remain disappointed. I must conclude that Utzon's departure was a tragedy. In all great buildings there must be certain relationships between inside and outside, between structural forms and building materials. At the opera house I, personally, do not feel this is the case. The spectacular promise of the exterior is not realised by the interior. If seeing the outside is one of the great moments of 20th-century architecture, the interior delivers one of the great anticlimaxes.

As the afternoon turns to evening I move on to view my third contender. This is, I admit, an unlikely candidate but, even if relatively architecturally underwhelming, it has a revealing and moving tale to tell. St James's Church is a relatively humble affair but the date at which it was built and the circumstances surrounding its design and construction make it fascinating and important. When the church was designed in 1819 Sydney was less than forty years old, its architect was an emancipated convict and the driving force behind its construction was one of the great men of early Australia – Lachlan Macquarie, who was then Governor of New South Wales.

I arrive outside the church as the sun sets. It is an amazing object, forming a group with the Hyde Park Barracks of the same date and by the same architect. When church and barracks were built Sydney was little more than a British penal colony, established in 1788 as a convict settlement at the other end of the world. But in this dubious and unlikely setting Macquarie and his architect Francis Greenway created buildings of the highest quality – particularly the church, which has a metropolitan dignity that must have been astonishing in its day. Its design is as fashionable and well detailed as any of the churches being erected at the time in the rapidly expanding cities of late Georgian Britain.

Francis Greenway was evidently an architect of great ability, and had trained with the London-based John Nash who was one of the leading designers of the Regency period. But Greenway got into difficulties with a building speculation and tried to avoid the shame of bankruptcy by forging a number of documents. His crime was discovered and in 1812 he was condemned to death but with the sentence subsequently reduced to transportation. When Greenway arrived in New South Wales he was fortunate to encounter the enlightened Governor, Lachlan Macquarie. After a military career – including time in India – Macquarie had been appointed Governor in 1810. Macquarie had a vision that embraced the nascent town and its community. He wanted to ennoble the town by creating a series of public buildings and to help rehabilitate convicts by recognising their talents when possible and by giving them responsibilities that would restore at least some of their dignity and self-respect. In these early days Sydney had a complex society, consisting of various levels of convicts and ex-convicts, and 'exclusives' – the free settlers who fancied themselves the aristocracy of the new land. These latter had a vested interest in keeping the ex-convicts down and so ensure that they offered limited competition for resources and power. To his great credit Macquarie insisted that emancipated convicts should be treated by their fellow colonists as social equals. All he wanted were the men to make his vision for Sydney become a reality, and when

My choice is the unassuming St James's Church in the heart of Sydney, designed in 1819 and made of handsomely coloured bricks. To my mind, its story most closely reflects the history of early Australia.

Greenway eventually arrived in Sydney in 1814 Macquarie had found his key man. During the next five years Greenway rose to the position of Chief Surveyor to Macquarie's little kingdom. But this admirable system was not to last. The 'exclusives' were alarmed by the liberties and opportunities that Macquarie offered the convicts and brought about his resignation in 1821. Macquarie's appointments among ex-convicts were also scrutinised and Greenway was demoted to be the subordinate to the Chief Engineer and, in 1822, dismissed from office – a year before the interior of St James's Church was completed. Greenway was a broken man. To have regained a professional life and dignity and then to suddenly have it all wrenched away proved too much. He stayed in Australia where he eventually died in obscure poverty. A tragic tale – but only in the short term. Macquarie and Greenway are now seen as early heroes of the country and, somewhat ironically for a man found guilty of forgery, Greenway's portrait has even embellished an Australian $10 note. So for me St James's Church – the story it tells and the attitudes it enshrines – is most special. It is a bold statement of confidence in the future and a declaration of intent. It proclaims that, from the start, certain men had a clear and enlightened vision for Australia. As I sit in the church I sense afresh the boldness of Macquarie's vision – the determination that this new country would rise above its difficult origins and eventually become one of the great and free nations on earth.

18 ABORIGINAL ROCK ART, KAKADU

Wednesday 21 July

It is, of course, one of the bitter ironies of history that the emancipated convicts and settlers of New South Wales could only begin to gain their identity by virtually destroying that of an earlier culture – the Aboriginal people. I want to find out as much as possible about these earlier Australians and so plan to go to Kakadu to see Australia's most concentrated collection of rock art. We fly to Darwin and into a world and climate very different to that of Sydney. It is hot, the landscape lush and empty. Kakadu is now a national park, returned to the guardianship of the families of the Aboriginal people that have lived in the area for as long as anyone can remember – and that's quite something because here memories seem to stretch back at least 20,000 years!

As we drive a termite city emerges from the wooded verge beside the road. I inspect one – it's a veritable skyscraper, soaring way above my head, an amazing object. I am deeply impressed by this example of insect enterprise and resolve to become more intimate with insects. This is about to happen in a way in which I could not have anticipated.

Soon we stop at a stall to buy fruit and I lean against a tree, but the trunk is alive with large green ants and I jump back. We contemplate them warily, wondering about the severity of their bite. Then Rod, our driver, walks up and says, 'Ah, green ants' – and promptly eats one. These creatures are popular with the Aboriginal people because their little green bodies are packed with vitamin C; as much in one ant, I am told, as in an entire orange. Yes – I have to try one. Suddenly this alarming sight, a tree crawling with ferocious-looking ants, becomes my food basket. I choose my target and chase the little fellow up and down. He sidewinds, changes direction and escapes. I select another victim. These ants are hard to catch. Eventually I get one and hold it by its head so that its green body presents itself. The desperate little ant battles hard to escape and wriggles its posterior at me in a strange and appealing manner. But to no avail. The moment is here. I bite. My first insect. It has a powerful taste – citrus, lemony, condensed vitamin C indeed. Not bad really. I try another, and another, until my tongue and gums become numb from the vitamin C. I am carried away by the novelty of hunting insects and eating them. Most humans have an innate fear of insects, a repugnance. Perhaps it's their resilience that frightens, the awareness that insects are a very superior life form, better adapted to life on earth than we are. Remorseless, almost indestructible. Perhaps this is the basis of my strange, elemental delight. I the hunted, the human usually beset by insects – be they mosquitoes or flies – have become the hunter. The worm has turned. If you can't beat them – eat them! The experience changes my whole perception of insects. They are a fine healthy food, protein and little else. And tasty. I begin to think that insects are the way forward. I wonder which others I can eat and resolve to keep my eyes open for opportunities.

Rod has lived with the local Aboriginal people for years and been initiated into some of their secrets – about which, of course, he cannot tell me. But he is willing as we drive to talk about other aspects of Aboriginal life. The term now used is 'Traditional Owners', or TOs. The people I'm to meet are from the Jawoyn tribe, who are the traditional inhabitants and guardians of the site we plan to visit at Ubirr. I probe Rod about 'Dream Time', the true reality – it is here that timeless truths, prophesies and fate are foretold – and the Creation Ancestors who gave shape to the world during the time of Dreaming. To the Aboriginal people the whole landscape is alive and tells stories of the past, the present and the future. Mounds, creeks, billabongs and caves are not only the work but also potentially the abodes of the Creation Ancestors. So all is sacred, the land and all that walks, crawls or grows on it, the sea and all that lives in it. Among these Creation Ancestors there is the Earth Mother called Warramurrungundji, who is said to have travelled through the world creating rivers, lakes and wildlife before turning into a huge rock – her 'Dreaming Site' – that the Aboriginal people believe is at Kakadu. Then

there is the Rainbow Serpent, who I find particularly fascinating given my recent encounters with rainbows and serpents in other cultures, notably that of the Inca in South America. Once again, I see strange connections between disparate places and people.

I will meet these ancestors – or at least ancient images of them left by man centuries ago – when I get to Ubirr, the site that contains the richest and most interesting collection of early rock art in Australia. Ubirr's caves and rocky outcrops contain thousands of paintings, some overlaid on others, some relatively new, others ancient almost beyond belief. Currently it is believed that some of the paintings could be as much as 50,000 years old with most of the early images dating from around 20,000 years ago. A number feature the long-beaked echidna that became extinct around 15,000 years ago. This is incredible. Some of these paintings make other ancient cultures seem almost recent. The first cities began

Some of these specimens of insect architecture in the Northern Territory rise several metres above the ground. Made of earth and saliva, it is a beautifully organic form. It is, I am told, roughly half as large again below ground, and when the upper portion is occupied during the rainy season, this particular mound houses up to 30 million termite inhabitants.

to emerge in the Middle East 10,000 years ago while the Pharaohs flourished in Egypt a mere 4500 years ago!

Before viewing the paintings at Ubirr we must spend the night at a camp nearby. Here I enjoy one of Britain's major cultural legacies to this great island continent – meat pie and chips. One home-made pie was particularly fine after being reheated within the engine of my vehicle. This refinement – a speciality of touring in the Northern Territory – not only gave the pie a satisfying all-through even temperature but also a slight hint of finely burnt petroleum spirit and high grade oil. Don't knock it 'til you've tasted it! On the journey I also manage to acquire another Australian speciality – a purse made from a kangaroo's scrotum, most useful for keeping round things in.

We arrive at Ubirr as the sun rises. Stunted rocks emerge out of the bush – one of them I suppose is the slumbering Earth Mother. We are introduced to our guide, one of the 'Traditional Owners' of the site. In fact this ponderous phrase turns out to be particularly appropriate. Natasha Nadji, who is aged about 20, is attractive and at first shy, but we soon warm to each other. 'How long has your family lived here?' I ask. Natasha looks at me as if I've asked a faintly silly question. 'Always,' she answers. It's an incredible thing to meet a young woman who believes that these images were painted by members of her family and for whom they are as alive now, as pregnant with meaning, as when they were first created.

The walls of the cave are thick with paintings, one overlaying another. Some are fresh and clear, others faded and confused. Some have clearly been retouched (they are a living art after all, relevant to the local people, not part of a museum), others bear the authentic hue of antiquity. More recent renderings contain abstracted images of European sailing ships and even firearms. Many metres above ground level is a faint image. It's a drawing of the Mimi spirits, Natasha says. They are frail, stick-like creatures with small heads perched on long, thin necks – they look incredibly fragile. Natasha agrees and tells me solemnly that they have to be careful because their necks can break in a strong wind. It sounds like she knows some Mimi personally. She says Mimi spirits taught the people how to draw and then the people started off by drawing them. 'So these must be very early paintings?' I ask. She shrugs. The precise dates of things don't interest Natasha greatly. I say they look rather like aliens. She smiles and says yes in a rather conspiratorial way. 'They are very naughty,' she says, 'very tricky.' I ask her directly if she has seen a Mimi. 'No – but my boyfriend has.' Natasha's boyfriend was out hunting, shot at his target and kept missing. He couldn't understand why until suddenly a cave opened up in a cliff face and a Mimi appeared. It had taken a fancy to the animal – a rock wallaby – and was protecting it. The young man realised the hunt must stop and as he moved away the Mimi and cave disappeared. A good story. We walk to the land above the caves, the highest point on the river, from which we can get a glimpse of the absurdly misnamed East Alligator River – home to much of the local crocodile population. Natasha points to smoke rising in the distance and says 'that's where we come from', meaning not only her immediate family but a family stretching back to the beginning of time. What an extraordinary sense of continuity – to be part of a culture that believes itself rooted in the mists and myths that surround the origin of human society on earth. To be part of an ancient people who, in their religious beliefs, have long ago transcended material concerns and operate in a landscape of rocks and mounds, pools and billabongs, all of which are at once simple and sacred.

As I walk down from the vantage point I spy a

Our guide is Natasha Nadji, one of the 'Traditional Owners' of Ubirr which contains the finest collection of rock art in Australia.

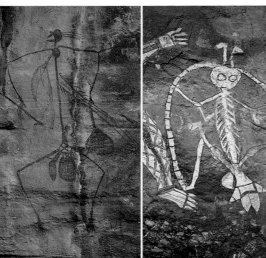

poem, pinned on a board, that tells me more about Natasha. It's written by her grandfather Bill Nadji and stops me in my tracks: 'But, now you know the story/You responsible now/You got to go with us to Earth/Might you can hang onto this story, to this Earth.' Once you know the story – the history, the meaning – you are responsible for it, you must play your part to keep it alive. It's quite a task that Natasha has shouldered. But it's a shared burden. This poem, I realise, is also a message to me – to everyone who knows the story of the earth. We're all responsible for its well-being.

Thursday 22 July

At last, it seems, the team has settled down, into harness. It has taken nearly a month – and there have been tremendous ups and downs along with serious logistical teething problems – but we seem to be pulling together, each in our different way. We mesh together more efficiently, work more easily without words – and mostly seem happier. As Nick puts it, we have become 'time-shifters' – we have left the ordinary cycle of events and now seem to float above reality. This is becoming a way of life, constantly thrilling, constantly stimulating. I am writing this at 5.45 in the morning in a hotel in Darwin and we are about to fly to Indonesia. But despite the early starts and hard work – mental as well as physical – I have rarely felt better. My problem is that I don't want to go home, back to the regular rhythm of humdrum life. I don't even really miss my friends! This could well turn into a serious problem.

We fly from Darwin to Yogyakarta on the island of Java. This is my first experience of Indonesia, and even as we load our vehicles to leave the airport I am overwhelmed by the sights, the sweet smells, the sound of bells and the beauty. Things bode well.

We travel to our first destination – the legendary 8th-century Buddhist temple at Borobudur. This masterpiece of symbol-loaded sacred architecture – one of the greatest buildings in the world at the time of its creation – was lost in the jungles of Java for nearly a thousand years and only rediscovered by the world at large in the early 19th century. The story is incredibly romantic, with a leading role going to the pioneering English merchant and colonial administrator Thomas Stanford Raffles who in 1815 explored and revealed the temple when Java was briefly a British possession. I half expect the temple to still be lost in jungle and am momentarily disconcerted when, arriving at our luxurious and sprawling hotel, I see the temple by moonlight – lurking at the end of the hotel garden. As I am constantly being reminded, I am in the modern world of mass tourism and holiday destinations.

Three examples of the Aboriginal people's rock art near Kakadu in the Northern Territory. The paintings have different ages, meanings and purposes with some believed to be up to 50,000 years old.

19 BOROBUDUR BUDDHIST TEMPLE, JAVA

Friday 23 July

We get up about 5.00 am so we can film the sun rising behind a huge volcano that stands opposite the temple. Although many kilometres away, the volcano – called Marabi – is ever present. Its perfect cone-like form soars to an unlikely height so that the plume of smoke that hovers constantly around its peak merges with the clouds. The sun bursting into life above this fuming monster should be a spectacular sight. But the morning is misty and as the dawn breaks the volcano starts to vanish into the haze. We hope the rising sun will soon burn off the mist. Perched on one of the terraces of the temple, we wait patiently, hopefully, for a moment that may not come. This is what filming is like. Unfortunately the mist wins its battle with the sun and the morning arrives without a visually dramatic sunrise. So we turn our attention to the temple and rush to film as much as we can before the tourists start to arrive in bulk.

The temple, or stupa as Buddhists would call it, is an astonishing affair. Built from *c.* AD 760 to 830 it is, famously, a diagram, a building with its meaning and message carved into its stones, its form and proportion. The temple is square in plan and takes the form of a step-pyramid. The square plan is a reference to the square mandala – the divine chart that informed the design and construction of Hindu temples and that was here inherited by Buddhist builders. The pyramidal form of the stupa is yet one more reference to the magic mountain found in most ancient religions – the pyramid being a man-made version of the mountain in which dwell the gods, that forms the axis of the world. The pyramid has more or fewer levels depending where you start and stop counting. Seven, eight or nine seem likely since these are sacred numbers in most religions. Buddha is said to have taken seven steps to the north immediately after he was born, and Buddhism has eight principles such as correct meditation, correct behaviour and correct action that lead to the goal of spiritual enlightenment.

I calculate that the stupa has nine levels, which appeals to me since King Pakal's step-pyramid tomb at Palenque in Mexico – of roughly similar date as Borobudur – has nine levels symbolising the nine levels of the Mayan underworld. I like connections like this.

Levels one to five are square in plan and are thus supposed to represent the material world, the world of form, in which we live. The sculptures or bas-reliefs on the wall of level one represent the world of the desires, and reflect the fundamental teaching of Buddha that all misery is caused by desire and that man cannot be free of suffering –

The Borodudur Temple in Java is a miniature Buddhist version of Mount Meru, the Hindu centre of the universe – the home of the gods. It appears to have nine levels, each moving closer to spiritual enlightenment.

achieve enlightenment – until desire is extinguished. Consequently these sculptures depict some lurid scenes, including erotic images. Unfortunately, these have now been screened by a terrace recently constructed against the lower level of one side of the stupa. Apparently the largely Islamic Indonesian authorities found these, when restored some years ago, a little too strong for their tastes. Level two shows the life of Buddha – from birth, enlightenment, to death, on his journey from earth to heaven. The 1200 carvings are of great artistic as well as spiritual power and are packed with exquisite detail. These are on the inner wall of the stupa, but the walkway of each level also has a high outer parapet and these too are loaded with carvings. These largely create a worldly context for the sacred images – they show daily life, people at work and prayer, and also, no doubt, now long-obscure parables. Levels three, four and five reveal the life, trials and tribulations of the pilgrim and disciple Sudhana on his quest for spiritual wisdom, enlightenment and truth. On level six Sudhana mixes with bodhisattvas (enlightened beings who have renounced nirvana to stay on earth to help those, like Sudhana, on the quest for spiritual wisdom) and achieves various insights and skills – there is a particularly charming panel showing Sudhana, now embellished with an aura, learning to levitate – before he finally achieves his goal.

What becomes clear, as the route around these lower levels is pursued, is that the stupa is intended to be a microcosm of the universe, a diagram of the route to nirvana – the place reached when all desire has been defeated, extinguished. And it shows the means by which enlightenment is to be achieved, with Sudhana representing everyman – all pilgrims – who set out on the quest for the secret of life, for escape from the repetitive cycle of life, death and rebirth. I suppose these lower levels of the stupa were open to all, with each pilgrim walking the route around each level, learning its lessons and then, informed, ascending to study the lessons of the next level, and so on up to level five.

The top levels of the stupa are entirely different in character, and must have been only accessible to those who had achieved enlightenment – probably only certain monks. These levels are circular in plan, not square, and so are seen as representing the spiritual

The top levels of Borobudur are circular and represent the spiritual world. Presumably they were accessible only to monks. At the edge of each level are rows of small bell-shaped stupas which each contain an image of the Buddha.

There are 1200 carvings at Borobudur, all packed with exquisite detail and showing daily life, people at work and prayer, and also, no doubt, now long-obscure parables.

as opposed to the material world. The walls here are plain – clearly in this rarified spiritual world there is no need for images to tell and teach stories. What these upper levels do possess, however, is perhaps even more visually striking than the carvings below. Set on the edge of each curving level are rows of bell-shaped stupas, each with its outer skin of stone pierced with small openings. These openings offer a glimpse of what lies within each stupa: an image of the Buddha. Then I notice that, in the three tiers of stupas, the openings in the lower are diamond-shaped while those in the stupas forming the top tier are square. Another secret of the stones, another hidden message? What can this subtle but significant difference mean? The best way is the most obvious. Ask a Buddhist monk. Although Borobudur was probably abandoned as long ago as the 11th century – long before the coming of Islam to the island and probably because of damage caused by earthquakes – the temple remains sacred to Buddhists. Since its rediscovery and restoration the great stupa has been the regular setting for Buddhist ceremonies, and monks abound.

I meet a monk from a nearby monastery and ask him about the meaning of Borobudur. He confirms the conventional interpretations of the place, is imprecise about the number of levels (I suppose each pilgrim sees the number he wishes or needs to see – although most locals I asked reckoned there were nine) and, charmingly, admitted to being baffled by much of the imagery on the lower levels. What about the diamond and square openings in the upper stupas? Ah yes, the diamond shape is a square standing on one corner – good but unstable, unsure, still able to lean one way or the other, towards good or back towards evil. On the other hand, the square standing on one of its sides represents stability, the goal achieved and no backsliding. So, if the great step-pyramid at Borobudur was not only to instruct pilgrims, but also to reflect their progress on their journey to nirvana, it would have been clear to all that the pilgrims basking on the topmost tier – next to stupas with square openings – were full of grace and standing at the gate of heaven.

Saturday 24–Sunday 25 July
The team flies to Bali en route to our next treasure, located on the nearby Indonesian island of Sulawesi. We check and go to see the town.

We wander around and soon find ourselves in a long street of bars and clubs. It's Dhyana Pura in the Seminyak district of Batu Belig. We enter a bar – chosen at random for all seem much the same – and I start to observe the scene. The customers are a mix of ages and races but it is not hard to miss a few dominant factors. There are quite a few middle-aged and not attractive white men escorting or leering at a large number of young, generally very attractive and spectacularly underdressed Indonesian girls. We have wandered into that frightful spectacle – the game that dare not speak its name – the sex tourist industry. I've never seen the like of this before. All of Bali is not like this, I'm sure, but it does seem a wicked world – and the main offender, it appears to me, is a certain kind of Western male. He has money to throw around on the pursuit of pleasures that are mostly illegal or morally frowned upon at home. As I travel around Bali I now view all Western men with suspicion. I suspect them all of entertaining unspeakable thoughts and desires and, what's really depressing, they – and the Balinese I meet – are probably having similar thoughts about me.

20 SPIRIT HOUSES OF TORAJALAND, SULAWESI

Monday 26 July

We meet in the hotel lobby at 6.00 am and fly into Makassar in the south of Sulawesi. Our destination lies at the centre of the island, in a remote region known as Torajaland. Sulawesi is in some turmoil. About ten days before we arrived a young female Christian preacher was shot in the north, it is supposed by a Muslim gunman. We have to be on our guard. No commercial flights currently land at the small airport at Pongtiku in Torajaland so we have to charter a small plane to make a journey that would take days if attempted by road. Our local guide and fixer Agustinus Lamba says not enough people want to come to Torajaland to make regular flights worthwhile. I'm puzzled. The country looks beautiful, the people I've met so far are extremely friendly. Does some danger lurk beneath the surface – is there something that people are frightened of? Admittedly, I have been attracted to Torajaland to see something many might think macabre, perhaps a trifle off-putting – in short I've come to meet death. Or, to be more precise, to see how people here deal with the presence and consequences of death, to study the rites and rituals of their extraordinary funerals, and to see the fantastic and artistic manner in which the dead are represented and their bodies interred. It must be said at once that, from the point of view of death, Torajaland is a strange and deeply unusual place. The religion here is ancient, a brand of what is known as animism, a religious conviction that all of creation – living and inanimate, man, animals, plants and rocks – contains the breath of life, soul and spirit. All is alive, all comes from and goes to the same place. This is much like the religion of the Australian Aboriginal people – but here animist beliefs have had very peculiar visual consequences.

With Agust leading the way we drive from the minuscule and moribund airport to our hotel. After a few kilometres the consequences of Torajaland's remoteness become apparent. The people wear traditional clothes and go about timeless pursuits in their fields – threshing rice or herding water buffalo. There are no advertising hoardings or the familiar strident trappings of material culture, roadside shops sell local products and crafts and there is a wonderful absence of the sort of ugly, quickly built concrete frame constructions that now disfigure most parts of the world. Instead there is something wonderful – and this is part of my treasure. The local traditional architecture is stunning. Buildings of any consequence are furnished with massive roofs made of bamboo thatched with palm leaves. These roofs turn up at either end so the whole affair looks like a boat or, perhaps, the massive horns of a giant water buffalo. As if the form of the roof was not dramatic enough, its eaves, bargeboards and the building below it, are all elaborately carved and painted in a tasteful range of earth colours. I knew of these boat houses of course, they are one of the reasons I'm here. But what I didn't realise is that

Everyday life in Torajaland – as we drive past in the background I glimpse the ordinary houses which blend in perfectly with the landscape – I am surprised to see that they are small versions of the treasure I have come to see.

they are everywhere – they are the standard type of building, merging magically into the jungle, standing in village clusters among rice paddies, or alone on vantage points – and serving all manner of uses.

We arrive at our hotel near Rantepao and to my amazement it is formed by clusters of these boat-roofed houses – the rooms are clearly relatively new, but beautifully made using traditional methods and materials of construction. But we have to dash off to our first appointment – a large funeral that has been going on for days. All, we are told, are invited! We drive for an hour or so through the lush landscape until the small crowded road, people strolling and sitting on each side, suddenly opens onto what looks like a village green. At one corner are men are crouched at some frantic activity. We get out to survey the scene and I wander by chance into a mound of green cattle dung – why is it this unusual colour and how did it get here? I look around and suddenly realise. It is the contents of the stomachs of numerous water buffalo, for ahead of me I see a mountain of butchered flesh and numerous massive skinned heads, with staring eyes and long horns. The frantic men are cutting up the bodies of buffalo that have just been sacrificed as part of the funeral rites. There are many dead animals – traditional tokens of wealth – many guests and a huge amount of funereal architecture. Surely this must be a communal funeral, I ask, but no. All of this is for one man. I plunge into the mass of still numerous guests to find out who this mighty man was – and to perhaps view his body.

In Torajaland death is the most important event in life. It marks rebirth, the return to the realm occupied by hallowed ancestors. When a person dies they are not at first regarded as dead. They are referred to as ill and kept among the living, perhaps in one corner of the home or in the family dead house or spirit house – a specially ornate boat house used for funerals and in which the dead, not the living, dwell. Only when the funeral is complete – perhaps lasting as many as nine days, and months after clinical death – is the person regarded as truly dead. Then their body is interred in a rock-cut vault, a cave or in a timber coffin hanging from a cliff face and an effigy (or Tau Tau) is erected near the burial site. This is ancestor worship of a familiar kind but, perhaps, with a special touch of magic about it, for clearly the effigies are not just memorials to the dead but are intended to be things of great power, totems or talismans for the living.

Most of this little village is temporary, erected solely for the funeral. The structures are two-storey with a gallery at ground level and balconies like boxes at an opera house at first-floor level, all to be occupied by guests of different status. From a first floor balcony I watch the people trickling away, each being given a part of the body of one of the sacrificed animals. The only permanent structure among all this is, as far as I can see, the massive boat house. This is the dead or spirit house of the deceased's family. I am seated opposite it and suddenly I realise that the box I am staring at contains the body of the dead man, placed on a first-floor platform in front of the building.

Part of the ritual of the Torajan funeral, this temporary village draped in red banners has been erected solely for the funeral of a man who has been dead for four years. Each guest leaves with a piece of meat from a buffalo or pig sacrified to accompany the dead man.

I leave to look around. Despite being a funeral all are happy, talking and laughing, and I am given palm wine to drink out of a bamboo pole. It's good – like very dry cider. A pig is brought to execution. It's a frightful business. The pig knows its end is near, squeals pitifully in terror and wriggles desperately on the pole to which it is tied. The executioner comes forward and slowly slides a long knife into the pig's heart. It is not a clean affair. Blood gurgles out, the pig continues to yelp, eyes swivelling imploringly. The knife goes in again and again. Before the pig has stopped moving the fellow disembowels it, and then chucks it onto a fire to remove the body hairs. While still smouldering, its blood still warm, the pig is butchered with its body parts added to a nearby heap of flesh that is being dispensed to departing guests.

I am desperate to know more about the great man whose funeral I am helping to celebrate and about the ritual I am witnessing. By luck I locate the son of the deceased. He is willing to have a chat. Yes, the father was a very important man – apparently in local politics or government and, to my surprise, died four years ago. It clearly takes a long time to organise a funeral like this, to give a man the send-off he not only deserves but, I expect, demands. The funeral has, it seems, been going on for several days and will continue for a few more, but this is the big day – with the sacrifices and even bull fights in the morning. He explains the huge importance of treating the dead with respect while confirming that, on Sulawesi, the dead are never really dead. I talk about the soul, the breath of life being in all things. He nods in agreement and then, remembering the poor pig, I ask why, since it has a soul, was it killed? 'So that its soul will go with my father.' It seems that the status enjoyed in life – reflected in the number of souls of valuable animals that the dead take with them – remains important in the world of the ancestors. The day is drawing to an end, the piles of meat dwindling rapidly and the opera boxes emptying. We leave the strange scene, presided over by the coffin of the dead man perched high on the towering spirit house.

The Tau Tau (images of the dead) at Lemo in Sulawesi stand or sit in cliff-face recesses. Carefully crafted, they have an extraordinary power over the onlooker.

21 THE TAU TAU – IMAGES OF THE DEAD

Tuesday 27 – Wednesday 28 July

This morning we are going to explore graves of the sort that the dead man of last night is soon to inhabit. These are, I'm told, works of art and expressions of culture and religious belief that are unique to Sulawesi. I'm excited by what we might discover when we penetrate the realm of the dead.

Our first location is no let-down. It is the cliff graves at Lemo in a region known as Pengumuman. We bump along a track through a straggling village and suddenly, ahead of us, see a cliff face in which a series of balconies have been cut at several levels. All are occupied by near life-size figures. These are the Tau Tau, the images of the dead. All stare into infinity and most have their right hands raised – in farewell or in blessing, it's hard to say. On closer inspection I notice the cliff face is dotted with square openings, only 60 centimetres or so across. These are the doors to the vaults in which the bodies reside. Some of these vaults are said to be huge and to contain the bodies of generation upon

Left A coffin awaiting burial in one of the caves or cliff-face vaults at Londa in Sulawesi.
Right I enter the largest cave at Londa and everywhere see skulls in various stages of decomposition, along with small offerings to the dead – cigarettes are particularly popular.

generation of the same family. The Tau Tau are made of wood with faces painted brown. They are all much the same in appearance, emblematic rather than actual representations of individuals. I wander around at the base of the cliff face, among the paraphernalia of many funerals and various offerings to the dead left by family members. There is a miniature boat house, seemingly forming a catafalque in which a body was carried. There is also a stack of coffins – I suppose bodies are brought to the site in these, then removed to be interred in the small vaults. Nevertheless it's worth looking inside. I open the first two – they are empty. Then I open the third and I get a surprise. It doesn't contain a body but a large rat caught in the act of giving birth on the stained coffin lining. I shut the lid quickly as I don't want to upset her. Odd – an unexpected metaphor of life in death.

We then travel to an even more bizarre location at a place called Londa. Here there are vault burials in the cliff face but also cave burials and hanging burials with coffins stacked on timber poles jutting or suspended from the cliff. There are also rows of Tau Tau – again in balcony-like recesses – but these are very different to those at Lemo. These have extraordinary – startling – power. They show men and women and are all clearly portraits – and very skilful too – of the dead. They have carefully modelled and painted faces, distinct and individual expressions, hair, in some cases spectacles, and wear what I can only assume are the clothes of the deceased. Some stand, some sit, some are rather grandly dressed, some are in simple local clothes and conical straw hats. But all stare fixedly forward, looking at something only the dead can see.

I have been brought to this site by three young men. It is the property of their families and they are happy to show the scene to me. They are proud of it – as one observes cheerily, 'This is where we shall all come when we die.' These boys, carrying hurricane lamps, take me into the largest cave. The scene on the threshold is a good sample of what is to follow. A couple of skulls on a wooden box surrounded by a few simple offerings – the means by which these local people believe they can persuade the dead to intervene for the living. I enter, and it takes a moment for my eyes to adjust to the light. Then I see an extraordinary sight. Stacks of coffins, from floor to the rocky ceiling of the cave, some fresh and new, others rotting and breaking open to reveal the decaying remains of corpses: peeling flesh, tangled hair and mildewed grave garments. And everywhere skulls – on rocks, on timber platforms, squeezed into stone crannies – and a wide variety of simple offerings. Cigarettes seem popular. One skull sits among a heap of them – presumably its owner had been a heavy smoker in life. Certainly it seems that the afterlife is a smokers' heaven. There are also bottles of water, a plastic doll for, I suppose, a dead child, and lots of flowers. Obviously this grave is constantly visited, evidence that in Torajaland, the dead and the living have a close and continuing relationship.

In one recess I see a small coffin embellished with a cross – clearly there is an interesting fusion of beliefs going on. I sit outside this open grave, both welcoming and sinister, and say goodbye to my three guides. I realise that the rocky arch of the cave is not just an opening into the grave but a window on an inner world. I have caught a glimpse of the soul of the Torajan people – of these pleasant boys who beam at me. They hold ancient beliefs and follow traditions that give Torajans a sense of continuity and distinct character. Modern values, overwhelming materialism and consumerism have been kept at bay. Paradoxically, the uncertainties and increasing violence in the world means that Torajaland is currently protected from commercial exploitation, from the bland hand of mass tourism. But, I wonder, for how long?

The day is drawing to a close and I still have yet to get a close look at a spirit house, my first treasure here in Torajaland. The best examples are in a remote village called Kete Kesu which, I am told, is still organised in a traditional manner and formed entirely of boat buildings. It is indeed authentic but intended to be something of a tourist trap – however, being Torajaland, there are virtually no tourists present. The boat buildings all look similar but fulfil three distinctly different functions. Most of the buildings on one side of the street are relatively small, although still embellished with fine carvings. These are rice barns – and rice here is virtually sacred, the means by which life is sustained. Facing these are the largest boat houses. They are the spirit houses, belonging to various local families. Most are decorated with many buffalo horns and one has a fine display of buffalo jawbones. These reveal the number of animals sacrificed at funerals and so reveals the wealth and status of the families that own the spirit house. The spirit houses – although splendid – are not lived in, so the villagers live and work in the third type of boat building that, in scale, comes between the rice barns and the spirit houses. I study the buildings in detail and reflect on their forms. Most of the spirit houses have large, bold and life-like carvings of buffalo heads on their front elevations, but also carvings of pigs – another valuable animal of sacrifice – and the cock. This is significant too, for Torajans – like many cultures – see creation as divided into three levels. At the top is heaven, the realm occupied by the dead, the ancestors. In the middle is the earth on which the living hold sway, and below is the underworld, the domain of demons ruled over by King Cock, Lord of the Underworld who goes by the name Pong Lalondong.

Each building – be it rice barn, spirit house or human dwelling – is designed to echo this hierarchy of worlds. Ground level – usually open and used for storage, work or for animals – is the underworld. The middle portion of the building – the first floor – is used to house or receive rice or people and so represents the world of the living, while the top

The village of Kete Kesu is formed entirely of boat buildings – I have come to see the boat buildings that are used as spirit houses or homes for the dead.

part, formed by the splendid boat, is heaven, the place of the dead. As I ponder these fairy-tale buildings – so packed with meaning – cocks strut and crow around the village, scratching up little clouds of earth. Yes – lords of the underworld.

As dusk falls we make the short flight back to Makassar, the main town and airport on Sulawesi. The somewhat ramshackle modernity of Makassar – concrete-frame buildings, bright lights, advertising hoardings and restaurants selling Western food (US-style fried chicken seems in particular to have a stranglehold on the place) – reinforces the special quality and fragility of Torajaland. It's almost impossible to imagine the boat buildings, the spirit houses, the Tau Tau and the venerated ancestors are only a few hundred kilometres away from all this.

Spirit houses in Torajaland are adorned with large carvings of buffalo heads and sets of horns – a measure of the wealth of the deceased.

The next morning we meet for breakfast and fly to Jakarta and then to Bangkok en route to Siem Reap, Cambodia. For me at least, the journey into Cambodia is something of a cultural assault. I thought it would be more remote – but instead we drive into a major tourist destination, down an avenue lined with recently built hotels and varied massive modern buildings. Will Angkor – a place that I have long imagined to be one of the most compelling historic sites in the world – turn out to be a disappointment?

22 ANGKOR WAT, CAMBODIA

Thursday 29 July

We get up well before dawn to be outside the temple of Angkor Wat at sunrise. The Khmer civilisation that created the monuments of Angkor flourished from 800 to 1400. It commanded the productive lowlands of Cambodia and achieved a surplus in rice – and with plenty, came leisure, the arts and the time to evolve a complex setting and symbolism for the Hindu religion that had arrived from India. The golden age of the Khmers' Angkor Empire was the 12th century and during this period a series of stunning structures was created over a large area – measuring 50 kilometres from west to east – with the best preserved and best known being Angkor Wat. It was conceived, like all great Hindu temples and Buddhist stupas, as a model of the universe, of the dwelling place of the gods, but also as both a temple and tomb for its creator – the deva raja or god-king Suryavarman II, who died in 1150 just as the Angkor Wat was completed. The king's name intrigues me – Surya is the name of the Hindu Sun god and varman the name of the rulers of Angkor – together they mean the Sun protector or shield. The identical name – and concept of royal pedigree and purpose – I found at the Mayan city of Palenque where its King Pakal was also the 'Sun Shield' of his nation and people.

I arrive alongside the wide, lake-like moat enclosing Angkor Wat just as a golden glow transforms the sky. But all is not peace. This is a tourist target, and sunrise and sunset the favoured moments for communion with history. And where there are tourists there are people dedicated to selling them things, mostly useless. My magic moment – the sun rising in a spreading golden haze behind the bulbous lotus towers of the temple – is made faintly comic as I and the team jockey for position with diverse tourists and have to do polite battle with the hawkers determined to discover exactly what it is that we crave – postcards, maps, water, fruit?

Before having a close look at Angkor Wat I want to get a feel for the site so I hire a motor rickshaw and go for a drive. The splendid Angkor empire collapsed in dramatic manner in the early 15th century, so its great temples and city were gradually enveloped by the jungle. They were only glimpsed by the Western world in the late 16th century and not fully rediscovered until the 19th century. What I was not aware of until I drove around was the mighty extent of the architectural remains of the empire, the sustained high quality of its monuments, and the way in which so much lies in picturesque decay with the jungle only just being kept at bay. And there is another, more serious problem gnawing away at the fabulous heritage of the Angkor civilisation. The region has recently seen 30 years of nearly continuous war and instability with temples – including Angkor Wat itself – occupied by North Vietnamese soldiers and by Khmer Rouge. The legacy of this fighting was chaos, lawlessness, looting and vandalism. Although peace now prevails, bad habits die hard and, among impoverished peasants, looting remains an employment which, although severely punished by the government, is an attractive option when faced with remorseless poverty.

As well as the quality and quantity of the built wonders in the area immediately around Angkor Wat there are two structures in particular that came near to knocking me right out of my rickshaw. My first glimpse of Baksei Chamkrong and Phnom Bakeng is a stunning revelation. They date from the 9th and 10th centuries and both are step-pyramids with flat platform tops – hauntingly similar to those being created a little earlier by the Maya in Central America.

And then I become aware of the scale of the waterworks – there are not only large moats around many of the main buildings, but huge reservoirs – the Barays – and evidence for an extensive canal system. To achieve this the Angkor kings utilised not only admirable engineering skills but also a fine understanding of nature. The Mekong River is the mighty heart of the region and it is the regular rise and fall of the river that filled – and continues to replenish – these great water features.

I return to the causeway leading into Angkor Wat and, with the sun now high above the temple, I walk over the wide moat along the straight path aimed at the heart of this cosmic construction. I feel as if I am on a pilgrimage, and everywhere there are signs and tokens that tell a story to those who know how to read them. Some even I can decipher. Across the causeway are numerous massive snakes carved in stone. These huge guardian

Angkor Wat, started in 1140, was intended to be a sacred landscape – a vision of heaven on earth and dedicated primarily to the god Vishnu. 'Angkor' means holy city and 'Wat' means temple. I had not realised that water would play such a powerful role in its design.

The apsaras at Angkor Wat in Cambodia have delicate, alluring and sensual features and still retain their power to enchant more than 800 years after they were created.

snakes are multi-headed – a familiar Hindu image – but the fact that each cobra has seven heads starts me thinking. I find a guide and ask him about them. To my amazement he confirms my theory. These nagas, he says, represent the rainbow, with their seven heads being the seven colours – these great serpents must originally have been brightly painted. So here we have it again, the rainbow associated with the snake – as in the Aboriginal people's imagery in Kakadu – and the rainbow representing a bridge between earth and heaven, a manifestation of the sacred – as in Inca theology. I suppose that crossing the causeway is to begin to cross the rainbow bridge from the world of man to the world of the gods, from the material world to the spiritual.

Somewhat amazed, I walk into the outer enclosure of Angkor Wat. Here it is easy to see that the temple is square in plan – a form inspired by the square mandala or divine chart used for the design of many Hindu temples. Within this outer enclosure is another smaller square where the pilgrim's path, carried by the causeway, becomes a straight corridor that penetrates to the heart of the temple. All is organised around this central and sacred axis. As I walk along it I look down smaller corridors and catch a glimpse of a huge and multi-armed image of Vishnu. Then on each side are sunken courts, the walls of which are embellished with images.

I am struck by a particular set of carvings. They show apsaras, the heavenly nymphs or celestial maidens who were consorts to gods, kings and heroes. In Hindu mythology apsaras were created during the great tug of war between gods and demons – good and evil – when the ocean of milk was well and truly churned; they used their female charms to distract the demons, thus helping the gods to win. In the complex ritual of Hindu temple worship apsaras were represented by dancing girls who were selected and guarded by Brahmin priests.

The route terminates at the centre of the temple where rises the towering central shrine in the form of a steep-sided pyramid. This is the heart of the complex and a symbolic re-creation of the holy Hindu Mount Meru – the home of the gods, the axis of the world.

I climb the dauntingly precarious, near-vertical steps to the heart of the temple – the shrine and mausoleum of Suryavarman II set below the tallest of the lotus towers. The carvings here are the most exquisite – especially the apsaras or queens. They have a contemporary appeal – when you stare them in the eye you almost fancy their staring back, faintly smiling, alive. They are in such striking contrast to the stylised Romanesque art being created at roughly the same time in Western Europe. These figures are lithe and vital, those in Europe powerful but symbolic rather than living.

23 STONE FACES OF BAYON, ANGKOR THOM

Friday 30 July

Adjoining Angkor Wat is the location of another of my treasures – Angkor Thom. This is a massive walled city – rectangular in form and 30 square kilometres in area – that was started in 1181 by King Jayavarman VII. It is a remarkable conception that was the product of turbulent times. The Chams, a warlike people centred in Vietnam, captured Angkor in 1177 but were quickly defeated and expelled from Cambodia. Jayavarman built the walled and fortified city of Angkor Thom both as a symbol of his triumph and as an attempt to ensure that his capital could never again be taken by an enemy.

Just entering the city is a heart-stopping experience. The walls are breached by five main gates, each of which – as a foretaste of things to come – have upper portions incorporating towers that take the form of gigantic human faces. These faces with their haunting smiles – benign or sinister depending on your frame of mind – have inspired the imagination of Western man ever since Angkor Thom was rediscovered. But before I even pass through the gate I am engulfed in an extraordinary experience. The bridge over the ditch surrounding the city suddenly comes alive – or almost. Its balustrades are formed by images of demons on one side and gods on the other, all pulling on a massive cobra whose head rears up at one end. It's the Hindu creation story rendered in colossal scale. I pass the grimacing and straining faces of the gods and demons, petrified in their never-ending struggle, pass beneath the ecstatically smiling faces of the gate and enter the city. The humble buildings of the city have long gone, replaced by trees and dusty tracks, but the great public and sacred buildings survive in part.

At the centre of Angkor Thom survives what was always its most important and most impressive building – the Bayon, a spectacular tomb and temple surrounded by a moat. This is the monument not just to a man, but to a nation and a religion. By 1181, when the construction of Angkor Thom started, the Angkor empire had replaced Hinduism with Buddhism as its faith, and everywhere in Angkor Thom the images of the two beliefs overlap and merge. This offers a clue to understanding the heads of Angkor Thom. Jayavarman saw himself as the compassionate Buddha, so the tiers of serenely smiling heads on the city gates and the Bayon can be seen as images of the compassionate

The Bayon at Angkor Thom, a strange example of anthromorphic architecture, is surrounded by a moat. It is a vivid and haunting place where you can feel the power of the past. It's almost as if the building is alive.

Buddha, or of Jayavarman in the guise of the compassionate Buddha, implying that he was a bodhisattva, an enlightened being committed to helping others. But it seems the Bayon could also have carried a political message, and as an expression of political worldly power, unified with spiritual power, the Bayon is hard to beat – more so originally when the long-lost crowning gigantic image of Jayavarman as a bodhisattva towered over the other heads to form the pinnacle of the structure. The triumphal and worldly aspect of the Bayon is reinforced by a large and powerful bas-relief that records in gripping detail the victory of the Khmer Angkor armies over the Chams. But this is still not enough to explain the extraordinary power of the place. I stand by the moat and look at the Bayon, the array of heads of the Buddha and of the god-king Jayavarman, and their reflections in the placid water. It seems as if the faces were meant to proclaim that the building was alive, a living thing in its own right, a sacred structure in which the very stones pulsed with energy. This strange idea seems tenable in the falling light, when I catch a glimpse of the mobile expressions of the faces reflected in the slightly rippling surface of the water. Who knows? But the sense of the works of man having the life of the works of nature is given another, more explicit expression at the next temple I visit.

Ta Prohm is a temple town founded by Jayavarman VII in 1186 in honour of his mother. It was, when new, like a religious factory with a large mixed population including farmers producing rice to support the priests, officials and assistants and 615 apsara-like dancing girls. It must have been wondrous to behold – rich in architectural detail, form and colour. Now it is fantastical – an astonishing ruin that reveals what most of the Angkor temples were like a hundred or so years ago. Mighty stone structures lie

Ta Prohm must have been exquisite when it was built in 1186. Now it is slowly being destroyed by vegetation. It is an amazing ruin.

in pieces – collapsed. Others stand as if in defiance of the laws of gravity with structural systems exposed to scrutiny – particularly fascinating are the vaulted ceilings formed of massive stones whose upper surfaces also form the roof surface. And everywhere is vegetation, with the roots of towering bodhi trees gripping, enveloping and gradually and remorselessly crushing the structures, like the tentacles of a giant octopus. This is how ruins ought to be – raw, authentic. But here an added and perverse thrill comes from the certain knowledge that what you now see and love – the organic architecture of nature merging with the architecture of man – can't possibly last. Like all living things Ta Prohm is in the process of dying. The vegetation is devouring it – but what a magnificent death. Go and see Ta Prohm now, before the great trees are destroyed, the roots removed and the toppled stones put back together. It will never look as good as it does now – perhaps never has. There is much, much more to see at Angkor but our time is up. The day is over and tomorrow we fly to Bangkok.

Left A bas-relief at Bayon records the victory of the Cambodians over the Chams in *1177.*
Right One of the gigantic human faces which have become the emblem of Angkor Thom. There are said to have been 54 of these faces.

24 GOLDEN ELEPHANT OF AYUTTHAYA, THAILAND

Saturday 31 July
Ayutthaya was once the capital of Siam (today Thailand), but is now a sad and haunted place, its ruins manicured and marooned in the midst of a sprawling modern city centre. The Ayutthayan kingdom was, for 400 years from around 1350, a great economic and cultural power in the region. In its heyday it had trading and diplomatic links with Holland, England and France, but there were enemies near at hand, and their actions eventually led to Ayutthaya being abandoned in 1767 in ghastly circumstances. It was sacked by a Burmese army which razed the city to the ground, killed or carried off 90,000 of its inhabitants as slaves and systematically destroyed art, manuscripts and records – everything that gave the Siamese a sense of national identity. But such brutal physical and psychological tactics did not prevail. Within seven months the Siamese, under King Taksin, had recovered and ejected the Burmese invaders. However Ayutthaya was not rebuilt or its site reoccupied – it was no longer considered an auspicious place for a capital city. What survives is an eerie landscape of structures that have been ruins for 250 years – scattered spectres in the modern city that still speak of the calamity inflicted by the Burmese.

These ruins are mainly of sacred buildings – mostly built of brick, and many containing the sad and stunted remains of giant seated Buddhas. Most striking are the chedi – needle-spired and bell-bottomed structures characteristic of Thailand. These

The ruins of Ayutthaya, capital of Siam until 1767, now mainly comprise distinctive sacred buildings such as this prang which also concealed a store of treasure, including the golden elephant I have come to see which was commissioned by King Boron Rachathirat II in the 15th century.

served as shrines, tombs or memorials and give Ayutthaya its memorable image. But I'm not looking for a chedi, I'm looking for a prang – a tower – that tells a very moving story and which held a very special treasure.

The Wat Ratchaburana that incorporates the prang I'm looking for stands in what now looks like a municipal garden. The place is dotted with ruins which still, if you study them, speak of the horror of that day of butchery and destruction in 1767. But the prang rises tall and firm and it tells an earlier story of the Ayutthayan kingdom. In the 1420s King Intharacha died and his two elder sons – Chao Aye Phraya and Chao Yi Phrayh – battled for supremacy and the crown. Their conflict ended when they both died during a duel, each mounted on a war elephant. The surviving younger brother – who became King Boron Rachathirat II – chose to commemorate his brothers' death, and I suppose his own good fortune, by building Wat Ratchaburana in 1424 on the site of the duel. The prang was to house the remains of the father while the ashes of the two brothers were housed in a pair of nearby chedi – one of which now remains, a ruin on a traffic roundabout. But the prang also contained a fabulous golden treasure including prized possessions of the father and brothers and, probably, exquisite gold and jewelled items commemorating the fatal struggle. The prang was not penetrated by the Burmese in 1767 and remained sacrosanct – few want to disturb the repose of the dead – until 1957 when tomb robbers burrowed into the bowels of the prang and made off with the treasure. It was usual in Buddhist stupas (and the prang is a type of stupa) to deposit precious or sacred objects in the foundation – but it was the quantity and quality that amazed. The nation sprang into action. The robbers were found and arrested but only some of the treasure recovered.

To see what was recovered I have to go to the nearby Chao Sam Phraya National Museum. I am led to a vault, sealed with a mighty steel door that, to my surprise, bears the British royal coat of arms. I suppose it's a British-built strongroom fabricated by a company with a royal warrant. Only the best will do. I enter, and am overwhelmed. The strongroom is dark but it glitters with gold. There is the royal sword, buried with the king in the 1420s, sheets of gold inscribed with Buddhist texts, varied ornaments and – what I really want to see – a small golden and bejewelled elephant. This is my treasure, an exquisite object, an amazing monument in miniature to the skill of the craftsman who made it. This golden elephant would have had special meaning and power – particularly since elephants carried the princes to their deaths. But there is only one elephant here and two brothers died. It's heartbreaking to contemplate the fate of the missing objects, and the theft remains an event of national sorrow in Thailand.

I have little time to look at other relics of Ayutthaya but manage to see Wat Mahathat, a temple complex dating from 1374 that contains a curious relic – a giant head of Buddha now engulfed and framed within the trunk and root-like tendrils of a giant bodhi tree. Clearly this head must be of some age to find itself in such a setting. No one seems quite able to agree its history but it has become a Buddhist shrine, not least because Buddha achieved enlightenment while seated below a bodhi.

As we make the long journey back to Bangkok our fixer begins to behave in a bizarre manner. All day he has been attempting to tell us what we can do rather than facilitate what we want to do. It soon comes to a head. My recent experiences with insects have

given me something of a new interest in the little creatures. I would like to taste a few more. I failed to find a tarantula in Angkor – a local delicacy – but know that numerous types of insect are eaten in Thailand including, I believe, scorpions. Tempting. We ask our fixer if he can help me find a stall selling insects after we check in to our hotel. It's not on our schedule, he observes. No, I agree, it's an idea that has only just occurred to me. We explain that spontaneous moments often make the best television. But at the hotel he suddenly turns into a government official. He announces that the day's filming – according to our agreed schedule – is over and it is his duty to seal our video tape cassettes, and the seal must not be broken until we leave Thailand.

The giant head of Buddha enclosed in the bodhi tree at Wat Mahathat at Ayutthaya.

What? There has clearly been a serious breakdown in communications. Yes, we hired and paid for this fixer but, he tells us, in Thailand he has a responsibility not only to us but to the government. No wonder he has been so anxious and obstructive during much of the day. A row ensues. The fixer bemoans his fate – his job is on the line, he will be blacklisted by the authorities if he fails in his duty. Then, when we agree to take his proposal seriously, he thinks we are trying to trick him by giving him old tapes to seal. We are indignant at this accusation of perfidy – and so the cycle of misunderstanding escalates. Finally an accommodation is reached, but it all leaves a bad taste. What on earth do the Thai authorities imagine we are up to? We fantasise, but in the end I suppose attempts to control the foreign media are now a routine activity of a surprisingly authoritarian regime. The video cassettes are sealed. The whole thing is absurd and has wasted too much of our precious time. So, much later than planned, we issue out on our bug hunt. I fancy a bit of scorpion, although any insect will do. We ask a cab driver to take us to the nearest hostelry or stall that stocks insects. No problem, he says. But the wretched fixer has done his job well. All the regular purveyors of insects are now closed! Insects will have to wait – I fancy China might have something to offer.

The next morning we make our way to the airport. Needless to say no one shows any interest in our tapes. We leave this strange country with troubled minds. Indonesia and Cambodia were delightful, the people open, charming and friendly. But the Thais have a certain hardness and cynicism. Perhaps it comes from the tough game they are playing with the West – wanting and getting high levels of investment and droves of European tourists, but at a price. These economic achievements enrich but also involve the exploitation of Thailand and its people. But then Thailand's history is different to that of its neighbours – it was never a colony of a European power or embroiled in a recent brutal war like Cambodia or Vietnam, so naturally its people will have a different attitude. And so we muse as we wait to board our next flight. I note that we are starting to communicate in a strange way. Sentences are started but do not have to be completed or, more odd, are started by one person but finished by another. A weird shorthand is evolving between us. We comprehend each other's thoughts and moods with the merest of words or gestures. As Nick says, the worrying thing is that soon we will be the only people who understand each other. To outsiders the chance is that we will make no sense at all.

The elephant was a sacred creature in Siam, and none more sacred than this exquisite golden elephant, thought to be one of a pair commissioned by King Boron Rachathirat II after he had succeeded to the throne.

HIDDEN WORLDS

Sunday 1–Monday 2 August
This is very exciting. A new and complex world awaits us and our treasures here are varied indeed. The drive into Tokyo is itself gripping. Passing over Tokyo Bay, where the old city was, there is nothing to be seen but recent buildings, a whole weird and wonderful architectural zoo, stark in its contrasts. It is visual chaos and architectural cacophony. Odd, I muse, in a culture that prides itself on harmony, balance and exquisite design. But the mix is stimulating, energetic and strangely liberating – it all seems to imply that the material world of building is only ephemeral, with greater truths lying elsewhere. As dusk falls we go out on the streets – we want images of modern Japan to contrast with our historic. I find myself in the Shibuya district – modern, commercial and brittle. The lights are bright, the young and fashionable on parade – the most vibrant part of one of the world's most modern cities. But as I look around, look more closely at the people, it is clear that all is not what it seems. In Japan modernity is little more than skin-deep. Below, are deep roots of tradition. I realise that I am entering a hidden world.

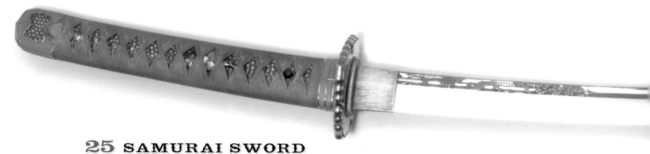

25 SAMURAI SWORD

Tuesday 3 August
After a day off in Tokyo we drive to Tochigi to meet Ritsuo Yanagita – a famed sword-master – to see how that great emblem of Japan, the samurai sword, is made.

Arranged around a courtyard off the main street of this modern and nondescript little town are a workshop, museum and shop. And in the workshop are a forge, a quenching trough and a small but beautiful Shinto shrine, a religion that venerates ancestors and nature. I meet the swordmaster and his two assistants – all dressed in white and flowing traditional costume, with the swordmaster wearing not only a type of kimono but also a small black lacquer hat that is constantly on the point of falling off. Clearly the making of a samurai sword is more than just a technical task.

The swordmaster shows me the various stages of manufacture. Everything must start with a prayer at the Shinto shrine, a request for a blessing for the enterprise. I watch the ceremony and see the workshop being prepared and begin to understand what is at the heart of the sword-making ritual. Coals – won from the bowels of the earth – are piled onto the forge, bellows blow air into the heart of the flame and water is poured into the quenching trough. Making a sword is, it would appear, the creative fusion of the four elements – and if made with care and due religious ritual it will have, in a sense, a soul of its own.

Then the swordmaster demonstrates the first stage of manufacture. He picks up a crude sliver of metal – roughly sword-shaped – heats it to a certain temperature, and then beats it on the anvil. He explains that samurai swords are made of two different types of steel – hard for the outer skin and edge so that it can have a razor-sharp blade, and soft for the inner core so that it is flexible and does not shatter in combat. These steels, he says, have to be hammered for hours – days – to remove dirt or air that could lead to flaws in the sword.

The final stage of manufacture arrives – the blade has to be heated for one final time and quenched. If this goes well – if the temperature and timing are correct – the steel will have realised its full potential and will be capable of being honed to a razor-sharp edge while retaining flexibility. This is a tricky moment – and the greatest test of a swordmaster's skill. If this stage is botched all could be wasted. This is the moment when craft secrets take over and many swordmasters guard their skill jealously. By tradition, this stage takes place at night or in a darkened room because the swordmaster needs to see the precise colour of the steel as he heats it. When it reaches a colour like the moon in August the moment has come. I watch and I strive to see the colour of an August moon – suddenly the swordmaster wrenches the sword from the flames and slides it quickly but carefully into the long thin trough of water. The water bubbles and hisses for a few seconds. It is all over. I look at the swordmaster, he looks at the blade and then he looks at me. A blank expression. Has it worked or not? His face erupts into a smile. The blade rings true. The four elements working together – and a little prayer – have created a sort of mineral life. But this object, of course, is intended to take life, in a most

The samurai sword has been made in Japan for more than 1500 years, the design and manufacture evolving over the centuries to reflect changing patterns of warfare.
Below I feel the samurai sword embodies the soul of Japan – I admire its elegant beauty and ruthlessly efficient function.

elemental manner, and its ability to do this must now be tested. This is the real moment of truth. The swordmaster can claim his blade is true, but only by using it against a set of specific targets can its inner character be revealed.

Traditionally this is a function fulfilled by a samurai, a member of the Japanese warrior caste dedicated to the bushido – the way of the warrior that promotes such qualities as perseverance, loyalty and endeavour. Such a fellow suddenly appears on the scene – a man past middle age, dressed in simple traditional manner, with a placid expression denoting inner calm and a plentifully scarred face. We stare – surely too good to be true. He takes the blade, scrutinises it and then walks slowly out of the workshop. In the past blades were tested on corpses or the bodies of condemned criminals. I anticipate something slightly less horrific but fear to see what the blade will be matched against. In fact the objects to be sliced are nothing more alarming than rolled rush mats and bamboo poles and the blade to be tested is not the one I have just seen completed but one made earlier. I feel a trifle disappointed, but never mind, the ritual looks promising. The samurai

The ceremonial testing of a newly forged samurai sword is done by a man trained in the martial arts who has the skill, reverence and control to handle and judge the sword. Yes, it passes the test.

breathes slowly, concentrates, stares at the rolled mats, strikes a series of elegant poses, draws the blade from its scabbard with steady purpose and then – in a flash of speeding steel – slices the mat and terminates in a posture at once sinister and graceful. After slicing a few more mats the bamboo is set up. This is also cut with aplomb. Another sigh of relief. This, it seems, is the acid test. Bamboo is tough stuff and – I am told – to sever the thick specimen in front of me takes the force and cutting edge required to slice through the bodies of two men! Really, I ask? Yes. I suppose it must be true although it seems unlikely. Anyway, the blade I have just seen tested is a great success. How long does it take to make such a sword, I ask the swordmaster. A hundred days he says. So each one is quite an investment and consequently expensive. The hope that I might be presented with a sword as a gift rapidly vanishes. Never mind. I hold it and examine it closely. On the tang is engraved the date of manufacture and the swordmaster's name while on the top of the blade is engraved a Buddhist symbol and a dragon. It is, after all, a sacred object. As I stare at the blade – a thing of elegant, minimal beauty derived from a quest for ruthless function – I feel that I am holding the soul of Japan in my hands. It is in this land the ultimate symbol of authority, of pedigree – a lethal object with a spiritual quality.

The swordmaster – a cheery fellow – appears in new informal garb. He wants to take us to lunch and I get into his car and off we speed. On the journey I discover that he has had a previous career as a crooner and we listen to several of his CDs. Rather good – a sort of Japanese Dean Martin. We arrive at the restaurant and gather around a large table in which the centre portion is a sunken barbecue. Various raw meats, fish and vegetables are produced and the swordmaster cooks them with great skill – rather like presiding over the forge I presume. I ask him who buys his swords. Retired policemen, he says with a smirk, but what is interesting is who is not allowed to buy them. Who, I ask? Yakuza, he says – gangster! Rather as if he were selling guns, the swordmaster has to declare who he sells his lethal weapons to and some people – or types of people – are prohibited by law from owning a killing-sword.

We return to the workshop and then I fall in love. In the window of the shop I catch a glance of a mask that has haunted my imagination ever since I first saw one many years ago. It has a horned head and an expression that is both horrifying and appealing – a sort of frozen shriek with lips curled and teeth exposed. What is this mask, I ask? The swordmaster explains that it is three hundred years old and is Hannya – a furious or jealous female spirit and a character in the ancient Japanese No theatre. If I can't have a sword I will have Hannya. The swordmaster understands my plight. Since I am an historian, and since I have recognised Hannya's virtues he will, he says, sell her to me for the same price he paid for her, even though she is part of his museum collection. I feel bad. I have asked for something that is not really available but which the swordmaster – out of hospitality – now feels obliged to part with. Have I made a blunder? I withdraw my request, the swordmaster insists. I can see he means it. Hannya is mine. She is carefully packed and I leave with the personification of female fury resting on my lap. I only hope she will grow happy and bring us good fortune

26 RYOANJI GARDEN, KYOTO

Wednesday 4–Thursday 5 August
We travel from Tokyo to the ancient city of Kyoto. I want to see what is perhaps one of the most revealing treasures in Japan – the garden in the Zen Buddhist temple of Ryoanji.

The garden, created in about 1520, is legendary. It is a tool for meditation, a means to enlightenment. It contains, I hear, a world of symbolism, it represents the vastness of nature in miniature, compressed within a universe of stone and gravel that measures only 20 metres by 10 metres. It is, as the temple guide explains, 'up to each visitor to find out for himself what this unique garden signifies'. The temple is part of the Rinzai school of Zen Buddhism – the school that believes enlightenment need not come gradually, after years of steady work, but can be the product of intuition, can come suddenly and dramatically, in a flash of awareness called satori.

Bearing all this in mind I'm in a highly expectant state when I arrive at the temple very early in the morning. All is quiet, no other visitors have arrived, and I make my way through the empty, spacious, timber monastic buildings. I arrive on a diagonal, at one corner of the garden. The first meeting is somewhat disconcerting. The garden, framed by a low, mottled wall made of clay boiled in oil, is immaculate and its crisply raked gravel is the exact colour of concrete hard core. It all looks a little too arid. Anyway, this is my honest first reaction. Bearing in mind the importance of intuition I try not to think, to theorise too much, and let my senses guide me.

Then mind games begin – first is analogy. The mind wants control, it wants to tell you

Before I visit Ryoanji I stop off at the Kodai-Ji Temple, a Buddhist retreat in Kyoto, famous for its immaculate gardens, shrines and tea rooms. It's like walking into a traditional watercolour.

Left *The temple
lake at Ryoanji,
a place for
reflection.*
Right *I sit a metre
or so above to
contemplate this
strange garden at
Ryoanji that
seems so little
and promises
so much.*

the garden is like something else. The stones are like islands, and the raked gravel like waves, the random patterns on the surface of the clay and oil wall are like landscapes and sunsets. Then the stones seem to map out the profile – the cardinal points – of a huge tree. It does indeed seem to represent the world, creation, in miniature.

Then I start to study and count the stones – contemplate their different colours, shapes, scales and textures and their relationship one to the other. I notice there are 15 stones but that only a maximum of 14 of them can be seen from any chosen spot. One stone always remains veiled. I also notice that the stones are arranged in five clusters – a group of five, of two, of three, of two and of three – and that in each group there is one large stone that is dominant in scale but not necessarily in interest. I also ponder the slight mounds on which the stones sit and the small clumps of moss that define the periphery of each group.

Then I start to appreciate the space in between the stones – the negative space becomes more dominant than the positive, the groups of stones subservient to the spaces they define. I remember having this feeling in Durham Cathedral. After looking at its stones for days – the forms they take, the carvings and patterns on them – I suddenly saw the space the stone walls and vaults enclose. In a cathedral it's this space that's important, at least as important, as the fabric that defines the space. It's the 'unseen' world that the Bible says is more important than the seen.

With this perception comes calm, and now, perhaps, I start to understand a little. Zen teaches that enlightenment lies everywhere, in the world, in life, in the ordinary. Just look and in the end you will see and when you see you will learn. As I stare at the garden I do start to see. The preconceived, the expected, start to recede. In the end the garden is no longer an analogy, full of meanings and associations conjured up by my over-active mind – it is not like anything else. It is just a simple garden containing 15 stones – one of which is always hidden from gaze. My time is up. It's true, the Ryoanji Garden is a haunting place.

As I sit by the temple lake, pondering the experience of the garden, I find myself picking up pebbles at random and arranging them in groups of two or three. I see them as objects, then I see their relationship to each other, and then I see the space they define. They make simple but strong compositions – compositions that seem to me to be, in their abstract simplicity, essentially Japanese. Odd this, a morning in a Zen rock garden and I am, as far as I can see, starting to develop a Japanese understanding of space – I even start to contemplate my pebbles in a Shinto light and see each as a little living thing, a repository of the spirit of nature. As I walk around the lake I see Buddhist and Shinto shrines – many with small pebbles on their door frames and arches, pebbles that have been tossed into precarious positions by various pilgrims and devotees. And I see little shrines containing miniature stone figures – hardly more than rough stones but with simple human heads – dressed in aprons. It is all rather moving – nature worshipped through one of its most simple and common creations – the ordinary pebble.

27 HIMEJI CASTLE

We drive to another ancient city to see one of the most familiar historic buildings of Japan – Himeji Castle. It's always fascinating to see, in reality, a building familiar from drawings and photographs – a building that lives in the imagination. Will it measure up to the image created, will it look bigger or smaller, will it thrill or be a sad anticlimax?

Himeji Castle looks fantastic in photographs and appears to be a paradox so characteristic of Japan – a stern and functional fortress, yet with a delicacy of detail, a fineness of form and romantic silhouette that make it look more like a fairy-tale palace. I've always wanted to see how, at Himeji, the worlds of architectural beauty and of military function are reconciled. And I know the castle will also reflect beliefs about correct orientation and propitious placing that relate to the Shinto vision of the power of earth energy and mental energy or ki.

I ask Chako, our fixer, about some of these traditions that, although ancient and mysterious, still discreetly govern design and much of life in Japan. She lists a whole number of traditions – religious rituals I suppose is a better way of putting it – that are taken for granted in Japanese society. You must never sleep with your head pointing north, until you're dead that is, and your body is brought home before cremation. I suppose the north is seen as the realm of the dead, a shadowland, because the sun never shines from the north. Also, while on the subject of north, lavatories should look north and contain walls with no windows. Chako is not quite sure how going to the lavatory and death relate, but feels sure they must. In fact a lot of Japanese customs seem to relate to death. Kimonos must wrap left over right and only ever right over left when a corpse is being dressed, and chopsticks must never be stood upright in rice lest, by looking funereal, they bring bad luck. We get on to other customs. As in all oriental countries, things that are being offered or given – be it a modest tip or something most precious – must be offered with both hands. Fingernails – often the little finger – are sometimes left to grow long to signify that the person so embellished does not come from peasant stock and does not have to do menial work involving the hands rather than the brain. I have not noticed this custom much in Japan but did observe it in Indonesia where many a customs officer flashed a long nail at me.

Friday 6 August
Fully armed, the time has come to tackle the castle. First, it must be admitted that its location is pretty alarming. Himeji, despite its ancient origins, now looks and feels like many other modern towns in Japan and the castle sits on the edge of the town looking, in its somewhat incongruous setting, a bit like a fantasy castle in Las Vegas. The best way to understand any fortress is to take it by storm and also to cast yourself simultaneously into the role of the defender. I start outside the main gate to the castle, and as I nerve myself for the attack I contemplate the place. To European eyes this is a strange castle indeed. Its little roofs are made of timber and tiles and its walls are painted white and look delicate, as if they are made of lathe and plaster. Warfare in Japan was clearly somewhat idiosyncratic in the early 16th century when Himeji Castle was last rebuilt. In the arts of war in Japan, as in other aspects of society, tradition prevailed and technical innovations, if not forbidden, were kept under strict control. Ideas and new weapons did

appear from the outside world but were applied in a strange and constrained way. This is particularly true of gunpowder weapons which were kept subservient to traditional methods of warfare, dominated by the sword, military codes and individual combat. So weapons technology was soon fossilised, with early forms of firearm such as matchlocks still being used in Japan when long superseded in other parts of the world, while certain types of weapons, such as heavy artillery, never came into favour. At Himeji there are no thick-walled casemates or fortified platforms for the location of heavy defensive artillery, as had been commonplace in European fortresses from the late 15th century. There was also no need to build defences against such frightful weapons so walls could be relatively slight and ornaments delicate and exposed.

So I start my assault. I cross the outer moats and arrive at the main gate of the outer wall of the castle. Himeji – as with contemporary European castles – is protected by concentric rings of defences culminating at the tall, central donjon tower. I push past the thick wooden doors of the gatehouse and enter the outer court of the castle. To have reached here an attacker would have had to weather fire from loopholes placed at regular distances along the parapet of the curtain wall. These form a pattern of three different shapes: triangular, rectangular and round. This seems so Japanese – a sense of

A sublime monument to the art of war – there is a thrilling harmony of purpose in Himeji Castle, a creation in which the demands of war, utility and beauty work together. The delicate exterior conceals a large and complex system of defence.

design, of refined aesthetics, even in something so utilitarian as the loopholes in a castle's wall. But then I realise that this rhythm of primary forms is probably to do with function rather than with a mere sense of form. I imagine some of the loopholes were designed to be used by matchlocks, others by bows. As I consider the loopholes in the walls I have taken I also notice those in the walls rising high in front of me. Below these walls, protecting them from direct assault, is a wide and deep pond. As an attacker, I am now in a deadly killing ground. Fire would be raining down on me. I would have to make a quick decision – a decision based on the numbers, armour, skill and spirit of my attacking force. To press on and hope to dislodge the attackers, or to retire? Staying where I am, inactive, would be intolerable. I decide to press on, but realise that as I pass deeper into the castle's defences I am perhaps doing what the defenders want most – to draw me into more killing zones, to ensnare me in a frightful trap where to attack or retreat could be equally painful.

I pass through a well-fortified inner gate and then up a ramp – all the time under fire from above and from the side. I then reach a corner where the ramp turns back on itself in a tight dog-leg. I peer around the corner, fearful of what awaits me. I advance and find my back suddenly exposed to further loopholes from above. An attacking force, unable to scale the walls, would find itself trapped under fire coming from several directions. I weather the storm and move ahead, towards my ultimate goal – the towering donjon. As I approach I come within range of its armaments – bows and firelocks. I advance – under an imaginary but withering fire – and find a moment's rest behind a wall. This, like the other walls of the castle, is painted white and looks delicate as if made of plaster. Now I discover that these seemingly fragile walls are thick in section, made of sand and clay bound with rice glue, are well able to absorb the shock of gunfire and are impenetrable to low-velocity matchlock balls. I also observe that the angle at which the castle's stone walls rise is well calculated and encapsulates the essence of the castle's design in which beauty and military science combine to make it not only functional but visually striking. So they rise in a shallow concave curve that starts at 70 degrees and gets gradually steeper so that, by the time the walls reach their full height, its sides are vertical – virtually impossible to scale.

The designer of this castle also utilised tricks of psychological warfare. The castle is – in many ways – a fortification of the mind. I see this as I move around and come to the main gate leading to the court below the donjon. It seems a soft target, but its seeming vulnerability is a lure. As the attackers reach the slightly recessed gate a trapdoor opens above their heads through which missiles or boiling liquid can be deluged onto them. Finally I reach the donjon itself. After making my way below alarming 'murder holes', visible on the underside of projecting eaves, and breaching a stout gate I enter the main ground-floor room. It was a store room with a ceiling supported by stout timber posts. As I work my way up, from floor to floor, more defensive tricks are revealed. The plan of the donjon is labyrinthine with a complex system of stairs to confuse and disorientate attackers and, in the four corners of each main floor, are Mushu-kakushi. These are, in effect, small strong points – miniature castles – in which a few warriors could lock themselves and fire into the interior of the castle through loopholes at attackers who had managed to penetrate the walls of the donjon. They are desperate places, essentially suicide posts, for these defenders would surely have had little hope of escaping with their lives.

Finally I make it to the top floor of the donjon, and look down on the cunning series of defences through which I have just passed. I am standing where no real attacker has ever stood because the castle was never taken by storm. In fact the existing castle was never attacked – which might suggest that all this elaboration turned out to be a waste of time and money. But not so. The best castle is the one that is not attacked – that's the sign of success. Ideally a castle's defences are a deterrent. This is the case with Himeji. In its marriage of the practical and the poetic Himeji has much in common with the samurai sword – both show that functionalism does not have to be visually arid.

Saturday 7 August

The following morning we drive from Himeji via Kobe to Osaka, from where we plan to fly to Beijing, passing through the industrial heartland of Japan. We move along an elevated motorway which, with its series of visually startling and long bridges, goes on for mile after mile. We sail above factory after factory. As someone observes, this is where virtually everything we use is made – our video and stills cameras, our recording equipment. The buildings are the usual wild eclectic mix of styles and materials, they appear so ephemeral, put up quickly and cheaply for a specific finite function. Here today, gone tomorrow, when technical or functional requirements change. Very unemotional, very practical. As with the sprawl of Tokyo I find the visual cacophony – almost brutality – of this industrialised world hard to reconcile with the exquisite delicacy of so much of Japan.

We arrive at Beijing in the early evening. The sky is grey, a mist hangs low and the avenues along which we speed are vast, with verges and central reservations beautifully planted and immaculately maintained. I become obsessed with this roadside horticulture that goes on and on. The plants are varied, often the central reservations are laid out as miniature ornamental gardens with clipped hedges and small trees as well as flowers. This all says a lot about China – what exactly? Pride in the city, a love of gardening? Yes, I suppose so, but these gardens also suggest a vast pool of cheap labour. My attention is drawn from these strange gardens – impossible to visit because they are moated by roaring traffic and almost spectral because they thrive despite the choking fumes – by another compelling vision. As the wide avenue nears the city centre huge and ungainly commercial buildings sprout on each side. The urban scene becomes more amazing by the minute – hotels, offices, towering commercial headquarter buildings – all glass and steel and rearing up on each side of this great international highway. I now realise that all this is politics. Beijing is demonstrating that modern and reformed China can beat Western capitalism at its own game. The avenue is the showcase of modern China and it says that Beijing is – or soon will be – the greatest modern city in the world, with more sparkling commercial buildings and more miles of wide straight streets than any other great city in the world. I observe the price that history is paying for this megalomaniac Soviet-style urban vision for, to left and right as I sweep along, are surviving fragments of the old Beijing – narrow streets of discreet courtyard houses that are being obliterated by the new roads and commercial towers. Soon Beijing will look more like the epitome of a capitalist city than anything in North America – already there are McDonald's restaurants and Starbucks coffee bars and even a chain of Playboy shops.

But this is consumerism and capitalism Chinese style. There is room for individual enterprise but officialdom and bureaucracy retain an enervating stranglehold. I discover the effect of this weird combination of Chinese-style communism and consumerism soon after I arrive at our very large, Western-style hotel. There is superficial order, regularity and calm but below the surface chaos and a lack of initiative due, I suppose, to years of draconian state control. Nothing works quite as planned or promised and it is soon apparent that an older world is at work.

After the ordeal of checking-in we escape and go for a drink in the bar with our new cameraman, Mike Garner. Mike – a veteran with much experience of foreign travel and passion for adventure – seems just the man we need. As we sit and chat I can't help but notice the way in which the bar is run. Moving so quickly from one country and culture to another makes it easy to juxtapose national characteristics. There's a risk of jumping to simplistic conclusions but it's an amusing game. After Japan, where polite behaviour is almost a religion, the atmosphere in this Beijing bar is strange indeed.

Virtually no one smiles and the waitress is irritated with a menu on our table, aggressively pushes it aside, and bangs plates together as she puts them down. It's impossible to imagine this crude behaviour in exquisite Japan. Perhaps politeness in Japan is exaggerated, superficial and hides a dark secret while the lack of welcoming smiles in Beijing is more honest, but as I sit in the chilly bar in Beijing I'm sure which of the two demeanours I prefer.

28 THE GREAT WALL OF CHINA

Sunday 8 August

The next morning we leave early to make the long drive to our first Chinese treasure – the Great Wall of China. The wall stretches for around 7240 kilometres and much of it is in an advanced state of decay and officially out of bounds to foreign tourists. And, I hear, the presentable sections are generally over-restored and characterless. I am intrigued to discover the truth when we arrive at the section at Jin Shan Ling that we have – for a hefty price – been given permission to visit. On the journey I chat with our fixer Andong. He is a highly intelligent man, probably in his early fifties, and a scientist by training. He is acting as our fixer because of family connections with a BBC employee in London. He is most friendly but seems constantly worried and on edge – rather like our fixer in Thailand. This makes me suspect that poor Andong has had a talking to from the Chinese authorities and is, in effect, also our government minder. By happy chance, Andong has brought along his 18-year-old niece as a general help. To our surprise she greets us in charming and immaculate English. Alice now lives in London and is a much needed and fluent translator who understands the strange complexities of

The Great Wall of China stretches around 7240 kilometres. We are taken to see one section of particular interest – a mini-fortress, an example of its clever system of defence. At various points the walkway turns into broad flights of steps separated by a number of landings protected by loopholed walls, offering a commanding position for the defender.

both the Chinese and the English thought processes.

After about a four-hour drive from Beijing we arrive at our section of wall. As we see it from a distance – snaking over the rocky terrain, as far as the eye can see – it is no disappointment. It is emblematic. It expresses China's unparalleled historic continuity and is bold physical proof that the civilisation of modern China stretches back at least 2500 years to the age of Confucius. The wall, built first by Qin Shi Huangdi from 220 BC, was extended and repaired over the centuries with the last major reconstruction taking place in the late 14th and 15th centuries during the Ming Dynasty. We approach from the outside, and see it from the perspective of the nomadic raiders it was designed to repel. It twists and turns to occupy ridges, to make the most of hills and natural gulleys so it commands the land before it. As I approach I also observe that the wall was only the main section of a system of defence for – at regular distances – isolated towers are set strategically on high points in advance of the wall. The wall itself is beautifully made. It rises about 7.5 metres high and here is made of large, square-shaped, very well-fired pale brown bricks. I walk through a gate – a postern – and climb a small staircase to the wall walk. As I look around a number of things are immediately clear. First, the width of the wall – the wall walk is as wide as a modest street – over 6 metres wide, I calculate – with the wall at its base being substantially thicker. The wall walk has parapets on both sides and towers placed regularly and at relatively short distances along the wall. Each of these towers, small, self-contained castles, would have contained its own garrison responsible for the sections of wall each side of it. So, if one section of the wall fell to attackers it could, in theory, be isolated as the defenders retreated into their castle-like towers on each side. If one part falls all is not lost for the wall is in fact a linear fortress made up of a series of virtually independent mini-fortresses.

As I contemplate the tower nearest me I suddenly realise its true genius. The enemy for the Chinese were the barbarians who roamed to the north, the nomadic tribes who fought from horseback, used shock tactics and favoured hit-and-run warfare. For this type of enemy the structure of the wall was a perfect defence. It absorbed the impetus of any attack, made cavalry warfare impossible and forced these mobile warriors to fight a static battle on terms dictated by the Chinese defenders, who could be reinforced at short notice by other garrison troops stationed on the wall or in camps behind the wall.

I climb to the top of the tower and survey the scheme. The wall is remarkable – not by any means an anticlimax, and even the recent restoration work is pretty good, discreet with proper materials and building techniques employed. The wall stretches away into the distance, following the ridges, climbing, tumbling, its straight edge broken by the sudden rise of towers. It snakes through the landscape and gradually disappears into the mist, like a great work of nature rather than of man. Imagine how the nomadic tribes viewed this spectacular creation when they ebbed up against it 2000 or so years ago. They must have thought it the work of gods, of giants, not of any mere earthly prince.

We drive back to Beijing and as we approach the city we enter a mist. A yellowy white sky hangs over all and the low sun appears as a pale yellow disc through the obscuring gloom. Smog, I suppose. It is eerie – the towers of Beijing appear as a futuristic megalopolis in a science fiction film.

29 THE FORBIDDEN CITY, BEIJING

Monday 9 August

Our permission for filming in the Forbidden City is very precise. We are granted only two hours, between 8.00 am and 10.00 am, are limited in access to only a few places and for this have, once again, to pay a large sum of money. This sum is to include a view of the Song and Ming porcelain in the City's museum where we have been granted permission to film after 10.00 am. We arrive at the City an hour early – just to make sure we are in and ready when the clock starts ticking at 8.00. A prompt start is essential for us because the City opens to the public at 9.00 and crowds are expected to flood in. Once again the sky is white and the weather overcast. We are ready to start by 7.30, waiting in a small court adjoining the main Palace Square containing the Hall of Supreme Harmony. We smile at the waiting officials and ask if we can start earlier. No chance. We are not even allowed to cross a theoretical line – drawn between two waste paper bins – to take a look at where we plan to film. We appeal to Andong for assistance but he is edgy and takes the side of the officials. Moving earlier is out of the question, he states. Oh dear. We are starting to get the feeling that China is a place where officials tend to say, 'the answer's no, what your question?'

At 8.00 we are allowed in – or rather hustled in. We are moved along the route that has apparently been agreed between Andong and the City officials. What we want hardly seems to matter – anyway, it is the only route available. We pass through small courts, between audience halls and suddenly find ourselves in the central court with the gate behind us and the mighty Hall of Supreme Harmony in front. The muted light, the mellow colours of the buildings – dark red painted wood, dull gold, deep orange terracotta roofs – look wonderful. But what no one bothered to tell us – and as we now find out to our horror – is that one long side of this central court is under scaffolding.

The timber and brick buildings are being repaired, or rather – to judge by the scale of works – being reconstructed. But worse is to come. We calculate an angle along which I can walk and talk without too much scaffolding in view and then discover that both our cameras refuse to work. The humidity in the air is so great that their delicate electrical circuits have closed down. At just about five

minutes to nine the warning lights in both cameras stop flashing and we are in business. I manage one walk and say a few words before the gates open and what appears to be a large portion of Beijing and much of the surrounding countryside flood in – led by a file of soldiers, marching neatly in pairs from the gate to the hall. We stare at each other in dismay and then Andrea grasps the obvious solution to our woes. Go with it, go with the scaffolding, go with the crowds, show the Forbidden City as it really is – a turmoil of visitors and a mass of scaffolding and reconstruction. Brilliant.

The Forbidden City is, in effect, the largest palace in the world. It is roughly square in form and isolated from Beijing by high walls and a wide moat. It covers 74 hectares. It is one of the great monuments of the Ming Dynasty that ruled China from 1386 to 1644. Most of the Forbidden City was built between 1407 and 1420 although much has been rebuilt over the centuries following fighting and fire. It is the most popular site in the country for Chinese and tourists who – as I can verify – fight to get a view and

The Forbidden City is now China's most popular tourist destination. We were rushed through and had to compete with the crowd for glimpses of many of its features.

photographs of the trappings of imperial power.

I extricate myself from the crowds around the Hall of Supreme Harmony and penetrate deeper into the palace. Now I become aware just how limited the access is that we have been granted. No, we cannot see any interiors, no we cannot deviate from the set route. Andong prefers not to fight our cause but simply explains that requests to see more are pointless. We have been given a route and that's it. He's no doubt right, but we don't want to fall easily into the authori-

tarian culture of China where, it seems, individuals feel themselves powerless when confronted by a faceless and all-powerful bureaucracy. We ask Andong to point out that, despite a hefty fee, we have been granted nothing beyond access to the general tourist route through the City and, with a heavy heart and slow tread, he goes off to plead our cause. Of course it does no good – the answer is no, we can see nothing beyond the public parts of the City. Time is running out so we rush on, mixing with the tourists, and hope we can grab some extra shots when we go off to film the porcelain in the museum.

I begin to get a sense of the place and relate what I see to what I know from studying maps and plans. The Forbidden City is – in its plan and buildings – an attempt to create an image of heaven on earth and as such is an expression of the Ming Dynasty's belief that its rule was the will of heaven. From the South Gate on Tiananmen Square, which is the main public or formal entry to the City, to the North Gate, runs a straight route that connects all the main elements of the City and which passes through seven courts and halls no doubt expressing the seven heavens. As I walk along this route I realise that the City is not only a diagram of heaven – with its straight north–south route marking a journey from this world to the next – but also an analogy of the human body. The straight route is the spine which connects the private imperial residential quarters in the north portion of the city to the more public reception hall and courts in the south portion. Of course the northern portion represents the head and brain where decisions are made, which pass down the spinal cord to the southern portion of the City which is the executive realm, where the imperial ideas and dictates are given physical and tangible expression.

One of the two lions – here the male with a paw on a sphere – which guard the residential quarters in the northern part of the Forbidden City. The other guardian is a female lion playing with her cub.

As my time draws near I approach the northern part of the city, passing between pairs of gilded lions, and walk briskly through the private quarters to my final – agreed – destination, the residential court of the Empress and of the imperial concubines. Amazing – official wife and official mistresses shared the same part of the City. But then it's 10.00 am. My time is up. An official appears next to Andong who, clearly in a state of anxiety, insists that we stop filming. It is all most extraordinary – the court is full of ambling tourists, we can go on gawking if we like, but there is no flexibility about filming. Finished or not we have to, we are told, honour the letter of our agreement and switch off the cameras at 10.00. Fair enough perhaps, but what about the City authorities' side of the agreement? We don't feel it has been honoured – certainly not in spirit – by taking our fee to film the Forbidden City and then ruthlessly restricting filming to such an extent that we have, we feel, been prevented from properly showing the place. Now, as someone observes, at least we know why it's called the Forbidden City. Then the increasingly harassed Andong reveals his terrible secret. For the last hour he has been in negotiations with the museum authorities and they have now finally announced that, despite our fee and agreement, we are not to be given access to the museum. The humidity of the air is too high, they say, to allow the porcelain to be displayed to us. Conservation arguments are always clinchers – of course we don't want to cause damage to these precious items – but none of us can understand how humidity can damage fire-hardened and glazed porcelain. We express our deep disappointment and request an explanation. No regrets or explanation are offered in return. That's it and, without any ceremony, we are virtually ejected from the City. We are baffled.

Chinese porcelain – a beautiful and for many centuries technically mysterious product that had such a huge influence on European taste in the 17th and 18th centuries – is one of my treasures. What are we to do? Some of the best examples are in the Forbidden City. But there are many other places in which to see it, not least the markets of Beijing. We resolve to go shopping.

30 CHINESE PORCELAIN

Thank goodness for the ordinary Chinese people. The faceless officials and bureaucrats may continue the old Chinese tradition for enigmatic inscrutability but the people we meet in the street are open, warm and direct. As I leave the Forbidden City I am surrounded by a group of students who insist I am photographed with them, and this popular enthusiasm for foreign visitors becomes a theme of our stay in China. I ask Andong and our drivers for advice about our porcelain quest and discover that Liu Li Chang market in the Xuan Wu district of Beijing is the place. The hunt is on!

Liu Li Chang turns out to be a fantastic place. It has – so far – escaped the attention of the avenue builders and high-rise developers – and is a long street of low-rise, old buildings. But, more to the point, virtually every shop appears to be selling antiques, or at least second-hand goods. Surely I can find some old, decent quality porcelain here that I can examine – even buy. As I get out of the car I'm surrounded by young men – shop and stall owners – who want to know what I am looking for. Old porcelain, I say. No problem, they announce, and lead me away. Excellent – but then there is a real problem. The camera appears and the crowd of formerly eager young men starts to melt away. The chap leading me starts to writhe as the camera is turned on him. No, he doesn't actually know where any porcelain is. Perhaps his friend can help. We focus on the friend – he giggles and runs for it. The camera is like a fly spray – wherever we turn it, the crowd scatters and quickly melts away. The eager throng of hustlers disappears. What is all this about? I conclude most Chinese have a natural and probably sensible aversion to authority and prefer to stay anonymous and pursue their livings in obscurity. They realise that if they appear on Western television, get noticed or put a foot wrong, then the game could be up.

Determined not to be disappointed a second time in my porcelain quest, I press on. I peer into various shops and in one see a good display of old porcelain. I enter. The shop assistants – a clutch of attractive young women – seem bemused and then horrified as I enter with a camera and sound men in tow. It is a bit discourteous I know, but I have to get my porcelain. This time I have a captive shopkeeper, they can't deny possessing porcelain because I have it in my hand – a rather nice example of a blue-and-white pattern, late 18th-century tea bowl, I fancy. One of the young women approaches. I apologise for bursting in, explain what I am doing and say that I hope she doesn't mind.

She gives me an icy stare. I enthuse over her porcelain, offer a few comments about it and ask a few questions. She warms a little. Then I explain that I not only want to film some of her stock but also make a purchase. Instantly our relationship is transformed. She flashes a smile – we are in business and fall happily into the relationship of eager salesgirl and erudite (I wish) customer. The only thing now is to find a piece that is good but cheap enough for me to afford to actually buy. In fact there is no problem – the stock is good and the prices not too high.

I look through her wares and discuss what they are. The origins of porcelain are obscure but reached a peak of excellence in China over a thousand years ago during the Song Dynasty when pieces of stunning beauty and sophisticated abstract simplicity were made. The secret of the beauty – the success – of porcelain lies not just in its design but in the materials and techniques of its manufacture and decoration. Porcelain is made from a particular type of clay – called kaolin in Europe and gaoling in China after the range of hills where it was first discovered. Kaolin – containing silicon, aluminium and iron oxides – when mixed with a little stone dust and fired at a high temperature becomes delicate and translucent. The most famous – for Europeans – examples of Chinese porcelain are the blue-and-white produced from 1385 to 1644 during the Ming Dynasty, for it was during this period that porcelain started to be exported in large numbers to an increasingly enthusiastic and eager European market. Europeans liked both the appearance and robust and practical qualities of Chinese porcelain. The fact that in Europe china is called china says it all. For over 200 years Europeans tried to find the secret and make their own versions of porcelain but it was not until the mid-18th century that the nature of kaolin was discovered and true European porcelain made.

The shop contains many examples of Ming period porcelain – good blue, bluish-white glaze and translucent when held up to the light. But eventually I settle on a blue-and-white slightly chipped tea bowl that, my by now most eager companion tells me, dates from the Qing Dynasty. These emperors ruled from 1644 to 1912 but I'm pretty sure my specimen dates from the late 18th century. I close with my delighted girl and, after a charming little haggle, we agree a price that makes us both feel good. By this time the entire shop has warmed to us. Before I can leave with my booty I sign a visitors' book – an unexpected request – and pose with all the assistants for a group photograph taken on a vintage Polaroid camera. So I have handled some Chinese porcelain – but this is the standard stuff. I still long to get a closer look at some of the best examples. We resolve to try and arrange a visit to another museum, perhaps the one in Shanghai which, I believe, contains some very fine examples.

Despite the disappointments of the day we feel pretty good. The Forbidden City was fascinating – what we saw of it – and the market exciting. And I'm pleased with my trifling purchase. Even Andong is lively and we decide to make an evening of it. The plan is to go to a restaurant that serves good but typical Beijing food. Andong rises to the

challenge and for once seems relaxed – this is, it seems, a commission he can undertake with no fear of compromise or embarrassing consequences. We go to a restaurant called the Old Beijing Noodle King, at the north-east corner of Heaven Temple, and it is a truly splendid place. As I enter the staff and some of the customers in the large, packed room cheer and shout. I'm taken aback, smile and bow. As we sit ourselves around a large table another group of customers enters. They are also greeted by shouts and cheers. So this is the custom of the place, and I notice – with a twinge of embarrassment – that these customers do not return the greeting but with cool and lofty demeanour assume their seats. Oh well, next time I'll know better. Food is served and it's astonishing – quite unlike the Cantonese food we usually eat in London – and incorporates a wide spectrum of tastes, textures and colours. It all arrives at once, plates containing sweet things and savoury things skidding onto the table at impressive speed and in apparently random order. There are cakes, soya bean curd (tofu), fried duck, spare ribs, pea cakes, a custard-like omelette with honey, and a sweet called 'donkey rolling' because it's dark in colour and with lots of sugar 'dusted' on it so it looks like a donkey that has rolled on the ground. We eat for twenty minutes and then comes the speciality of the house – lashings of fresh noodles served with a light, tasty and clear sauce. As the noodles arrive the waiters cheer once again and clash the plates together – the atmosphere is heady, other customers join in the celebrations, there are smiles, nods and waves all around – this is splendid theatre!

31 THE GROUNDS OF THE SUMMER PALACE

Tuesday 10 August

We drive a few miles to the Summer Palace, the imperial residence outside Beijing. Once a royal haven, this huge park with its lakes and ornamental buildings is now a much-loved public park and retreat for the people of Beijing. It dates back 800 years as a royal residence. Within the grounds were over a hundred exquisite and inventive examples of exotic garden architecture – once, at least, forming the finest collection of its kind in China. Most of them date from the second half of the 18th century and nearly all have been almost entirely rebuilt in the 20th century following two destructive attacks – in 1860 and 1900 – by Western forces.

As I walk through the palace gardens all seems authentic and charming. It is full of visitors as many use the grounds for their morning exercise. One group of happy women are dancing in formation, swinging their pink pom-poms in a most pleasing manner. I come to a splendid multi-arched bridge that, a sign tells me, was built in 1755. It has ornamental dragons at each end. There is also an 18th-century life-size bronze ox – one of the Chinese birth signs – looking over the placid waters of the lake. Well, these are two items that appear to have escaped the European soldiery. I take a ferry in the form of a dragon ship across the lake and discover yet more fine mid-18th-century garden buildings, including a long ornamental corridor with delicate painted scenes on its inner walls and ceilings and a richly decorated pagoda. And the names of the buildings are charming and thought-provoking – the Hall of Embracing the Universe, the Dragon King Temple, the Hall of Foresight, the Tower of Moonlit Ripple, the Chamber of Heartfelt Contentment.

The story of the Summer Palace is entwined with the story of the Empress Dowager Cixi, one of China's most fascinating historic characters. Born in 1835, she was a powerful and charismatic woman who became the real ruler of China in the late 19th century by exercising fierce control over her Emperor nephew, who she had put on the throne when he was only three years old. The West saw her as devious, even treacherous,

for the role she had played during the Boxer rebellion but, in China, she was known as the Holy Mother.

I make my way through the gardens towards a structure with which the Empress was intimately involved. In 1755 Emperor Qian Long ordered the construction of a small island in the form of a marble boat in one of the palace lakes. It was a birthday present for his mother and, as such a boat could not be capsized, a symbol of the everlasting stability of the Qing Dynasty. This sturdy structure – protected in the moat-like lake – survived the Western invasions, although its timber superstructure was destroyed in the devastation of 1860. The Empress Dowager was particularly taken by this agreeable symbol of Qing continuity and had it restored and transformed in appearance into a modern paddlesteamer that would look at home on the Mississippi. So, although a guardian of the traditions of the Celestial Empire, Cixi was clearly not entirely adverse to, or ignorant of, the modern world. On this boat the Empress Dowager would dine – accompanied by her own image reflected in a mirror placed opposite her seat. I suppose she thought that only her own company was exalted enough to join her at the table.

My imagination running wild, I finally arrive beside the boat. Crowds throng all around it but nobody is on board. Why? I'm haunted by memories of the Forbidden City. Sure enough we are told, despite what we took to be previous agreements, despite paying a fee, we will not be allowed on board. It is too precious and fragile, they say, for us – a mere Western film crew – to enter. We ask Andong to plead our cause, he – under stress – tells us it is impossible. Tim Dunn snaps. Harsh words are spoken in anger – someone must lose face. This is a bad business in an oriental culture. But, to my amazement, it does the trick. A compromise is rapidly reached that seems calculated to let all sides proceed with dignity. I alone can go aboard the Marble Boat – a privilege, I am told by a woman with a very straight face, that is usually only granted to very important people. Have I just been insulted, I wonder? Anyway, this will do because the boat is only a few yards from shore and I can be seen easily by the camera and make myself heard.

As I enter I notice old signs directing visitors and discover that the interior is in shabby condition. Evidently the boat has been open to the public in the past – not just to VIPs – and is now presumably closed awaiting repair. I realise that the authorities are

The Empress Dowager Cixi diverted money earmarked for modernising the Chinese Navy for the restoration of this boat and the Summer Palace gardens. The dramatic consequence of the reconstruction of this symbolic craft was the humiliating defeat in 1894 of an antiquated Chinese fleet by the Japanese Navy.

probably preventing our filming the interior because they are embarrassed by its poor condition. For them to admit this would, of course, be a great humiliation.

I walk through the dining room, paint peeling but huge mirror still in place, step on to the stern platform and stand next to a massive rudder tiller carved out of marble. I look at the crowds swirling on shore and they look expectantly at me. What am I to say? It seems obvious. The boat embodies old and new China – and makes the connection between these two very different worlds. Originally it symbolised the unsinkable power of imperial China and stood in a pleasure garden open to the elite of the land. Now the boat is a precious symbol of modern China, a national shrine that stresses cultural continuity and pedigree, while the once exclusive gardens are a much-loved popular resort. What a strange ship of state this must be – staying afloat even after the world that created it, that its stability was meant to symbolise, has long been swept away. We leave the garden, spread below the now familiar white and misty sky of Beijing, and head back to the heart of the city and the roaring bustle of the 21st century.

Nick and I made a couple of friends a few days earlier as we walked around the streets near our hotel and when we return we discover that they have left a note for us at reception. It's a curious and revealing story. As Nick loitered – looking every inch an Englishman – two demure girls approached and announced that they were students studying English and art and, as luck would have it, they, their fellow students and art master happened to be holding an exhibition of their work in a gallery nearby. Would we like to see it? The girls – who chose to call themselves Sophie and Angel – seemed very straightforward and decent and, having time on our hands and not a little curious to see the work of young Beijing-based artists, we agreed to go. The studio turned out to be a room behind the steaming kitchen of a dubious-looking restaurant – but why not? We entered and there was their master, having a cup of tea, and the walls were loaded with paintings and drawings in many styles, all more or less traditional. They showed us their work, their friends' works, their master wrote our names in highly decorative Chinese characters and, yes, of course, we felt charitable and bought a couple of drawings for a very reasonable price. We were happy, they were happy and we told them where we were staying so they could collect our business cards as mementos. All was well until, the following day, and the day after, we were all accosted in the street by delightful young people – always in couples – who also were art students, studying English and whom, by happy chance, just happened to have an exhibition on around the corner. It was, as the Victorians used to say, a lay. Nick and I had been had. But never mind, it was a gentle con. The drawings remained pleasant – although clearly mass-produced rather than the work of Sophie, Angel or their friends. Nick and I were intrigued to see these two young women again – to try and penetrate a little below the surface. We wanted to discover if they were hard petty fraudsters with a veneer of innocent charm or just a couple of well-educated but poor provincial students seduced into the role of confidence tricksters, preying on hapless foreign dupes, to earn a little extra money to help pay for their studies. I like to think the latter.

They turn up at the hotel as their note promised and we walk the few hundred yards to their 'gallery' because I want the word 'dream' drawn as I saw it in the Zen temple in Japan. This the master does beautifully and presents to me as a gift. We talk to the girls and slip in the fact that we have met many other students with exhibitions, but Sophie and Angel remain calm and unflustered. They must realise that they have been rumbled but give no sign – they are the same eager and innocent little students. But we are cunning. We tell them that we plan to film in the market later – I am going on a hunt for bugs to eat – and would like their help as translators. We will pay them. They giggle with excitement, flash a glance at each other, and agree to meet us at their gallery an hour later. We turn up with the rest of the crew and – you've guessed it – Sophie and Angel are nowhere to be seen. The gallery – the spaces left vacant by the work we purchased now filled by virtually identical drawings – is empty. I go into the kitchen and find the 'master' slumped on a bed. He jumps up, alarmed, and agrees to hunt for the two girls. We wait, he soon returns alone, shrugs, and vanishes. So, like the hustlers in the market, Sophie and Angel don't want to be captured on film. We rather admire Sophie and Angel – they are clever girls. As Nick says, their air of natural innocence persuaded him to put his usual suspicion and cynicism on hold and give them the benefit of the doubt. It was the same with me. It felt almost perverse to doubt them.

Wiser men, we commence our hunt for bugs. Having been disappointed in Thailand, and denied the delights of spider and scorpion, I persevere in my quest. Suddenly a range of ghoulish stalls appears. On display is a wide range of food that would cause dismay in some quarters: dog meat, snake skin, frogs and – most strange – huge, puffy, silk-worms or silkworm larvae, which are large, ball-like and not quite the insect I had in mind. I fancied something crisp, crunchy and more obviously healthy such as protein-rich locust. But silkworm is all there is in the insect department. I fear the silkworm may prove rather chewy and anyway feel bad about eating one because I love silk and revere silkworms – they are fine and industrious creatures. But there can be no retreat. I order a skewer of worms along with a helping of snake skin and of frog. I falter at the dog meat – I'm British after all, and to eat a dog is little different to cannibalism. Now that's a thought. Cooking my titbits involves nothing other than placing them on a well-greased metal plate below which roars a flame. First I am given the snake skin, wrapped around a barbecue skewer. It's dripping with oil and fat, chewy and rather tasteless. I feel short-changed. What's happened to the snake meat? I'm afraid I can't recommend the skin. The frog is alright but rather skinny, undercooked and no comparison with the tasty and succulent frog legs served in France. Last comes my row of silkworms. I bite into one. It's like biting into a dense ball of cotton wool – into a ball of silk actually – but through a hard, leathery and tasteless outer skin. I chew, spit out the skin and make some headway with the inner goo. It's a bitter disappointment. Not particularly disgusting – just nothing. Perhaps it's the way the worm's been cooked. No, silkworms are not for me. So my quest for the perfect insect food – tasty, crunchy, nourishing and healthy – must continue.

32 THE TERRACOTTA ARMY, XI'AN

Wednesday 11 August

We fly to the old capital of Xi'an, in central China, and then drive to a site about 30 kilometres from the city centre. We have come to see one of the great cultural wonders of the world – the army of larger than life-size terracotta figures created 2200 years ago to accompany the First Emperor of China and builder of the Great Wall – Qin Shi Huangdi – to the grave.

This army – perhaps amounting to 8000 figures – was arranged around the tomb of the Emperor in four separate divisions, ordered as if awaiting battle. There were ranks of infantry, cavalry and chariots, a headquarters with commanders, all placed in subterranean galleries covered with timber and earth roofs. The Emperor's tomb itself remains a magnificent affair, a huge squat pyramid, rather like some I saw in central America, that is earth-covered and as yet unexcavated.

This great army – presumably intended to accompany the Emperor to the next world and to fight his battles in heaven – was discovered by chance in 1974. Preliminary excavations soon confirmed that this was one of the greatest archaeological discoveries of the 20th century. Around 1500 figures have so far been unearthed – for reasons of conservation the figures are excavated slowly and painstakingly – and mighty museum halls have risen over the separate pits in which the army was buried.

We have arranged to film the army but as soon as we arrive at the museum it becomes clear that our task is not going to be easy. Our arrival coincides with closing time, as planned, but as we unload we are directed to one of the halls and are told we are to be allowed to film there and nowhere else. We ask Andong to explain that we have come to film the army – which is dispersed in three halls – and not only one portion of it. Our complaints mean nothing. We fume, but after a quick look at the two out-of-bounds halls realise that all is well for our hall is by far the best and most exciting. When the army was originally dispersed in its four pits the divisions were far from equal. The pit surrounded by the hall in which we are to film is the largest and contains rank upon rank of infantry, arranged in columns as if for battle and all looking east – towards the rising sun and rebirth. Officers stand leading their men, soldiers at the sides of the ranks look sideways – to the earthen walls of the pit, as if on the lookout for a flanking attack – while, at the rear, guards look backwards in readiness to issue warning in case of a surprise attack from behind.

So we are happy with our hall, but our troubles are far from over. The figures on display are magnificent but fairly remote. We are perched on an upper walkway and want to get a trifle nearer. Walking among

Below Such is the skill of the craftsmen who worked on the Terracotta Army, the figures almost seem alive.
Over Each figure has different features and a slightly varied posture. Each was fired with clay which turned into a terracotta of great strength, able to withstand damp and flames.

The architectural remnants of the communist era blend with Shanghai's more capitalist present. I am surprised by the blatant commercialism of the new China.

the figures would be ideal but is out of the question in case we, by mischance, cause some damage. This restriction I understand but not the ban on observing from the lower platform. Eventually it is agreed that I alone can stand on the lower platform. As I move there we are told that while it is permissible for us to film the figures we are not allowed to take still photographs. Why? Then the rate of payment is discussed in detail. We are to be charged not by time spent in the hall, but by the number of minutes of film shot – seems reasonable in principle, but the rate per minute is high. Oh well, we will have to be very organised and controlled and – counter to our usual more spontaneous working method – will have to rehearse each take before actually filming it. As we start, the museum authority – in the person of a rather sinister director wearing black tee shirt and dark glasses – reveals his arbitrary nature by suddenly decreeing that the crew can join me on the lower platform. As Nick suggests, he's behaving like this simply because he can. We are going to have to watch out for this fellow.

Despite this unpleasant atmosphere the figures capture and hold our attention. They are compelling. They are clearly mass-produced but not repetitive. Each figure is different, very personal, with the heads almost certainly being portraits of individual soldiers. It is quite amazing. You can see regional and ethnic differences in styles of hair and facial features and each seems to possess an individual personality. Investigation has suggested that about 85 master workmen were responsible for the creation of this terracotta army that looks – in certain lights – as if it were made of living men about to spring into action. These masters made the heads – many are signed works – while 1500 men of lesser skill mass produced the hands and bodies, moulding or hand-working the clay. Each figure was painted and some even retain elements of pigment. What has disappeared almost entirely are the weapons with which this mighty army originally bristled – swords, spears and crossbows. Being of wood and iron these have long ago rotted or rusted away but the empty hands of the soldiers still grasp or embrace their invisible arms. They still look menacing. The ranks I look down upon are in wildly different states of preservation. The ones in the front, nearest me, are complete for they have been skilfully repaired and conserved. The ranks in the middle distance lie in shattered heaps, as most of these figures were found engulfed and damaged by the collapse of the roof and earth above them. At the rear the statues lie mostly still buried, and not to be exhumed until money is available and conservation techniques and technology improve.

It is nearly 9.00 pm and they want us out. But now a new battle begins. We say how much film we have shot and explain how its duration in minutes can be counted on the camera. Our sinister director appears not to believe us – which really is quite an insult – and insists on watching and counting every frame. It seems that he is convinced we have in some way cheated – or perhaps he is simply vexed by the fact that we have worked efficiently and so owe only a minimal fee for less than half an hour of video shot. He looks at the footage, is surly and, finally, demands an additional fee to cover our rehearsal time. The whole thing is outrageous but, we realise, a ritual that has to be endured. Andong fights back and finally, after over an hour of viewing and negotiations, a fee is agreed.

We leave exhilarated by the army but exhausted by the process by which its wonders have been glimpsed. As with the Marble Boat we have become aware that, in China, truth and honour are subtle things that are not finite or objective. We feel dismayed because the contract we believed we made was not honoured, and because the director virtually accused us of attempting to cheat the museum. But, I suppose, for him, as with the people at the Marble Boat and the Forbidden City, there was a greater truth and a greater honour at stake than that to do with us and our disputed contract. The greater truth is to get as much money out of us as possible – I hope and assume for the sole use of the museum. And the greater honour is that of China – they wanted to control our access to parts of the museum because they thought the disarray revealed in some parts would show China in a poor light. I really don't know. It puzzles me deeply.

Thursday 12 August

In the afternoon we fly to Shanghai which is, by any account, one of the most peculiar cities on earth. Development is dense to put it mildly, and as we drive from the airport it is virtually impossible to see a piece of ground that is not built upon. I go to the Shanghai Museum and ask to film some of their finest porcelain. In contrast with Beijing all is relaxed. We go in and film some choice pieces. So I get to see at close quarters – if not actually handle – some of the best porcelain produced in China.

In the evening we go to Pudong – the commercial heart of this astonishing high-rise city – and are amazed. This is socialist China but, as with parts of Beijing, all reeks of consumerism and exudes capitalist values. I'm being naive, I know, but I am surprised by the blatant materialism of it all. I stand on the Bund, as dusk descends and a storm blows up, and wonder about it all. Modern China is the fruit of an ancient civilisation, and it possesses a cultural continuity going back well over 2000 years. Yet the view from the Bund is the epitome of the modern commercial world of consumerism. All is strident, materialistic, sensual. I think of Mao's huge portrait, raised above the gate to the Forbidden City and looking down upon Tiananmen Square. He smiles benignly, a face from another age, seemingly robbed of meaning. In this new, modern China Mao's once mighty and powerful visage is reduced to little more than a Pop Art image. It's easy to be cynical about the way things have gone here, as capitalist values replace communist. But some things appear to remain the same. There are the outward trappings of consumerism normally associated with Western democracies but there is, of course, no tradition of democracy in China. This means that there is little regard for the views – or rights – of the individual. Thus is created the atmosphere of restraint that I witnessed among our fixers, the sense of powerlessness when faced by a great and faceless bureaucracy that is answerable to no one. But all is not as simple as it seems. I know from my recent experiences that here – as in Japan – old values live on. For an outsider, relationships and actions are hard to fathom. This is truly an ancient world of secret or hidden meanings and beliefs that I have skidded over, sometimes feeling delighted, at other times confused and baffled. I feel embarrassed by my anger and impatience of the previous days. I just didn't understand what was really going on. Under provocation I have behaved just as a westerner is expected to behave. I have been two-dimensional in my vision, simplistic in my expectations of literal – superficial – truth and honesty. I have not read the subtlety of the situation, not responded to cultural peculiarities, not recognised the hidden messages. I feel plodding – like a bull maddened irrationally by a mere shred of flapping red cloth. I have reacted according to type. It's bad – there is still much to learn.

At last in the Shanghai Museum I am able to see some of the finest examples of Chinese porcelain – some up to 1000 years old. The secret of making this elegant and translucent porcelain was kept in China until the mid-18th century.

HEAT AND PASSION

33 THE GODDESS DURGA, CALCUTTA

Friday 13–Saturday 14 August

Calcutta has always been a most curious and enigmatic creation and I'm on a quest to find the heart and soul of the city. As a coherent international trading city it started life in 1690 when a merchant named Job Charnock obtained a lease from the local Muslim nawab on an unlikely piece of marshy land beside the great river Hooghly. Charnock was acting for the English East India Company and this is where he planned to create a trading post. The enterprise flourished and a small English trading town and fort arose as spices, fabric and dyes such as indigo were shipped to the West. But a later nawab – Siraj-ud-Daula – took offence at what he perceived to be the presumptuous behaviour of the British and in 1756 sacked the city and imprisoned a number of its British residents overnight in a small cell near Tank Square, the centre of old Calcutta. This incident, quickly dubbed by the British as the outrage of the 'Black hole of Calcutta', was promptly avenged. The young, energetic and bold Robert Clive – formerly an East India Company clerk and now its leading general – marched north from Madras and swiftly retook Calcutta and the fabulously rich and mighty Mogul city of Murshidabad. In the process of this stunning victory, and in his amassing of personal and company wealth and power, Clive resorted to subterfuge, cunning and trickery that shocked his foes and that eventually led to a court of inquiry in Britain. To this day Clive remains an ambivalent figure in Calcutta. He is admired for his military and political genius, but held in contempt for his treachery. He is, arguably, the father of the British Empire in India, but because of his amoral methods the empire was tainted at birth. For most Indians Clive simply didn't play with a straight bat – he did not live up to the high standards and traditions of an English gentleman.

But, morally flawed as it was, Clive's victory led immediately to the creation of a new and far grander Calcutta. In the late 1790s Calcutta's proto-imperial ambitions were given splendid expression when the Governor-General Warren Hastings commissioned the construction of a huge and impressive Government House, designed along the lines of a great and palatial English mansion. Calcutta and its trading possessions in Bengal were ruled by a trading concern – the East India Company – which was now to have the imperial flavour of a national enterprise.

The story of Calcutta's creation, history, people and architecture has long fascinated me. It is one of the great and compelling cities of the world. To walk around and through it, to penetrate its secret and hidden parts, to enter into its life, to get to know it, to see it as a great living organism – at once strangely European but also quintessentially Bengali – is an incomparable experience. In the past I have come to Calcutta looking for many things. This time I come to find the city's great Hindu goddess and protector – Durga.

We drive into the city centre from the airport at Dum Dum and pass along the edge of North Calcutta heading for Chowringhee, the European quarter on the river Hooghly. As always, the air is thick, warm and pungent with the smell of perfume, spice and decay – the smell of humanity, I suppose. The streets teem with life, people walking, working, living on them. I have seen this scene many times before but there is always something new to observe. All of human nature is on show – its strengths and weaknesses, its joys and its sorrows, comedy and tragedy, beauty and beastliness. You just have to have eyes to see. As we drive along the congested Sri Bannerjee Road, Damyantee, our fixer, points out the location of the last legal opium parlour in the city. This is a new one for me. Does it really still exist? I strain to see the sign above the door she points to, and miss it, but Damyantee squeals in delight as she spots it and confirms that this unlikely establishment is still in business.

As usual, there is little time to wander around this enthralling city. We must start our quest for our treasure. Every year in October Calcutta celebrates its patron goddess during a three-day festival – the Puja. Images of Durga, wrought in mud and bamboo and straw, are made in their thousands, set up in shrines throughout the city, worshipped and then – in an ecstatic frenzy – taken to the Hooghly where they are submerged, the blessed mud of the image returning to that of the sacred river. We want to see these images being made, to see where they will be put on display and to learn as much as possible about Durga and the ancient ceremonies and rituals of this celebration. We start by going to the area in North Calcutta where the image makers live and work. At this time of year the narrow streets in this part of the city present one of the most extraordinary sights on earth. Everywhere, in all the close-packed workshops, are images of Durga and other Hindu deities in all shapes and sizes, in varied postures and states of ornamentation and of undress. It's extraordinary, walking along these alleys between towering, mud-coloured, naked images of Durga and of her more sinister manifestation Kali, which still await their vivid hues and gorgeous clothes.

My treasure is Durga, Calcutta's patron goddess, and the ritual of the Festival of Durga held each October. Thousands of images are made of mud, bamboo and straw, dressed and worshipped for three days, then plunged into the river Hooghly. Durga protects the city from evil.

Durga is an incarnation of Parvati, one of the great Hindu goddesses and the wife of Siva who, with Vishnu and Brahma, forms part of the mighty triad of great Hindu gods. In images Parvati is presented as a fair and beautiful woman, a calm and balancing consort to Siva who is a god of fertility, of action and of destruction, albeit destruction that is positive and part of the cycle of life and death. But Parvati can assume some of the attributes of her husband when she manifests in the forms of Durga and Kali. Then she becomes a powerful and ruthless warrior who first appeared on earth for the destruction of demons that were 'obnoxious to both gods and men'.

Durga – despite her violent posture – is also depicted as a beautiful young woman, usually of a golden colour, with a benign smile playing about her lips even as she thrusts her trident into the body of a demon. But images of Kali are very different. She is black of hue, heavily armed, wild of appearance and is shown caught in a moment of violent ecstasy – dancing in triumph with blood smeared on her naked body, festooned with corpses and severed heads and with her tongue protruding in a way that is at once grotesque and lascivious. Kali's frantic and violent actions and her evident state of trance have given her a fearful reputation despite the fact that it is evil that she slew. The views expressed by W.J. Wilkins, writing in 1882, are typical. There can be no doubt, wrote Wilkins, 'that human sacrifices were formerly offered to Kali, though now they are forbidden both by British laws and [in more recent] Hindu scriptures…In the [ancient] Kaliika Purana…nothing could be clearer than the instructions regarding this cruel practice'.

To find out more about Durga and Kali I tramp the streets of North Calcutta. In every street are shrines, some no more than crevices in the facade of a building, others merging with the roots and knots of sacred road-side trees, many to Durga or Kali. Also the great

I love Calcutta, and know it well. It has life, passion and humanity. There is always something new to see and learn. I make my way through these crowds and meet a passer-by on the way to the Kali Temple.

houses – no matter how ruinous or sub-divided – generally retain their puja halls or chapels in good condition and these present a rich repository of shrines. During the time of the Durga Festival these shrines are joined by up to 2000 temporary shrines containing the mud and straw images I saw being made.

I gain access to a small 18th-century palace owned by the Ghosh family. They kindly show me their puja hall in which images of Durga and Kali are in course of production and I ask the family to explain what the festival means to them. It has been celebrated in their house, and by their family, for 280 years. During the festival each Hindu household welcomes Durga as a member of the family, like a cherished daughter returning home after a year-long absence. She stays for three days with her children – Ganesh, Lakshmi and Saraswati – and then re-ascends to the realm of the gods. I ask why Durga is so important to Calcutta – what does she represent? It seems a silly question as I ask it. Durga is Calcutta, she is an elemental force beyond analysis or question. Mr Ghosh smiles patiently and explains that she is the destroyer of evil and, quite simply, that the prosperity of the city depends on her. Also she is a great uniting force. Each image must incorporate all, from the high and sacred represented by the pure mud from the Hooghly to the low and profane represented by mud 'blessed' by a prostitute. All of the city – of creation – has to be involved in this festival. Mr Ghosh has one more thing to reveal. His family owns a Siva temple that, he claims, contains the largest Siva lingam in the world. I have to see it.

A street or two away, I come upon a cubical building from which a frantic, clamorous noise is issuing. I throw off my shoes and enter and there is a gigantic lingam rising to the ceiling, so tall that those venerating it have to climb a step ladder to pour their liquid libations over the tip of the mighty erection. The lingams are an abstract representation of Siva and – since he has much to do with fertility – they are quite obviously phalluses. But they are more than just phalluses. The great shaft of the tapering lingam rises from a round dish with a spout at one end. This is a symbol of the yoni – the female genitals. So the lingam is male and female force combined – the symbol of creation through sexual energy. I watch agog at the celebration taking place around the towering shaft. Men and women are clambering up the ladder to bathe the lingam with milk and deck it with flowers, while below men sing hymn-like budgens and women sponge and kiss the lower portions of the phallus and collect in jars the milk as it flows from the spout of the yoni dish. Intoxicating stuff indeed.

Leaving this strange scene, I head towards Kalighat, a teeming quarter to the south of the city centre. As I make my way along the crowded streets I am reminded again why I love Calcutta. All around is decay – buildings crumble, rubbish festers – but from this

physical decay springs life and spirit. I can't help feeling that somewhere in Calcutta, down one of its dark alleys, lies the secret of life. Perhaps in Kalighat, for here, located on a tributary of the sacred river Hooghly, stands Calcutta's great Kali Temple, a sprawling place last rebuilt in 1809. There is nothing quite like this in India. It's the last official location of blood sacrifice in the country – buffalo are regularly slaughtered to gratify the goddess – and as I arrive the evening puja is just getting under way. People are shoving, pushing, shouting – there seems to be a sense of hysteria, most suitable for the highly emotional cult of Kali, the frenzied goddess of ecstasy. As I stand gawking I am granted a sudden vision of Krishna – an incarnation of Vishnu. A being painted in blue with exotic make-up and playing a pipe dances towards me, and when face to face smiles through bright red lips and yellow teeth and puts a hand out for money. I can only return the smile and pay up. Is it a man or a woman, I wonder? I struggle to join a line weaving into the shrine and, after much manoeuvring, get inside. But I manage only a glimpse of the image of the goddess. It is almost abstract, little more than a huge head and massive protruding tongue atop a body swathed in an orange robe. Almost before I can take this in I am pushed on by the eager, chanting crowd behind.

My last destination in the city is the bank of the Hooghly, the place where the images are cast into the river. All along the river bank are shrines and the eerie and rotting remains of many an old mud-made image. Some stand, almost intact, in small gardens, others lie in decomposing heaps of mud with only a sparkling, red-lined eye or fragment of dark visage to show these were once representations of the great goddess Durga or Kali. Perhaps most disturbing are the images that have been robbed of most of their attire. Here they sit, smiling seductively, with full heads of hair and well-formed breasts visible beneath stained, ragged and tight, jewel-encrusted bodices. The Hindu faith is 4000 years old and Durga – that ancient goddess – reamins very much alive in Calcutta.

Sunday 15 August – Robert Clive's house, Dum Dum
About three years ago I was involved in a BBC programme, as part of *The House Detectives* series, about Clive's House in Dum Dum, which was then occupied by squatters and in an advanced state of decay. A fascinating story emerged. Clive had acquired the Dum Dum building in 1757 and transformed it into an elegant villa that reflected European Classical taste but also local building traditions and habits. In it, he lived like a Mogul prince, receiving in his throne room and with a ballroom above, as was the custom in Indian mansions. As I worked on the programme and investigated the house it became clear that this building – said to have been an old Dutch factory – was far older and much more significant than generally believed. It stands on part of an

Images of Calcutta during preparation for the Festival of Durga.
Left *Many-armed Durgas waiting to be ornamented.*
Right *Is it a man or a woman I encounter in the image of Krishna holding out a hand for money?*

Three years ago, in The House Detectives, *I investigated Robert Clive's house in Calcutta, prompting repairs to the house which unearthed valuable artefacts believed to be from the 11th century.*

extensive mound – itself an indication of age and high prestige in Bengal – and has a mighty water tank nearby. I took Mr Uta from the Archaeological Survey of India around the site and what he said was a revelation. Many of the bricks, and much of the house itself, were Mogul and dated from the 16th century while, all over the mound, were fragments of early pottery. Mr Uta was convinced it had once supported a great temple or palace and that it could go back well over a thousand years. I was dumbstruck at the time – not least because I realised that this discovery could prove the salvation of Clive's house. The state authorities were not prepared to save the house just because it had belonged to Clive – he remains a fairly unpopular figure in Calcutta. But if the house stands on the site of a long-lost but significant ancient building, the discovery of which could rewrite the early history of Calcutta, then there was a chance that it could be saved and reused to serve as a museum for the site.

As I left Calcutta three years ago, Mr Uta started to excavate and made a number of significant discoveries that appeared to support his initial analysis. I am intrigued to find out what happened since. I wind my way through the narrow streets of Dum Dum and suddenly break into a familiar open space. There is the house, still standing and looking much the same. I approach and to my gratification see a welcome sign. It declares the building a scheduled historic monument and warns of the dire consequences that will be visited upon anyone who damages it. Wonderful – the house is saved. And there is more. There are stacks of newly made but authentic-looking Mogul bricks and mounds of lime mortar. Repairs are under way! I enter the central throne room. Last time I was here it was metres deep in rubble. This has now been moved and old timbers and joinery have been extracted and set to one side for reuse. I am approached by a site guardian and told the story. The house is being repaired and, as I had hoped, is to serve as a museum showing the finds made on the site. And these turn out to be of extraordinary importance. There is evidence of building and burials from as early as 200 BC and a number of exquisite terracotta and stone figures have been unearthed, including what could be an image of Durga that, if dating from the 11th century as estimated, is one of the earliest known representations of the goddess. I pick up a booklet from the site office. It states that the 'excavation of Dumdum mound can be considered as a milestone so far as the history of the origin and antiquity of Kolkata is concerned'. Golly – history has indeed been rewritten, and all because of *The House Detectives*!

Monday 16 August

We fly to Bangalore and then on to Colombo, Sri Lanka. We arrive in the late afternoon and, on the drive to the hotel, get an intriguing glimpse of the city. Colombo is a rich repository of the Raj – in the city itself is an impressive array of majestic 19th-century Classical public buildings, including the former Government House, the Treasury, the Museum of 1877 and the magnificent St Lucia's Cathedral. But this jolly ex-colonial atmosphere is veiled by more sinister modern concerns. Everywhere are road blocks, sandbag redoubts and soldiers and police carrying AK47s. Colombo is clearly a city under siege – a victim of the 25-year struggle between the government and the separatist Liberation Tigers of Tamil Eelam, better known as LITE or the Tamil Tigers. At the moment things are reasonably quiet as the talks between the two sides continue, but impatience is growing as major issues remain unresolved. The entire conflict is a sorry tale of mismanagement and misfortune that, sadly, has its roots in commerce and British colonial rule. In the mid-19th century the British attempted to grow coffee in Sri Lanka but this was a failure. Then they introduced tea which was – and remains – a spectacular success. But the wages offered by the British planters were so low that the native Sinhalese did not want to work on the plantations. So Tamil peasants – willing to work for the wages on offer – were brought over from south India. No doubt the seed of ill will, between the Buddhist Sinhalese and the Hindu and Christian Tamils, was sown at this time. The Indian Tamils – together with native Tamils – had grown into a significant minority population, based in the north of the island, by the time independence was gained from the British in February 1948. But after independence the frictions between the two communities mounted – there was even talk of deporting Tamils back to India. These problems were compounded by the 1972 constitution that confirmed Buddhism as the 'foremost' religion of Sri Lanka and Sinhala as the official language of government.

And so in the early 1980s the battle for a Tamil homeland in the north of the island was launched. Around 50,000 people have been killed during the 25 years of conflict, with the increasingly fanatical Tamil Tigers resorting to ruthless and bloody terrorist tactics, and many historic Hindu and Buddhist temples have fallen victim to savage attacks from both sides. I realise that my travels around Sri Lanka will be coloured, perhaps even controlled or curtailed, by the continuing threat of violence and by the high level of security.

34 THE PALACE OF SIGIRIYA, SRI LANKA

Tuesday 17 August

We spend the night in Colombo and then travel through the rich and varied landscape of Sri Lanka to the ancient city of Sigiriya. The city suburbs give way to rich farmland, the road winds high through jungle passes and then down to flatter and lower terrain. Sigiriya makes its first appearance in a most dramatic manner – a great slab of flat-topped rock thrusting up 200 metres from the plain. It was here, from AD 477, that King Kasyapa created his city with his fortified palace placed on top of the looming rock, with rooms and passages cut within it. Strange legends surround this place and the man who created it. Kasyapa is said to have had the blood of his father on his hands – murdered in savage manner to pave the way to the throne – and a powerful and calculating wife. The hill-top palace was, perhaps, built as an act of penance for the death of his father as well as defence against the righteous wrath of his gathering enemies, which included Kasyapa's own brother. It was also, some say, a place of hedonistic and sinful pleasure

A site of worldly pleasures or of spiritual enlightenment? I wonder. King Kasyapa's palace at Sigiriya sits on top of a 200-metre high rock, his own sacred world – an acropolis.

or, alternatively, a world of magic, for Kasyapa fancied himself the incarnation of Kubera – a yaksha or nature-demon in Hindu theology, the keeper of the treasures of the earth.

I want to investigate the remains of Kasyapa's fantastic creation to see if this was no more than a place of worldly pleasure, wealth and power, or if the king was also pursuing, through the making and placing of his city and palace, some type of spiritual quest.

I approach the great rock and begin to spy out the remains of its

Right *More than 500 of these apsaras were painted on the walls of the Cave of Heavenly Maidens at the palace of Sigiriya. Only 15 remain, but they are beautiful.* Opposite *One of the pair of enormous lion's claws which guard the entrance to the palace at Sigiriya. A new staircase has replaced the huge lion's jaw through which visitors used to enter the palace.*

citadel and palace. But before I reach its base I walk through the remains of the city that Kasyapa built at the foot of the rock. It's a fantastic place, approached through a series of moats and brick-built walls. The form of the city is my first clue. All is ordered, with junctions set neatly at right angles.

I study my rudimentary plan with fresh interest. Suddenly I understand. The city takes the form of two right-angled enclosures, one on each side of the towering rock. The enclosure to the west is square and contained sophisticated water gardens and royal buildings. The enclosure to the east is half the size of the western enclosure, a double square in plan, and set on the same axis as the main square. Indeed the centre of this axis is the palace on top of the rock. Kasyapa was using Hindu temple geometry and had surely created a model of a sacred world – with himself at its peak. It was his own Mount Meru.

Is this all some kind of ancient blasphemy? This type of planning – using square mandalas, or divine charts representing the realm of the gods – was reserved for temple building, with the god or the king who held himself to be divine set at the centre. But Kasyapa was a patricide and possibly a sinister sensualist worshipping material power and riches – perhaps he saw himself as a servant or manifestation of a dark god. His religion is hard to pinpoint – there is Hindu and Buddhist imagery here.

I press on past the remains of the strange king's city. It is clear that this was a place with an organisation and water system of Roman standards. As I begin my ascent of the rock, a wide brick and stone staircase snakes up and I find myself on a terrace from which rises a spiralling modern steel staircase. This carries me up Sigiriya's most obvious visual treasure. I walk along a gallery that takes me past a wall of polished plaster – incredibly, dating from the 5th century – on which is scrawled some ancient erotic graffiti, and then up more steps and into a grotto formed by a rocky overhang. Here are paintings of what are generally referred to as heavenly maidens. These are females that are at once realistic – painted with a sense of perspective and shadowing – but also idealised. At least I assume they are idealised – unless all maidens in Sri Lanka 1500 years ago had perfectly formed but huge breasts, tiny waists and wore incredibly tight and revealing bodices and impossibly languishing looks. These young ladies are one of the reasons why the palace of Sigiriya is assumed to have been a lustful pleasure ground,

with these the portraits of Kasyapa's courtesans. But it is clear that this is not the case. These delightful females are apsaras, the celestial maidens of Hindu theology, who were created during the tug-of-war between gods and demons, good and evil, that I saw illustrated in Angkor Wat. Apsaras are divine in every way and are seen as the consorts of gods, of great heroes and kings. Kasyapa had more than five hundred painted in this grotto and the painting stretched for 140 metres and rose 40 metres high. It must have been an incredible sight – a whole rock face of delicately painted and coloured beautiful young ladies, floating 100 metres or so above ground level. The fact that these figures are heavenly apsaras and not merely courtesans is significant. Evidently Kasyapa did indeed see Sigiriya as a sacred creation with himself as the focus for his flock of apsaras, and not just a place of earthly pleasure.

I have to double back to continue on my journey and soon reach a court, about half-way up the rock, where an amazing image confronts me – a pair of gigantic lion's paws with exposed claws, partly hewn out of the rock and partly formed with brick and plaster. The name Sigiriya means 'lion mountain' and this creation is the emblem of the palace and of Kasyapa. Originally these paws supported stout legs and between the legs was the head of a crouching lion with jaws wide open. This is the entrance to the palace proper, and all who wound their way to the heart of Kasyapa's domain had to do so by passing through the mouth of a roaring lion – an overwhelming image of power and kingship, and not a little daunting. Although the brick and plaster upper portions of the lion have long crumbled, the staircase that winds up between his paws survives, and I ascend. As I do, fellow pilgrims panic – what on earth can the matter be? 'Hornets!' goes up the cry and I am told to rush down – I do, followed by many others. Where the lion's head would have been now live – in massive pendulous hives – ferocious hornets that occasionally descend upon noisy and disrespectful travellers and do them great harm. So this is still a dangerous place to enter.

The hornets eventually settle down and I resume my journey upwards, to the heaven or the hell of Kasyapa. When I reach the top, enough of Kasyapa's palace remains to make me realise that I have entered what was a magic world perched among the clouds. Even at this high level there were baths, fountains powered by windmills, ornamental pools and drainage and cooling mechanisms. The palace contained one of the world's most sophisticated and ingenious hydraulic systems so that 1500 years ago Kasyapa and his court enjoyed bodily comforts more usually associated with the 20th century. I wander among the fragments of palace walls and the pools – still containing water – and look down on Kasyapa's kingdom. Immediately below is his city, a sacred precinct from which rises this mighty acropolis – the god-like dwelling Kasyapa created for himself, his own peculiar heaven on earth. The place is deserted, the shadows are long and the wind whistles. I must descend before it is dark. I re-pass the frightful pods of the hornets and down and down to regions of the ruins I have not yet examined. There is just enough light left to make out the remains of buildings – temples, perhaps a throne room – and then I see a mighty form rearing out of the gloom. It's a huge cobra, about 15 metres high, with hood outstretched, ready to strike. As I get near I see that it is carved out of the side of the rock. It must be a shrine. Is this where an image of Siva once sat – the Hindu god of fertility associated with the cobra – or even that of the Buddha, who sometimes reposes beneath a cobra hood?

Again I see Sigiriya as a sacred landscape, even if one that appears, to many, to be weirdly skewed, one in which the physical and the spiritual, the sexual and the sacred, are intricately entwined and inter-related. In Hindu religion sex is part of life, of the life of the gods, the means through which procreation is celebrated and achieved. Perhaps this marriage of the sacred and the profane is a clue to the meaning of Sigiriya.

And what happened to Kasyapa? It's a sad story. He either committed suicide when confronted by the powerful army of his vengeful brother Moggallana or, according to another version, was poisoned by his wife. Whatever the truth, he was dead by AD 495 and his city abandoned. I re-cross the moat at last light. Sigiriya is a strange place. I'm not sorry to leave.

35 THE GREAT BUDDHA OF POLONNARUWA

Wednesday 18 August

Breakfast is an intriguing affair, with new foods on offer. Pride of place goes to the hopper – a pancake made of rice flour, served with a fried egg on top and with a dab of chilli samba. More familiar is the chapatti, served with grated coconut. With a bit of fruit, it's light, wholesome and delicious – and the tea, of course, is excellent. In good spirits we drive to our next treasure – the ancient city of Polonnaruwa. The history of Polonnaruwa is, effectively, the history of the ancient kingdoms of Sri Lanka and of their relationship with their giant neighbour to the north – India. Ancient ruins – Hindu and Buddhist temples – abound here, but my particular treasure is a giant figure, one of several I meet on this journey. I have seen the enigmatic Moai on Easter Island, Christ the Redeemer at Rio de Janeiro, the Giants of Tula in Mexico, the Statue of Liberty in New York, all with their different meanings – and now I'm going to see a massive reclining figure of Buddha.

Polonnaruwa dates from the 10th century when it was a possession of the Hindu Chola kings of south India following their conquest of the northern portion of Sri Lanka. Polonnaruwa was then retaken by the Sinhalese King Vijayabahu I in 1070 and became his capital with palaces, Buddhist temples, huge water tanks and parks being created. Mighty as these works were, the golden age of Polonnaruwa came in the late 12th century under King Parakramabahu I when it became one of the great cities of south Asia. In the 13th century Hindu rulers again gained control of Polonnaruwa, adding another layer of complexity and culture to the city.

I walk through the sacred heart of the ancient city – a group of temples raised on a quadrangular platform which reflect the religions, and fusion of beliefs, of the warring Indian and Sinhalese dynasties. Indian Hindu temples sit side by side with Sinhalese Buddhist shrines and, in the case of the Vatadage or reliquary, four images of Buddha sit in a structure the doors of which are ornamented with Hindu gods. There is the spectacular Hatadage in which Sri Lanka's greatest Buddhist treasure – the tooth of Buddha – was kept in the 12th century, and nearby is one of the most curious structures in Sri Lanka. Called the Satmahal Prasada, dating from the 12th or 13th centuries, it is a pagoda-like step-pyramid. It reminds me of similar structures that I have seen in central America, Cambodia and Egypt. There is nothing else like it in Sri Lanka and no one has the slightest idea what its function was. For me, it's yet more strange but compelling evidence for long-forgotten cultural and religious connections between distant lands and peoples.

I reach the Gal Vihara, the Cave of the Spirits of Knowledge – my treasure. There are three colossal Buddha images here, carved in the 12th century out of the granite cliff face. In the centre, one stands, 7 metres high, with arms crossed across his chest – a most unusual stance for the Buddha. It appears to be

The Standing Buddha, one of three giant Buddhas at Polonnaruwa, the ancient capital of Sri Lanka. This 7-metre-high image is carved into the rock and has crossed arms, a most unusual pose for the Buddha.

The Reclining Buddha at Polonnaruwa is the treasure I have come to see. The detail of the carving is beautiful, capturing the moment of utter peace and release from earthly troubles. As a sacred work of art, it has an almost tangible power for those who come to worship and seek spiritual help.

looking to one side at the mighty image of the Buddha that is reclining to the right. This is 14 metres long and a sublime work of sacred art. The Buddha, his features finely cut from the hard rock, appears to be in a state of transcendental peace. It's now assumed that these two images show Buddha at different moments of his life, with the standing figure contemplating his quest – the moment of enlightenment, of nirvana. To the left is a more conventional seated Buddha, smaller and less finely carved than the other two images. Size is important in Buddhist art, for largeness of scale is seen to reflect largeness of heart, of devotion, of sacred power and importance. Parakramabahu wanted to build a gigantic stupa to reveal the scale of his devotion and of the effort and sacrifice he had made for his religion. And here is a gigantic image of the Buddha – beautiful to behold, yet a strangely materialistic monument for such a fine and non-materialistic faith. Such colossal images of the Buddha are a relatively late arrival within the Buddhist faith, dating from only 1700 years or so ago. Before that, the Buddha, who died 2500 years ago, was invoked in a more abstract form – a wheel, a pair of feet, a column. These seem to me to be more appropriate images for a faith the main protagonist of which is not a god but a man who, through meditation, achieves divine understanding.

As I stand contemplating this enigmatic figure I am reminded of its continuing power. It is not primarily an attraction for tourists or historians, but for devotees. Suddenly I am surrounded by dozens of worshippers and the benign smile on the face of the reclining Buddha takes on its real meaning. It is giving encouragement, beaming love on those who come in search of help. I retreat, leaving the Buddha, suddenly alive, to his devotees.

36 THE BUDDHA'S TOOTH, KANDY

Thursday 19–Friday 20 August
My pursuit of the Buddha does not end at Polonnaruwa – which is perhaps understandable in Sri Lanka, for it is the country with the oldest continuous Buddhist history in the world, the faith having arrived in the 2nd century BC. I plunge into the heart of the island, to Kandy, the capital of one of Sri Lanka's independent Buddhist

The entrance to the Temple of Buddha's Tooth in Kandy, Sri Lanka. This symbol of nationhood is hidden away in a golden casket and rarely shown. I am disturbed that such an important object of devotion has assumed a political symbolism.

kingdoms for nearly 2000 years until finally conquered by the British in 1815. At the time of this conquest Kandy had, and still retains, the greatest Buddhist relic in the world – what is alleged to be one of Buddha's teeth. Four teeth are said to have been taken from Buddha's funeral pyre in 543 BC and this tooth – supposed to have been brought to Sri Lanka in the 4th century AD – is the only one still known to be in existence. For Buddhist Sinhalese, at least, this tooth is a tremendous symbol of national identity.

Kandy is a very pretty town, nestling within jungle-clad hills and straddling a river. At its heart is the Temple of the Tooth, made up of a collection of traditional buildings with steeply pitched roofs. For safekeeping, the Tooth Relic was brought to Kandy in 1542, but the repose of the tooth in this stronghold in the centre of the island was not to last. In 1594 Portuguese attacked and captured Kandy and the temple was destroyed. The Portuguese were pragmatic adventurers and profit-seeking merchants – but they possessed a missionary zeal when it came to religion. They would not tolerate what they perceived as paganism and were determined to impose Roman Catholicism, even if the price of saving a human soul was death. Buddha's Tooth was seen as a frightful item of idolatry and to be destroyed.

From this stage a certain ambiguity surrounds the tooth. The Sinhalese claim that the tooth was saved with a false tooth being surrendered to the Portuguese, while the Portuguese claim the tooth was seized, taken to Goa and incinerated. No one now believes that the tooth was destroyed – and certainly its guardians are said to have saved it from Hindu fanatics by the same deception technique.

And that's not all. The tooth is a target once again because it has assumed huge political importance for Buddhist Sinhalese as a symbol of nationhood. In 1998, in response to the tooth's status as the symbol of Buddhist political dominance in Sri Lanka, the Tamil Tigers detonated a large truck bomb outside the temple gates. Bystanders were killed and maimed, the temple damaged – but the tooth survived, although now confirmed as a secular and nationalist symbol as much as a religious one.

I must say, I wonder what I am actually going to see and feel when I enter the temple to witness the morning service when the tooth – kept within a series of seven golden caskets – is exposed for public veneration. Will it feel tainted by the fact that the tooth is now firmly rooted in the world of politics and violence? It's worrying. Predictably, my first experience is security. Streets around the temple are closed, armed guards patrol and

I am searched thoroughly as I enter. What a bizarre situation, what irony – the Temple of the Tooth has become one of the most dangerous rather than most tranquil and peaceful places on the island. What would Buddha, the champion of tolerance and non-violence, make of all this?

Eventually I enter a huge hall. Everywhere people are gathering, holding offerings of flowers for the Buddha. When the hour comes for the service to begin, monks and musicians emerge from the ground floor of the temple and drums are thumped and trumpets blown. But what is really important happens upstairs. A door is opened to reveal a first-floor room of the shrine and within the room the sparkling, bejewelled and golden outer casket of the seven is exposed. That's it – no more. The tooth is far too precious to show. But it is enough. Devotees queue and push to see the casket, to grab a blessing from it, to place their offering or to sit quietly and chant or pray towards the tooth-containing casket. I watch and wonder. Just why it should be such an important object of devotion for a faith that promotes not the material but the spiritual is a great puzzle. Perhaps it's just the presence of the security men that disturbs, but it all seems a little strange – this militant Buddhism.

After the service when the door closes and the casket is once again concealed, I walk around the temple to look in other buildings. I enter a modern shrine within the temple complex. At one end is a giant image of the Buddha, and from the walls hang instructive paintings telling the history of the Buddha, of the tooth relic and, in a slanted way, the history of Sri Lanka. Tourists mill around and then a large party of schoolchildren enter, are sat down at one end of the room and are lectured. I wander over to listen and as I walk through the buildings I look at the images. The message carried by them becomes increasingly alarming. I see a particularly ferocious painting showing violence, men being killed and buildings burnt. I read its caption: 'Patricide King Rajasingha (AD 1581–1593) embraced Saivism [Hinduism] to save himself from sin and attacked to destroy Buddhist temples, burnt Dharma books and tortured Bhikkus and therefore the Tooth Relic was taken to the up-country for safety.' Good heavens, what inflammatory stuff. It implies that in Hinduism patricide is acceptable and states that Hindus tortured good Buddhists, burnt temples and wanted to destroy the Tooth Relic. I don't know about the historic truth or otherwise of this story but what I see with my own eyes is that schoolchildren are brought here to be indoctrinated. If they are Buddhists it can only inflame them, if Hindus it can only alarm, shame and alienate them. I watch the children being instructed, being shown the paintings. It has a horribly familiar feel – this seems the stuff of racism, of religious warfare. Where will this end? Sri Lanka is, by nature, a paradise and its people are delightful. But there is very clearly a dark side – a shadow that threatens to turn this paradise into a hell.

I return to Colombo to brood. We are all to have a week off – a little bit of R & R – but I now see everything in a slightly different, more menacing, light. As I drive into Colombo my vehicle is waved down at a vehicle checkpoint. I am surrounded by armed police, questioned and my passport examined. All the police are correct and polite, all is understandable given the circumstances and – most sad – I'm not even surprised. Already I have grown to accept this type of desperate action. Sri Lanka is a country at war.

We stay in the Mount Livinia Hotel, south of Colombo. It's a rather grand, sprawling place with its own private beach, prowling security guards and an air of exclusivity. After so much travelling, it feels most strange to be still. I'm not used to doing nothing. After a day or two I want to be on the move – to get the adrenalin pumping again. I get my wish. On 25 August we leave the hotel to spend the night at the Taj Hotel near Colombo airport. We have a 5.45 am flight back to India, back to what has become our reality – on the move, a different bed virtually every night, constant novelty and stimulus. We are going to see Madurai, one of the greatest Hindu temple complexes in south India.

37 MEENAKSHI TEMPLE AT MADURAI, INDIA

Thursday 26 August

We arrive in Madurai at lunchtime and go to our hotel on a hilltop overlooking the town. From there we can clearly see the temple, its dimensions marked by the series of towering gopurams, pyramid-like towers that define the temple's boundaries and mark its major gates and shrines. The temple is huge, a town within the teeming city.

In the afternoon we go into Madurai – not initially to the main temple but to a shrine on the edge of this vibrant manufacturing city. Today is a festival and a special service is being held in honour of Madurai's presiding god and goddess – Sundareshvara and Meenakshi. These are curious beings with charming characteristics. They probably began life as Tamil deities but centuries ago were enlisted by Brahmin priests into the Hindu orthodox pantheon. So Meenakshi is regarded as one more of the many manifestations of Parvati, while Sundareshvara (which means 'the handsome one') is her husband, Siva, in yet another guise. Meenakshi is the major deity of the pair, the protectress of the city, and she is a most singular creature. She has eyes the shape of a fish, smells like a fish and has three breasts. Siva's powerful, abstract symbol, the lingam, rises from the Hindu representation of the female genitals – a yoni – and, it seems to me, the yoni relates to Meenakshi's eyes. They are almond-shaped, a form called the vesica piscis which is, arguably, used in Christian art to signify the passage through which the Saviour reached mankind – the Virgin's vulva. And curiously, the early Christian sacred symbol of the fish was formed by a vesica piscis – the shape of Meenakshi's eyes – but with the arcs continued at one end to represent the fish's tail. All most intriguing.

As we arrive at the shrine the service is in full swing. Siva is reputed to have worked a number of miracles in and around the site of modern Madurai and this shrine marks the location of one of them, where Siva taught a proud ruler – who oppressed poor holy men or sadhus – a stern lesson in proper behaviour. Consequently, as I arrive, the very

The temple complex at Madurai in southern India mixes the sacred and the profane. It is huge, a world within a world. The brightly coloured paintwork tells the story of the whole of Hindu life.

image of a vain ruler, dramatically made-up and sitting on top of his elephant, is waiting in the wings to be taught his lesson as the pageant unfolds. Within the shrine are a number of images highly ornamented with jewels and heaped with flowers. These are Meenakshi and Sundareshvara and they are about to be carried – on litters – the 4 kilometres to the main temple. Crowds push and manoeuvre to see, to be near, to touch, the images. I get caught up in the melee, carried past a pair of temple elephants – one of which gives me a blessing by wrapping its trunk around the top of my head – and am suddenly eye to eye with the images. I stare at them, they – with dark, red-rimmed eyes in brazen faces – stare back. Somehow the images are extricated from the teeming crowd and the procession weaves its way into town. We make our own way to the temple and arrive there some hours before the images, which make numerous stops en route, to be refreshed and to offer blessings to the people.

The temple is a huge affair, comprising numerous courts, halls and shrines, all within a walled enclosure punctuated by gates topped with towering gopurams. Great south Indian temples like this one at Madurai were conceived as sacred cities, worlds of their own – microcosms of the world of the gods. Usually they take the form of a series of concentric enclosures, which get increasingly more sacred and exclusive, with only the most holy or esteemed able to reach the central shrine – the holy of holies. Madurai temple was conceived on this principle but not fully realised. It seems to mix various ideas that have evolved over the centuries. A temple was probably founded on this site in the 12th century but the existing buildings date mainly from the 16th and 17th centuries onwards.

I try to make sense of the spaces in this temple. It is not really a series of concentric courts, although there is clearly an inner court – instead, it seems to me, the temple offers a sequence of spaces and buildings that suggest a route around or through it. I ask the young man who the temple has provided as my guide to explain the meaning of this confusing place. He takes my notebook and in it draws a small plan – a simplified and idealised version of the organisation of the temple. The spaces are, it seems, modelled on a human body – or rather the body of a god. At the top is a square court and building containing a major shrine, that of Sundareshvara or Siva. This is the head, connected via a narrow passage to the main, larger rectangular court. These represent the neck and body. Below this is an image of Nandi – Siva's bull, a temple flagpole and, below this, another shrine. These, says my guide with a strangely triumphant smile, represent the navel, the male organ and the feet. Of course – the temple is not only the image of a body, but a fertility symbol. In fact sex – or fertility – is absolutely everywhere, not just in the plan of the temple, but in its decoration and symbols. My guide starts talking about sexual energy and the chakras and how routes through the temple simulate, and help release, this explosive physical and spiritual energy. He confides a secret to me – 'sex life is divine life'. True perhaps – certainly this temple, in all its parts, seems to be proclaiming this – but sex as a means to an end, never an end in itself.

I pass by a wide passageway filled with stalls and people squatting, sleeping, talking and selling. To the side of this passage is one of the great architectural glories of the temple – the Thousand Column Hall. This was the ceremonial heart of the temple, completed in about 1570, and the gift of one of the Nayak's – the ruling dynasty's – most powerful ministers, so there is more than a hint here of politics, power and well-placed patronage. The columns facing the passage are among the best. They show a number of beings who are crucial to the meaning – to the life – of the temple. My attention is drawn to a figure at the far end, a striking young woman, naked from the waist up with monumental breasts and admirable nipples. In one hand she holds a sitar, its neck grasped firmly between her delicate fingers. She's a dhasi – a celestial maiden, a dancer, rather like an apsara, and it was for her earthly equivalents that the Thousand Column Hall was built. The Brahmin priest who controlled the temple would collect young girls, keep them secure within the sacred precincts, and train them to dance. These girls would dance for the gods, the princes of the land and – I suppose – for the Brahmins. Dance was the force that ordered the world, the rhythm of creation. My guide smiles at the lovely girl and whispers to me what I had already imagined. 'These dancers were also concubines – for the king.' Yes, celestial concubines. Music, dance, religion, sex, power, life and creation – it's all there. Oh, yes – and beauty.

I penetrate further into the cavernous, womb-like hall. The central avenue of the hall is lined with yalis – lion, ram, bull and lizard combinations – all with the sexual organs of well-endowed men. These creatures that, like the Sphinx, combine the essential characteristics of primal animals, were well loved by the Nayak rulers. I gaze along the ranks of this bizarre monster – some lion-faced, others more like rams. They are amazing representations of fertility, worldly

I have chosen the Meenakshi Temple because it is so full of life. In the Thousand Column Hall, the erotic heart of the temple complex, there are statues of animal and man combinations and exquisitely wrought celestial maidens and dancers. This statue portrays one of the young ladies whose virtue is put to the test by Siva.

power, the wisdom and forces of nature. Opposite is a statue of a gypsy that appears to be carved out of one stone – which makes the fact that certain parts of it are hollow rather puzzling. But more curious still is the fact that when the gypsy's right hand is struck the statue rings out a perfect note. This – weirdly – is a musical instrument. This, and other columns in the hall, can be played, with their different parts producing different but harmonious notes. One can only imagine the sort of events that took place here 400 years ago. Dancers rotating to the movement of the earth – with the building itself a musical instrument. Extraordinary.

I walk on and discover yet stranger images. On one square column at the far end of the hall are carved two young ladies in advanced stages of sexual excitement. Their trousers are falling down, one covers her pudendum with her hand and the other – rather brazenly – exposes herself, with her vulva carved in loving detail, like a yoni on a Siva lingam. On a third side of the column is carved a near-naked man. My guide tells me that the man is Siva who, to test womankind, sought out the wives of sadhus – humble Hindu holy men – and tempted them. The wives, being only human, fell in lust with Siva, although he was in the guise of a beggar. So we see the women in the moment of their fall – one grasping a phallic-like spoon with which she was proposing to offer food to the beggar-god, both a-tremble. The message of all of this is clear. Sexual energy is a power to be reckoned with, it's the currency of the gods, it's the currency of mankind. But it can be negative as well as positive. It's to be controlled, to be used creatively, not abused. For humans, of course, it's easier said than done. But that's the test. Unlike these wives, you should rise above temptation. That's the lesson written in the stones.

Time to move on to the main event. The images have arrived at the temple – the pair are home – and the nightly ritual of uniting Meenakshi with Sundareshvara is about to take place. They are a happily married couple and although they usually spend the day apart – he in his shrine and she in hers, being decked in jewellery or exercised on her swing – each night they are put to bed together. I wait until 11 pm – by which time the temple has emptied considerably – in the cavernous and raw space outside Siva's shrine. Then suddenly – pandemonium. The door of the Siva shrine swings open and a couple of men burst out carrying a palanquin with a curtain lowered to conceal its contents. This, I know, is Siva/Sundareshvara on his way to see his wife. The two fellows run through the temple, followed by devotees and accompanied by a clanging of bells, to Meenakshi's shrine. Meenakshi and Sundareshvara are together until the morning, when the ritual is reversed and the loving couple part, each to their different daily duties. It's nearly midnight – with the bedding of the couple the day ends for the temple. I walk through its dark and echoing halls and courts, past the statues – now with people sleeping between them – and into the city streets. I am stunned by it all. I love these Hindu temples, in which ancient gods – older than the long-dead gods of ancient Greece and Rome – still lead active daily lives, are still worshipped as living beings, still have the power to move and to be part of the daily life of millions of ordinary people.

Friday 27 August

Today we are to take a train towards our next destination – the ancient port of Cochin. But first, one last look at the temple and lunch. South Indian food is incredibly wholesome. We sit in a restaurant, overlooking the temple, and indulge in an orgy of vegetarian delights – vada made from chickpeas and flour, rice flour idli, utupam made from tapioca, delicious curd rice, coconut chutney, crispy dosa and thali with samba. Wonderful – and so is the train. We board it at Madurai Junction where the station name is, rather oddly, written within a graphic device based on the circle and bar logo of the London Underground! Such is the legacy of the Raj.

The train is a sleeper of the wide-gauge variety. In the past I have spent weeks in these Indian wide-gauge sleeper carriages. On long journeys they become communities as the six or more passengers that squeeze into each compartment get to know each other during journeys that can last for days. As I sit in the carriage awaiting departure, two faces suddenly appear at the slatted window. One of the chaps asks me where I'm from and my name. I tell him and we nod and smile at each other. He then asks me if I like trains. I say yes. He asks me how much I like trains. I say very much. 'Very, very much?' he asks. Yes, I answer, 'very, very much'. He rocks his head from side to side – in that universal Indian gesture that can mean many things – smiles again, and says 'Good'. The train pulls slowly away, editing this pair of smiling faces from my view. I lean forward to wave goodbye. They run along with the train for a little and wave back. Travelling by train in India is always like this – strange, wonderful.

Eventually we transfer to our cars and arrive in Cochin just after nightfall. We drive to the centre of this ancient trading city and discover that our hotel – in a sprawling 17th-century mansion once belonging to a rich merchant – sits next to the old town square with, across from the hotel, a mighty and ancient church. It could be an English village green – except for the palm trees and tropical vegetation, the somewhat parched grass and the decidedly foreign look of the church.

Cochin – recently renamed Kochi – is probably the oldest international port in India. It's the gate through which, over the centuries, not just goods but ideas, religions, different peoples and conquerors have made their way into the subcontinent. Those using the natural ports around Cochin in Kerala have included the Phoenicians, Syrians, Egyptians, Romans, Arabs, Chinese and, from the 16th century, the European colonial powers. But it was not only a point of entry. More importantly Cochin was a port from which precious goods were exported from India – and most precious of all in the past were spices. These were of huge importance. They served as medicines and tonics, as food flavouring of course and, perhaps most important in world history, they helped to preserve food or, more precisely, helped to make long-stored food healthy and edible. This last function had massive consequences. If food could be stored man escaped from the remorseless cycle of food production, from living hand-to-mouth, from winters of want. Food could be produced in bulk when conditions were right and then stored, leaving time for leisure, for reflection, for the growth of civilisation. Also the ability to store food made it possible for man to explore, to travel long distances by sea, to open trade routes, to spread ideas and technologies.

Ginger, turmeric, cardamom, nutmeg, mace, mustard, cloves and cinnamon were all traded through Cochin. But it was pepper in particular that the world craved and that made Cochin famous and rich. It was known as black gold. I have come to Cochin to discover the physical and cultural consequences of the spice trade, to see a city that was, in the past, one of the most important trading places on earth, a great crossroads of the world-embracing Spice Route.

38 THE SPICES OF COCHIN

Saturday 28–Sunday 29 August

Cochin has something of the quality of Venice. The old town – Fort Cochin – sits on the end of a peninsula with the sea on one side and a great sheet of water on the other. In this water is a partly man-made island-cum-peninsula called Willingdon Island and beyond this is another sheet of water and then the mainland. And through these slivers of land run watercourses, mostly providing access to warehouses. I make my way to the harbour in old Cochin to get a boat. I want to experience some of these waterways, to see the old city as it was meant to be seen, to see the face it presented to the world, to traders arriving in their great vessels. On the way my attention is gripped by one of the famous sights of Cochin – the mighty fishing nets that line the harbour front. These are massive boom structures, made of slender timber poles, which pivot in the centre. At one end of the boom is a net, which is counter-balanced by stones attached to the other end. By merely pulling on a few ropes the boom – and net – can be lowered into the water and, when the time is right, the ropes can be pulled again and the boom rises – theorically with a net bursting with fish. These impressive structures are called Chinese fishing nets, and are meant to be a legacy of the Chinese traders who used Cochin from the mid-14th century. I watch these great machines at work – they are effortless and elegant, but none brings up many fish. I fear that nature is not as abundant, or the location as fruitful, as it was 500 years ago.

The entrance to one of the main spice warehouses in Cochin – the architecture is in Classical style, and the limewash colours on the exteriors are vibrant.

I get on a small boat and sail along the backwater. This offers an incredibly romantic view of this ancient port. The Portuguese founded a colony here in the very early years of the 16th century and were replaced as masters by the Dutch and then the British. But this diversity of ownership is not clear in the waterside architecture. What emerges is a coherent image of rustic yet erudite vernacular Classical architecture. Most buildings are brick-built, covered with render and then lime-washed with yellow ochre. This mellow stone colour is usually offset with brighter colours – pale blue, deep red or green – used on joinery. The visual effect is magical. Most of the buildings I see must date from the years of Dutch dominance, some with charming baroque details – playful curving gables that you might see in Amsterdam or Delft.

I land by one old warehouse to see how these buildings worked when this was the spice trading hub of the world. It's a sad wreck but still retains a smattering of elegant details.

Left *The Chinese fishing nets in Cochin harbour date from the 14th century. Sadly, there are few fish caught in them today.* Right *Sorting pepper – known as black gold – in Cochin. It is still done in the traditional way.*

Tragically, much of old Cochin is now in this condition. I move on, down an alley, to the main warehouse. It's a massive place, its high, gaunt limewashed walls covered by a handsome timber roof. But most exciting are the mountains of sacks that rise inside. I can smell the contents – dried ginger and turmeric in some and, yes, black peppercorns in the others. These are the spices that the world has craved for thousands of years and here they are, being stored and prepared in the traditional manner – a woman sits on the floor sifting peppercorns, men haul and load the sacks that are destined for the ever-eager global market. I pass into a small yard, through a gate and into the street, and see similar ancient and grand establishments. Palaces of commerce indeed. I'm standing in Jew Town Road, in the Mattancherry part of town. This is not only where the spice warehouses are but also – as the road name implies – the home of Cochin's long-established Jewish community.

At the end of the road stands the splendid Paradesi synagogue, founded in 1568 and rebuilt in glorious style in 1760. I visited ten years ago and found it a miraculous place – largely because of the Chinese blue and white tiles that cover its floor and the light that floods in through its large windows. But things are different now. The Jewish community is tiny – said to number only 14 – and defensive. Most have long ago taken up the right of Jews to residency in Israel and have abandoned their native home in Cochin. I knock on the door to ask if I can enter and film inside. This produces great anger – mostly directed at me by men speaking in American accents. This is the Sabbath, they point out, why can't you leave us alone? I apologise, but persist. It is clear that I am dealing with a group of American religious tourists who appear to have appropriated the synagogue for the day. They turn not only me away but a group of local visitors who want to see their own heritage. It all seems a little rum. Eventually I manage to secure an interview with a local gentleman, who appears wearing a skullcap and clutching an Old Testament. He is the head of the synagogue and is polite but very short with me. The answer is no filming and no visitors on a Sabbath. You need a permit from the state government to film the synagogue he says – and then adds that, 'even if you get one we would still refuse you permission to film'. He then stalks away. It's all very sad – but I suppose the small community feels threatened, vulnerable and fears attack – and so one of the most curious, historic and beautiful synagogues in the world retains its secrets.

I walk back to my hotel by the green – enjoying the street life, the smell of spice, the vigorous and inventive Classical architecture and the beautiful limewash colours on the buildings. When I get to the green my spirits pick up. The scene is complete. Local boys are playing the great game – cricket. I watch in admiration. India is, of course, one of the great cricketing nations and many of its star players have, over the years, learned and honed their skills on simple wickets just like this. To say all this is the legacy of the British

Raj is true – but that is to miss the point. Cricket in India is far more than just a colonial hangover – it's transcended all of that. It is the supreme national sport and now plays a major role in the expression of Indian national identity and pride. The energy and attack with which the boys play express all this. Tim Dunn and I admire the game for a while and then ask to join in. We are welcomed with glee. I am put in to bat. Excitement mounts – a sudden India versus England friendly is under way. I knock a couple of balls around – even score a four – but am soon bowled out. These boys of the Star Eleven are good and full of spirit. We all pose for a team photograph when the game is over. It makes such a perfect picture as the sun sets over the green – the crack of the cricket ball on willow, the studied stance of the batsman, the mannered gait of the bowler and the shouted appeals of the fielders. And in the background the antiquated bulks of once-great houses and the church.

I walk to the greatest of the houses and see, at once, both that it is a wonderful thing and that it appears to be derelict. I find the front door open and enter a large rectangular hall with the remains of one of a pair of ornate Classical doorcases on its inner walls. Behind and on each side of the hall are further rooms, with a long wing extending from the rear of the house into a deep garden. It is fantastic, complete, unspoiled. As I ponder this wonder the security guard suddenly appears. He is in a state of high excitement – and truly delighted to see me. It is called David Hall, is built of bricks brought over as ballast from Holland, belonged to a Dutch merchant called Hendrik Adriaan van Reed of Drakestein and is to be made into a museum.

My last object is the church. Surely it can only prove an anticlimax after David Hall. It doesn't. St Francis Church is a startling, cavernous place dating back to 1502. Consequently it is the oldest continuously operational Christian place of worship in India. It was founded by the Portuguese, taken over and altered first by the Dutch and then by the British and has gone from a Roman Catholic to a Protestant place of worship. Much of the fabric dates from 1516, when the original timber church was rebuilt in stone, and it is a wonderfully gaunt place. First I enter a vestibule – ornamented only with simple Doric columns – and then cross into the long, aisle-less nave of the church. I am looking for one gravestone in particular – and suddenly I see it. On a simple stone slab, on one side of the nave, inscribed in primitive letters, Vasco da Gama. Here was buried one of the great adventurers of the 16th century. Da Gama came to Cochin in 1500 in search of pepper, returned in 1502 to help establish the port as a Portuguese colony, and died and was buried here in 1524. His body was taken back to Portugal in 1536 but his empty grave remains – a place of attraction and contemplation for all who ponder the European role in the shaping of modern India.

Different nations from the West brought trade, religion, technology and advanced

Left The flamboyant Baroque style of Our Lady of Life Catholic Church in Cochin recreated in the early 20th century a Catholic church in Mattancherry demolished by the British in the 1790s.
Right We join the boys of the Star Eleven cricket team for a group photograph after our India versus England friendly.

political beliefs, but they were selfish and greedy benefactors. As well as giving they took – in plenty. It's true the British created modern India – they forged many different and fractious states into an empire, and that empire became two nations in 1947 – Pakistan and India – three when Bangladesh later emerged out of East Pakistan. The British also established noble concepts – that perhaps existed more in principle than in reality – such as equality before the law and freedom of worship. But I – like many who stand in front of this empty grave – wonder, and ask the obvious question. What if the Western traders and colonisers had not come? How would this mighty subcontinent have pursued its destiny if left to itself? I brood on this. Who knows, but probably these intruders have made relatively little difference to life in India. All these once-great European powers have come, bustled, connived, thrived, and then gone with their legacies being absorbed, reworked or ultimately rejected by the great and natural force that is India and its peoples. It's like the cricket. It's only here because of the British but only survives and thrives as a sport because the Indians have taken it to heart. It's now their game.

39 THE JANTAR MANTAR OBSERVATORY, JAIPUR

Monday 30 August

Jaipur is one of the most extraordinary cities in India because it is, in a way, so un-Indian. It's a perfect, considered, jewel-like, geometric and powerfully symbolic creation – the vision of one man.

It was founded in 1727 and its creator was Maharaja Sawai Jai Singh II. He wanted to create an ideal city that was a fusion, in its inspiration and plan, of Eastern and Western urban traditions and of Islamic and Hindu imagery. The city is organised around a right-angular grid – like avant-garde European Classical cities of the time. But it is also square in plan, a form inspired by the sacred mandala used in the design of Hindu temples. Jai Singh was a Hindu prince and, like the Mogul rulers he replaced, a man of great intellectual complexity with an ever-inquiring mind. I want to find out more about him, to understand what inspired him and, in particular, to see his mighty observatory with astronomical instruments and sundials of such huge scale that they look like massive works of abstract art. The city is my treasure but, I feel, the observatory will be my treasure within the treasure.

Despite neglect, overcrowding and much unwise rebuilding, Jaipur preserves its architectural coherence, with its main roads still lined mostly with 18th-century buildings, many sadly battered and with a very lived-in look. As much as anything the visual harmony comes from colour. The local sandstone used on most of the buildings is pale pink while plastered walls are also painted pink – an idea that dates only from 1883 – so Jaipur now glories under the title of the 'Pink City'. It is a visual thrill to drive through the place in an open rickshaw, to look along the wide, straight avenues and up to the balconied buildings, and then suddenly to see an architectural tour de force like the towering Hawa Mahal, with its veil of ornate masonry that makes the massive structure appear light, playful and almost transparent.

It also becomes apparent how extraordinary the square plan of the city is. It is divided into three tiers of three lesser squares – a sacred plan – and this sub-division is expressed in the city's street network. Such ideas are found in the *Shilpa* and *Vastu* shastras – Hindu texts that deal with town planning and the relationship of architecture and planning to the cosmos. It begins to dawn on me that it is not just the observatory in Jai Singh's Jaipur that relates to – or is inspired by – celestial bodies. Everything here is to do with the planets and the stars, not least because Jai Singh believed that he – through his divine ancestors – was descended from the Sun. This familiar conviction is revealed

by the image of a jauntily mustachioed round visage, beaming solar rays, that decorates many a building and lamp post in Jaipur – Jai Singh as the sun god. In Hindu temple planning, each of the nine squares has a different attribute or is the domain of a different god, with the highest god occupying the centre square. In Jaipur, Jai Singh's town palace and ornate gardens occupy the centre squares. There is also another, rather charming, detail about Jai Singh's vision for his ideal city – it didn't quite fit the terrain available. One of the nine smaller squares – that occupying a corner – collided with natural features and so was displaced, to hang from the corner diagonally below it. Sounds complicated but it's not; since Jai Singh and his Bengali architect Vidrahar Bhattacharya accepted this compromise, so should we.

I arrive at the square containing the observatory – the Jantar Mantar as it is called. Work started on the observatory even before it started on the city, with construction beginning in 1718 and continuing until 1734. It is the most extraordinary place, with curious structures whose strange, generally large, abstract forms and seemingly discordant positioning are dictated almost entirely by their function as instruments for observing planetary movements. In this small park resides the whole universe, astronomy and astrology combined. This was, for its day, pioneering science allowing for detailed observations of stars and planets.

The most immediately striking of the instruments is the Samrat Yantra – which is, quite simply, the largest sundial in the world. It is a wondrous and beautiful thing. Nothing is arbitrary about this instrument – nothing can be. Its exact form and orientation are dictated by the turning of the earth, by the planets – by the works of God. A massive ramp rises to the height of 27 metres – this is the gnomon. It is aligned north–south and points directly towards the North Pole – Polaris. This is all necessary if the dial is to work with accuracy – and this it does to a remarkable degree. On each side of the ramp – aligned east and west – are huge quadrants. The gnomon casts its shadows along these quadrants, and the edge of each quadrant is calibrated. I look at them. There

Jaipur, the celestial city, is a diagram of the universe. The Hawa Mahal is an extraordinary sight with its pink stone and elaborate carved masonry. The Jantar Mantar Observatory is my treasure.

The Samrat
Yantra at the
Jantar Mantar
Observatory
at Jaipur. This is
like nothing else I
have seen – built
between 1718
and 1734, its
astronomical
readings are
accurate to within
two seconds.
I am struck by
the powerful
abstract
architectural
quality and
overwhelming
beauty of the
instruments.

is a series of bands, each containing a scale. The inner band is divided into a series of boxes and these boxes record minutes of the day, for it takes one minute – 60 seconds – for the shadow cast by the gnomon to enter and leave each box. But this was not accurate enough for Jai Singh. Below the minute band is a six-second band and a two-second band. Incredible. This sundial is accurate to within two seconds per day and still no one knows how such accuracy was achieved around 280 years ago. It's a mystery.

A large portion of the park is occupied by 12 instruments, called 'equatorial' sundials that are, in form, miniature versions of the great sundial. Each is aligned to a different constellation and each sundial is – as I observe as I walk around – named after a different sign in the zodiac. This is the point. Each of the 12 sundials becomes operational when the constellation that corresponds with its zodiac sign is on the meridian. This reveals the true purpose of these instruments. They are for detailed observation of the constellations of the zodiac and give precise information for the casting of detailed horoscopes. There is nothing else like them in the world.

Most tantalising is a complex instrument that Jai Singh is said to have designed himself. It is called the Jai Prakash Yantra, and takes the form of two hemispheres, side by side and each sunk into the ground. They are clearly two halves of a single map of the heavens for each offers a fragmented map and, if you look for a moment, it is obvious that the portions missing in one are present in the other. This instrument was intended as the master instrument of the observatory – to check the accuracy of the other instruments. Like so much of the Jantar Mantar, the Jai Prakash Yantra is unique and an impressive example of the learning and erudition of Indian princes.

As I contemplate this complex invention I can't help but feel sad. As Jai Singh lost himself in such learning, as he strove to understand the stars, the origin of man, the will of the gods, people were plotting to rob him of his birthright, to overthrow this sun god. This didn't happen at once – Jai Singh died in 1743, with his state intact. But the plotting continued among the greedy, materialistic men who wanted to possess the soul and spirit of this exquisite domain, to turn it from a place of intellectual pursuit and beauty into a place of trade and profit, and ultimately they prevailed. And who were these greedy plotters? Europeans, of course – adventurers, merchants, soldiers and ambitious politicians. They all, in their turn and in their different ways, hammered a nail into the coffin of this magical kingdom – this place of the stars on earth, this last domain of the sun god.

In the evening we drive to Agra to see one of the most famous buildings in the world, indeed a building supposedly dedicated to love – the Taj Mahal, a tomb built by Mogul ruler Shah Jahan for his favourite wife, Mumtaz Mahal. I wonder if reality can possibly measure up to the fantasy. I'm almost sorry that I'm going to see it, to be disappointed. A poem, a prayer, in stone – surely it should exist only in the imagination, in dreams, not in the harsh and unforgiving world where all decays, all corrupts.

40 THE TAJ MAHAL, AGRA

Tuesday 31 August

We rise very early, before dawn, so as the sun rises I find myself living the dream of many. I am standing in front of the Taj Mahal as the first flickers of red-tinted sun touch the white marble of this most venerated of sepulchres. The first impression does not disappoint. I have passed through a mighty gate to get my first view, and entering this portal is indeed like entering into paradise – a paradise in which everything is ordered and surgically symmetrical. That, of course, is the impression that was meant to be created. In front of me lies a garden – with its four rectangular slivers of canal invoking the four rivers of paradise mentioned in the Old Testament and the Koran. I contemplate the tomb from a distance, across the garden – a perfect piece of primal geometry. It is in two distinct parts and occupies the volume of two cubes – one placed upon the other. Within the volume of the bottom cube sits the building proper – this takes the form of an irregular, eight-sided figure, an octagon, in which four sides are long and four are short, and long alternate with short. Set in each of the four long sides is an iwan, or arched recess – a route of penetration. Above this octagonal base, and occupying the volume of the upper cube, is a dome. But not just any dome – it is of that variety beloved by Islam and looks, in form, like a turnip or onion. Islam must have been deeply impressed by the great domed early Christian churches – the Holy Sepulchre in Jerusalem and Hagia Sophia in Istanbul – and soon embraced and developed the form, with the

No building is more romantic or more tragic than the Taj Mahal, built by Shah Jahan for his favourite wife, Mumtaz Mahal. Completed in 1653 it took 22 years to build. Its emotional impact comes not only from its powerful symmetry and dazzling white marble but also from the simplicity of its form.

*As you move
closer to the Taj
Mahal you see
the lettering
and decoration –
the marble is
ornamented with
28 different types
of precious and
semi-precious
stone. The scale
and craftsmanship
are overwhelming.*

Dome of the Rock in Jerusalem of the 690s being one of the earliest and best domed Islamic sacred buildings. For both Christians and Muslims the circle or the sphere symbolises the heavens, God's creation, the world of the spirit. And this is the case at the Taj Mahal. The dome – a three-dimensional permutation of the circle – represents the realm to which the spirits of the dead ascend. The square represents the material world and so the octagonal lower portion of the Taj, a geometrical form derived from two squares turned at 45 degrees to each other, represents the world of man, the cycle of life and death. So the Taj Mahal carries – in its geometry – a powerful message about life, death and rebirth. It squares the circle – it's a symbolic passage reconciling the material world with the world of the spirit.

I approach nearer and begin to see some of the detail on the building. There is not much, but what there is makes its point through delicacy of execution. The whole thing is exquisite – white marble embellished with 28 types of precious and semi-precious stone, jade and crystal from China. There is a jewel-like perfection about the structure, it feels like a mighty and rich casket rather than a building – a casket made to contain the emperor's greatest jewel. It took, it is said, 22 years to build this structure and the toil of 20,000 workers.

I enter – and this is my greatest surprise. Of course the tomb is dark, sombre – it is to do with death. There is no direct light, instead it filters in through a series of grilles. But what I didn't expect is the sound. The building is alive – it speaks, or rather groans. It's not the echoing reverberations one expects from a masonry-built, domed structure – it's more than that. I walk around the tombs inside. There, in the centre, is the simple table-tomb of Mumtaz Mahal with, to one side, the tomb of Shah Jahan himself. And as I walk, the building wails. I suppose it's the wind, entering through high louvres and then rolling around the underside of the dome. I don't know, but the Taj Mahal – seen from the outside, a perfect, almost arid jewel box of a building – certainly packs an emotional punch when experienced from the inside. It makes death tangible and the grief of Shah Jahan eternal. I have to tear myself away. Being inside, the solemn light, the rhythmic sobbing and sighing of the stones, is hypnotic. I wouldn't have believed it – the over-exposed and world-famous picture-postcard Taj Mahal is not a disappointment. In fact it's better than I expected.

I go to the nearby massive fort, a series of spectacular palaces, to see where Sha Jahan spent the last eight years of his life. After the death of Mumtaz Mahal and the completion of the Taj, Shah Jahan's life became terrifyingly turbulent. His sons fought for power, one killed another, and Shah Jahan's realm was reduced to one palace within the fort. Here he remained until his death. I make my way to this palace, to see Shah Jahan's diminished world. It's haunting. I see the pavilion in which he slept and the loggia where he would sit in contemplation of his great creation. I sit where Shah Jahan sat. The distant Taj – shimmering in the light, reflecting and reflected in the waters running below its dome – looks magnificent, ghostly, unreal – indeed a thing of dreams, a phantasmagoria. Its construction is generally seen as an act of devotion, as a memorial for a dead and loved wife. This it certainly is. But perhaps Shah Jahan is interred in the Taj not simply as a consequence of his fall from power and his inability to build a great mausoleum for himself. Perhaps he always intended it to serve as his own tomb. If this is the case then the Taj is not such a selfless act. Shah Jahan saw it as a mausoleum to his wife but also, and ultimately, as a monument to his own taste and power. Ethereal as it may appear, the Taj Mahal is also very much of this world.

As always, India has been a powerful, intoxicating experience. As always, a place of stark contrasts, from Calcutta, where life grows out of death and decay, to the Taj Mahal, where death dwells in a carapace of serene geometric beauty. There's no doubt about the India that moves me – the warmth, the savage, raw beauty of Calcutta. For me, it's the eternal spirit of India.

TRADE ROUTES

Wednesday 1 September – Uzbekistan

We leave Delhi at 9.00 in the evening. This journey is going to be a hard one. Uzbekistan Airways flies old Soviet Aeroflot Illusion 62s and everything is ramshackle to say the least. As I walk down the aisle of the plane I am surrounded by what appears to be smoke. It turns out to be the air-conditioning system coughing into life, pumping cold, damp, vaporising air into the stuffy interior. I tell you it's scary before a flight – it makes you imagine frightful things. And then I discover the seats are broken, I observe that the lavatories are packed with goods and the hostesses look world weary, exhausted and sullen. I only hope the plane's engines and electrics are not in the same tired and emotional state. There is no safety briefing before flying and then the plane rattles down the runway with overhead lockers clattering. We are airborne, thank God.

We arrive at Tashkent airport and are bustled into buses by humourless staff that shout instructions at us. This is still the old Soviet world – where hirelings with their petty power are answerable to no one and ordinary people like us have recourse to no one. We can hardly take our custom elsewhere – there is no elsewhere. For us – the hapless herd – it is take it or leave it. We grumble and move on to passport control. Queues here are scrums. It's the survival of those fittest to duck and dive to the front – a ritual that is interesting to observe, but somewhat exhausting to be involved in, especially at 5.30 in the morning. Finally we get through, collect our luggage and as a pleasant and fresh dawn breaks we drive to our hotel.

41 SAMARKAND, UZBEKISTAN

Thursday 2 – Friday 3 September

This inauspicious start launches us on a new phase of our journey. The next set of treasures lies along ancient trade routes – those arteries that once linked and nourished the world, the routes along which not only wealth and trade travelled, but also ideas, religions, civilisation. We will see places – now, long backwaters – that were once central to the world's economy, cities that were key trading centres along these routes, buildings and souks that housed the riches of the world.

I get up at 1 pm – still feeling dazed – and start the long drive to the ancient, almost legendary trading city of Samarkand, once the capital of the great and cruel lord Tamerlane – Timur the Lame – a name that still invokes dread. The road is straight, wide, well maintained – and virtually empty. Clearly something is strange here. I talk to our local fixer. Yes, she says, for many, life was better in Soviet times. The economy of the region was boosted by Soviet visitors and businesses and there was security. Now all is uncertain and the country's main exports – cotton and silk – do not really compensate for the investment that has been lost. Russians hardly visit Uzbekistan any more, she says, they can't afford to. Things are clearly very difficult here. Will this long-term economic plight, coupled with isolation, confirm the country's already somewhat authoritarian approach to government? I wonder, as the country finds its feet, what fate will befall its people. Those I meet appear to have embraced Western attitudes – clothes are fashionable, new freedoms are clearly being enjoyed and, as I observe, trade is the essence of life. Buying and selling forms the soul, the very structure, of the country.

Eighty per cent of the population of Uzbekistan is Muslim – but by no means fundamentalist. Religion here seems a relaxed affair, no doubt the consequence of decades of Soviet rule during which religion was far from a priority. This strange journey I am on throws up stark contrasts, weird juxtapositions – I travel at speed between such different worlds, such different existences. Sometimes I feel like a disembodied spirit, gliding over the globe – observing in a dispassionate way the oddities and absurdities of human existence and utterly detached from the life I see around me. I'm tired – but gripped by what I see, by what I have recently seen and experienced. The contrast between Uzbekistan and India could not be more extreme. In India there are shrines, temples and churches everywhere – the sacred is part of daily life. There is colour, noise, people bustle. Here, there is no sign of the sacred – no mosques present themselves, there is little colour, occasional groups of low, white-painted houses cower as if afraid. There are few people to be seen, little activity. We glide on, for mile after mile, and occasionally catch a glimpse of another, ancient time: young shepherds tending their flocks of sheep and goats, seemingly oblivious to the modern world in which they find themselves.

Two thousand years ago Samarkand was a major cultural and commercial centre on the Silk Route – in the Arab world it was known as the 'Gem of the East'. What's left of all this, I wonder, as I make my way towards my destination. Not much, I guess – most buildings are modern, neutral and orderly, the product of Soviet town planning. And then I catch my first glimpse of my treasure. At the heart of the city is a series of public buildings – mosques, madrasahs and tombs – that owe their origin to the conquering triumphs of the great Tamerlane, who seized power in 1365 and exercised it with breathtaking ruthlessness to amass an empire stretching at its zenith from Persia to north India. Myths vie with facts to explain the extraordinary nature of Tamerlane's power and conquests. He is reputed to have killed 17 million people during his reign, to have slighted and destroyed hundreds of towns and cities that challenged or disobeyed him, to have erected pyramids of skulls, of living men. Terror was a tool of state – a mechanism of politics, power and rule. Tamerlane seems to have sold his soul to Satan – but things are not so simple. If, to Tamerlane, terror was one weapon in his political arsenal, so was beauty, and to make the monuments to his reign as beautiful as possible Tamerlane collected architects, painters, craftsmen and scientists from all over his conquered lands and brought them to Samarkand. Beautiful architecture carries power and status. Tamerlane knew all this, and so he created within his capital a series of noble structures – buildings among the most beautiful on earth that made Samarkand in the 14th century the finest city in Asia. The heart of his city was Registan Square – here triumphal armies paraded their prisoners and plundered treasures, and here mass executions took place, blood flowing within this flower of urban beauty.

My excitement mounts as I near this terrible place – what can it be like today? I should have guessed. There lies the square – framed by astonishing and beautiful Islamic buildings – but all has been done, consciously or unconsciously, to rob the Registan of its meaning and power. It is now the centrepiece of a small and dreary urban park – no longer joined to, or part of, the city it adorned. It is virtually deserted. The glazed tiles on the buildings sparkle like jewels in the early morning sunlight. The blue of the tiles merges with the strong blue of the morning sky and makes the buildings seem light, translucent – almost unreal.

Although Registan Square is the vision of Tamerlane, none of the existing buildings was constructed by him and only one is from his time. The earliest is the Ulug Bekh Madrasah – built in 1417, 12 years after the death of Tamerlane, as a religious

The Sher Dor Madrasah (1619–36) is one of three magnificent buildings which show the scale of Tamerlane the Great's architectural vision on Registan Square, Samarkand. Today this majestic building stands in a small park isolated from the city proper.

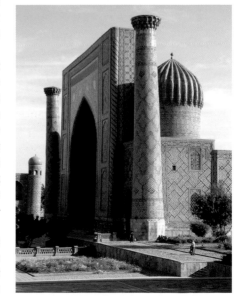

Opposite *The use of glazed tiles on the Tilya Madrasah (1647–1660) in Registan Square reached new heights of artistic and technical brilliance with an almost magical quality. The colours are powerful – deep blue prevails – and the tiles both reveal and reinforce the forms of the architecture and carry messages from the Koran in their varied motifs.*
Below *Over the portal of the Sher Dor Madrasah are images, most unusual in Islamic architecture, of a huge tiger stalking a deer. Sitting on the tiger is a white human face radiating solar rays, another personification of the Sun and an indication that 400 years ago the Islam of Tamerlane's empire had accommodated other deities.*

school with dormitories by Ulug Bekh who was Tamerlane's grandson and a great scientist and astronomer. The building has a very striking form. It presents a virtually square central elevation that promises a vast cubical volume behind and on each side are minarets ornamented with tiers of lozenge shapes, formed out of tiles, that appear to imply a double spiral. This motif fascinates me – a similar pattern is on two of the early 12th-century nave columns in Durham Cathedral, a building greatly influenced by Islamic ideas brought into Western Europe by early Crusaders. One key to understanding the use of this abstract pattern is the Old Testament and the biblical description of that seminal sacred building, Solomon's Temple in Jerusalem. Solomon and his temple are held in high esteem by the Judaic, Christian and Islamic faiths because all three believe that the temple was built according to God's instructions and – in its forms, details and proportions – held divine secrets and enshrined immutable laws of creation. Details within the temple seem to have included not only cubical spaces but also spiralling columns and – in particular – a pair of columns framing the approach to the Holy of Holies which, in themselves, contained the mysteries of creation. I walk through the iwan. Sadly, there is no vast cubical volume – the square facade is theatrical, merely a screen. Instead there is a courtyard, handsome but something of an anticlimax.

Opposite is the Sher Dor Madrasah, built 200 years later but obviously designed to harmonise with the Ulug Bekh Madrasah. The Sher Dor Madrasah is clad with tiles, with blue being the dominant colour, but the motifs are strikingly different – even shocking. At the two top corners of the main facade – above the iwan – are images. Images! The Koran is very critical of images so in virtually all Islamic sacred – and even secular – art and architecture, from the earliest times, images of living beings – human or animal – have been excluded. In place of these traditional motifs Islam developed abstract, geometric forms – often based on plants – and, of course, used lettering as an architectural ornament. Indeed, such has been Islam's distaste for images of living beings that from time to time the creation of such images has not only been outlawed but existing or ancient images destroyed. So to see images given pride of place on this religious structure is most revealing – it tells us about attitudes to Islam in Tamerlane's former imperial capital 400 years ago – clearly older ideas of the gods lived on.

The last structure in this group defining the square is the Tilya Madrasah which, built between 1647 and 1660, is also the cathedral mosque of the city. It, like its neighbours, presents a tall, square face to the world but here there are no framing minarets. Instead, to one side, stands a tall, blue-tiled dome that rises over the mosque. I pass through the iwan and enter an arcaded courtyard. This was once accommodation for the madrasah but, to my surprise, each cell now contains a shop – yes, here is trade, at the heart of Samarkand's most sacred buildings. The shops sell ancient carpets and fabrics, outlandish hats – some massive and shaggy affairs, each seemingly the larger portion of a sheep's back, others are pointed or fur-trimmed red felt creations – the headgear of mystic Sufis, I suppose. It is all very tempting, but I must move on.

My next stop – a little distance off in this sprawling city – is the Gur Emir. This is the mausoleum built by Tamerlane for his grandson who died in 1404 but, much more significantly, it was used to house the tomb of Tamerlane himself, who died the following year. I study the minarets that rise to each side of the tomb. They are fascinating. Those at Registan imply spirals, whereas these minarets are embellished with complete spirals, formed from tiles, that snake around their shafts. The spiral is a powerful motif in sacred art. It is the image of a journey, a pilgrimage, and is found around the world and in the most ancient religious sites – those far older

than Christianity or Islam, in Bronze Age labyrinths, in the 6000-year-old Sumerian cities of Mesopotamia, and carved on ancient stone circles. Do these minarets suggest a connection with the spiral columns of Solomon's Temple, or is Islam here connecting with older religious traditions to suggest the journey of the soul after death? I enter the tomb of this awe-inspiring man. In the centre of the space are the tombs of Tamerlane's two sons and grandson and, beneath a 2-metre slab of jade – more precious than gold in the ancient world – lies the body of Tamerlane. The actual tomb is simple. It had to be. What in death could have increased the glory that this man – the terror of the world – had achieved during life?

I leave the tomb and walk through the nearby bazaar in search of the commodities that once helped Samarkand to be one of the richest cities in the East. But those days appear to be gone – my search for silk is in vain. Sad. Will this be the case elsewhere in Uzbekistan? I will soon find out because my next destination is another of the great trading cities on the route – Bukhara.

42 OLD CITY OF BUKHARA

Saturday 4 – Sunday 5 September
Early in the morning we leave Samarkand and drive along the ancient Silk Route, wondering what Bukhara will have to offer in the way of trade. I know that architecturally it is a fascinating place because, although of ancient origin, in the 16th century much of the city was rebuilt with trade in mind. Most striking is a series of structures built to accommodate different merchants or craftsmen – jewellers, silk weavers and carpetmakers. These are domed, like mosques – an appropriation of a sacred form that seems almost to raise trade in Bukhara to the level of a religion. These trading domes – and the world they dominate – are my treasure. But will they still be flourishing?

As the sun starts to set we arrive at Bukhara. I am desperate to get a sense of the place so straight away we make our way to the old centre. The first thing we see is the extraordinary and organic ancient citadel – called the Ark – with its high, sloping walls and bulbous towers that swell out at the bottom and then taper towards the top. It all looks and feels strangely sinister. We head towards a structure that dominates all around. This is the famed Kaylan Minaret. Brick-built and completed in 1127, it stands 47 metres high and was one of the early generation of giant minarets – others stand at Ghazni and Jam in Afghanistan and at New Delhi in India. This one, when complete, was one of the highest structures in Asia. So astonishing was it that it was virtually one of the wonders of the Asian world. Minarets are odd things – they were used as platforms from which to call the faithful to prayer; they are also staircases to heaven marking the site of the mosque as a sacred place, an axis mundi around which the world turns.

I climb this minaret and, as the sun sets and colours fill the western sky, I reach the gallery at the top and glimpse a wonderful world. Immediately below me is the vast Kaylan Mosque, completed in 1514, with a domed sanctuary and huge court capable of accommodating 10,000 worshippers. And in the distance I can see other domes – some adorning mosques and madrasahs, while others are the famed trading domes, once home to merchants and craftsmen. Around these domes I can still make out the remains of the Old City – now sadly fragmented in parts but still significant, arguably one of the most impressive historic city centres in the Near East. I see mud-coloured walls, narrow alleys and wide streets, and austere facades of houses hiding generous private courtyards. As I stare, the image of this exotic city starts to dissolve before me – the light has gone. I creep down the stairs of the ancient minaret in the dark and fumble my way onto the roof of the adjoining mosque, along which I must travel to reach the ground. Already the moon is rising, casting a strange light over the landscape around me. The mosque is roofed with what feels like earth, and from this seemingly solid terrain erupts scores of regularly spaced pustules. These are the small domes that decorate the cells below. It all looks most peculiar – a world that is organic yet regulated and geometric. I pick my way around the domes, that recede in neat rows and disappear into the dark.

What can these trading domes hold in store? They have different names that reflect their original functions: the Dome of the Moneychangers, the Dome of the Hatsellers and the Dome of the Jewellers. The Dome of the Moneychangers stands on the edge of

Even though this is a fine example of organic architecture, I find the Ark, the exterior of the Old City of Bukhara, faintly sinister, and can't wait to move on.

the old fortified suburb and rises from four huge pointed arches. These stand between four piers so that, in plan, the dome sits over an octagonal base, and crowns a crossroads. These roads are lined with shops and vaulted, and the piers that support the dome are honeycombed with vaulted shops. It's all very architecturally impressive. It was the work of Abdallah Khan II. He ruled from 1583 and presided over the reconstruction of the city's bazaars in this rational and convenient way.

As I wander around I discover that this Dome and its related buildings originally contained a community of uses, not just shops and places of business for the moneychangers, or the sarraf, as they were called. There was also a small mosque or temple and a bathhouse that must have formed the heart of their world – it was surely here that deals would have been done as these men steamed and cooled themselves in intimate circumstances. Today the domes and adjoining shops remain lively, even though the moneychangers have long gone. Instead it is carpets, hats and CDs that are on sale.

There is another domed building, a caravanserai, or merchants' inn. I go inside and it is splendid. Here are dozens of shops selling silk and even – in one corner – silk fabric being woven on a huge, ramshackle loom. I rummage around in the mounds of old fabrics for sale and I find an old Suzanne, a pattern of cotton fabric that is native to Uzbekistan. It is of faded pink and full of holes – it's wonderful. It's embroidered with emblems and motifs symbolising prosperity and plenty – appropriate since Suzannes were usually made to be part of a bride's dowry and were hung from the wall in the married couple's home. I buy it for just a few dollars.

Trade is in the air – and in the blood of the people of Bukhara. All have something to sell. I walk back through the square and am swamped by chirping and cheerful young girls, most of whom seem in their early teens. They giggle and swagger – they all want my attention, and they all seem to be the proprietors of shops, stalls or merely a patch of ground on which a cloth is spread and goods displayed. And, perhaps most amazing, they speak English very well indeed. I resist but in the end surrender and am dragged off to see their wares. They are selling fabrics, old and new, cotton and silk, and all manner of hats – mostly hairy – that are clearly one of the specialities of Bukhara. These girls love to sell – but more, they love to bargain. I get drawn into the game. One young thing offers me a black cotton scarf. I show interest, she states a price that seems fair, I begin to agree, but she tells me in a most stern manner – she can't be more than 12 – 'This isn't a supermarket – you have to bargain.' So I bargain – and everyone is happy.

Before I leave Bukhara there is one more domed structure I must see. It is far older than the trading domes – indeed it's arguably the oldest intact structure in central Asia, one of the almost forgotten wonders of the world, a lonely survivor of Bukhara's early

Opposite When it was completed in 1127 the Kaylan Minaret in Bukhara was one of the highest structures in the Asian world. When Genghis Khan attacked the city in the early 13th century he was overcome by astonishment and spared the minaret although the rest of the city was levelled. I climb the internal spiral staircase to the top and see all of Bukhara.

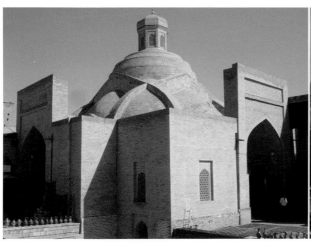

Within the Old City of Bukhara are the famous trading domes (left), an unusual architectural form which borrows from religious sacred domes – the material world afforded a spiritual context. Right The interior of the Dome of the Money-changers is still a lively centre of trade.

golden age as a trading centre. The Mausoleum of Isma'il Samani stands in a small park near the Ark. It was built in the 10th century and, like many Muslim mausoleums, has a cubical lower portion topped by a hemispherical dome – but it's the details that grip my attention. Here are motifs that found their way into Western Romanesque and early Gothic sacred architecture – chevrons and spirals and simple pointed arches. Small but important buildings like this mausoleum, placed along the ancient major trade routes, had a tremendous influence on the minds and imagination of Western travellers and merchants. They would have seen these forms and details, admired them and carried these ideas home to influence their own building. From this minuscule seed of a building great architecture rose in the West. Did the Benedictine Order that created Durham Cathedral know this little mausoleum? Did its monks, on pilgrimage, trade or diplomatic missions, pass through Bukhara? Without doubt. This is one of the ways in which sacred geometry and symbols became a common and shared currency in the Middle Ages and Renaissance – used by East and West, Muslims and Christians alike.

43 FIRE TEMPLE, BAKU, AZERBAIJAN

Monday 6 – Tuesday 7 September
We rise at 2.30 in the morning for our early flight to Baku, Azerbaijan. At the airport I am reminded that the lumbering and demotivating mentality of the USSR lives on in the minds of at least some of the people here. We have to fill in forms in duplicate, queue and deposit the forms with surly and uncaring officials who, without glancing at our documents, stamp them and file them away. I suppose there are rooms in some government building where these useless documents are stored. In years to come some official will be able to tell exactly in which hotel I stayed and for how long. Vital stuff.

We arrive at Baku in the late morning – the atmosphere here is even more peculiar. Baku retains, I have been told, one of the most complete and curious ancient city centres in Asia dating back, perhaps, 3000 years. So I am full of curiosity to experience this wonder, perched on the shore of the Caspian Sea. But the old streets are mostly deserted and many buildings are derelict. Something very wrong is going on. We make our way to the waterfront and see one of the problems besetting Baku – oil. The water glistens with rainbow colours and black sludge sticks to the sea wall. Vast oil tankers slumber and slink along the horizon and in the distance are oil derricks, some nodding rhythmically, others frozen as if in mid-motion. Baku is the birthplace of the modern oil industry, producing 50 per cent of the world's oil in 1910.

What we see as we wander around the city centre is the detritus of the period of Soviet rule. Vainglorious monuments to Soviet power stand among the sad remains of this ancient and once-proud and independent trading city. All seems ominous, threatening, depressed. The new buildings we see must be for those canny entrepreneurs who are making oil fortunes since Azerbaijan gained its independence from Russia in 1991. But looking around it is clear that this new wealth is going only to a tiny proportion of the population. Virtually all the people I see in the street look miserable and far from wealthy. Certainly strangers are not made to feel particularly welcome.

In the evening we drive out of the city to see something most peculiar. Thousands of years ago pilgrims came to the region to see fire, the product of ignited natural gases, belching from the earth. This natural fire was seen as sacred – an incarnation of the Sun, of the divine power and force of nature. One of the pilgrims was a man called Zoroaster. He came probably from northern Afghanistan, born in about 630 BC. By around 600 BC he was near Baku and here saw God's fire issuing from the earth. As Zoroaster contemplated he had a vision. Fire, he suddenly perceived, is the symbol and manifestation of a powerful, elemental and omnipotent single God who could guide man to salvation. As Zoroaster's vision quickly spread, this God became known as Ahura Mazda and his symbol was a winged solar ring – an ancient sacred image. But the great days are long gone. Once Zoroastrianism was the religion of princes and of the Persians – but it has long been eclipsed by the dominance of the three great monotheistic religions – religions whose doctrine and ritual it did much to influence.

We are now going to see one of the sites that, perhaps, inspired Zoroaster over 2600 years ago. It's at a place called Yanar Dag and – we are told – here fire bursts from the side of a hill, from the ground on which you walk. Sounds extraordinary. But all debates about what is in store for us are eclipsed by a vision of a reality that I can only call hellish and profoundly disturbing. Azerbaijan has been exploited – abused – for its oil deposits for well over 100 years and, in the early years of the Soviet era, when Baku supplied 50 per cent of the USSR's oil, this was done with a cynicism and disregard for ecological or environmental concerns that is now utterly breathtaking. We pass through some of these early oilfields. The ghastly vista stretches as far as we can see. Literally thousands of antiquated and generally abandoned derricks stand – almost side by side – each presiding over a hole in the ground and an oily pump, tangles of rusty and useless metal piping, and puddles of mud, oil and cracked, reeking earth. We look on in horror – none of the locals even seem to notice. Staying alive is the concern here – caring for the environment is a luxury few can afford.

Just outside Baku, a once-fabulous trading city, is pollution on a scale that is hard to imagine – derelict oil derricks preside over the waste-land of the world's first oil boom. The earth has been poisoned and the natural beauty of the country ravished.

What an incredible irony – that the land that inspired Zoroaster to see God in nature and the elements should be reduced to this. It's too cruel to contemplate – such tricks do the gods play. During the last two months I have seen many attempts, by different peoples and different faiths, to create heaven on earth. But this is the first time I have seen such a determined effort – albeit unintended – to create an image of hell. I walk between abandoned buildings and reach a viewing platform. Below me, bursting fitfully from the side of a low mound, is fire. It looks most strange. The side of the mound contains crevices and small hollows and it is from these that the flames issue. I approach to what I think is a safe distance – but it's difficult to judge because the flames burst forth and recede, ripple, move and burst forth again in an almost but not quite regular pattern. It's as if I'm observing the respiration of the earth – but an earth with breathing difficulties. And the smell – it's not oily but faintly toxic, pungent, earthy. I suppose what's on fire is methane gas – the waste of microbes, the result of millennia upon millennia of rot. I peer into one of the crevices, trying to see the source of the fire. This is a mistake. The earth dragon suddenly breathes out – a fire gushes from the crevice, I leap back, but too late to fully escape the effects of the blast of heat. I am left slightly scorched. The pulse, the breath of God – maybe. Perhaps I'm labouring under the influences of what I have so far seen today but the image of these flames erupting spontaneously from the earth seems like yet one more image of hell in this sadly benighted land.

But I'm being too gloomy. After all, fire has without doubt had a long and illustrious history in this part of the world and is the vital force behind the next treasure.

We drive to a temple 30 kilometres from Baku called Suraxam Ateshgyakh. It's an odd-looking place. It sits in a desolate location surrounded by semi-derelict old buildings and half-complete modern buildings, but is a most powerful composition. It's an irregular pentagon in plan, with windowless outer walls that define a courtyard. Set off-centre within the sloping ground of the court is a small domed and arcaded cubical structure – it's clearly a shrine. To one side of it is what looks like a well. But this is a

most unusual shrine and a well like no other because, from the centre of the shrine and from its four upper corners, and from the centre of the well, gush flames. The exact origin of the temple is unknown but it is assumed to originally have been the site of a Zoroastrian temple, perhaps 2500 years ago. What exists today was, it is said, built in the early 18th century by Hindu merchants and pilgrims who also saw the fire as holy. I walk around the temple and ponder the shrine and the adjoining well of fire. It's curious. In the past oil and gas – and the bounty and fire they produce – were venerated as the gifts of nature, as aspects of the divine. All was seen as beauty, as spiritual, evidence of the wondrous ways of creation. But now these natural resources are merely brutally exploited as material assets – and the result is devastation and unspeakable ugliness. As I look from the roof of the temple and see decaying oil derricks and a bleak, menacing urban wasteland I can't help but feel our world has lost its soul. And the final insult – as I leave I discover that exploitation of the oil and gas reserves of the area has after all these centuries robbed the temple of the source of its sacred fire. The flames that I have been admiring have been produced by burning piped-in gas. If ever there was an emblem for our sad times this must be it. The fire that was famed for being eternal has gone out.

44 BISITUN CUNEIFORM, IRAN

Thursday 9 September
After a welcome day off, our journey through the extraordinary country of Iran begins. I wonder what we will discover. Tehran is very cosmopolitan, sophisticated. Courtesy is a custom that I have grown to expect in this part of the world where there is a strong tradition of hospitality and welcome to strangers – even when, as is the case with me, I come from an 'enemy' country. The ordinary Iranians I met in Tehran seemed not in the least swayed by government propaganda – and I saw a lot of it – against Britain and the West. Instead all were warm, and even showed genuine pleasure that someone from Britain was visiting Iran. It felt good – certainly safe. But things outside the sophisticated environs of Tehran might be different. We will see.

We fly to Kermanshah and then make our way towards the border with Iraq. We have come to see the bas-reliefs at Bisitun – an ancient carved document that holds the key to understanding life and politics in this region 2500 years ago.

Bisitun stands on what was, once, one of the great trade highways of the world – the Silk Route. It also stood on an important national and cultural frontier. Empires, be they Assyrian, Babylonian, Egyptian, Persian or Greek, expanded and contracted at such a rate in this region that most political frontiers were only temporary. But the frontier at Bisitun marked the meeting of two worlds. It stands just east of the Tigris and is where the people of Persia – modern Iran – came face to face with the people of Mesopotamia – modern Iraq. The location may now seem remote but, when the bas-reliefs were cut, this was virtually the centre of the known world, a key location on route from China via Babylon into the remote and barbarous parts of Western Europe.

The bas-reliefs are an amazing piece of work. They were made in 522 BC on the orders of Darius the Great, the ruler of the Persians and what was then the most powerful empire on earth. Carved into the side of a massive cliff face, the bas-reliefs stretch 20 metres in length, 8 metres in height and now stand more than 60 metres above the existing road. So important was the message they enshrine that, at Darius's command, it was written in the three main languages of the region – Old Persian, Elamite and Neo-Babylonian. All are written in a form of text called cuneiform, the earliest known type of writing that seems to have emerged in Sumeria – in the south of Mesopotamia – around 8000 years ago.

The images carved on the bas-relief show Darius standing in triumph over his defeated enemies, including a number of rebels or 'false' kings. The text starts with the declaration: 'I am Darius, the great King, the King of Kings, the King of Persia...' The prime meaning of this monument must have been – and remains – clear to all. To reveal the power and glory of Persia and to warn would-be rebels of the inevitable perils that would befall them.

I look at the monument and wonder who – despite its size – could have read these texts 2500 years ago. I can hardly see the individual cuneiform characters let alone begin to decipher their meaning. Was there once a grandstand built opposite so that passing travellers could ascend and read what is, in effect, a massive and permanent poster – a declaration of intent? Perhaps, but a simpler solution is that the road was much higher – and therefore nearer to the bas-reliefs – 2500 years ago. Well, be that as it may, I can't see them properly and will have to climb nearer. Now, this presents certain difficulties. There is no permanent route up to the inscription. A narrow ledge runs below part of it

Opposite The Fire Temple at Baku – I am horrified to discover that the sacred eternal flame is now produced by man.

Darius the Great's statement of power carved high in the rock face at Bisitun shows Darius backed by courtiers looking down on his defeated enemies – the nine 'false' kings. The figures are still in fine condition.

but the path was destroyed after the bas-relief was completed, presumably to ensure that no one could easily get near this inscription to deface or alter it. The physical isolation of the bas-reliefs has always proved a problem, and finally led to one of the most heroic – and epoch-making – episodes in early archaeology.

Henry Rawlinson – a soldier working for the East India Company and, in 1835, based in Persia – rode out to see the Bisitun bas-reliefs and became fascinated. Here was a huge and tempting challenge – first to gain access to this remote and dangerous monument and then to discover the meaning of its text. Cuneiform was clearly of ancient origin and, being found in those parts of the Middle East that had been home to once-great but largely enigmatic civilisations, it was assumed that their secrets could be discovered – perhaps the origin of man glimpsed – if these texts could be read. Using ropes and ladders he gained access to the ledge and then started the huge task of copying each letter in the inscription. This went on for over a decade. One part of the ledge had collapsed so Rawlinson had to crawl across a ladder – and nearly fell off. Another portion of text was placed too high to reach and at a precarious angle so he hired a 'wild Kurdish boy' who was lowered on a rope from the top of the cliff and then made papier mâché casts of the inscription. As he copied the texts he observed that – although all written in cuneiform – they were in fact three different languages and all appeared to be saying the same thing. Rawlinson realised if he could read one of these he could ultimately read the others. All this was achieved by the early 1850s, nearly 20 years after Rawlinson had first stood in awe before Bisitun. Now other Assyrian, Babylonian and Sumerian texts could finally be read – and they proved sensational, for they included fragments of the world's first known book – the epic of Gilgamesh that seems to have been composed in Sumeria about 4700 years ago – and sacred writings that anticipated biblical accounts of the flood and the Garden of Eden.

So I stand where Rawlinson stood – and stare. The images and slabs of lettering above me are as important to the understanding of our past – the history and aspirations of mankind – as is the far better-known Rosetta Stone that unlocked the secrets of Egyptian hieroglyphics. Now my only problem is to get a clear look at them. Some repairs have been undertaken in recent years and a rickety-looking scaffold remains in place. We make our way up. The ledge below the inscription appears reachable, by a leap and a scramble across a rough rocky ledge that would not prove an obstacle if there was not a 60-metre drop below. Having come this far we have to go on. A young Iranian soldier has been sent with us and, seemingly fearless, leaps onto the rock and shows that it can be done. Mike – almost equally fearless – strides across but I and the others cling closely to the soldier as we cross the divide from this world into that of Darius.

It's breathtaking – standing on the irregular, 1-metre-wide ledge, to where Rawlinson climbed and crawled, enjoying the vast landscape in front of me and the bas-reliefs close behind. The height makes me dizzy, I can't really look and walk – but I can now see everything very clearly. Five and a half tall slabs of text in the centre, written in Old Persian, are the key inscription. Here I finger the opening cuneiform letters that read 'I am Darius, the great King, the King of Kings ...' – chilling and haughty words from the past that still grip the imagination like talons of ice. To the left and high to the right is the same inscription, written in Elamite. I can't get near the portion of text to the left because the ledge between me and it has crumbled. It was while bridging this gap that Rawlinson nearly tumbled to his death. I look to the rocky ground far below. Golly, Rawlinson had some nerve, he was audacious and brave in the pursuit of his goal. So, by the way, is Mike, for now he suddenly scales a rusting scaffold tower to place his camera on the boarded platform to get a better shot. I'm full of admiration and am thankful that there is no earthly reason for me to join him. I look away – the drama of the scene is too much – and continue to study the bas-relief. High on the left, set at an angle that must have made the inscription virtually impossible to read from the ground,

Cracking the cuneiform code was one of the great challenges of the mid-19th century – it took Henry Rawlinson 20 years to decipher this curious writing, so called because of the cubical form of many of its characters. I sit precariously on the 1-metre-wide ledge beside the text from where Rawlinson painstakingly copied each letter. Whole tracts are now impossible to read, eroded by weather, moisture and salts oozing from the stone.

is the version in Neo-Babylonian or Akkadian. And then in the centre, set above the slabs of Old Persian text, are the figures. Above the dejected enemy and in front of Darius floats the ring emblem of Ahura Mazda – the omnipotent God of the prophet Zoroaster that was worshipped by the Persians.

I stand and look to the west, towards the Tigris, Baghdad and Babylon – towards Iraq, only a few miles away but now a land I cannot enter. I was in Iraq just before and just after the fall of Saddam Hussein but now it's too dangerous. It is, I feel, absurd to make a journey like mine – in quest of the world's great cultural, man-made treasures – without going to Iraq, but there it is. I, like many before me, am a victim of history, of bad timing. I can only ponder and regret. Iraq, or Mesopotamia as the Greeks called it, was arguably the cradle of civilisation, certainly all things the West associates with civilisation started here, some 8000 years ago: writing, agriculture and irrigation, mathematics, the wheel and related tools, urban living, arts and crafts, many of the fundamental doctrines and myths of much theology. Here, on the fertile land between the rivers Euphrates and Tigris, thrived the nations and empires of the Sumerians, the Babylonians, the Akkadians, the Assyrians and where the Tigris and Euphrates meet near Basra was, some say, the biblical Garden of Eden. It's a land in which myth, imagination and fact flow effortlessly together. If I were at liberty I would plunge back into this magical country – return to the ruins of the 6000-year-old ancient city of Uruk, where Gilgamesh once ruled, to the 4500-year-old ziggurat at Ur and to the astonishing, elemental 9th-century spiralling minaret at Samarra. As I look towards this land – near yet so far – I wonder what the future holds for this tragic country.

To complete my forlorn thoughts I receive a call from the BBC's security consultant. He tells me that my planned trip to Afghanistan has to be postponed. I want to go to Kabul to see the 1800-year-old Bactrian Gold – comprising 20,000 ornamental items that may have been saved when the country's culture came under attack during the civil war in the 1990s and after 2000, during Taliban rule. I also want to see the remote 12th-century minaret at Jam. But the BBC now regards the country as currently too dangerous for us to enter. This is a massive blow for me. Due to war and international politics, I am denied access to two countries through which I roamed freely, and with relative safety, only three years ago. Is the world becoming better and safer? Evidently not.

We fly back to Tehran and then on to Isfahan. We have come here to get to the heart of Islam. Isfahan contains one of the greatest, most majestic mosques in the Muslim world. I hope to penetrate deep within the mosque – and to speak to clerics – to grasp fully the meaning of Muslim sacred architecture. Also, I want to start finding out more about one of the most characteristic objects from this part of the world – the carpet.

45   EMAM MOSQUE, ISFAHAN

Friday 10 September
We arrive in the centre of the city. It's thrilling. I am about to confront the powerful urban vision of Shah Abbas the Great – the ruler who made Isfahan his capital in 1597 and then set about its transformation into one of the greatest cities in the Muslim world. Shah Abbas was the most successful member of the Safavid Dynasty that ruled the land from 1501 to 1722 and although his new city of Isfahan – attached to an existing ancient city – is his most obvious triumph and glory there is yet more to his legacy. He encouraged trade with Europe – and cultural connections – and was particularly successful in promoting Persia's export of silk and carpets. Indeed it is from Shah Abbas's time that Persian carpets, once the rare and prized possessions of European royal households and the very rich, became more commonly available. Now I am to meet the great works of this man – to see him, as it were, face to face.

First I walk through a huge, architecturally handsome and bustling bazaar – vaulted, domed where streets intersect, with shops on each side and many packed with very tempting carpets. The place is bubbling with colour, music and sweet spicy smells – life. People look, smile, are warm – delighted when we stop, ask a question, a price. This is wonderful. Then I see a large pointed arch, a gate at the end of the great bazaar, through which light floods in and makes the metal goods on display sparkle. As I get nearer, the view through the arch becomes more distinct. I see that I am looking into a huge rectangular space – this is the core of Shah Abbas's creation, his sublime city. Emam Khomeini Square (originally called the Maidan-i-Shah or Royal Square) was started in 1611 and measures 500 metres by 160 metres. Entering into it – vast, geometrically pure and light – from the dark, meandering constraint of the bazaar is one of the great urban experiences. Drama, symbolism – it's like the act of birth. The proportion of the square – roughly 3 to 1 – is significant as this is one of the key proportions of Solomon's Temple in Jerusalem. I am entering the square through one of its short sides. The other short side – way in the distance – is closed by the Emam Mosque, one of the most evocative mosques in the world that was built, from 1611, by Shah Abbas. Mosque and square are one conception – they are intimately connected. The centre of the great square is occupied by a formal garden with pools – a familiar Islamic image of earthly paradise. But the buildings that define the edge of the square – generally simple and uniform in the extreme – contain shops. Worldly and spiritual activities meet again. It was a prelude to the Emam Mosque – the journey across the square was intended to give worshippers coming from the bazaar an opportunity to compose themselves, to detach themselves from the material world before entering the House of God.

I continue my way towards the Emam Mosque, Shah Abbas's masterpiece. In form all mosques, no matter how large and grand, are essentially simple houses – the House of God reflected through the re-creation of Mohammed's house in Medina. So, like the traditional house of man in the Middle East, it has an entrance gate, leading to a central courtyard off which are placed subsidiary rooms and courts. Water is used to chill the air, and cool interiors are created by the use of lofty ceilings and high, screened windows to keep out direct sunlight but allow breezes to waft inside. As I near the entrance gate I see all reflected in a small canal that lies before the mosque. It's marvellous – the material House of God hovering against the infinite blue sky, an ethereal image in a shimmering sheet of water.

As I approached the mosque I noticed that the main domed sanctuary, with its minarets, was set at a diagonal to the axis of the square – it is oriented so that the mihrab it contains faces directly towards Mecca. What I did not quite expect was the dramatic nature of the switch of axis and the powerful – theatrical – architectural consequences. I walk through the main door on the axis of the square, look across a vestibule and into a curved, tall and partially vaulted recess. But the moment I am across the threshold I am in another world. The world of man – represented by the geometry of the great square I have just crossed – is superseded by the geometry of God. All within the mosque is organised around the axis determined by the alignment of the mihrab with God's gift to mankind – the veiled, sacred stone that is the cubical Ka'bah in the centre of the square of the Great Mosque in Mecca, the physical focus of the Islamic world. The point where these two axes meet – of man and of God – is in the centre of the curved and vaulted recess in front of me. I enter and find the exact point where man, leaving his world, turns to God, looks towards Mecca. From this vantage point the sacred geometry of the mosque becomes explicit.

I now advance into the central court. In the centre of its four sides are four iwans. One frames the high recess I leave, the iwans to the left and right mark entrances into cubical and domed sanctuaries while the iwan in front leads to the main sanctuary – the sacred heart of the mosque. So the court is divided into four quarters – as, according to the Old Testament and Koran, is paradise. Indeed to reinforce the symbolism of the court the iwan on my left is decorated with large flowers, realised in coloured tiles – the blossoms of paradise. Somewhat to my surprise – in fact, dismay – the court is covered with a temporary awning to protect pilgrims from the heat of the sun. Curious – does this need for the creation of ad hoc cover reflect a design fault in the traditional, arguably God-inspired, organisation of the mosque – or is it just that pilgrims aren't as hardy as they used to be? Or perhaps there are more of them these days. In the centre of the court is a

The Emam Mosque in Isfahan, one of the greatest mosques in the world, is a vision of paradise on earth. The geometry of the mosque is dramatic – in form it is simple and elegant while the surface decoration is lavish. I see it reflected in the small canal in front of the mosque.

Dazzling tiles clad the mosques of Isfahan. Left The dome of the Sheikh Lotfollah Mosque appears to float and shimmer in the blue sky. Right The interior decoration in the Emam Mosque, in keeping with Islamic tradition, is geometric and abstract, and loaded with levels of meaning, some explicit and some more complex and mysterious.

pool – to cool the air and provide water with which worshippers wash their hands, feet and faces before they pray. In Islam godliness and cleanliness go hand in hand.

Inside the main sanctuary all is still, the cubical lower volume topped by a huge dome. The interior of the dome is spectacular: clad with a scintillating skin of tiles incorporating geometric tendrils and a crowning star, it offers a glimpse of nature and the cosmos with, at a high level, shafts of light entering through small windows – God's light. On the far side of the sanctuary is the mihrab, facing towards Mecca, and next to it the minbar, or pulpit, reached by a tall flight of steps. To each side of this sanctuary are large and shady halls, each bold in form – a double-square in plan – and simple in detail. These are powerful places of gathering and of prayer. A few people are sitting and strolling. This is one of the best things about great mosques like this. They are truly public places in which people feel able to relax, sit, talk, pray – to pursue their lives in the House of God. All seem to be welcome – certainly we are. People approach us, chat, offer help, offer greetings. I'm intrigued by the way the mosque is used. On the threshold of one of the halls a row of young women, dressed from head to toe in black cloaks called chadors, all kneel towards Mecca and pray, their heads touching the ground. It's a poetic sight, these slight and mysterious black forms set against the brightly coloured tiles and delicate architectural details, all bowing and swaying together. I watch, transfixed. One girl suddenly turns towards me – she is not offended, she flashes me a smile – and then gets back to her prayers. In the main sanctuary a family gathers, in the most informal way, below the minbar. One child suddenly climbs it, sits on a step, and goes on talking, playing. The minbar is just about the holiest thing in a mosque – in theory no one, except the prophet, is permitted to stand at its top. But here no one cares about the minor transgression of this child. No insult is intended – God, 'the compassionate, the merciful', is certainly not going to be affronted by humans being mildly human.

My last mission is to talk to a cleric about Islam for I am intrigued to hear what a Shi'a thinks about the events unfolding in Iraq. A young man arrives, a mullah named Mahdi Sadr. He is charming, relaxed and friendly. Islam is, he says, about love, peace and tolerance and he is saddened by the way it is now often misrepresented as the creed of fanatics and fundamentalists. I say that, to some, the Koran can seem rather vengeful, like the Old Testament, rather than forgiving like the New Testament. I wonder if Islamic fanatics are not encouraged by certain texts in the Koran. He says all people of the Book – Christians and Jews – are accepted by Islam although they are seen as erring. Mohammed is the 'seal' of the Prophets, the last word, with the Koran correcting faults

– the result of human error – that taint the doctrines of the Jews and Christians. Mary, exclaims the mullah, is the greatest woman that ever lived and Jesus Christ a prophet – but not the son of God. If there is only one God – essential to Islamic faith – what is one to make of a son of God? To Muslims, the Christian Holy Trinity – the Father, Son and Holy Ghost – seems confused and to whiff of blasphemy, the product of human folly in misunderstanding the words of the Prophets. At the end – says the mullah – Christ will return, proclaiming the words of Mohammed. It's heady stuff – in the glittering light and rich yet sombre shade of this great mosque, in this world of exquisite man-made beauty in service of the abstract ideal of God and faith. We end on the subject of violence. I ask him about Najaf, about the possibility of Western-backed forces attacking holy sites in this Iraqi city. He is not to be bogged down in worldly politics. He merely says that if Muslim fighters are trying cynically to use the shrines in Najaf as a cover for their own violent actions then they are a disgrace to their religion. Islam, reasserts the mullah, is about peace not war, love not hate, life not death. And so we part – he back into the peaceful shade of the mosque, me back into the sunny glare of the city.

Saturday 11 September – Reflections on the veil

We travel to Shiraz. It is a day of reflection. I ponder our experiences so far in Iran. The country has proved delightful, the people friendly, no animosity whatsoever, and Tehran immensely cosmopolitan in feel. But one thing worries me – nags. Iran is a theocracy in which sharia law prevails, which means that civil law is based on the strictures of the Koran and, more to the point, interpretations of the Koran and precedents established over the years by clerics and lawyers. So all women are compelled to wear scarves to cover their hair. In Iran it has become a custom – imposed by law – for a woman to wear a headscarf, a hood called a maghnaeh or an all-enveloping cloak – usually black and called the chador – stretching from the forehead to the ankle. These garments can obviously be uncomfortable, hot and restrictive, but there is no choice in the matter. The benefit most quoted is that they give the wearer status, dignity and protection from the unwanted attentions of predatory males.

What lies at the root of this Islamic tradition? Well, the first point is that it is not specific to Islam. In many times and places other faiths have taken this same attitude or at least those religions that are of the Book – that is the Jewish and Christian faiths. All three religions have the same source, the books of the Old Testament, share many of the same prophets, principles and tenets. The Koran is, after all, viewed by the Muslims as essentially a revision and addition to the Old and New Testaments and Mohammed as bearing the last and definitive word on God's will. And all these religions of the Book have a similar and rather sinister attitude towards women. In ancient times, in the Middle East and in Europe, the Great Goddess – Mother Earth – ruled. Creation and the creator were seen as essentially female. But the Old Testament offers a very different – a very male – view of creation with females cast in a distinctly unfortunate light. From the Book of Genesis onwards women are portrayed as the weak vessel, as the medium through which evil triumphs, as the tempters and seducers of men, as the spawn of Satan. In any culture where these tales are accepted as part of the basis of religious belief and in which men dominate, women are bound to be repressed.

This was the case in Europe in the Middle Ages – it's surely no coincidence that the Iranian black chador looks much like a nun's habit – and is still the case in certain orthodox Jewish communities. So this is why I find the maghnaeh and the chador disturbing. My mind goes back to the story of the Hindu celestial nymphs, the apsaras, whom I met at Angkor Wat. Here female sexuality and beauty – far from being a thing Satanic – saved the world from evil. I go to bed much agitated of mind.

46 PERSEPOLIS

Sunday 12 September

Persepolis was one of the great cities and power hubs of the ancient world. The 'City of the Persians' looms large in poetical fantasy. The very name Persepolis evokes dreams of power and ancient legends of conquest and empire.

The city was founded in 512 BC by Darius the Great, and was built during the following century and a half, largely by his son Xerxes I. It was the centre of the greatest empire in the world. Like the inscription Darius was to cut a few years later at Bisitun, Persepolis was to make a statement about power and kingship. This city was to celebrate Persian achievements and to serve the king as a comfortable and elegant summer capital, notable not for its fortification but for its palaces, fountains, orchards and – a delight pioneered by the Persians – formal gardens. The very concept of a paradise on earth – comprising delightful gardens – is of Persian origin. Persepolis was indeed to be a paradise, a tribute to the world order Persian power had created and, more particularly, to Darius. He had grabbed the throne in the confusing tussle following the death in 529 of Cyrus the Great and the subsequent murder of Cyrus's two sons. After this violent interlude Darius revealed himself to be not so much a man of action but of administration. He failed in his attempt to conquer all of Greece – stopped famously by the Athenians at the Battle of Marathon in 490 BC – but Darius was determined to hold on to what he had seized by his coup and to establish his legitimacy.

I arrive at sunrise and circle the city. Its retaining walls are impressive, but clearly ornamental rather than functional fortifications – as revealed by the main entrance to the upper level, to the world of palaces. Rather than a strong gate, or defences in depth, there is a pair of broad staircases, leading away from each other, each turning 180 degrees at

Persepolis was not a city of commerce or military triumph. It was a display of Darius the Great's absolute power over most of the known world. Built on a massive terrace 15 metres high, Persepolis is surprisingly small, but even now the ruins possess a sense of menace.

a half landing and then running towards each other to meet at the top of the plateau on which the city stands. It's very nicely done – the start of an extraordinary journey that led to the epicentre of world power. The route is calculated to impress and intimidate – many of the people using this staircase were under the power of Persia, they were the conquered, and they were being brought here under protest, as supplicants or to pay tribute and homage to their overlord – the king of the Persians. They were going to see a mortal presented as a god who had the power of life and death over them, perhaps over their nation. It must have been a terrifying experience, with all the architecture calculated to increase the sense of awe and powerlessness.

I walk up the majestic staircase from the world of mere man to the elevated world of the king of the Persians. As I walk I notice a strange thing. The steps are wide but they rise in a very gradual manner. This makes my steps slow and slightly awkward. I am being paced! The humble tread of a supplicant is being forced on me. I reach the great Gate of all Nations, where the ceremonial route splits in two. One leads along a processional way to the Palace of One Hundred Columns, built by Xerxes. The other leads to the double staircase leading up to the Apadana or Audience Hall. This hall was at the time the most extraordinary structure in the world – a space designed to truly amaze and daunt. It had a huge cedarwood roof supported on 20-metre-high columns and its shady and mystic volume could accommodate up to 10,000 people.

I make my way towards the Apadana and to reach its higher level I have to travel the staircase. Here all is made explicit. There are in fact two staircases – both beautifully carved with figures and both very similar although not identical. Together they are among the great wonders of the ancient world and are my treasure in Persepolis.

Each staircase is peopled with a microcosm of the Persian Empire. Here we can meet those who Darius and Xerxes ruled, and see them bringing tribute to their ruler. This is the world – captured in stone 2500 years ago – as ordered by the Persian kings. Here are their 23 subject nations, all bringing their tribute to the Persian court. It's amazing. As I walk the staircase I walk alongside, am as one, with these men as they journey to their master. All the figures appear calm and peaceful – they are portrayed as having accepted their lot and each group of tribute bearers is led in paternal manner by a long-robed Persian official. It all looks childishly charming – if one didn't know of the blood spilt to achieve this harmony, this Persian peace and order.

The figures are incredibly well preserved – they were buried beneath sand for centuries until excavated in the 20th century. I ascend the eastern staircase, which is the better preserved. At its southern end I pass Ethiopians bringing their tribute of a mini-giraffe and tusks, Libyans with chariot and mountain goat, Zaraganians of Sistan, Arabs and then Macedonians. I stare into the faces of these men – for Persia these are the Pale

The figures on the processional stair-case at Persepolis showing the different peoples over whom Darius ruled, and the objects which they brought to pay homage are incredibly well preserved. I am impressed by the artistic language and conventions used by these artists 2500 years ago.

Riders of the Apocalypse, death and hell followed after them. But these placid Macedonians just give me a stony stare – they are biding their time. I can't see the future in their faces. Then the images of the nations are stacked in tiers of three. These include Scythians, Indians bearing spices and leading a mule, Gandarians, Heratians and Bactrians from present-day Afghanistan, people from Samarkand leading a camel, Egyptians, Ionians, Assyrians carrying cloth and gold vessels, Cappadocians from modern Turkey, Babylonians with cloth and a buffalo, Elamites, Armenians and Medes. As well as portraying the subject nations of Persia in Xerxes's times – and revealing the geographical extent of an empire that stretched from Turkey to India – these figures also offer a fascinating insight into what they reared, grew or fabricated, and so we can see what they would have traded. Of course – spices from India, ivory from Ethiopia, cloth from Babylon. They are reminders of the almost sacred nature of trade in ancient times. Trade produced wealth but also it was the measure and currency of power.

I now enter the Apadana. Little is left beyond a few rearing columns. I try to reconstruct the interior – the experience – for tribute bearers. The hall would have been vast and dark with its flat cedar ceiling, 20 metres above, lost in the gloom. Guards would have lined the walls, with Persian officials gliding silently around in their long robes. You'd have approached the great presence, knelt, crawled, laid down your tribute and backed away, trembling, in case the tribute was not enough.

Beyond the Apadana and the Palace of One Hundred Columns were the more private parts of Persepolis, including the Palace of Darius. I make my way towards it. The palace – relatively well preserved – is a curious marriage of Egyptian with what would become known as Greek Classical architecture. Coved lintels, supported by stout stone posts, create openings that define the form of the palace and frame a central hall. Now open to the sky, this hall was originally roofed with a plaster ceiling, supported on long-lost timber columns and with its stone walls so highly polished that it was known as the 'Mirror Hall'. In the openings, on the surfaces of the thick stone posts, are delicate carvings. Most show Darius in his power and pride, killing a sacred lion much as Gilgamesh does in his epic journey in search of immortality. The epic of Gilgamesh was an ancient text in the time of the Persians and no doubt Darius would have read it. Astonishing – to be standing in Darius's home, looking at the images he would have seen still virtually in the condition he would have known them minus their gold ornaments – and to be pondering his reading matter, to know a little of what he would have been thinking about, imagining.

Many beautiful objects were constructed at Persepolis by Darius and his son Xerxes. These symbolic creatures were probably protectors of the world over which they presided as well as figures of power and virility.

But all was soon to turn to dust. The mighty Persian Empire was itself laid low when Alexander the Great defeated its armies and looted and burned Persepolis in 330 BC in vengeance for Persian outrages in Greece. Alexander's slighting of Persepolis was absolute. Its treasures were carted away, its buildings burnt and tumbled to the ground. Alexander destroyed one of the most beautiful products of civilisation on earth. As I look at the ruins for which he – as much as time – is responsible, I feel a shiver of anger. What irony that a man who we now associate with the high values of Greek civilisation should have committed such an act of brutality and vandalism.

As I brood within Darius's palace – and imagine Alexander's men rushing through it with torches and tearing the gold from the bas-reliefs – I spot a party of young Iranian tourists. I wonder what these modern-day Persians feel about the destruction of this great city – do they still feel anger? Of course not, they are laughing and flirting. Most daringly the girls whip off their headscarves to be photographed, with their rich dark locks flowing, as they pose next to carvings of Darius dispatching a lion. Life goes on – I'm foolish of course to get morbid about an event that took place 2300 years ago.

My last mission of the day is to see Darius's tomb. It's a rather bleak affair now, no more than an empty, echoing tomb cut high up in a cliff side. But its composition is reminiscent of the staircases in Persepolis. Stairs to heaven, I suppose – which, perhaps curiously, I have seen in Inca, Moche and Aztec art and architecture in South and Central America. But I have also seen this step motif somewhere else – it's one of the standard geometric patterns on certain types of Persian carpet. This implies that some designs do go back at least 2500 years. Golly – I must find out more.

We return to our hotel in Shiraz. Perhaps it's the gloomy story of the destruction of Persepolis but this evening I feel that I've reached a new threshold of pain. It's been about three months since I left home and now I'm starting to wonder and worry a little. I suppose it's a combination of wanting to go home and fearing what I will find. It will be hard to fit into the day-to-day banal regime of sedentary life – worrying about small, domestic things. I have got used to the broad sweep. To be in one culture or country at one moment, to immerse myself in it, work hard and then, in a few hours or days, move on to another country or culture. And to do this week after week, month after month, always on the move, always fresh, startling, stimulating things to see, smell, hear, experience. Yes – it will be hard to stay still. But there is yet much work to do.

47 PERSIAN CARPETS, SHIRAZ

Monday 13 – Tuesday 14 September
Today some of my questions about Persian carpets should be answered. They are one of my treasures because they have long fascinated me. They are ancient in origin – more than 3000 years it is said – and I saw a continuity in design at Darius's tomb that suggests that this claim may be no exaggeration. They are beautiful, robust objects that are also functional – they were probably made first by nomads using the wool of their flocks to create portable shelter and covering. What also seems certain is that they very soon became objects of trade so that patterns and techniques, whether they arose in China, Egypt or Persia, rapidly became known internationally and they became objects of high status. It is recorded that Cyrus the Great – the most powerful monarch in the world when entombed around 530 BC – was covered by a pile of Persian carpets.

I go to the bazaar in Shiraz and see a treasure trove of carpets – they cascade from shop upon shop, stand in huge piles and hang from the walls. I look and talk to the traders, to learn more about these wonderful things. They are a feast. Regional in origin, or related to family and religious customs and beliefs, they can be abstract and geometric as in mosque architecture or show living beings – animals, birds or even humans – in ways rarely found in the arts and crafts in Islamic countries. As with magic carpets in fables, they can transport the mind, you can get lost in their subtle array of pattern and colour.

From the technical point of view the Persian carpet is hugely impressive. Most are made using long, soft, silky wool – called kush and sheared in spring from the bellies of sheep – but also goat and camel hair is used and, occasionally, for the finest decorative carpets, silk. The wool or hair is tied by hand to the warp thread in a knot formation – called a Sinneh knot. When a row of knots is tied, perhaps using many different coloured threads and following a complex pattern, all are compacted using a comb to form a dense pile. When this is done the next row of knots is started. This is what the word carpet means – *carpere* in Latin, to pluck or seize – and then to tie the wool or hair to the weft and warp frame formed by thick threads of wool. Dyes are also very important to achieve beautiful colours that are stable and last. Most are of vegetable origin – roots,

Making a Persian carpet: these women tie about 9000 knots a day. I do a quick calculation – it would take at least 60 to 80 days to complete this carpet, of a type called a Gaber, which will have a star-like motif in the centre and in each of the four corners.
Right *I admire the carpets in this warehouse in Shiraz, but the prices are very high indeed.*

flowers, barks, leaves, but also some are from animal products and insects. These natural colours, if they fade, become yet more beautiful of hue. Quite literally, an old carpet, providing it's not worn through, improves with age.

Broadly, the quality of a carpet is determined not only by the complexity of its pattern, but also by the number of knots per square inch, which can be as many as 330 in the finest work. In ordinary carpets this is far lower, perhaps around 50, but even to achieve this a carpetmaker is expected to tie about 10,000 knots a day. The artistic and technical high point of the Persian carpet was arguably achieved in the 16th and early 17th centuries, during the Safavid Dynasty when Shah Abbas was creating Isfahan. The characteristic colours are burnt-red for backgrounds, dark and light blue and brown; characteristic patterns and motifs that emerge – varying from region to region – are flowers linked by tendrils, geometric arabesques, diamond shapes and, of course, the step patterns I saw at Darius's tomb.

The day ends with a purchase. What to buy, how much to pay, how to get the carpet home. One trader takes me to his warehouse. Vast piles of carpets greet me – room after room of them. I wade through them, examine and discuss. He's asking prices that would be high in London. I look down in despair – and suddenly see what I'm standing on. A delightful little carpet covered with images of living beings – naughty in Islam – that show pairs of birds facing each other. Love birds, set against a background of deep red. It must have been for a harem or a hammam. How much is this, I ask? He looks surprised, then amused – it's nothing, just a few dollars. We close on the deal, I whip up my prize in a cloud of dust, and am off. I stride back though the bazaar and reach a bench outside a mosque. I unwrap my carpet to look at it – the doves perch among flowers, the bench on which I sit is surrounded by polychromatic tiles showing huge blossoms – the doves are in paradise and so am I.

Before we leave for Syria we have an appointment to see carpets being made. We arrive at a gaunt modern yard and on its concrete floor sit two women clad in bright red shawls, enlivened with small gold ornaments and their hair uncovered. These are nomadic women from Fars – the Beni Abdullah or Children of Abdullah – and they sit side by side in front of a large frame on which are stretched weft and warp threads. They are knotting a carpet. I ask them, what do they feel when making a carpet – is it tedious? They agree that it offers escape – the repetitive work is like prayer or meditation. I observe that they, from time to time, tighten the threads, increase the tension. Yes, they have to 'tune' the carpet – of course, it's like an instrument, it has to sing. As we talk they knot, draw the knots together with a comb, adjust the warp and weft occasionally, and knot on. I watch these women putting their hearts and souls into this carpet, this finely tuned instrument. Magic carpets – yes, I begin to understand.

48 DAMASCUS SOUK, SYRIA

Wednesday 15 – Thursday 16 September

Today we fly – via Dubai – to Damascus, Syria. This is where I will really get to grips with trade. For well over 2000 years Damascus was one of the great trading cities of the world, its markets and souks were legendary. Goods would arrive in Damascus from all over the Eastern world, enter the markets and then be dispatched to the Mediterranean coast to be shipped to Western Europe. It was one of the great commercial and cultural centres of the world – I want to see what remains of all this.

I know Damascus a little and have longed to return because here history is not frozen. Damascus is, arguably, the oldest continuously inhabited city in the world – founded perhaps 7000 years ago – but, although ancient, it is no museum city. Here the past is very much alive. I have two specific targets in Damascus – one of which will be my treasure. Both are streets and both tell the tale of Damascus and trade. One is Straight Street and the other the al-Hamidiyeh Souk.

Straight Street was one of the most famous streets in the world 2000 years ago. It was Via Recta, the main street (the Decumanus) of Roman Damascus and cut through the city, straight and true, from one gate to another. It was the great street of merchants and trade. Here people gathered, from all over the known world, to buy and sell, to meet, to look and to wonder. The street is even mentioned in chapter nine of Acts of the Apostles in the New Testament as '...the street which is called Straight...', for it was here that Paul – after his dramatic conversion on the road to Damascus – found lodgings and had his eyesight restored by a Christian named Ananias. I want to experience this great street.

We start by the impressive 3rd-century AD Roman gate and, as I walk on, to my right are a number of handsome houses, with large balconies and ornate timber embellishments. They date, perhaps, from the 18th or early 19th centuries. Many are hopelessly derelict. Why? My fixer tells me that this used to be the Jewish Quarter and many houses here have been abandoned since their occupants fled the city at the time of the 1967 war with Israel.

Ahead of me stands one of the architectural monuments of Straight Street – a Roman arch that marks roughly the centre point of this ancient thoroughfare. So far things have been pretty quiet but, up ahead, I can see they are very different. The road is vaulted over, with sunlight beaming through small square windows and casting beguiling slivers of light onto the dark pavement below. This is the Midhat Pasha Souk that occupies much of the remainder of the route of Straight Street. Already I can see that it is heaving with life – vehicles loaded with merchandise pushing slowly past shops and shoppers packing the straight, but very narrow, street ahead. This is good, because I have a particular shopping mission. Tonight I am going to a very fine hammam – to soak and steam my troubles away – and I fancy being properly attired before being stripped naked. So I am looking for a comfortable silk robe. Since I'm a fairly large fellow this could, I realise, be a bit of a problem – certainly it has in other countries. When I soiled my shirt during the making of the sword in Japan the courteous and concerned swordmaster wanted to help by lending me one of his shirts. He stood back and surveyed me. 'Ah, big body,' he murmured as he shook his head from side to side, and eventually produced a blue tee shirt the size of a sack – goodness knows who it had belonged to before, a sumo wrestler I suppose. And later, when looking for a shirt in the Hogg Market, Calcutta, a stall holder rather than asking my dimensions merely said, 'Yes, elephant size.' Much amusement for all – even me, but I don't

The 3rd-century Roman temple gate through which I pass to the Great Mosque from al-Hamidiyeh Souk. In this market I saw the riches of the Middle East on display much as they would have been 1000 years ago.

The courtyard of the Great Mosque of Damascus lies within the 3rd-century Roman walls. People come here not just to pray, but also to meet and relax in the shade of the arcades that surround three sides of this huge space.

particularly want to go through this experience again. So, with some trepidation I look for shops or stalls selling men's clothes – hoping against hope to see one specialising in out-size garments. We wander off into narrow winding streets and courts, some sheltered by generous domes. Everywhere goods are on sale – here a street selling silks, nearby metalworkers. Some streets contain remarkable houses, with enclosed balconies, austere facades and small entrance doors that open into large and ornate courtyards with central pools or fountains. The buildings, the light filtering into the narrow streets, the call to prayer echoing from afar, the bustling people and the bright and intriguing goods on display together weave an intoxicating spell. It is magical.

And so on to the Souk of al-Hamidiyeh. My first sight of this strange street is awe-inspiring. I stand with my back to the roaring traffic and rearing tower blocks of modern Damascus and stare into a wondrous cavern – dark, mysterious, pulsating with life, inviting. I am looking into the past, into the heart and soul of man. The curving street is dark because it is roofed over with a ribbed and opaque semi-circular vault through which light occasionally sparkles, like stars in the firmament sparkle – it's incredibly organic, it's like entering the bowels of a beast, but also incredibly romantic, picturesque. This is the beginning of the al-Hamidiyeh Souk. I enter the maw of the beast and, as soon as I am out of the sunlight and enveloped by the shade of the roof, I can see all.

The souk was built on part of the site of the Roman fortress in Ottoman times and the two-storey shops that frame it date from the 1780s, the cast-iron roof from the 1880s. I wander along this street transfixed. Each shop is a different world of activity, of produce – some selling damask, cotton fabric with silk thread embroidery that is the traditional product of Damascus. Small streets make their way into the gradually curving line of the souk as it snakes through the city. Then, suddenly, I see light at the end, an image framed by the shops and curving iron arches of the vault. It's extraordinary – a whole series of things happen in quick succession. As I move forward I walk into the sunlight – the vault stops and in front and on each side of me are the heroic remains of a huge Classical colonnade and portico standing to one side of a small square. It's spectacular – coming out of the darkness and intense activity of the souk into this bright, open and relatively tranquil space. This complex of buildings formed the sacred heart of Roman Damascus. The story of these buildings tells much of the story of the city. The

Romans built their temple on the site of a 9th-century BC temple to the god Haddad. In its turn, in the 4th century AD, the temple of Jupiter was converted into a Christian basilica dedicated to St John the Baptist and then, following the Muslim conquest of Damascus, the basilica was, from 709, transformed into a huge mosque. And the outer walls of the temple survived all these transformations, although being pierced with new doors and sprouting a series of towers and minarets. I stare at it in wonder – what a moving monument. There's no doubt about it – walking the length of the shady and sinuous al-Hamidiyeh Souk, mingling with vibrant humanity going about its worldly business, and then bursting out into this space, at different times sacred to so many faiths and religions – is one of the greatest experiences to be had in any city on earth.

I head to a street lined with shops selling carpets – this is the carpet bazaar and the goods are most tempting – but time is pressing on and I plunge on in search of my garb. Eventually, I find a likely shop. I enter and enquire. The assistant looks me up and down and claims to have a robe that is large enough – but only one. It is duly produced, voluminous and reaching to the ground, made of silk – which is good – but with a thin pink stripe – which could be very bad. I am dubious, but it's all they have and my time has run out. I try it on and it fits, that's a move in the right direction. I leave the changing room and no one laughs aloud. Another good sign although, I must admit, I feel rather like a large ticking-covered pillow. But I buy it and we are off – to the hammam.

It's located near the souk. Nick, Mike and Tim Dunn are my companions and we enter through a small door and find ourselves in a splendid cubical, domed space. Chaps loll on benches and on divans set in adjacent rooms and alcoves. I imagined I would have the opportunity to wear my new pink-striped robe – the attendants are looking at it approvingly – but not yet, for a towel is wrapped around my waist and we are ushered into the bath. Here I take a shower, kneel by a basin in the shape of a giant shell and pour cold water over my head. Then on to the next stage – the steam room. I enter the door – my God, it's hot. Steam fills the rooms so that it is impossible to see more than a few feet, I'm being boiled, it's impossible to stand it for more than a few seconds. I last a few minutes, retreat, and then return to be boiled some more. I can't say it's enjoyable – I suppose it's doing me good. Then the massage! Off the cold room are a series of small alcoves in which stand beefy men – the masseurs, all armed with oils and salty unguents. I glance in one of these and see a chap lying flat of the floor, on his stomach, with a masseur pounding away at him. The chap on the floor is moaning and rivulets of oily water appear to be oozing out of his convulsing body. Most odd – not quite for me. In my alcove there is a bed – I get on it and the fellow works on my back and legs – not bad although he bends my legs in directions that, I'm sure, nature never intended. Eventually I am released. Do I feel better? Not sure. Do I feel alright? I think so – providing my legs stop shaking soon.

Now the best bit – I re-enter the domed vestibule and in an instant my wet towel is whipped away and I am wrapped, from chin to toe, in a massive warm towel, another is wrapped, turban fashion, around my head, and I am led to a bench where a blanket is tucked around me. I am cocooned. It's bliss – I'm heated by an inner glow, the cold chill kept at bay, my muscles relaxing. We all four sit in a row – what a sight, like four huge bugs. I free an arm and order a tea and a narghile, a water pipe. It's time to reflect. I have seen much – and there is still much to see. But I am on the road home, for the Silk Route on which Damascus stands is the route that leads, ultimately, to my home in Spitalfields, the area in London in which raw silk from the East came to be woven into fine fabric.

In the East hammams or bath houses are a part of daily life. They briefly enjoyed a vogue in London in the late 17th century, but soon acquired a reputation as places of debauchery. All very proper here in Damascus though.

HOLY LANDS

49 HOLY LAND MOSAICS, JORDAN

Friday 17 September – Madaba and Mount Nebo

We drive south from Damascus towards Jordan. The landscape is monotonous. To our right, in the far distance, I can make out the Golan Heights, the rich, high land lost to Israel in the 1967 Six Day War. I wandered across this commanding plateau a couple of years ago looking at crusader and Arab castles and the debris of the more recent fighting. Then, I looked down from those heights into Syria and Jordan – now, I look up towards them. On both occasions what I saw seemed impossibly far away – because there is no border crossing between Syria and the heights, and no chance of one while bitterness continues between Israel and the Arab world. I am on my way to Jerusalem, a city in which the tension between Israeli and Arab, Jew and Muslim is made manifest in the most dramatic way, for it is played out against the stupendous backdrop of history. Indeed history, or rather the conflicting interpretation of history, occupies a pivotal position in the current conflict which will, I fear, give the theme to this chapter. This is, historically, the Holy Land but, at the moment, there is little holy about it.

We cross the border into Jordan with ease and drive towards Madaba on one of the most ancient roads in the world – the King's Highway, once a great trade route and, according to the Old Testament, the route by which Moses intended to lead the Children of Israel out of Egypt to the Promised Land. So even the roads here play their part in the often doleful story of the Holy Land. There is only one thing I want to see – an object that should throw fascinating light on this region 1500 years ago. I enter the Greek Orthodox Church of St George, which was rebuilt in a pleasant but undistinguished Classical manner in the 1890s. I cast around for what I want – and then see it before me, spread all over the floor. It is a remarkable thing – a map of the Holy Land, rendered in large scale as a mosaic floor, which originally adorned a basilica that stood here in the 6th century. The map was only rediscovered in 1884 and large sections are missing, but never mind, much is there – including an astonishing portrait of Jerusalem. I stand in front of the map, looking towards the altar in the church – it's as if I'm hovering at a great height above the Mediterranean coast, looking south-east over the Holy Land. To my left is the river Jordan running into the Dead Sea – complete with ferry and ferryman – and to my right is the Nile Delta. At the top are the Mountains of Moab and the location of Madaba. I feast on the details, over 120 cities and towns are named – in Greek – and many of them illustrated. But it is the image of Jerusalem that overwhelms. It is oval in shape and defined by its wall. I can make out the domed Church of the Holy Sepulchre but not, of course, the Muslim Dome of the Rock for it wasn't yet built. This map shows the Holy Land before Mohammed was born – in the age before Islam. Here everything is Judaic and Christian. In a little over 100 years all was to change dramatically and forever. This map captures a vital piece of the world on the cusp of change, just before those divisions which have caused – and continue to cause – so much misery were put in place. It's a fantastic and moving document.

We drive a few miles further on – we are going into the mountains. The sun is starting to set and I am on Mount Nebo – standing on one of the most extraordinary sites on earth. To my side is another church, adjoining a Franciscan monastery, in part truly ancient, the remains of a once-majestic basilica. I go inside in quest of another mosaic floor, this time complete and of the highest artistic quality. This floor marks the site of the baptistery and was made in AD 531. In the early Christian church baptism was the most important ritual for it was seen as the moment the soul of a pagan or idolater was redeemed, won and secured for Christ, for the promise of life eternal, for paradise. So the mosaic shows, from top to bottom, the struggle between man and beast – no doubt the battle between Christ and the old gods. Then a pastoral scene with a shepherd tending his flock, which must represent the love and teachings of Christ with, along the bottom, what is surely a scene of paradise – all of God's creation living in peace, harmony and beauty. Quite some vision. The church is dedicated to Moses – and that reveals the focus of this location. Many believe that Moses is buried below this church and from this site he was granted, by God, his one and only view of the Promised Land. The story's explained in Deuteronomy 34:1–5: 'And Moses went up from the plains of Moab unto the mountain of Nebo...And the Lord said unto him, This is the land which I sware unto Abraham, unto Isaac, and unto Jacob, saying, I will give it unto thy seed: I have caused thee to see it with thine eyes, but thou shalt not go over thither. So Moses the servant of the Lord died there in the land of Moab.'

I walk to where Moses must have stood – on a rocky outcrop in front of the church – and contemplate the scene. The view is astonishing. It is the mosaic map of the Holy Land, but in reverse. Rather than looking to the east I am looking to the west, towards the setting sun. In front of me is the glassy water of the Dead Sea. To my left is Bethlehem, to my right is Jericho and to my front – just 40 kilometres away – is Jerusalem. So near, so far. It is a world away. Between Jerusalem and where I am standing are borders, the gated, guarded and fenced-about territory of the West Bank – and mountains of anger and hate. The Promised Land is responsible for so much of the violence and hatred in the world today. Those ancient words in Deuteronomy still have political power and relevance for they offer spiritual and moral justification for Israeli possession of much of the Holy Land. Because of this text Jews believe this land is their rightful possession – their birthright promised by God. Because of this divine promise to Abraham they feel justified in uprooting the people – the Palestinians, both Muslim and Christian, and other Arab nations – that have been in possession of the 'Promised Land' for centuries. This radical action – pursued since 1947 with vigour and sustained through a series of wars – has provoked a violent and vicious response and sparked anger and discontent among Muslims around the world, has indeed now polarised the world to a terrifying degree. Where is the right and where is the wrong in all this? Where is the sense? How can the seemingly incompatible aspirations of two peoples be reconciled? I ponder these impossible questions and as I stand where Moses stood when this fateful promise was confirmed, the vision before my eyes starts to fade. The sun goes down behind Jerusalem – darkness engulfs the Holy Land.

Left The map of the Holy Land as a mosaic floor in the Greek Orthodox Church of St George in Madaba, Jordan. It names 120 towns and the wall of Jerusalem is clearly defined. Right On Mount Nebo the church houses another mosaic floor dating from AD 531 showing the struggle between man and beast.

50 PETRA

Saturday 18–Sunday 19 September

We overnight in Amman and long before dawn drive south to one of the most famed ancient cities in the world – Petra. I want to see it for many reasons – not least to discover how it's dealing with the hordes that every year tramp over its stones. Tourism brings money and life but it can only prove to be deadly, with tourists literally destroying the things they come to see and obliterating any sense of magic. With a sense of dread I go to see how Petra is bearing up, the fear gnawing at my heart that the programme I am making will only encourage more people to visit this precious place. Petra reached its peak around 2000 years ago but was only rediscovered by the West in 1812, after being largely abandoned and forgotten for centuries. Since then its strange location – secreted within a lunar landscape of mountains and reached via a long, deep and twisting gorge called the Siq – has given Petra a compelling romance. And then there is the material from which the city is made. The word Petra means rock, and the rock from which the city is built – carved is nearer the truth – is extraordinary and beautiful. It is red-hued primary sandstone that erupts into marble-like swirls of colour, the result of iron oxide and water mixing within the grain of the stone. Add to this the quality of the surviving architecture – finely detailed Classical compositions cut within the faces of the cliffs that frame the city – and it is clear that, of all the ancient ruined cities of the world, Petra is in a league of its own.

Before the mouth of the Siq is reached the long winding road along the bed of the Wadi Musa valley – stretching for nearly a mile – has to be traversed. In time-honoured fashion we hire horse transport – not an Arab stallion which would probably toss me off in embarrassing circumstances, but a somewhat prosaic horse and carriage. In I bundle and off we trot. Earlier I noticed that most carriage horses have blankets tied over their rumps – odd, I thought. Now I find out why. Horses in Petra are given to frightful flatulence and the rug is evidently intended to mitigate the unfortunate consequences. It doesn't. Poor beasts – they must have a grim diet. So, amid gushes and rumbles, I make my way sedately along the wadi. Oh well, it's all part of the experience, I suppose. Quickly I tell the driver to stop – not because of the pungent cloud that surrounds me – but because of what I see. Death, ancient death, is all around – everywhere.

Petra is, in many senses, the great city of the dead. Not only has this once-thriving city been long abandoned – in 100 BC it had a population of around 30,000 and controlled the valuable trade route between Arabia and Damascus – but its people were deeply enthralled by a death cult. The Nabateans – as the Semitic people of Petra were called – had occupied the site from the 7th century BC and had a religion that was influenced by those of the great and ancient civilisations of the region – Egypt, Assyria and Babylon. Their deities were often worshipped through abstract, featureless upright stones, some looking remarkably like Siva lingams, called betyls. But it was the cult of death that led to Petra's most enduring monuments – thousands of rock-cut tombs, some of spectacular grandeur, that rise above and surround the site: the city of the dead standing guardian over the city of the living. This all reminds me of the rock-cut tombs I explored a few months ago in Sulawesi, Indonesia. Outside, some of the tombs have ornate architectural embellishments. A few have abstract step motifs cut in panels above the door. This not only reminds me of the motif I saw on the tomb of Darius the Great in Iran, and on some Persian carpets, but also of the step motifs and step-pyramids or ziggurats of Central and South America and Iraq. I suppose a step is an ancient, universal symbol representing the ascent of the soul after death, the stairway to the stars.

The Wadi road leads to a small clearing; in front of me is a vast crevice – inviting, almost livid in hue – and in I plunge. The narrow and winding defile is nearly one and a half kilometres long, its walls about 100 metres high and it varies in width from 3 to 11

The Treasury at Petra. It is exquisite. The architecture is Roman in influence but the playful details and its east-facing aspect towards sunrise indicate it was a temple to female fertility, regeneration and rebirth. It can also be read as a calendar. I find it fascinating.

metres. Suddenly I understand why the great God of Petra – Dushara – is called the lord of the mountain. He is not symbolised by the mountain – he is the mountain. With the Inca and many other ancient people, mountains were not only where the gods resided but were in themselves divine, living gods. Here in Petra the mountains – rock and stone – were holy. The people were surrounded by their gods, placed their dead within the body of their gods. Fanciful? Perhaps, but certainly not unprecedented. All pyramids from India to Egypt, from Mexico to Iraq, are accepted as man-made sacred mountains – the Gods of Greece lived on Olympus, in India the sacred Mount Meru was the centre of the universe. The quality of different stones has haunted man. I have seen rocks set up as shrines in Shinto temples in Japan and used as objects of meditation in Zen temples; in Britain specific stones were transported hundreds of miles, at great difficulty I would imagine, to be set up to help form Stonehenge; in Egypt different stones were chosen and used with great care to express the powers of the Pharaoh; in Mecca it is a huge stone that is prayed to by Muslims as the gift from God; and in the Old Testament it is put most simply (in 2 Samuel 22:32): 'For who is God, save the Lord? And who is a rock, save our God?' No, man has always found mountains and stones extraordinary, magical, divine – symbols of truth and reliability – immutable. And if the mountains around Petra are the bodies of the Nabateans' gods, then what of the Siq that penetrates it, that carries on its walls the conical, domed and somewhat phallic forms of the betyls? Is the whole of this ancient city a huge fertility symbol, with the tube-like Siq allowing man to penetrate – to in some way impregnate – the rocks, to bring about the rebirth of the dead entombed within them? Can trade be central to all this – could the spices and particularly the incense, the myrrh and frankincense that the Nabateans traded, carried in vast quantity down the Siq and that are associated with the birth of Jesus, have been part of the ritual of impregnation? Enough questions, no answers, and my head is in a whirl from these fevered speculations.

The Siq takes its last turn and I am confronted by a stunning image. The cliff leans to one side, shadow falls on the other and Petra's most famous elevation is revealed, framed, in a deep gorge yet glowing in the mid-morning sun. It is magical – and unbelievably beautiful. The elevation is that of the Khazneh – or Treasury – an absurd name given to it centuries ago by the Bedouin who fancied that every old structure or tomb must contain a secret hoard of treasure. In probability it was a tomb that dates from the 1st century BC to the 1st century AD. I approach the building – well, hardly a building, more a sculpture carved out of the living, sacred rock. It is an erudite, rather flamboyant design in the spirit of Roman provincial architecture. But it is the detail that grabs my attention. Motifs are grouped to suggest the elevation is a calendar – four

eagles, seven cups – so all marks the passing of the ages, it is a time machine. Also the details are rich and feminine – so it comes as no surprise that most of the carved images on the building are of goddesses or legendary females. I notice other details – the central door surround is embellished with egg-and-dart carvings. A conventional Greek Classical motif but here – suddenly – given new meaning. What could be more emblematic of fertility than an egg, and what more phallic – piercing – than a dart. I stare into the room these doors frame. The walls are carved with Classical detail and explode with a swirl of natural colour. It all seems symptomatic of the energy within the rocks – of a life force. Suddenly I fancy I see the room as the Nabateans saw it – yes, a tomb as well as a temple, but really a place of rebirth, where the body and the soul gain new life.

One road leads through Petra and I follow it along a winding valley. It's a linear city and down this road the people and traders travelled, heading towards what is now called the Lower Town, about a mile distant, which is where most people lived and worked. I suppose there would have been some houses and shops here but virtually all evidence of them – the city of the living – has gone. What survives is the Great Necropolis. Next to, and rising high above the road, sometimes in deep tiers, and in all sizes, are tombs. It's an incredible scene – an incredible thought. The city of the living surrounded, dwarfed by the city of the dead. Some of the tombs are monumental pieces of work – notably those speculatively dubbed the Royal Tombs, loaded with columns, pilasters and entablatures, many originally partly plastered and painted, I suppose. The Nabateans would have travelled and lived along this road looked down upon by the ages – their ancestors dwelling in palaces.

The day is going fast so I press on. I exchange my carriage for a donkey to complete my journey. I want to reach one of Petra's sacred High Places – the abode of its mountain gods – before sunset, but it is at the end of a mountain path that winds up for almost 2 kilometres. My donkey is a strong and worthy beast and clearly knows the route well. Off he goes, with no directions from me, and picks his way along the path, up steps, slithering over the rocky parts, walking at a good pace along the flat portions – some of which are on the very edge of steep gorges. I'm trusting this donkey with my life – and I hardly know the fellow. But he never falters. I peer over the edge of these rocky inclines while my admirable donkey – without instructions of any sort – pirouettes around corners and heads upwards, ever upwards. It's like being on a magic carpet with a mind of its own.

Eventually it ends. I reach a small plateau on the peak of Jebel al-Deir, dismount and walk ahead of me and then I see it – the massive rock tomb that the Bedouin call al-Deir – the Monastery. It is astonishing to see such a thing in such a place. It's a larger and

Left On one of the High Places above Petra stands the Monastery – a large, more masculine version of the Treasury. It faces west – towards death. Right Seated against a camel's saddle I enjoy a Bedouin feast of coffee, meat, rice and, best of all, sheep's testicles.

somewhat more robust version of the Treasury – built, most think, a hundred or so years later. This huge carved facade faces west and there are huge discs carved in the frieze of its upper entablature. The Treasury is ornate and feminine and seems to celebrate birth. The al-Deir is plain and masculine and looks towards the setting sun, towards death. These two elevations – cut out of the divine rock – seem to mark the beginning and end of a journey. Birth in the hidden womb of the city and death on this High Place, near the gods. As I sit here at the end of my journey through Petra – having, it seems, unwittingly followed the path of life – an Arab starts to play a pipe. The sound is piercing, haunting – stranger still, he has clambered to the top of al-Deir to play, to take one last look at the sun before it dips below the horizon. He is playing a lament to the setting sun, to the death of yet another day, to the remorseless march of time. We listen in silence, each with his own thoughts, and then steal away before night descends.

But the day is not over. I have a dinner date – with Bedouin. Petra was lost and forgotten to all for about 700 years – except to these nomadic people. They passed through it, stayed when its shelter suited them, grazed their flocks among its tombs, moved on and, when it was convenient, returned. This cycle went on for centuries – it was their secret city. I drive to Little Petra – a place of tombs some distance from the city. It is dark but there is a bright moon and, in a clearing between rocks, an open-fronted tent. I am welcomed by two aged Bedouin – both are warm in their greetings. The food is good and plentiful – a huge plate of seasoned rice acting as a bed for the corpse of a well-cooked sheep. Most of the body of the beast appears to be strewn around the large plate – legs, great chunks of muscle and in the centre its head. I stare at it, the head stares back fixing me with a watery and mournful gaze. Sheep's eyes – delicious. I am exhorted to eat much – and the best bits. Suddenly something rotund and yellow is placed before me – the sheep's testicles, complete with voluminous scrotum. My favourite. I put one in my mouth. Succulent indeed, dense and sweet meat. These are the best testicles I have eaten for a long time. I devour another – then more appear. How many testicles did this ram have? Even I can't manage more than two – they are more than a mouthful. I decline the second pair, my hosts insist, I decline again. And so it goes on.

Then, in front of the fire, we fall to talking. I ask the pair about Petra. Did you experience anything unusual among the tombs? Yes, one of the Bedouin says and, the smile of the perfect host falling from his face, he tells me the tale. When we slept in the tombs or walked out at night they would throw stones at us. Who, I ask? The spirits, the spirits of the dead. We look at each other. Did it happen to you? Yes, he says, and in such a way that I believe him. Where do this spirits live, I ask? In the rocks, he whispers. Yes, of course in the rocks, like the Aboriginal Mimi ancestor spirits. Clearly the Bedouin have inherited the belief that the rocks in Petra are sacred, alive. He tells me more – a secret. He lowers his voice and moves closer. When it happened, he confides, I fell down and didn't move for a day, until the next night. He looks at me – there is significance in this, but he sees I don't quite understand what it is. He gives me a clue. The same thing happened to a friend of mine, and he wasn't the same afterwards, it changed him, he couldn't live with his family. Silence. I look at him again, then around the empty tent. There's no sign of a family here – was there ever a friend, I wonder? And now? We still go there, he reveals – but the spirits don't appear. Why? Perhaps they are overwhelmed by the crowds of people now in Petra, perhaps they have been driven away by the call to prayer from a nearby mosque – he doesn't know.

To spend the night in Petra would certainly be an interesting experience – a challenge. But I can't enter at night – the gates are firmly closed and the dark mountain passes fatal to all but Bedouin familiar with the trails.

To reach Petra's High Place I entrust this donkey to make the climb. It's obviously experienced at scaling steep rocky gorges.

51 TEMPLE MOUNT, JERUSALEM, ISRAEL

Monday 20 – Tuesday 21 September

After a day of rest in Aqaba, we are off. We make the short drive to the Jordanian–Israeli border. All is quiet – in fact deserted. We pass through the Jordanian checkpoint with no trouble and then enter the no man's land that separates the Jordanian crossing point from that of the Israelis. We are greeted by polite Israeli security personnel – a good start – who explain with regrets that every item has to be X-rayed and then hand-searched. 'Such times,' one of the men shrugs. We agree. It takes an hour or so, my passport is scrutinised, I explain what we are doing, it is stamped and we are off.

My treasure here is, perhaps, mythic rather than actual – the Temple of Solomon. But whether an idea or an actual building, the temple has had a profound effect on architecture around the world – arguably it is the most influential structure ever built by man. And upon this treasure sits another – the fabulous late 7th-century Dome of the Rock, one of the earliest and most haunting sacred buildings of the Muslim world.

But to see these treasures in Jerusalem – a city divided by fear and suspicion – is a major problem. Israel, of course, controls Jerusalem and the area around the Temple Mount, which includes the world's most sacred site for the Judaic religion – the Wailing Wall. This lies in the Jewish Quarter to the south-west of the Temple Mount. To the north and north-west of the mount is the Muslim Quarter of the Old City and the top of the Mount – loaded with Muslim shrines since the 7th century – is administered by a Muslim Trust. So the Temple Mount is in the thick of it – if anything goes wrong in Jerusalem it is pretty quickly felt here. We have secured permission from the Israeli authorities to film around the Temple Mount. We have also got permission from the Muslim Trust to film on top of the Temple Mount and, I think, in the Dome of the Rock – a triumph if true and a thing achieved by few these days. But all these agreements are fragile, non-binding, subject to the atmosphere of the day, the whim of the moment. If there is trouble in the city, if someone suddenly takes a dislike to us, gets nervous, then all could be off.

We start by tackling the most important thing first – access to film the top of the Temple Mount and the Dome of the Rock – and meet an uncertain reception. It is not

The Dome of the Rock on top of Temple Mount, Jerusalem – the most sacred site on earth. It is truly breath-taking. For centuries its proportions have inspired designers of sacred buildings around the world. Among its treasures was the Ark of the Covenant.

Left *The Dome of the Rock is a perfect geometrical space. The design of the building is based on the number four – the square, the circle, the cube and the sphere. The interior (right) is serene, harmonious and sophisticated – organised around the floor of the rock on which Abraham was to sacrifice Isaac.*

clear at first that we are expected. Negotiations start, letters are shown, people appear and an agreement – seemingly quite separate from the one I thought we had – is forged. Yes, we will be allowed to film, under the supervision of a party of unsmiling men, but there must absolutely be no 'acting'. We explain that we are making a documentary not a drama and I have no intention of acting. 'Yes – but no acting,' we are told again. Soon we overcome this language problem and discover what the instruction really is. No talking. I can see the top of the Mount, be filmed, but not say a word. A terrible blow – I explain why – but they do not relent. The men from the trust are becoming impatient. We sense that if we do not agree to this almost impossible condition the whole enterprise might be off. What are we to do? We agree, get our foot in the door, and hope something turns up. So we walk west across the Temple Mount on which – once – stood Solomon's Temple. My emotions are aflame.

The Temple of Solomon lives in the mind – in the imagination – as not only the world's most inspirational, but also as one of its most ancient, architectural creations. But the temple is not just a figment of the imagination. It also exists in the tangible world – mysterious, much altered, rebuilt and – as we are now having confirmed – a much troubled archaeological and religious site. The reason is, of course, because it is of intense religious importance to all three religions of the Book – Jews, Muslims and Christians. Put simply, all three faiths embrace the idea that the temple was an exemplary structure, designed to God's orders, in which many of the secrets of creation were said to be enshrined and revealed – in its forms, in its proportions, in its details and in its contents. But, to make things more confusing there were, according to biblical accounts, three material temples built on the same site, one after the other.

Solomon's great creation is thought to have been completed in around 953 BC but it was not destined to remain intact for long. Some speculate that Solomon himself sent the sacred heart and power-base of the temple – the Ark of the Covenant – to Ethiopa with the son he had conceived with the Queen of Sheba. All accounts suggest a right-angular building of precise proportions (2:1 and 3:1 being consistently used) that became the essence of Classical design. Then in *c.*586 BC the temple was destroyed, what remained of its treasures seized and the Jews carried into exile by the Babylonian King Nebuchadnezzar. This seems to have been the end of the first temple – but a second was soon built. Cyrus of Persia had defeated Nebuchadnezzar and captured Babylon and so was, as the biblical account makes clear, able and willing to bring forth, '…the holy vessels which Nabuchodonosar (sic) had carried away from Jerusalem'. But nothing much happened during Cyrus's reign, largely because most Persians feared what would happen if the Jews were once again settled in Jerusalem with a rebuilt temple. But eventually one of the royal guards – Zorobabel – won a competition seeking wisdom set by the Persian king Darius. The reward Zorobabel requested was for Darius to honour Cyrus's earlier vow to rebuild the temple in Jerusalem. So in *c*.515 BC (just as Persepolis was being started) the second temple was built and it is often called Zorobabel's temple.

The appearance of the second temple is hinted at in Ezra chapter 6:3–4, or at least the appearance it was meant to have when initially envisioned by Cyrus: 'Let the house be builded…the height thereof threescore cubits, and the breadth thereof threescore cubits.' So the new temple at Jerusalem was to be – essentially – a massive cube! It was Zorobabel's second temple that was repaired – some believe rebuilt – by King Herod in 20 BC. The existing retaining walls – including the Wailing Wall – date from this rebuilding. And it was Herod's grandly enlarged temple – by some called the third temple – that the Romans largely destroyed in AD 70 to punish the Jews for rebelling against Roman rule. A historically important moment and the root of so much modern misery. The destruction of the temple was not the only punishment inflicted by the Romans: Jews were exiled from their own city – their own land – and so started the Jewish Diaspora that allowed their ancient homeland to become the homeland of others.

It is across the foundations of these mighty and magical buildings – some say the work of divine intelligence and once housing the mysteries of creation – that I am now walking. I pass the Dome of the Rock. Can I go inside? No, they say, the el-Aqsa Mosque first. I walk and look, being filmed – but then am told abruptly to stop. Another official has appeared and is taking a dim view of proceedings. Things have suddenly just got much worse. He orders that not only is it forbidden for me to talk to camera but I must not walk in front of the camera. That is, he says, also acting and I suppose, in some ways, it is. What we do could be thought of as idolatrous because cameras are, after all, making images of a living being. We protest vigorously. Tempers flare – we are appeased by being told that we have permission to film inside the Dome of the Rock. That's good. No acting – very bad. So we take ourselves off, both sides bristling. Then something incredible happens.

We are leaving the mosque and one of our guides rushes back at us shouting and waving his hands: 'You should be filming them,' he screams at us. And then points accusingly at our fixer. 'She's a Jew.' We are aghast, what on earth is going on, what has provoked this extraordinary outburst? Then I see. A small group of orthodox Jews, escorted by heavily armed soldiers, is walking in front of the mosque, they are walking across the Temple Mount. The Temple Mount is open to the public and they are, I guess, beating the bounds, making it clear that the top of the mount may be in Muslim hands but only because the real master – the state of Israel – permits it. This is all highly provocative; I'm shocked. Things look like they might get nasty. We are hustled quickly to the dome, away from the shrieking Muslims and hunched-up, marching Jews.

We enter the dome. It is the most surprising of places. An exquisite piece of geometrical design, conceived in the 690s, clad in delicate tilework, yet sitting over a huge and rough-hewn lump of rock. But it is this rock that the Temple of Solomon is all about – indeed what much of the Jewish and Muslim faiths are about. It's an incredible story.

Even after the temple buildings were destroyed and control of the top of the mount lost, the temple site remained – and remains – holy for Jews. Why? This is because of what lies within. Jews pray at the Wailing Wall but not to the wall itself – they pray towards the sacred heart of the Temple Mount, towards Mount Moriah which the Temple Mount embraces, towards a rock within that, to the Jewish faith, is the foundation stone of the world, where God started His creation.

This same rock appears on the surface of the mount and here is believed to be the stone on which Abraham planned, at God's bidding, to sacrifice his son Isaac. It is the tip of this rock – the would-be sacrificial altar – that is now covered by the Dome of the Rock (the Qubbat al-Sakhra). Since the Jewish and Islamic faiths have the common root of the Old Testament texts it is only to be expected that Muslims – like Jews – identify Abraham as the key prophet and patriarch, from whose seed the Messiah will spring, as promised by God. So, naturally, for both faiths this same rock is intensely sacred – as sacred as the mountains around Petra were for the Nabateans. In addition, Muslims also believe this is the rock from which the prophet Mohammed ascended to heaven – leaving behind a faint impression of his foot!

Standing beneath the dome, I contemplate the serene interior of the building – people are praying, coming and going in peace, escaping from the hostile world. It all seems so, so sad. Judaism and Islam have the same foundation, and yet in this part of the world, on a site sacred to both, they are divided by a hate fuelled by a battle for land – a desperate battle for survival really – and by conflicting political ideologies. What this means, ironically, is that things which should pull these faiths together force them apart. The very fact they have so much in common yet currently cannot happily co-exist in the Holy Land means that sites like this – sacred to both – become a battleground, yet another source of fury and conflict – I've just witnessed an example of it.

All I can do is to contemplate the architecture. The square and the circle – and their three-dimensional equivalents the cube and the sphere – are the basic building blocks of the Dome of the Rock. As I walk around the building I realise that I'm walking through a perfect geometrical form. Judaism, Christianity and Islam suggest that God's creation is ordered around numbers, and that mathematical and geometrical proportions and ratios are the essential language of creation, of God himself. So, for example, a building organised around the number four evokes and possesses the power that the number four expresses. And, as I've seen in many buildings during my journey, number four – the square – is the material world – the four seasons, the four elements. On the other hand the circle or sphere – a perfect and continuous geometrical shape without beginning or end – expresses the spiritual realm, the world of God. I saw this at the Taj Mahal, at Isfahan and at Samarkand. So, at one level, the Dome of the Rock – its hemispherical dome sitting upon a base formed by two squares – is the fusion of the worlds of man and of God.

But our time is up – our nervous guides have decided it is the moment for us to be ejected from this paradise. As I leave I turn for one last look at the dome – its skin of blue tiles and marble sparkling in the sun.

Wednesday 22 September – Ethiopia

This is a day of travel. In the morning we fly to Addis Ababa, the capital of Ethiopia. We meet our fixer – Samson Mekonnen – as we leave the airport and then wind our way to our hotel in the heart of the city.

We are here on a quest. Ethiopia is the oldest independent country in Africa and home to one of the world's great, lost and ancient civilisations. It has a history going back to the time of Egypt, is the only country in Africa to possess an alphabet more than 2000 years old and, according to the Orthodox Church in Ethiopia, this has been a Christian country for at least 1600 years. But there are legends suggesting that one of the religions of the Book – Judaism – was here long before that, perhaps nearly 3000 years ago, in which case Ethiopia would be the oldest biblical country in the world. And that brings me to one of my quests – the Ark of the Covenant. Was it lost or destroyed in remote antiquity, did the Knights Templar find it in the early 12th century – did it ever exist? According to one account – recorded in a remarkable 13th-century Ethiopian epic text called the *Kebre Negast* (The Glory of Kings) – the Ark was acquired by Solomon's son Menelik, who was the fruit of Solomon's intimacy with the Queen of Sheba. Menelik is said to have taken the Ark home to his and his mother's native land – according to Ethiopian tradition, in present-day Ethiopia. A nice and ancient story. But there is more. In Axum is a shrine and housed in this shrine – according to the Ethiopian church and to all Ethiopians to whom I speak – is the Ark of the Covenant. Being the guardians of this sacred object – God's Seat on earth and containing the tablets of the Law – makes Ethiopians the Chosen People. It's incredible – this small shrine contains the heart and soul of the Ethiopian people. Over the years many have asked to look inside, to see the Ark, but all have been refused. Is there something to hide or, more to the point, nothing to hide – in fact nothing to see?

But there is more – much more – to see in Axum. It was an ancient city and spectacular fragments survive, notably a collection of tall stone stelae – or monolithic obelisks – that seem to mark a great and royal necropolis. All who see these mighty monoliths are, I hear, overcome and awed. I, too, want to be transported.

Thursday 23 September

We fly from Addis to Axum. The flight is a revelation. Most think of Ethiopia as a land of poverty and starvation – a desert. But it is a place of beauty – or at least the northern part over which I am now flying. It's magical. Steep mountains thrusting up from plains coloured with a beautiful palette of pale greens, dark yellows and brown, deep gorges, mystical and isolated plateaus seemingly inaccessible to man, meandering rivers – and everywhere fertility, fecundity, and much more luscious green than I ever imagined. It's a paradise and, along with southern Mesopotamia, is one of the contenders for the site of Eden.

We land on a small airfield and drive into town. We bump along the dusty road, people straggle each side, some carrying huge bundles on their back or heads, a few leading heavily burdened donkeys and mules. There appear to be no carts or carriages – no wheeled transport on the road except occasional motor vehicles. Strange – the land may be one of natural beauty but there is serious poverty here, want, almost despondency.

We reach Axum and check into our hotel. I want to get to the cathedral as quickly as possible – to find the shrine, to sound things out and, if possible, start negotiations for entry. We walk to the cathedral and, on the way, collect a swarm of young men all anxious to sell trinkets. Indeed they are most insistent, in the most charming way possible, that it is absolutely essential that we purchase their wares. It seems to be incumbent upon us, our duty. Perhaps it is – but most of the things on offer are truly dreadful. I stride ahead. We enter the compound in which the cathedral stands and the hucksters fall away and we are besieged by beggars, some most genuinely distressed and unfortunate. Money is dispersed, thanks and smiles given, and we move on, along a path. At its end, sitting in a sentry box, is a guard, in a sort of uniform that is mostly disguised below a large shawl. He looks exhausted but hauls himself out to question us, picking up an aged and somewhat rusty-looking AK-47 assault rifle. This man might look relaxed – indeed virtually asleep – but he has the power to hurt. And his job is vital – he is guarding the pride of the nation. As he ambles towards us I notice, over his shoulder, what I have

The Holy of Holies, the shrine – what is claimed to be the resting place of the Ark of the Covenant in Axum, Ethiopia. It is an unlikely building, relatively modest and topped by a rather mean-looking Islamic-style onion dome.

Street scenes in Axum, Ethiopia. I am charmed by the brightly coloured houses and friendly children.

been looking for. In front of us is the low and ancient church of St Mary, a structure distinct from the new and showy cathedral. And I know the shrine of the Ark is near St Mary's.

Samson explains our mission to the guard. He says in a rather matter-of-fact way that we wish to speak to someone in authority – a senior priest preferably, or monk – about viewing the Ark of the Covenant. He makes it sound as if we're on a humdrum sort of mission, nothing very special really, we've just popped across to see God's long-lost gift to man – do you mind opening up, there's a good fellow? Well, it's a tactic, it might even work. He says he'll see what he can do – and as he stands there doing nothing, another victim appears. This time we strike lucky. He is an official in the church – his name is Mezemer Kokeb Sadok – and he explains the situation to us. Yes, the Ark of the Covenant – the Ark brought back to Ethiopia from Jerusalem about 2950 years ago – is in the shrine opposite us. How can we get to see it, I ask with an air of innocence. You can't, he replies. We are talking in stilted English with Samson helping out so there is a lot of room for misunderstanding and manoeuvre. No, I say, you don't understand. I want to know how we can manage to see it, we have come a very long way. You can't, he replies. I register dismay and deep shock – both at once – and, I think, innocent disbelief. We can't, I splutter, what do you mean? This decent man then takes the trouble to explain in detail. The Ark is in the shrine. No one can see it – not the President of Ethiopia, not the Queen of England, not the President of the United States – not you, no one. It is guarded by a single monk, he lives in the shrine and the Ark will tolerate only his presence. He lives in there until he dies and on his deathbed he will name his successor. That's it. I goggle, what's my spiel going to be? I ask if there is a senior priest or monk I could talk to. The chap says yes and that he is most happy to conduct me to him, but he will want to be paid for his time. I'm a little surprised but agree and so off we go. To my astonishment this visit entails a car journey. Evidently this important cleric does not live on site. We clatter through the town and nose down impossibly picturesque side streets lined with mud-built houses painted in beautiful hues of blue and ochre. In these streets cattle and goats wander around and bright-eyed children play, watched over by mothers, their heads draped in light, white cotton shawls and many with huge blue crosses tattooed on their foreheads and between their eyes.

Eventually we stop in front of a house – the home of the high priest. Children are hanging around in front of the door, women look at us from the windows. It all seems a little unlikely, but we are strangers to the customs of this land, who knows? But where is the priest? No one is sure – and then a man of middle years comes into view, driving home his sheep and cattle. This is him? Apparently so. Things are getting odder still –

we shrug at each other and wait. Our helpful man from the shrine asks the priest if he will talk to us. He agrees, but insists that we give him time to change into his priestly attire. We do and within a few minutes are ushered into the yard. As we approach the door to the house our priest bursts out – now clad in a voluminous white robe and turban – and, with glittering eye, utters in a curiously deep and Transylvanian voice a greeting that proves memorable: 'Welcome, welcome…welcome to Axummmm.'

This is the full extent of his English so we stand on the porch and have a three-way conversation with Mezemer from the shrine acting as translator. We get nowhere. I don't seem to be getting the answers to the questions I'm asking. I try to end on a positive note. Can we meet by the shrine tomorrow to continue the discussion. No. Why? Because I never go to St Mary's. What – but you're the high priest, aren't you? Of course he's not. He's a choirmaster, and when I note down his name – Likee Mezemer Sadok Fischa – I discover that he's the father of Mezemer, the man who brought us here. We smile at this mild deception. I suppose he could have helped us. We pay the modest fee requested and the fellow chants a beautiful song about Solomon. We stand in the twilight in the yard and listen, with the beasts and children gathered round. Yes, it's worth every penny – and there's always tomorrow.

52 THE AXUM STELAE

Friday 24 September

We postpone our pursuit of the Ark of the Covenant and go to investigate my real treasure in Axum – the mighty and enigmatic stelae. In such a humble setting these tall, heroic and perfect ancient structures are utterly unexpected, amazing. They look indeed like objects that have wandered in from another world – certainly another age. There is one that really impresses me – a monster, fallen now and shattered, it must be all of 30 metres long and weigh 500 tonnes. What people could have carved, transported and erected this massive single stone? What engineering and technical skills – what audacity. It is assumed these stelae are the work of the Kingdom of Axum that arose in the 4th century BC, grew rapidly to be a power that vied with that of the Greece of Alexander the Great and the Eastern Roman Empire, reached a peak in the 3rd and 4th centuries AD and, then, in mysterious circumstances, declined in the 7th century and fragmented, with other centres in Ethiopia, like the Christian kingdom at Lalibela, rising as regional powers. But the kingdom of Axum had nearly 800 years of glory and these stelae are, it seems, its most powerful visual memorial.

Beyond being evidence of a once technically advanced civilisation operating in this region no one knows much about them. Did these stelae once stand in isolation, marking a sacred site? Did they – cut in fine stone, monuments to the permanence of the gods – rise in stark contrast above the transitory city of man, made out of mud and timber? If myth is true these monuments should be Christian. The Ethiopian Orthodox Church sees itself as the fountainhead of the three great monotheistic religions – Judaism, Christianity and Islam – the fusion of many of their doctrines, and with a history stretching back at least to Solomon. But historical evidence found so far suggests that if Christianity was followed in Ethiopia as early as the 4th century it was confined to the royal household and the nobility and only became a popular religion during the late 5th century following the arrival of nine Syrian missionary monks.

So these stelae, if their speculative dating is correct, could stand on the cusp of change, at the end of the age of the old gods or on the brink of the new Christian age. It makes them particularly fascinating and rewarding to study. It seems that, at least in some key details, they are pre-Christian. For example, they feature carved discs, rather like those

Evidence of a once technically advanced civilisation, little else is known about these mysterious stelae or monolithic obelisks at Axum. The site is packed with them, some standing, most toppled. This most striking stela stands 21 metres high, weighs 150 tonnes and is covered with abstract carved images suggesting windows, or crosses. At the base is a false door.

I saw on the entablature of al-Deir in Petra. Do these solar discs imply that the stelae are to do with the worship of the sun? Their orientation also suggests this, for the fronts of all the stelae here face south and so confront the sun on its daily journey across the sky. And some stelae are crowned by a carved stone of an unusual but compelling form. It's a crescent or semi-circle supported by two quadrants. It could well be a solar image and, intriguingly, is much like the Egyptian hieroglyph for sunrise, which is a semi-circle placed over the bottom corners of a triangle or pyramid. Before the Christian cross started to appear on Ethiopian coins in the 4th century, they bore the disc and crescent symbol. It would seem that the crescents and the discs on the stelae are royal images – representing the sun god – from pre-Christian Ethiopian civilisation.

But Samson tells me what, by tradition, the people of Axum think this crescent shape means, indeed what the stelae mean. They think it looks like the dome of a penis and that all the stelae are in reality phallic symbols and to do with fertility. Perhaps they are, or to do with the worship of the Sun or of the dead – possibly all these things at once and so are monuments to the natural cycle of life, death and rebirth. What they don't seem to have to do with is Christianity.

If not Christian in origin do these stelae carry Judaic imagery? This would support the idea that the Ark of the Covenant, from Solomon's Temple in Jerusalem, was lodged nearby – in all its spiritual glory – when these stelae were carved and raised. I study them and wonder. Not as far as I can see. Perhaps this means the story of the Ark in Ethiopia dates from a period after these stelae were erected and not from nearly 3000 years ago – perhaps from as late as the 13th century when the *Kebre Negast* chronicling the story of the arrival of the Ark in Ethiopia seems to have been composed. This seems highly possible but as yet I can't be sure. I must continue to collect information, to look and listen.

In the afternoon I pursue this quest by returning to the shrine containing the Ark. I can imagine what is within – the Bible tells me what to expect. The Ark is a cubical box as broad as it is high with a length that is nearly half as long again as the breadth and height. To be precise it is one and a half cubits in breadth and in height and two and a half cubits in length or, to use modern measurements, a box approximately 75 by 75 by 125 centimetres, a proportion approaching that of the golden section. In I Kings 8:7, we are told that the Ark was guarded by cherubims that 'spread forth their two wings over the place of the ark'. Instead of celestial beings there is now an aged monk who, if he really is in that chamber day and night, must be going quietly insane.

I have an appointment to meet Mezemer Sadok, my friend of yesterday. This time he will, I am assured, bring a top man. At the appointed time my friend appears with a priest called Kese Berhane Wolde Gorgise. I start from scratch. Can I enter? No, and so it goes. But two interesting things emerge. I am forbidden entry not because it is the

Orthodox Church's policy to hide the Ark from mankind, but because it is protecting me from a terrible fate. If I approached the Ark I would be punished – the theory is that it would become invisible and unleash upon me its terrible power – I would be killed outright, probably incinerated. So now, bizarrely, I have to thank the priest for NOT letting me see the Ark. Also, to my amazement, I am told there are many exact copies of the Ark, which are placed in the Holy of Holies – the sanctuaries – of all Ethiopian churches. But these have each been blessed by a bishop, have been consecrated, and so have the powers of the authentic Ark or tablets, and are venerated by the people as almost living things. Even seeing one of these could prove fatal. This is confusing – so many near-nuclear devices standing around in the churches of Ethiopia? Surely not. But the game's not over. I may not be able to see the original Ark but perhaps I could yet see a copy.

We walk back to our hotel and as we leave the cathedral compound something strange happens. A young man approaches Samson, they talk for a moment and then Samson explodes into fury, shouts at the fellow and belabours him. Apparently he had offered to sell us a small-scale reproduction of the Ark – a sort of tourist trinket – and this provoked, in Samson, the violent response I witnessed. I can only assume that Ethiopians believe that to see – let alone possess – even one of these replicas can be dangerous. Even they can have power. Golly – I must keep my eyes peeled – one of these scale models could be as near to the Ark as I'm going to get.

This evening we talk it through over a wholesome Ethiopian meal. I notice Samson asking for awzea – a paste made with chilli, onions, garlic and ginger – to go with his already burningly hot meat. The fellow's like a dragon. I ask him if all Ethiopians want to fill their bodies with fire. He roars and tells me of a yet more potent dish called kekela, made with boiled lamb – preferably meat from the leg – chilli, onion, ginger and butter. It's very good for 'jiggy, jiggy', Samson tells me. I don't have to ask what he means because the euphonious words are accompanied by explanatory physical movements. 'The girls say you burn me,' bellows Samson. Yes, Samson likes his meat, and he likes it hot. He's a good man.

53 ILLUMINATED MANUSCRIPTS OF DEBRE DAMO

Saturday 25 September

Today I continue my quest for the Ark, for the origin and meaning of the stelae, by going on a pilgrimage. We are travelling to the mountain-top monastery of Debre Damo – said to date from the 5th century and so to be the oldest monastery in Ethiopia, and to possess the country's oldest church, dating from the 6th century. In this monastery is an ancient library, paintings and learned monks that could help me with my search. In particular I want to examine a very early – perhaps the original – copy of the *Kebre Negast* that is lodged at Debre Damo. But there are a number of problems. The monastery is near the border with Eritrea and relations between Ethiopia and Eritrea – which declared its independence from Ethiopia in 1993 and took the nation's coastline with it – remain very tense. The border is in effect a military zone in which violence occasionally flares and where troops from both sides go on aggressive patrols. We will have to be cautious. But the real problem is the library and the monks. There was recently a fire and some books were destroyed – it is not clear which. And access to the monks is limited – sole entry to the monastery is via a rope dangling down a 20-metre slab of vertical cliff. If the monks don't want us all they have to do is pull the rope up.

With these concerns on my mind our little convoy of two vehicles makes its way north through an astonishing landscape. It's like driving through an enchanted country – a

Left *The 6th-century church at Debre Damo. The library at the mountain-top monastery tells the story of Christianity in Ethiopia. It contains an amazing collection of illuminated manuscripts and books.*
Right *Access, however, is for men only. I make it up the 20-metre cliff face in a rope-pulled harness; and find descending is just as tricky.*

fairyland. Miniature mountains with near vertical sides and serrated tops – the sort a child would draw – thrust themselves up from the plain, singly, in bizarre pairs or in groups. But the roads are getting steadily worse – soon they will be no more than tracks. We start to climb up towards the mountains and wind along narrow roads through high passes. The views are spectacular and then, in the distance, I see our destination – a squat, flat-topped mountain, an amba as they are called in Ethiopia. It is still an hour or so away.

The story of this monastery is, essentially, the story of Christianity in Ethiopia. Christians here hold sacred their 'Nine Saints', the Syrian missionaries who came to the country in the 5th century and spread the court religion of Christianity among the people. One of these missionaries – perhaps the most charismatic – came to Debre Damo and founded the monastery we hope to visit. His name was Mikael Aragawi – now known in Ethiopia as Abu, or father, Aragawi – and his legendary route to the top of this inaccessible plateau is almost predictable. The serpent – the earth spirit, the bridge between this world and the next, familiar from Aboriginal and Hindu theology – appeared to Abu Aragawi and it was by climbing up the length of this prodigious creature that he reached the plateau. This became Abu Aragawi's heaven on earth and, for many Ethiopians, it remains the most sacred site in their country, one of the most sacred in the world.

Soon we are below our amba, which rises 2200 metres above sea level. All we have to do now is negotiate our way up to the plateau on which the monastery is located. In fact this stage is not a problem. The monks wave us up – clearly this is the etiquette here. Climb first and talk later. The ascent looks tough. The 20 metres that has to be ascended is indeed vertical with only a few toe or handholds. But fortunately the monks have a tried and tested solution. They lower down a leather harness and, safely bound in this, visitors make the ascent, secured and assisted by monks pulling from above. We all want to go up but, to her dismay, Andrea is forbidden. Nothing female – not even female animals – are allowed on top. Poor Andrea. She had to put up with being forced to wear a scarf in Iran and now, again, she is a victim of a male-dominated religion that views women with suspicion. It's very bad. As we console her the leather harness descends, I am tucked into it and off I go. Actually it's quite difficult. At first I try to climb using the handholds but that is a mistake, for as soon as I get my hand or foot in place I'm pulled up by the monks. This leaves me dangling in space – most uncomfortable and undignified. But I quickly grasp the technique. Embrace the odd situation, trust the monks and harness, lean back and, well, as far as possible enjoy it and walk up the mountainside. I am quickly at the top, grappled by a group of aged, smiling monks, and

pulled through a door of sorts onto solid ground. We all make the ascent successfully –
and not too painfully – and Samson puts our case. Yes, we can visit the library and talk
to the monks. All seems well. However we are taken not to the library but the church.
Confusing – but fascinating. I enter the oldest church in Ethiopia, and in the shallow
narthex talk to a monk. Like many of my conversations with Ethiopian clerics it is
somewhat baffling but the conclusion is that the *Kebre Negast* can't be seen – whether
because it is somewhere else, has been burnt, does not exist or just simply cannot be seen
never becomes absolutely clear.

As we talk I look around and there, beyond the small nave and through a narrow
opening in the curtains, I see a huge heavily draped object lurking in the dark shadows
– an Ark of the Covenant. Dare I ask? No, stick to the books. Finally the monk agrees
to let me see a very special book – the best book in the library – that, he says, is over
1000 years old. The text, on parchment, is handwritten – in the Ethiopian Ge'ez
language – and there are numerous painted illustrations. The book seems to be an
example of a favourite Ethiopian type dealing with the Glory of Mary. She and the infant
Jesus are illustrated in a charming manner along with a rather startling image of what, I
assume, is God and, more curious, several of those enigmatic Ethiopian images that seem
to refer to pre-Christian beliefs. There are Suns with smiling faces – angels, I am told –
and even humanoid squares. Could these, I wonder, be references to the spiritual power
of the cubical geometry of Solomon's Temple and of the Ark? No one is sure. I admire
the book, ask some questions and suddenly it is over. The book – a sacred thing, in its
way alive in the eyes of the monks – is snapped shut and taken back to its solemn place
of repose. How odd – a long journey out, a long journey back, and no more information
about either the Ark or the *Kebre Negast*. The book was interesting – I doubt 1000 years
old – but not what I was looking for, not the *Kebre Negast*. The sun is getting low and
we want to face the mountain passes before nightfall, so it is time to leave. Fascinating,
but all rather unsatisfactory, all rather confusing.

As we drive back to Axum I ask Samson why we are having such difficulties. Are
people hiding the truth from me, protecting the Ark and the secrets of their past and
religion from inquiring strangers? Silence for a bit then, confides Samson, Ethiopia is a
strange country – we live in the past. I know, I say, that's why I like it here so much –
history and tradition still alive, continuity. No, Samson cuts me short. We really live in
the past. In Ethiopia it's now 1997 not 2004 and, looking at my watch, he says that for
Ethiopians it's not 7.00 pm but really 1 o'clock in the morning because the day starts
when the sun rises and ends when it sets. When my watch says 6.00 in the morning it's
really 12 o'clock in Ethiopia. What? A strange tale unfolds. Ethiopia still uses the Julian
calendar – abandoned by other countries
centuries ago – so that it has a 13-
month year – 12 lunar months of 30
days plus one month of five or six days,
depending on the leap year. The Julian
calendar started seven years and 113
days after the Christian age, hence in
Ethiopia it's 1997 not 2004 – and the
113 days, Samson points out to me
with a significant stare, means that
New Year in Ethiopia falls on 11
September. Does all this answer my
question? Not really, but it does
perhaps help explain why Ethiopia is
such a magical place – wonderfully
out of time with the rest of the world.

*A book, in the
library at Debre
Damo, said to be
1000 years old;
not what I had
come to see, but
interesting
nonetheless.*

54 THE LALIBELA CROSS

Sunday 26 September

We have chartered a plane to fly us to Lalibela where a nationally important festival starts later in the day. I have two quests in Lalibela – two treasures. I want to see the new Holy Land – to see how Lalibela was conceived and re-created as the New Jerusalem by a pious Ethiopian monarch in the 12th century. I also want to see an object almost as sacred in Ethiopia as the Ark of the Covenant, an object that is God's direct gift to the 'Chosen People' of the land – the Lalibela Cross. And I mustn't miss this festival because this is the one time during the year when this precious and revered cross is displayed in public, in fact paraded through the streets.

We arrive over Lalibela and I see the New Jerusalem laid out below me. On each side of a meandering rocky gorge that could once have been a river are churches – many representing sacred sites in Jerusalem and the Holy Land, or dedicated to key figures like the Virgin and St George. But these churches are all most odd. Cut from the rock of the hills that rise on either side of the gorge, each sits in a hole in the ground – like the tombs at Petra, they are huge sacred sculptures rather than buildings. And the tiny gorge? I find it on my map as we pass over. It's called the Yordanos or, more familiarly, the river Jordan.

Lalibela is a homely sort of place. It might have been the New Jerusalem 800 years ago – the heart of a new Holy Land – but now it is decidedly a backwater. The road leading to the town is lined with humble structures, many of them the stalls of local traders hoping to sell trinkets – crosses, paintings and old family Bibles – to those coming to the festival. In the centre of the town there is a sort of informal square and this is the location of increasingly frantic activity and excitement. A huge bonfire is being constructed and this will form the focus of the main phase of the festival. People are bringing bundles of twigs, faggots and bunches of flowers to the bonfire – clearly its construction is a communal affair. It celebrates an important event in the evolution and establishment of Christianity – Queen Helena's search in the Holy Land for the true cross. Helena – the mother of Emperor Constantine who tolerated Christianity within the Roman Empire from AD 313 – is a key figure in the Oriental Orthodox Church and associated with its belief that Christ was a god and to be worshipped as had the gods of old. This view may not now seem exceptional to most people but it almost tore the fledgling Christian church apart in the mid-5th century. This interpretation was opposed by the Occidental Church of Rome and Constantinople which argued that, in fact, Christ had two natures – divine and human but in a single divine body. The schism has rumbled on through the ages, and when the people of Lalibela celebrate Helena's quest they are asserting their church's recognition of the true nature of Christ. Helena's search for the cross, so legend says, proved successful, and she also identified the sites of Christ's crucifixion and burial and upon them had built the Church of the Holy Sepulchre in Jerusalem. The celebration of this successful quest is held in Lalibela because part of the true cross in said to be kept in one of its churches, and it takes the form of a bonfire strewn with flowers in commemoration of the legend that Helena undertook her search by the light of bonfires and burnt incense as she prayed for divine assistance.

We stand and watch the pyre get higher and the crowd denser. There is a mounting air of anticipation. The day is drawing on. I ask if the fire will be lit soon. No – tomorrow. So the expectation is not prompted by an imminent kindling. I wonder what is about to happen. Then shouting supplies the answer. Behind me, within its

The Lalibela Cross, God's 'gift' to the Ethiopian people, is said to be made of solid gold, the decoration symbolising Christ flanked by the Twelve Apostles. I see it on the one day of the year it is paraded in the streets. The priest who carries it allows me to inspect it closely.

cutting in the ground, squats a huge church – Beta Medhane Alem, the largest rock-hewn
church in the world – from which now issues a procession of clerics, all gorgeously
attired. They stroll towards the bonfire in leisurely fashion, chatting, greeting members
of the crowd that gathers around them, some seeking shelter from the sun below
umbrellas. Some of these men exude power and intoxicating confidence – you can see
plainly what an authority they and their church are in this community, in this land. It's
fascinating to watch.

One chap – clad in fine clerical robes and hat – is almost swaggering, his face set-off
by a handsome pair of fashionable sunglasses. He seems to be drawing special acclaim –
I suppose it's his urbane self-confidence that attracts. But as I get nearer I see there is also
something else – the chap's carrying the near-legendary Lalibela Cross, said to be made
of solid gold. I thrust my way towards it – it's hard work, people swarm around the
priest. Other monks gather in groups and long tracts of scripture are read out, in
between readings a female choir sings, and men play instruments. And all the time the
crowd is building up. There's a good feeling – and tomorrow will be a public holiday
with, I am told, lots of eating and drinking. There's a carnival atmosphere about the
whole event.

I ask Samson to find out if it will be possible for me to interview the priest and have
a private moment with the cross – perhaps tomorrow when there should be more time.
But now I must grab the only chance I might have. I walk across the open space in front
of the bonfire and ask the striking priest for a blessing. He stares at me – I can't see his
eyes for his dark glasses so am not quite sure what sort of look he is giving me – and
then he points to his neck. He wants to see if I'm wearing a cross, whether I'm Orthodox.
I'm not, all I can think of saying is that I was born a Christian. He looks a little longer
– only a micro-second, sizing me up – and then breaks into a broad grin. With something
of the air of 'what the hell' he lowers the cross in my direction, I get a good eyeful, and
then I do what I have seen the other supplicants do. I ask its blessing with a silent prayer,
kiss it, and back away respectfully. And that's it – nothing to do now but think about it

all. The crowd goes on growing, the singing and readings continue but we retreat. The churches we will see tomorrow and, with luck, the priest.

As we walk back to our hotel we discuss the recent history of the Lalibela Cross. It's a curious one, already full of mystery and legend. In 1997 it was stolen from Beta Medhane Alem in very suspicious circumstances – suggesting some sort of inside job – and eventually turned up in Belgium. Some say customs officers, aware of the presence of something strange, found it in the bag of a returning tourist; others allege that the thief found it too disturbing an object to retain and orchestrated its return. So the cross was flown back to Addis Ababa where the authorities wanted to place it in the guardianship of a museum. But the cross would have none of it, making a nuisance of itself by causing accidents and the like, so the museum authorities were only too eager to send it home to Lalibela. What a good yarn. I could, I suppose, undertake some research to verify what really happened, but why? If this story is not true, then it should be. But perhaps – if he sees me – I'll ask the priest about it all.

Monday 27 September

Good news – the priest will see us, and bring the cross with him. We are meeting inside Beta Medhane Alem. It is dark, massive, plain. I sit and wait for the priest who is busy with a party of people. I observe the gloomy, cave-like space. Really, it's like nothing I've seen before – virtually everything here is the opposite to conventional building practice. This church was not constructed, it was carved – one great lump of stone that has been sculpted. Here structure does not create and define spaces. Instead spaces have been excavated to create and define structure. What is positive in conventional buildings is here negative. It's an amazing thought. The Bible makes it clear that it is the unseen world that is more important than the seen, the immaterial and spiritual that is more important than the material and worldly. 'Look not at the things which are seen, but at the things which are not seen for [they] are eternal' (II Corinthians 4:18).

I notice, to my amazement, that at least one window is in the form of the crescent that topped the stela in Axum – a semi-circle supported by two quadrants – and is virtually the precise negative image of the Axum crescent. What is made of stone on the stela is here space defined by the cut stone of the wall of the church. What message does this stone – in all likelihood a pagan Sun sign – carry in this Christian church? At the very least it implies a continuity between Axum and Lalibela, between the old religion and the new.

My mind is racing, but I am called to talk to the priest, Kese Gebze Getia Hargwoin – the guardian of the cross. He lets me inspect the cross very closely and tells me its history and of its power. It is 900 years old and is a gift of God to the people, it was given to King Lalibela. I gasp – from God to Lalibela. Yes, confirms the priest. My word! King Lalibela – after whom the town was named – is the powerful and inspirational monarch who reigned from the late 12th century and who conceived the powerful political and religious idea of declaring his realm the new Holy Land with his capital the New Jerusalem. Yes, of course he would have received a gift from God for his trouble. But can this object I'm staring at – a complex design typical of geometrical Ethiopian crosses – really date from Lalibela's reign? I ask of its powers. It is miraculous, answers the priest. It has the power to heal, to free people from fear and shame. Shame? How unexpected. I ask about the circumstances of the theft and the version I heard yesterday seems positively tame in comparison with what the priest tells me. According to him the cross was not apprehended by customs officials in Belgium but virtually brought itself home after causing justified mayhem in Addis when bureaucrats tried to impede its progress. Whatever the truth, it's home now where it belongs – a living thing, not a museum piece, and playing a key and positive role in the life of thousands of people – as it has done for centuries. It's a wonder to behold.

55 ROCK CHURCHES OF LALIBELA

Tuesday 28 September

Having seen the cross I must now see the New Jerusalem over which it presides. I walk back into town, to the 'river Jordan', before exploring the churches because, in its heyday about 800 years ago, Lalibela was a place of pilgrimage and there is a route, of sorts, to follow.

King Lalibela's vision is extraordinary – and still far from fully understood. Some churches could be as old as the 6th to 8th centuries and so were old structures that were adapted and incorporated to play a role in Lalibela's grand design. Some may have started life as houses or refuges. And then there are the deep trenches, cuttings and long and winding rock-hewn tunnels that surround and connect some of the churches and sacred sites. Some are, of course, the consequence of construction, the result of excavating the church from out of the ground. But many others are mysterious indeed. The remains of ancient defensive systems or pilgrimage routes that burrow through the sacred rock – avoiding the profane surface paths trod during daily life – to allow pilgrims to move from church to church in a state of uninterrupted religious ecstasy?

King Lalibela's creation of this new Holy Land seems to have been as much a political action – to legitimise his reign and dynasty and secure him in power – as an act of divine homage. The great kingdom and empire of Axum had finally fragmented and some of its power, customs and prestige seem to have come here. But Lalibela didn't have that symbol and attribute of kingship – the Ark of the Covenant. The Axumite kings, according to the *Kebre Negast*, claimed their right to rule through their descent from Solomon's son Menelik I and that gave them, through Solomon, a lineal connection to the House of David and, ultimately, to Christ. They not only ruled by divine right, they were divine rulers. All King Lalibela had to do was to give his land the necessary attributes and himself and his dynasty the necessary pedigree to make him the new Solomon and his capital the New Jerusalem. The mechanism by which Lalibela did this can be seen in paintings plastered over the walls of most tourist shops in the country. There sits Solomon flanked by two women, each carrying a baby. One is Sheba with

St George's Church is carved into and from the surrounding rock. It has a series of Greek crosses within each other on top. The precision required to build this church is remarkable.

Left *The beautifully executed windows are a feature of Beta Maryam.*
Centre *In Beta Golgotha, another rock-cut church nearby, there are, to my surprise, life-size carvings of saints on the walls.*
Right *At last I see an Ark of the Covenant.*

Menelik and the other is Sheba's maidservant, dressed as an Agew woman from the Lalibela region, and it is from her son, so the story goes, that the Zagew Dynasty is descended. As simple as that, and so was established a continuity of sorts with Axum and a direct connection to the royal and sacred fountainhead of Solomon.

I arrive at the Jordan and here King Lalibela's sacred world – his Holy Land – divides. On the north bank is the re-creation of the physical, terrestrial Holy Land. The churches include the Beta Maryam and Beta Golgotha. On the south are churches that represent the celestial, spiritual Holy Land. In addition there are sites marking other holy places – the Mount of Olives, Bethany, Mount Tabor and Bethlehem.

In addition to the ten Holy Land churches – made or remodelled by King Lalibela, some as free-standing monoliths others little more than embellished caves – his widow created one more, as a memorial to the king after his death in about 1220. This is St George – and this is the church I'm really longing to see.

But I restrain myself and begin my journey by going first to Beta Maryam. In the east wall of the church have been cut a dazzling array of windows – sculptural, geometric, beautiful. They light the Holy of Holies in which the energised copy of the Ark is placed. Ah – the Ark. Who knows. The windows are linked to form vertical compositions with, from bottom to top, a square window with thick stone tracery in the form of a Maltese cross, a squat semi-circle-topped Axum window, an oblong window with stone tracery in the form of a Latin cross and, at the top, a simple square window. How extraordinary this array of different crosses must look from within, what strange light they must give. I go inside – but the power of the windows is swamped by the power of the paint, the dark, rich and sombre colour. Much is damaged and faded but I spot, high up, Mary on a donkey, accompanied by Joseph and the Annunciation. But, good as these are they are conventional – to be expected. Other details are not. There is the six-pointed star of the Star of David or the Seal of Solomon embracing a Maltese cross, representing Jewish and Christian doctrines combined and, most intriguing, a yellow disc with a smiling human face – the Sun – flanked by eight-spoked wheels or chakras that are Hindu or Buddhist in feel.

I move on to Beta Golgotha, and receive a shock. The walls are embellished with life-size bas-reliefs of saints carved into the walls. They are powerful pieces of art and incredibly rare in Ethiopia where, as in Islam, figurative art was avoided in religious buildings. Why are these permissible here? No one knows And why are there not more bas-reliefs elsewhere? As I ponder this puzzle I suddenly notice something momentous.

This church contains the tomb of King Lalibela. Standing over the tomb is a large bulky object draped in a heavy yellow cloth. An Ark of the Covenant. I approach it, so does a priest who is prowling nearby. Before I can advance again he orders me to retreat. I do, and goggle from afar. A step nearer – but still I haven't got my hands on one of the things. Perhaps tomorrow.

I make my way through town, through the deep cuttings and tunnels, and eventually arrive in front of the church. Well, in front is not quite correct. I arrive on a piece of sloping rock above the town and find the roof of St George's at my feet. The church stands in a 20-metre deep hole in the ground, the cutting from which it was excavated. It is a remarkable site, a Greek cross in plan, with the upper face of each arm of the cross more or less square in plan and equal in size to the square that forms the roof over the centre of the church and from which the arms of the cross radiate. It's like one giant cube laid flat. I've seen such drawings in Ethiopian bibles – five squares arranged in the pattern of a Greek cross and each square containing a human face. I suddenly see it, this church, apparently the last created here, is the culmination of Lalibela's heady enterprise to create the new Holy Land and to establish his family as the new Solomonic dynasty. St George's – in its abstract way and perhaps executed by his widow to help secure the family in power – is the new Temple of Solomon, the New Jerusalem. It's a Greek cross in plan but a mighty cube in spirit – and the Book of Revelation explains the meaning of vast cubes: 'And I saw...the holy city, New Jerusalem, coming down from God out of heaven...and the City lieth four square and the length is as large as the breadth...the length and the breadth, and the height of it are equal...'. New Jerusalem is a geometrical concept – a huge, perfect cube.

I ponder the difficulty of carving a thing of such geometrical precision and symmetry, and with no possibility of correcting a mistake. The workmen first had to conceive it in its every aspect, plan carefully, excavate the basic form of the church – this huge cross – and then, with patience, stamina and great care had to carve into this form to create volumes and details. Miraculous, this great sculpture – in which art, theology and function combine so brilliantly – is a treasure indeed.

I clamber down a steep ramp and enter the base of the cutting from which the church rises. Ancient burial chambers are cut into the rock face all around me and not all are empty. I pass one to see a skull poised, rather theatrically, at its entrance, and the soles and toes of mummified feet. Extraordinary. Then I enter the church. It is very plain. A priest, who is standing in front of the curtain screening the Holy of Holies, is happy to show me his books and charming paintings – of the Virgin and, naturally, St George.

As we exchange nods and pleasantries and get on famously I notice a large wooden rectangular chest, lying longwise, in the shadows of one of the arms of the cruciform church. Looks like a vestry chest, I think. What can it be? Can it be...? I walk quickly towards it, the priest follows. I ask him what it is, he answers by unscrewing a huge wooden shaft, with a beautifully cut thread, from the top of the chest. It's an ancient locking device, clearly used for securing the lid and protecting what was placed inside. I look at the priest, he smiles politely at me. Dare I touch; he raises no objection. I lay my hand on the ancient wooden surface of the chest, I scrutinise it closely – yes, the side boards are square, it is as broad as high, I use my forearms and fingers to measure off the lengths in cubits. Yes, it is. It is an ancient Manbara Tabot, an Ark of the Covenant. I manage to open it and look inside – there are no tablets of the law, no Tabots – no secrets here of what was and what will be, no divine and immutable laws of beauty and creation. Just a little dust; how very sad.

What has happened, why has this once sacred vessel lost its power, why has it been pensioned off and left to lurk in the corners of this church? No one can tell me. Perhaps no one living knows. But I have found what I have been looking for. I have seen, I have touched, an Ark of the Covenant.

WATER AND LIFE

56 DJENNE MOSQUE, MALI

Saturday 2 – Sunday 3 October
We leave the hotel in Bamako, Mali, at 6.00 in the morning to board a charter plane that will take us to Mopti. It's a good flight and eventually we see the legendary river Niger. Around it all is fertile – particularly so at this time of year when water is plentiful – with flood plains stretching far from each of the river's banks. It's hypnotic to follow the meandering course of this great waterway, particularly since water and the life it brings are the theme of this portion of my journey. Yes – here water is life.

We land and drive to Djenne. Now we are introduced to the buildings of the region. Water not only brings life and prosperity – but also architecture. The buildings are made of mud. Or, to be more precise, sun-dried clay mud bricks covered with a coat of clay-based render. Water for all this is, of course, essential. The forms these buildings take are deeply satisfying – thick walls, undulating and organic – but often with surprisingly delicate and well-judged detail. The Friday Mosque in Djenne is made in this manner – said to be the largest mud-built structure in the world.

Djenne was once a key location on a great and ancient trade route through Mali, but is now a small and dusty provincial town in which the buildings are virtually all of traditional clay mud construction. Outside a small mosque boys sit in the shade, learning and reciting prayers. Girls, dressed in vivid colours – startling seen against the dung-colour of the mud walls – pass by, selling creamy white milk. Goats are corralled in pens, asleep, or wander the streets. The streets and alleys I pass have surfaces of beaten mud, and down one flows an open drain that carries still and stagnant water of a beautiful dark green colour. Walking through these streets is like walking back into another, more ancient world – a world we all came from. It almost brings back memories.

Mali is a fascinating land – once the heart of a great African empire that stretched to the west coast of the continent, it was evangelised by Muslim missionaries and traders during the 13th century and by the 14th century was a key part of the Muslim and Arab world, with strong trade connections to the north and east – connections maintained and developed by inland rivers, like the Niger and its tributaries. But the empire fragmented, imploded, there were incursions and conquests from all sides and finally it was gobbled up, along with much of north and west Africa, by the French during the 19th century. However, people here have the memory of Mali's days of greatness, its centuries of culture, wealth, power and independence.

After lunch we walk to the Friday Mosque. It's a mighty and impressive affair – a double cube in shape with a series of bastion-like towers that carry minarets, all well over 10 metres high. It has an elemental quality, its forms abstract and timeless – an incredibly powerful presence. The walls of the mosque are smooth, but undulate slightly in an organic, almost sensuous way and are pierced by rows of protruding palm tree trunks. Called torons or horns, these act as permanent supports for scaffolding, for all mud buildings require frequent and regular maintenance as a way of life. With it they will last indefinitely, without it they will rapidly wash away and crumble in the

The life-giving river Bani at Djenne, a tributary of the river Niger – I can see how, over centuries, the course of these rivers has changed dramatically as it found new and more convenient paths across the plain. Foundations of once large riverside towns, now a long way inland, were consigned to oblivion when the river moved.

rains. So, after each rainy season – sometimes more often – workmen dangle from these poles and give the mosque a new mud-based skin.

The first mosque was built here in the 13th century by King Koy Konboro immediately after his conversion to Islam. So enthusiastic was the king about his new religion that he demolished his own palace to make way for his mosque. But what I see before me is not King Koy Konboro's pioneering and great Friday Mosque, although it stands on its site. The original mosque fell into ruin after a petty Islamic fundamentalist called Sekou Amadou seized power in the region in 1819. He was shocked by the way the ancient mosque was being used by the community of the town, it was too worldly for his liking – it stood in the market place and people danced and drank millet beer on its very threshold. Amadou decided the mosque was defiled beyond saving and in 1834 had a new mosque built a little to the east. But Amadou's mosque also fell out of favour. The Koran specifically forbids the demolition of mosques but, for mysterious and dark reasons, both of Mali's early mosques were destroyed. No one suggests that the present Friday Mosque, built in 1907, incorporates any fabric of the 13th-century mosque, although it is possible that its plan reflects the original.

While I contemplate and consider all this, I wait. Ousmane, our fixer, is having great trouble getting us in so we wander off into the town – implored from many quarters to purchase a whole spectrum of goods, including carved wooden masks. I see a shaman selling his wares by the road – spells, potions, medicines for most things. There are dried roots and sticks, bags of herbs, the feet and legs of long-dead and desiccated dogs, lizards' heads and parts of sundry other creatures. The chap is very helpful. He asks my ailment. I say I am a little anxious and tired, he nods and gives me a small bag, to be taken mixed with water. I thank him, pay and walk away. God – what on earth can it

The mud-built Friday Mosque at Djenne was built on the site of the original 13th-century mosque in 1907. The thick earth walls and small windows keep the interior cool during the day – they are about 2 metres thick.

The exterior walls of the Djenne mud buildings are protected by render – lots of it and often applied. Boys carry tubs of render up to the roof. The plasterer (left) stands on protruding palm logs (right) to apply the plaster to the face of the building.

be? Toads' legs, I speculate. I look inside. Just dried leaves – Ousmane inspects them and declares them very good. We should, he says, consume them later.

Then the decision. We are in – but we have to go now and we only get ten minutes. Ousmane implores us to move fast – I can see he has taken the challenge of getting us in very personally, his honour is at stake. It's easy to react to a complex building you have never seen, but quite difficult to explore and explain it cogently, especially when working under such terrible time pressure. Anyway, I have a go. The interior is incredibly crowded. Not with people – there are just a few men sitting or sleeping on the carpeted floor. No, it is crowded with huge square piers, closely packed to create a very mysterious, gloomy and cave-like interior. The atmosphere is remarkable. Tranquil, of course, in comparison with the market outside. Not only is building with sun-dried clay brick and mud very economic and ecologically sound – no valuable resources or non-replaceable sources of energy are consumed – but also very functional and appropriate in a hot climate for it keeps it cool during the day. But at night, the heat stored in the walls can also make it stuffy. I look up, and in the centre of the ceiling between each cluster of columns is a hole – ventilation. How are they opened, I ask? From the roof, I am told. Is there time to go up and see? Our minder is hesitant – perhaps he's just trying to remember the word 'no' in English, because our ten minutes is up. But we take this delay for a 'yes' and hurtle up the staircase.

There are three minarets, and now I can see something I hadn't noticed from ground level. On each sits a large, egg-shaped object – ostrich eggs. They must be memories of the old, pre-Islamic religions of the country, signifying plenty and fertility. The mosque is a wonderful marriage of traditional building practice with Islamic conventions – the whole culture of the country is a creative fusion. Things have changed little since the 14th century. Tomorrow we're off to see the Dogon people, where the old values and rituals survive – and thrive, I'm told – represented through dance and the making of sacred masks.

Later on Nick and I go for a walk to investigate the masks we saw on sale earlier. In and around the town centre – in shops and on stalls – there are literally thousands for sale. Mask making is clearly quite a national industry and obviously most are made for tourist sales or export. But among the many modern blank-faced, brass inlaid and characterless tourist masks I see some that could perhaps have been used in sacred dance or hung in sacred places. I talk to the owner of one stall about what I'm looking for and he takes us to his storeroom nearby. We enter and are met with an astonishing sight. As the light goes on score upon score of masks are staring at us. We stare back. They are made by many different tribes – Bambara, Malanquit. I select some. They only cost a few dollars each but a lot of intense bargaining goes on – it's the custom and, anyway, I've got used to it. I don't know if the masks are old or authentic – or even if they are what the chap tells me they are – but they are individual, very different to the mass-produced samples I have seen, and each has character. Some sprout exuberant and extravagant horns – male fertility gods. They're to give Hannya – my horned Japanese female No mask – some company.

Before leaving we have one last walk around Djenne. I happen to see a mud-built house being repaired. This is a good opportunity to find out a little more about this ancient, traditional building technique. The bricks are firm to the touch, but heavy and still full of moisture. Although their surface is hard they wouldn't last long in the rains without protection. This finishing coat is amazing stuff. I stick my hand in one of the buckets and grab a handful. I rather wish I hadn't. It absolutely stinks – clay, some straw or rice husks – and dung. The mix is allowed to go off for a couple of weeks before it is used so it's pretty rank by the time it gets to the building site. I look from the roof top, and as far as the eye can see, to the mosque and the river in the distance – all is mud-built. Wonderful.

57 THE DOGON MASK, BANDIAGARA

Monday 4 October

Early in the morning we drive some hours to the Dogon country to meet our Dogon hosts – to learn about them, their masks, and to see them dance. We have another fixer with us as well as Ousmane. His name is Boukhari – and he is a Dogo. This will, we trust, make life easier. We arrive at the village, which has two parts – a high and a low. Twins – pairs of related things – are sacred in the Dogon land, as in many other cultures – the Sun and the Moon, night and day, life and death.

The Dogon is an ethnic group located mainly in the Bandiagara district, numbering around 250,000 people. They are now, and have been for centuries, agriculturists growing crops and raising goats, cattle and poultry. What gripped me about the Dogon when I read their history is their creation story. It has so many similarities with the stories of other ancient peoples. They believe in a single god called Amma (a name uncannily close to the name of the great Egyptian god Amun) – who created the heavens, the stars and the planets. The earth he created in the form of a woman – so the Dogon conceived a Mother Earth, the great fertility and nurturing goddess. In union with Amma she bore the first sacred twins – the Nommo. Then Amma created a human couple from clay but they were hermaphrodites, with the foreskin being the feminine part of the man and the clitoris the male part of the woman. The foreskin and clitoris were removed making each a fine example of a single sex and it is because of this story that circumcision and clitoridectomy are still important rites of passage at puberty. This couple rapidly produced eight children – who are the original Dogon Ancestors. Having descended to earth on a rainbow, the seventh ancestor turned itself into a snake – the Lebe – reminiscent of the Aboriginal Rainbow Serpent Creation Ancestor.

The Dogon believe they were led to Bandiagara by Lebe and so for them this particular Ancestor has special meaning. As I walk through the village I see Lebes everywhere, adorning the mud-built walls of granaries and houses, carved on timber doors. Villagers are proud and pleased to show us their houses. I enter one small yard and see, in font of me, a mud-made honeycomb wall. It's a 'dead house' – a reception hall for dining feasts with the dead,

The Dogon masks can be decorated with shells but are predominantly painted red, yellow, blue, black and white, and many of the painted shapes are abstract, evoking elemental things that can't be shown in figurative pictures and likenesses.

The Dogon masks are living things; they are mostly of the large, robust, box-like sort with basic features – holes for eyes sunk in deep vertical grooves – with their individual character coming from the colours and patterns that appear to have been dashed over them, as if by someone in a trance.

with ancestors. This is incredible. The Dogon religion has to do with nature, the cycles of life, with fertility and crops, the spirits of the dead, the ancestors – things familiar from so many ancient religions – and now this dead house. My mind races back to the ancestor worship of Sulawesi, Indonesia with its spirit houses and to the Great Necropolis I saw at Petra, Jordan. Such compelling connections.

But what about our dancers? We go to find Boukhari and have a strange journey. In front of us lies a huge rock – a cliff really. At its base is the mouth of a long tunnel – presumably the work of nature – and at the end of this tunnel I can see a light. We walk towards it. There are children milling around – all girls – and as we get to the tunnel mouth they coalesce into a group – a choir – and start to sing. It's a traditional song of welcome, they are welcoming foreigners – white people – to Africa. I wonder how many meetings, between the people of Mali and Europe, this bright song has floated over – and I wonder how many of those meetings matched in warmth and honest intent the words these girls are now chanting so charmingly.

There are many types of mask in Mali and many types of Dogon mask, nearly 80 I hear – but the ones I am about to see in operation are very special. The Dogon elder who keeps me company tells me that these are too powerful to be handled and can only be seen during the dance, and then only at a great distance by women. Are they, I ask, in the likeness of things – do they represent things, are they symbols? The answer I get is riveting, uncompromising. The masks represent nothing, they are not symbols. They are the thing they show, with all its powers and attributes. Masks are living things. I'm taken aback. I've heard of 'Nyama' – the life force in masks – but never conceived of it in such direct and dramatic terms. What happens when they are not in use? It slumbers, he says. So there it is – this object, of wood, paint, fabric and feathers – imbued by ritual with Nyama – slumbering in its hiding place, its power present but latent and only to be awakened in all its elemental glory when a dancer puts it on – and then the mask gives the dancer its power, makes him perform the dance the mask dictates. My word – and this is the dance, the ritual, I'm about to see.

The time has come. We walk briskly to a clearing on the side of a football pitch. At one end of the clearing stands a row of elders, one with a drum and next to him an old chap with a stick. In the distance, on an outcrop of rocks that overlooks the clearing, sits a group of watching women. Suddenly the fellow with the stick starts to wail and his neighbour starts to beat his drum. The dancers are arriving – in small groups of two or three, more and more of them – all wearing a variety of masks, red raffia skirts, baggy black trousers and all bedecked with white shell beads. When each group nears the clearing – nears the beating drum – it seems to quiver, the dancers shake and arch themselves like cats, seem to throw off their bodily selves, let the mask take over; they leap, whoop, and gyrate across the field. When all are collected in a group, swaying, shaking, lowering and raising their masked heads, the dance begins in earnest. They form into a swirling line – like the writhing body of a snake I suppose – and dance in front of the elders – in front of us. All, as they move round and round defining a large circle, lift their knees high, beat the ground with their feet, suddenly leap bodily into the air and let up shrill cries. But all do other things as well. One pair of dancers has impossibly tall masts on top of their masks, each several metres high. As they dance they rhythmically raise their heads – so the masts seem to touch the sky – and then lower their heads so the masts rub clouds of dust from the ground. The dancers are clearly working themselves into a frenzy – the afternoon is hot, they are sweating, the enclosed and large wooden masks must be heavy and constricting – yet they dance on, the circle ever moving, they are indeed dancing to confirm the cycle of life, to quicken Mother Earth.

Finally the dance ends, and I am given permission to approach and talk to the dancers who stand, sweating and swaying, just coming back from their strange journey. I can barely make out their eyes through the slits of the mask. Are these the same young men who, just an hour or two earlier, were slouching around in Western clothes, trying to persuade me to buy their trinkets, wheedling and coaxing? One mask boasts a pair of huge goitres. What on earth can this mean? Ousemane questions the Hogon – the priestly chief – closely, this is clearly a little complex, and then tells me, rather primly, that it shows the 'social inclusion of handicapped people' in the ritual of the dance. Admirable. Then I meet the pair with the tall crests. They are 'levels of knowledge', explains the Hogon, the spiritual body going up to the sky – and they are also the snake, Lebe. Finally I come upon the men on stilts, with breasts strapped to their chests. I observe that women can't join the dance or even watch it from close by. Yes, he agrees, it is not for women to dance, but they have most important work to do. I now push my luck a little; I'd like to see where the masks are kept. No, says the Hogon, that is top, top secret. And with that, all is over. The dancers now leap into the air, whoop, shake their tufted masks, and are off. With rhythmic, swinging gait they make their way back to the material world – no doubt I will be meeting some of them again, very soon.

We go back to the hotel and are quickly surrounded by youths intent on selling their wares. I scrutinise them. They must be the dancers – who so recently were as gods. Then something troubling happens. I go into the hotel shop. It is packed with masks and I want to buy one more. I receive a shock, but for which I was partly prepared. While waiting outside I saw a young man enter the shop with something in a large yellow plastic bag – one of the masks from the dance, one with an antenna, one of the masks that I have just been told are too powerful to touch, that are stored in a top, top secret place. Now here it's in this shop, on display, for sale. What in heaven's name is going on? Do these masks have power or not, I demand of the slightly taken aback shopkeeper – why are you selling this? Yes, he says, the masks have power – just because they are in a shop doesn't mean they are dead, their power is just sleeping. Would it be bad luck for me to buy a mask used in the dance, I ask? No – you are a foreigner, it wouldn't matter for you. A kind of answer I suppose, but I am still in shock. Pointing to the one fresh from the dance, I ask him why is this one for sale? He ponders for a moment, and then says sadly that he supposes the family needs money. Money, of course, and this is how ancient cultures and beliefs die – gradually, with a whimper. Things once sacred, precious and priceless become a mere means of entering the material world. And, I realise, it's people like me who are to blame. Yes, I am the tempter – I am the demand that prompts the supply that gives the mask a monetary value. And, I'm sorry to admit, I do buy a Dogon mask – but not the one I saw in the dance, I wouldn't dare. The one I buy shows, the shopkeeper whispers to me, the Dead. And that night, in my little domed bedroom, I contemplate my dark prize, its power dormant. In the middle of the night I am woken by a loud crash. The room is pitch black but I see in front of me a circle of pale light – like a huge, plaintive, all-seeing eye. I fumble and find the light switch – a timber shutter has fallen out of the orifice that houses one of the round room's rather quaint porthole windows. Strangely, I find it difficult to get back to sleep.

At the shop near the hotel beside the Dogon village I am shocked to see one of the sacred masks from the dance for sale.

58 CIRCUMCISION PAINTINGS, SONGHO

Tuesday 5 – Wednesday 6 October
We leave at first light. At the village of Songho, not far from Bandiagara, are some Dogon rock paintings I want to see.

We stop by the village – a perfect place of cylindrical, conical-roofed, mud-built huts and cubical granaries – and climb to a grotto, scoured out of the cliff face. This site is used for the ritual of circumcision and, I hear, there are paintings here that could date back to the 13th century – when the Dogon were still nomadic. This, for them, is an ancient and sacred site, where generation upon generation of young men have passed from childhood to manhood, where they have learned the history of their people, have faced their gods. My guide from the village says the site is still used. Every third year boys come here, he says, aged between about 8 and 14, and they stay a month, being taught, initiated. I ask him if he came here. He says yes. Suddenly we reach the grotto and, on a wide and sweeping section of smooth rock face, is a baffling array of images, one painted over the other. Some could be old but others are obviously very new. My guide explains – the paintings are recoloured by the different groups, and new ones added. These paintings may, in some cases, be ancient but they are not museum items. To the Dogon who come here they are vital and alive – a repository, a record, to keep alive, to enrich with their own experiences.

Many of the images on the wall are by now familiar – the sinuous Lebe, masks with aerials, a face with horns, strange lizard-like creatures and hundreds of renderings of pouches holding medicines and spells. I suppose these creatures and pouches are tribal symbols. Extraordinary – it's like a site from a culture long dead, like ancient cave art, but many of these images were made, virtually, yesterday, and they still bear the meaning that they have had through the ages. As the Dogon say, when a man dies, with his memories and stories, it's like burning a library. These paintings are a way of keeping memories and stories alive. But, I wonder gloomily as I make my way back to our vehicles, back to the tempting modern world, how long will these memories and stories last, how long will they retain meaning and power? It all seems terribly fragile – horribly under threat from the world that I inhabit, of which I am a part.

The circumcision paintings at Songho are extraordinary and remind me of ancient cave art, but most of them are relatively new and represent stories of the circumcised boys. Here the Lebe serpent writhes above tribal symbols.

59 LEPTIS MAGNA, LIBYA

Thursday 7 – Friday 8 October

Tripoli is an enthralling city. At its heart is the walled Medina – or old town – built next to the Mediterranean, complete with fortress, winding streets, small squares and souks. Beyond the walls is the sprawling modern city, a place of strange character – once an Italian dream town, the jewel of Rome's new 20th-century empire. There are baroque squares, palazzos and an absolutely huge domed cathedral. And then there is the architecture from the later period of Italian domination – from the Fascist years of the late 1920s and 30s. This produced long city-centre avenues – all furnished with spacious and sheltering arcades – of bold Classical design. The material – stones and marbles – are generous, the few details excellent. The 20th-century Romans may have proved inept and unlucky empire builders but, my goodness, they knew how to build delightful cities.

Tripoli, however, is not my treasure. We are here to see Leptis Magna – one of the greatest, most complete and most evocative ruined cities from the Classical world which lies on the coast just a little distance from Tripoli. The city has a long history – a history founded on water-borne trade. There was a Phoenician settlement on the site by the 10th century BC and it was a great trading centre under the control of Carthage as early as the 6th century BC. But the golden age of Leptis dawned in the early 3rd century AD, during the reign of Emperor Septimius Severus, when the population neared 80,000 people and it was the great gate through which commodities were traded between Africa and Europe. Leptis was by then a possession of Rome, part of the province of Africa and enjoying, since the early 2nd century, the status and numerous privileges of an official Roman colony. This was essential to its success but the key thing is that Septimius Severus, a protégé of Marcus Aurelius who reigned until AD 211, was a native of the city. He did all he could to make his home town great.

This I discover immediately on my arrival at the perimeter of the city. I leave the vehicles, walk a few hundred yards and then I come upon the mighty arch of Septimius Severus. After being finally abandoned in the 7th century the coastal sand drifted over the city and buried it so that what is now visible through excavation sits some feet below modern ground level. For this reason this imposing arch rises out of a shallow depression

The arch of Septimius Severus at Leptis Magna – most unusually for a Roman arch it includes four arches, one on each of its faces, rather than two, so it is really a quadruple gate, each opening framed by columns and commanding the crossroads.

in the ground – and so is not seen to its majestic advantage. But never mind – it is an original and impressive Classical design and it tells a fascinating story. The Decumanus Maximus passes through it – that is the main street of the city – as does the Cardo, the once column-lined main shopping street of the town that leads to the markets and, ultimately, the harbour. So trade – the lifeblood of Leptis – is honoured by the fact the main street of trade passes through a gate that is dedicated not only to the Emperor of Rome but also to one of its great gods. This is confirmed by a much damaged bas-relief that is placed within the arch. It shows the living emperor Septimius confirmed as a god – a concept still novel even to Rome – and he is shown in the form of the mighty Jupiter, seated and as if blessing the traders and shoppers as they pass along the Cardo.

Before walking along the Cardo I explore the portion of the Decumanus Maximus nearest the arch. It's peculiar, walking along this deserted street – thronged with people 2000 years ago and now a mere cutting through banks of wind-blown sand. Here the past seems very far away – until I reach a corner of the Decumanus and suddenly see a stone street sign as fresh and direct as the day it was carved. It shows a huge and erect penis – a mighty phallus – running along on legs. Romans, and people of the romanised world like these North Africans in Leptis, liked such fertility symbols. It's charming – suddenly I feel this slightly arid ruin coming alive. I like these people.

I return to the Cardo and stroll down it, towards the sea. I pass the remains of the merchants' exchange and then, on my right, is a large, 2000-year-old market square with the ruins of a pair of circular pavilions. In one of these cloth was sold, and the cloth measures still in evidence offer an insight into the different peoples who traded here. On the one stone are three scales – the Punic and Alexandrian cubits and the Roman foot. The cubit was a traditional linear measurement based on the human body – the length from the elbow to the tip of the middle finger – usually between one foot eight or nine inches or about 52 centimetres. I place my elbow at one end, extend my middle finger and, to my surprise, discover that my forearm and open hand measure exactly one ancient Punic cubit. So, with an arm of the perfect Leptis measure, I am really beginning to feel at home here. I feel that I ought to imagine myself as a citizen of Leptis, a merchant, and live a typical working day. So, I've been to the market, now I'll go to the bath to refresh myself, to the main forum and basilica – a great public building in which, among other things, law cases are heard – then to the harbour to check my cargo and, finally, to the theatre. In Leptis all this is still possible – albeit in a rather ghostly way – just as it was 1800 years ago. So, first, off to the bath.

I cut across the Cardo, greet a few friends, and then make my way to the huge public baths that were – and still are – one of the great wonders and ornaments of the city. A resident of Leptis might have lived in a small house or apartment but, if of sufficient status to be granted access to the bath, he lived like a king. These were the great social heart of the city and where, of course, in intimate and relaxed settings business deals could be hammered out. The existing baths were given to the city by the Emperor Hadrian in AD 126, just after the people of Leptis had built themselves a huge aqueduct to bring plentiful water to the city and, when complete, were the finest baths outside Rome. I walk past a huge rectangular exterior pool once surrounded by porticoes and colonnades and then enter the first hall of the baths. The light, filtering from above, would have been soft, mysterious, the atmosphere tranquil, reverberating just a little with the echo of the talk and laughter from the adjoining rooms and those using the small pools at either end. I wouldn't linger long here, but plunge into the hot room, the caldarium. This was barrel-vaulted and domed like a hammam – magnificent, but now much ruined. I notice the shattered recesses and wall areas, and see evidence of an extensive system of pipes carrying hot air and steam from furnaces and cauldrons in subterranean chambers. There are smaller side rooms – these were the laconica or sweat baths and, 1800 years ago, it would probably have been as hot here as the steam room

I endured recently in the hammam in Damascus. From these rooms, near-smoking bathers would have staggered back to the hot room to receive vigorous massage from muscled and expert masseurs. Now, to the cold room – a plunge in the pool to wake myself up – to the apodyteria to dress, and out.

Feeling much refreshed, I'm ready for business in the basilica, but if by sudden chance a bodily action has to be accommodated, the baths are furnished with a splendid public latrine – and public is the word, for around 30 people could use the room at once. It's a fine hall and, although only the seating now survives, it is enough to reveal how the room functioned. Below the elegant seats – essentially holes cut in long pieces of marble – is a large stone trough, while in front of the seats is a smaller stone trough. Water would have run through both constantly. The larger trough carried the bodily waste away in an instant, while the water in the smaller trough was used to cleanse a small brush that would be inserted in a convenient orifice cut below the latrine seat and used to scrub the buttocks. Public baths in Roman cities were generally used by both sexes but, fortunately, rarely simultaneously.

I leave the baths feeling like a new man and make my way to the forum – I have a court case to settle. Like so much of the monumental and public architecture of Leptis the New Forum, started in AD 203, was created by Septimius Severus. It is as much a monument to him, his family and their power as it is to the wealth and prestige of the city but, although a work of colossal vanity expressing worldly ambition, it is almost heartbreakingly beautiful, haunting. It was when new – and remains – one of the greatest pieces of city landscape in the world. I walk through heaps of carved stone and marble

Although in ruins, Leptis Magna remains one of the most impressive city landcapes ever created. The basilica of Septimius Severus is roofless and now a partly collapsed ruin, but still a magnificent building. The two apses on the short ends retain much of their decoration, including tiers of figures that tell two tales – one of Hercules, the other of Dionysius, the patron gods of the Severan family.

Left *A stone street sign at Leptis Magna – an image that brought good luck, a timeless token of plenty, of fertility.*
Right *The theatre at Leptis Magna is one of the best preserved in the Roman world. Its architectural scenery creates an impressive Classical world in miniature.*

– these ruins of a spectacular architectural dream – and pass the podium of a lofty temple that once presided over all this. This was its crowning glory – a cult temple dedicated to Septimius Severus and the 'genius' of his family and his divinity. At the height of the city's wealth the people of Leptis must have felt that they had it all – money, beauty, recognition and protection from the god-like emperor who was, after all, not just the most powerful man in the world, but one of their own, a local boy. It must have felt good to be in Leptis in about AD 210, just as this forum was being completed and Septimius still alive – you've have looked around and believed yourself at the centre of the world.

Opposite the temple is my destination – the basilica – which occupies one entire side of the forum. Basilicas were the most important public building of any Roman town or city containing law courts, public meeting rooms, shrines and even markets and exchanges. They were of a particular architectural form and have given their name to a type of plan with which anyone who has been inside a Western Christian church will be familiar. Basilicas – including this one at Leptis – are generally rectangular in shape, with apses at one or both of the short ends, with a nave running along the long axis that is divided from side aisles by a screen of columns or piers. I look around, glory in this sombre yet magnificent ruin, read its stones, experience its spaces, wonder which part the law courts would have occupied, and then move on.

One of the main reasons for the decline of Leptis was the silting-up of the harbour. I walk down to the quay where merchants' ships would have docked, to see the evidence of this creeping calamity that overtook the city. I pass the remains of great warehouses where the wealth of the world would once have been stored, on its way into or out of Leptis – olive oil, grain, wine, glass, textiles, slaves, wild beasts for the amphitheatres of the empire, gladiators too. Now silent, deserted.

But I shake off these morbid thoughts. For me the golden age of the city is not yet over. The year is AD 210, I have seen my ship come in, my fortune flourishes and I'm off to the theatre. I walk back into the city and then up to, and into, the theatre – one of the oldest, largest and best preserved anywhere in the Roman world. What I see in front of me, all around me – a massive semi-circular cascade of seats topped by small temples – was built over a period of years, much in the first year or two AD, with elements added or altered during the next 140 years or so. Here all the emotions were put on display – tragedy, comedy. It sounds so lofty which, in fact, mostly it wasn't. More often than not this haughty setting was home to the pantomimus, a most popular entertainment in provincial Roman cities and much like a modern day rumbustious costume musical. It's sunset, and the stone and marble of the ruins start to glow. The low evening shadows hide much of the desolation, and the fiery orange sun illuminates the standing columns with an eerie precision. Gaunt buildings, mere husks an hour ago, now appear whole and complete. It's as if the great city is stirring back to life, struggling to free itself from its sandy burial mound. We walk back through its empty streets, along the Cardo and through the arch. It's twilight now, that strange and magical moment when the world seems to stand still and when – in such a place as Leptis – the past, in all its vivid complexity seems, for a fleeting moment, to become almost visible, almost tangible.

60 BERBER GRANARY, QASR AL-HAJJ

Saturday 9 October

Today we are in quest of a treasure that throws light on the character and history of the Berbers, the once-great power in this region and a people that were partly responsible for the eclipse of Leptis Magna. Before Arabs flooded along the north African coast in the 7th century, carrying and spreading their new Islamic faith, the Berbers ruled the land, but there were many different tribes and cultures in the region. Some have been virtually lost to memory, for the Arab Islamic culture that has dominated the land for nearly 1500 years has evolved its own view of history – a view that almost excludes the existence of an earlier world. The consequence in Libya of this amnesia is a determination not to support, barely to recognise, certainly not to protect, Berber culture or traditions. Berber dialects are not taught, their language is not in official use – road signs even in Berber areas are in Arabic – and Berber customs are gradually but ceaselessly replaced by those of the Arab world. These actions – overt and covert – may well result in the sought-after cultural coherence for the Arab nations of north Africa but much of the history, the complexity and the richness of the region will be lost in the process.

The Berbers are the original inhabitants of much of north Africa and their history in this region is thought to date back 5000 years. They were a nomadic culture, moving their livestock through the land to a pattern dictated by the seasons. A route of movement would be followed, year after year, and along this route the Berbers constructed villages, where some would stay, and citadels. These structures were to serve primarily as granaries or store houses – to ensure survival during winter months – but also as

Today I'm in search of the remains of the Berbers. This amazing granary, used to store food, is built of rubble rendered with a gypsum plaster so it has an organic, undulating surface – like that of a cliff face – that is in wonderful contrast to its perfect circular, geometric form. The effect of the apertures is incredibly pleasing, like a huge – and entirely unselfconscious – piece of abstract art.

These little storerooms in the granary are wonderful examples of really well thought-out and functional design achieved with minimal means. The thick stone and gypsum walls of the rooms, with only small areas exposed to direct sunlight, mean that the interiors are cool, dry and with a constant temperature – excellent conditions for preserving most foods.

refuges in times of war. And it is a Berber citadel granary – nearly 900 years old – that I am now going to see.

We drive through flat lands parallel to the coast, and then branch south to the highlands of the Jabel Nafusa, the Berber heartland. This is terrain fought over by the German Afrikakorps, Italian and British forces during the Axis retreat after the battle of el-Alamein in October 1942, and there are, our fixer warns us, still plenty of mines around, especially in the remote places where we are going.

We arrive at Qasr al-Hajj, seemingly a small, anonymous modern town, but then I see a collection of low, vaulted courtyard houses – mostly in ruins – and then a large circular structure looms into sight, standing in proud isolation. This is the granary. It's spectacular. At first glance it looks like a fort out of fairyland – tall, with few external apertures and a small, easily defensible gate. As I approach this gate I know something wonderful is about to happen. This is a very distinguished vernacular building, built by a local leader – Sheikh Abu Jatla – for communal use, for a very specific function. Here the precious foodstuff for the community was stored and guarded, and here safety was sought in time of turmoil. This was a sacred place. The survival, the future, of the people that built it was trusted to its stones. I pass through the gate – on each side are alcoves in which the guardian of the citadel would sit – and enter the great cylinder of the court. I'm stunned by the strange mix of organic form with Euclidian geometry, and the way in which tiers of apertures – the doors to the individual storerooms – follow a very relaxed approach to architectural propriety. The openings attempt no recognisable symmetry – they are like the burrows made in a cliff face by some wise creatures, and they follow an order higher and older than the servile law of symmetry. It seems to be dealing with essential things, almost like an expression of the origin of architecture. Looking at the elevation of this court – this perfect O, this little world – is to see man-made architecture emerging out of the forms of nature. But, as if all this was not enough, there is more. I have been told there are 114 openings. A random number – yes, but also maybe no. There are 114 suras, or chapters, in the Koran and by the early 12th century the Berbers were under the sway of Islam, so this citadel – among many other things – is a muscular prayer in stone, a monument to God and a plea that the life within be given divine protection. And its name – Hajj – means pilgrimage, the name of one of the suras in the Koran. Does this name mean that coming to this structure, a building in which the bounty of the earth was stored, was like going on pilgrimage?

I look inside some of the storerooms. Many, it appears, are still in use. In these, traditionally, Berber families would store grain, wheat, beans, barley, dates, figs, dried meat and olive oil. Each of these self-contained, cave-like storerooms was the property of a different family. In many of them the floors are awash with barley. Also, I notice small windows in the door and the outer wall – to encourage cross-ventilation to prevent mildew and rot. Also, the fixer tells me, the daylight at the small window attracts any insects that might be lurking in the darkness, and gum and poison around the window aperture trap and kill them.

I want to see more, and enter some of the abandoned storerooms. In these I find ancient containers – including massive conical amphorae – strewn around. To pass the threshold of these storerooms, to push aside their gnarled and ancient palmwood doors, is to travel by time machine to a remote world. All around is as it would have been a thousand years ago. That these rooms were once occupied – or intended to be – cannot be doubted because there is evidence that their doors could be secured from the inside as well as the outside. In times of extremis, if the community was under attack and sheltering within the citadel then, I suppose, these little rooms would have become home to the families, their last and individual redoubts, places of final resistance – if necessary.

I climb a staircase to the narrow wall walk that surrounds the citadel, and then clamber onto the vaulted roofs of the upper storerooms. From here I can see the town, with the ruined courtyard houses below me. These houses were once occupied by Berbers, but they were moved out years ago. And the new houses in the town, who lives in them I ask? Arabs I am told. What happened to the Berber families? My guide smiles and shrugs. He doesn't really know – but they've gone, long gone. But some still come back here to use these storerooms I ask. He agrees – they do. All is unspoken. I realise the fate of the Berbers is a difficult issue in Libya – it has to do with politics and that, here, is a subject that it is wise to avoid. But what is clear is that, in this ancient town of the Berbers, in the Berber heartland, the Berbers are no more. They are, I fear, yet one more ancient people being squeezed out of existence by the pressure of the modern world. The Berbers are a fiercely proud and self-reliant people to whom 'nif' – honour, virility – is all-important, the ability to retain dignity and outface your enemy or your difficulties. They are a people who would sleep in the tombs of their ancestors to receive inspiration and guidance. But, in the thrusting and shrinking modern world, 'nif' and ancestor veneration are, sadly, commodities of dwindling value.

Sunday 10–Monday 11 October – Egypt

Another ghastly early start. We leave our hotel in Tripoli at 1.00 in the morning for our flight to Cairo. But at least this means that we arrive early in the city and have nearly a full day to prepare for what is to come – a plunge into the intense, complex, exciting and enigmatic world of ancient Egypt. We plan to meet Cheops, Tutankhamen, Ramesses II and his great wife Nefertari and the Ptolemies. But before meeting these rulers and their gods we have to meet a new member of the team. Tim Dunn is leaving us in Cairo – he is going back to London to sort out the urgent and vital business of editing the vast amount of material we have shot so far. In his place as producer we are to have Jonty Claypole – a charming young man with whom I have worked before.

We are in a modern hotel, in the centre of Cairo and overlooking the Nile. I enter my room, walk to the window and stare at the wide and placid waters below. This river is the reason for it all. It brought life to this hot land – trade and ideas travelled along it, and nearly 5500 years ago it stirred into life the most haunting, enigmatic – perhaps greatest – civilisation the world has ever known. A civilisation that – despite many ups and downs – enjoyed a cultural and political continuity that lasted over 3000 years.

The Museum of Egyptian Antiquities is not only one of the greatest museums in the world, but also one of the most charming, occupying a wonderful late 19th-century building purpose-built for the collections it houses. But, as I approach, I see that all is not as it should be. It now looks more like a barracks than a museum. As I pass through the gate from my hotel I see a fellow clad in bulletproof vest and steel helmet and clutching an AK-47. Is something dreadful anticipated or is it always now like this? Yes, this is normal. Good Lord – what a world. I suppose it's the mass of foreign tourists who visit the museum that are the potential target for terrorists – and there was an attack here a few years ago – but I tremble for the precious contents of the museum.

I am here to see the boy king – Tutankhamen – and the enigmatic and often maligned father, the 'heretic' Pharaoh Akhenaten. I walk straight across the central atrium, to Room Three, and there I see four colossi of Akhenaten, each over 3300 years old, that show this strange Pharaoh as no other Pharaoh was shown before or would dare to portray himself afterwards. Akhenaten looks like a hermaphrodite, with wide hips and budding breasts – or perhaps this is an image intended to imply that the Pharaoh is a divine being, in which both male and female qualities reside, the quintessence of creation. But this is not all – the elongated shape of his face, his almond-shaped eyes and strangely pronounced features make him look like a life form from another world, a human in the image of the gods. Since the images of Akhenaten and his family were discovered in the late 19th century at his long-lost capital of Amarna, debate has raged about the meaning of this art, about this man and his radical reform of Egyptian theology. He swept away the many traditional Egyptian gods and replaced them with just one – the Aten – and Akhenaten's motto, his pithy defence of the Aten, was that he was the 'Living Truth'. Perhaps Akhenaten applied this motto to the way he was rendered. Rather than being shown in the usual stylised, ideal form Akhenaten had himself portrayed as his weird, and somewhat wonderful, real self. So, along with the traditions of Egyptian religion Akhenaten perhaps also jettisoned the ancient traditions of Egyptian formal and sacred art. But it's not just Akhenaten who is shown in a peculiar, unconventional manner. Renderings of his family also have an air of oddness about them, particularly the two daughters he had with his Great Wife Nefertiti, who both are shown as possessing peculiar elongated heads that make them look deformed or, more bizarrely, like aliens. Even the arguably most beautiful portrait bust ever found in Egypt – that of Nefertiti unearthed in Amarna – is weird. The bust appears to be the individual life-like portrait of a very beautiful woman – not a rendering of a royal ideal or stereotype. But the head is sitting upon an impossibly – eerily – long neck.

I walk quickly to the darkened room in which resides the most famous single item found – the golden mask that sat over the mummified head of the boy-Pharaoh. I stare at it, into its eyes. The expression is passive, blank, he is – as he should be – staring into eternity. His features are regular – in no sense grotesque or bizarre like Akhenaten. The kingdom Tutankhamen presided over was very different to that left by his father – perhaps this explains the difference in the way they are depicted. Tutankhamen's face is unexceptional, bland – it gives nothing away. But the items the boy is wearing – their materials, design and detail, reveal a great deal, there is a story here to unravel. But not yet. With one last look I leave – but I shall soon return.

We have a day without filming – which is good, for it gives me time to improve my acquaintance with this strange royal family from Amarna. Akhenaten started his reign with the name Amenhotep IV and with – outwardly at least – a conventional belief in the traditional religion and arts of Egypt. But, in an amazing leap of insight, of the imagination, he launched a religious revolution. In place of many gods there was to be one – Aten – whose symbol was the solar disc. In a sense Akhenaten chose to worship nature in its most visible and dramatic manifestation, the flaming disc that was reborn each morning, bringing life to the earth, that established the hours and the seasons, confirmed the cycles by which humans live. After coming to the throne he changed his name to Akhenaten – 'it is beneficial to Aten'. In one dramatic leap, Akhenaten intro-duced the concept of monotheism and swept away the idea that multiple gods should be shown as many and varying images all with different powers, responsibilities and attributes. And he built a new city on a virgin desert site, Amarna, where temples were simply huge walled enclosures, full of god's light and open to the sky, to the life-giving rays of the Aten.

But things started to unravel fairly quickly. Akhenaten failed in his duties as a temporal ruler. He could not lead his armies or pursue effective foreign or domestic policies, he could not visit his great cities and people or appeal to the disgruntled priests of the old religion. He made many worldly enemies and did little to win friends. It all seemed doomed to come to a sticky end – and it did – but the legacy of Akhenaten's vision is huge. It seems clear that it had a profound influence on the formation and doctrine of later religions, notably the Zoroastrian, Judaic and Christian. To suggest that this so-called heretic Pharaoh is the root of the world's three great monotheistic religions may seem shocking, but among the things that my recent travels have revealed to me are the curious and complex connections that appear to exist between religions around the world. A dispassionate analysis of evidence suggests that few religions are the direct and dramatic revelation of God to a prophet but an accumulation, adaptation and reinterpretation of existing doctrines and stories. One possible exception to this is Akhenaten's vision of the Aten. Yes, aspects of the cult of the Aten were based on the old god Re – but the radicalism and purity of Akhenaten's perception is utterly astonishing when set in the context of the times.

When Akhenaten died his radical religion died with him. Egypt was in chaos, tributes were not being paid by its vassals and its borders were under threat from its enemies. Rapidly Akhenaten was demonised. The old gods could, it seems, only forgive Egypt if all traces of Akhenaten and the Aten were destroyed – as if they had never existed. They were to be removed from memory. No trace has ever been found of Akhenaten's body – perhaps it was never placed in his tomb.

It was into this world of chaos that, in about 1333 BC, Akhenaten's son stepped – the ruler by divine right of a kingdom that was in shock, that was tottering, busily wiping all trace of his father from its memory. He was only nine years old, yet the role ordained for him was to put the world to rights, to re-establish the old order that his father had rejected. And one of the first things this boy Pharaoh had to do was change his name. He had been known as Tutankhaten – 'the living image of Aten' – but two years after he came to the throne he was renamed after the old great god of Thebes, Tutankhamen. He was now the living image of the god his father had tried – and failed – to eradicate.

61 TUTANKHAMEN'S MASK, CAIRO, EGYPT

Tuesday 12 October
We enter the museum as the last visitors leave and ascend to the Tutankhamen galleries. Before looking at the mask I view other items found in the tomb. I am entranced by some of the furniture, decorated with telling images. On the royal throne Tutankhamen is shown with his wife Ankhesenamen, who was probably his half-sister. The informal intimacy of the scene – Ankhesenamen is adjusting her husband's collar – is typical of the art of the Amarna period. And in their headdress, and on the back panel of the throne, are images of the Aten disc. This imagery is extraordinary in the circumstances. It suggests that the spirit of the age of Akhenaten was not quite dead, or at least did not die until Tutankhamen – the last of the Amarna period Pharaohs – and his wife did.

I then come to the series of huge gilded timber shrines that had covered the sarcophagus, coffins and body of the Pharaoh. There are four, each decorated with hieroglyphs, and they diminish in size because each fits within the other – like a series of giant Russian dolls. Then there is the quartzite sarcophagus – still in the tomb – and within that three coffins, the last of solid gold, and then the golden mask. So, including the mask, the body had nine covers. Why nine? I've come upon the number nine before in royal tombs – the 1300-year-old step-pyramid of King Pakal in Palenque, Mexico, has nine levels representing the nine levels of the Mayan underworld. As I ponder this it strikes me that these box-like shrines are familiar. Of course – most are larger in scale but there is no mistaking the fact that their proportions are much like

Tutankhamen's mask – made of gold, a traditional funeral material for kings, and encrusted with turquoise, lapis lazuli and cornelian – acted as the final barrier of preservation against spiritual attack from malignant forces or dark powers.

those of the Ark described in the Bible. So, the precious body of the dead Pharaoh – the Son of the gods – is placed inside an Ark in the same way as Moses's precious tablets of the Law – the gift of God – and at roughly the same time, certainly in the same time period.

I now enter the darkened room that is dominated by two of the coffins and, in pride of place in the centre of the room, the golden mask. I approach it. The boy is still staring into eternity – into infinity. He died at about the age of 19 after fewer than ten years on the throne. He had presided over Egypt's return to religious and cultural orthodoxy – old gods and the priests were back in their temples, the land was more stable. But this must largely have been the work of his veteran and experienced advisers – notably Ay, who had once been close to Akhenaten but seems to have become a leading force in the counter-revolution that swept away his legacy. Men like Ay must have organised the young Pharaoh just as they reorganised his kingdom. Tutankhamen as an individual seems to have made little impression besides the spectacular accoutrements of his funeral, but even this was organised by others. Whatever promise the young Tutankhamen may have shown as a man and as a Pharaoh was, it seems, left largely unfulfilled by his early death.

Knowing this, the passive expression on the Pharaoh's golden face assumes a melancholy air. But what can this mask tell us about the boy and about his beliefs or, to be more accurate, about the beliefs and intentions of those who orchestrated his lavish – but seemingly hasty – funeral? Did the Pharaoh take secrets to the grave? Is there any whiff of Amarna, of Akhenaten's god Aten about all this?

The first thing is the gold. It was precious to the Egyptians because it seemed evidence of the divine – it did not corrode so it spoke of eternity and its colour and sheen seemed of the Sun. Could wrapping the boy's head in 11 kilos of solid gold be seen as a sign of continuing homage to Ahkenaten's religion?

As well as the gold, the mask is decorated with turquoise, cornelian and lapis lazuli, all of which – as well as looking beautiful – must have had precise magic powers to those who made it. Around his neck is a broad collar, not an unusal ornament for a Pharoah, but Akhenaten presented gold collars to those who embraced Aten. The collar includes inlays of turquoise, lapis lazuli and cornelian arranged in 12 concentric rows that produce bands of red, and pale and dark blue. Surely these materials and colours – and the number 12 – must have had magic and protective qualities for ancient Egyptians. Certainly the number 12 could refer to time and so to cycles of the Sun, to the Aten. The origin of our calendar is ancient and the oldest Egyptian 12-month calendar could date back to 4241 BC, but was certainly in use in the Old Kingdom from around 2658 BC. Can the numerology of this mask form a calendar and, if so, what purpose does it serve? Perhaps it's a time chart intended to guide the Pharaoh's soul in the afterlife, charting his journey to the stars. Looking at the mask from this perspective it's like a helmet worn by a traveller to give protection on the journey, to help guide the soul to its ultimate destination. Indeed, inscribed on the back of the mask is a spell from the Book of the Dead, a text compiled to prepare the living for their death, instructing them how to conduct themselves in the underworld, how to approach their judgement before the gods.

The more one studies this beautiful object the stranger it seems. Tutankhamen's tomb was entered at least twice by robbers in ancient times but very little was taken and the Pharaoh's body not disturbed. The theory is that the robbers were frightened off – they even discarded some of their booty as they fled. Did the mask and the spells do their magic job? Perhaps so, to judge by the fate suffered by some of the archaeological team that finally disturbed the Pharaoh's rest in 1922. Within six months Lord Carnarvon – the financial backer of the excavation – died in Cairo from a mosquito bite; the secretary of Howard Carter – the man who led the dig – died in peculiar circumstances in the Bath

Club in London; while Carter's right-hand man – Arthur Mace – sickened and expired even before the tomb had been cleared. And what of the death of Tutankhamen? There has been much speculation that he was murdered, by a blow to the back of the head or by poison. This seems possible, even probable, but no one knows for certain.

62 THE GREAT PYRAMID, GIZA

Wednesday 13 October

This morning we make the brief journey to the western suburb of Cairo. We pass sprawling modern housing developments, shanty housing and shops, humdrum and ugly and then, suddenly, above this world of modern urban chaos burst three vast expressions of pure, elemental, geometrical perfection, beauty and harmony – the pyramids at Giza.

They stand on a plateau, raised slightly above the city which laps up to their very feet. It's strange – on one side of the pyramids is the modern world of concrete buildings and advertising hoardings, while on the other is desert, the tranquil and wide horizons of eternity. There are three pyramids, all aligned – the pyramids of Cheops, Chephren and Mycerinus – and they are the last surviving wonder from the ancient world – a title that gives a hint of their antiquity because they were mysterious and ancient structures 2000 years ago, impossibly old even in the age of Tutankhamen.

But to reach these pyramids I must walk past the Sphinx – that most enigmatic and inscrutable of all the creations of the ancient world. What age is it, who built it and why? The answers to these essential questions lie, it seems, in the realm of speculation. It gazes east, towards sunrise and so is to do with rebirth; it's the guardian of the pharaonic temples and tombs over which it presides, of the gates to the underworld; or it's the mystic protector of the secrets of creation. The riddle of the Sphinx is that the Sphinx is always a riddle. It provokes questions but never gives answers.

With these thoughts on my mind I walk towards my destination – the pyramid that is now known as the pyramid of Cheops – the Great Pyramid, the largest and evidently the oldest of the three. As with the Sphinx, we know so little about this vast and perfectly formed construction. We don't really know when it was built, by whom, for what exact

purpose and – most gripping for me – how it was built. Nor do we understand the relation these pyramids may have with the step-pyramids, or ziggurats, of Mesopotamia – some of which could be 6000 years old – or with the much later step-pyramids of south and central America and south and east Asia. After two centuries of Egyptology and of close examination of the Great Pyramid and of documents and artefacts relating to it a story has emerged that sounds convincing – and is accepted by most – but which is, in the end, still only informed speculation. It is now generally accepted that the pyramid was built by the Pharaoh known as Cheops or Khufu, from the Old Kingdom fourth dynasty, who appears to have died in around 2528 BC. It was to serve primarily as his

Building the Great Pyramid involved moving and shaping 7.5 million tonnes of stone. It remains a great mystery. It is thought to have been achieved using levers, rollers, rockers, ropes and ramps of earth with the stones shaped to perfection by hammering with harder stones or scratching with bronze chisels.

tomb and perhaps as a Sun temple and was built using conventional Bronze Age technology and techniques. This all sounds reasonable but even a quick glance at the Great Pyramid's vital statistics and main characteristics raises some basic problems with this profile, along with a lot of questions.

First, just consider the pyramid's astonishing scale – and I do just this. I walk along the plateau and enter the pyramid's long morning shadow and see, as I move forward, the sun disappearing behind one of its sloping sides. I look upwards, along its huge cliff-like sides of stone, my eyes squinting in the sun.

The Great Pyramid rises 137 metres, but was originally 146 metres high before its capstone – the pyramidion – was removed. This stone, now lying shattered at the foot of the pyramid, was, in a sense, the essence of the pyramid. It's a little pyramid in itself and must have had a sacred purpose. If, among other things, the pyramid was a temple to the sun god Re, then the pyramidion marked the dawn of each day for it caught and – with its skin of gold or of a gold and silver alloy called electrum – reflected the first rays of the dawning sun. It was the herald of Re's daily rebirth, and the living image of the Egyptian hieroglyph for sunrise – a semi-circle rising over a pyramid. The pyramid covers 5 hectares of ground, has sides each 230.3 metres long, contains around 2.5 million blocks of stone, each weighing on average 2.5 tonnes, rising in 203 courses. The total weight of stone used is calculated to be about 7.5 million tonnes.

The construction project is truly vast, outstripping virtually any other comparable single-building scheme in the ancient or modern world. Was it really just to bury a Pharaoh and, perhaps, to guide his soul to the next world? It seems that the Great Pyramid must have been built to serve, at least in part, as someone's tomb, for in its heart it contains a heavy, solid stone sarcophagus-like chest that could only have been inserted during construction. But surely this pyramid must have been something else as well – something of such importance that it justified the investment of vast amounts of time, energy and resources in its construction.

It's not just the quantity of materials used that impresses – it's also the quality of construction. A quality that is not just overwhelming but entirely baffling. Indeed the construction is virtually perfect and of a standard of precision way above that which could, theoretically and logically, be achieved by the Bronze Age building technology assumed to be available around 4500 years ago. And there is more. The orientation of all three pyramids is very precise. The four corners of the Great Pyramid define the four cardinal points of the compass with an accuracy of within one twelfth of a degree, and it has been calculated that the main, and originally hidden, entry to the interior passages of the pyramid is aligned on the position the Pole Star would have occupied around 4500 years ago.

The relation between the three pyramids and the form of the Great Pyramid is also very precise and must carry a message – if only we could read it. The sloping sides of the Great Pyramid now rise at an angle of 51.51 degrees. But they are ragged, stripped of their facing stones over a thousand years ago, so it must be assumed that the original angle was closer to 52 degrees. This is fascinating because, if a vertical and horizontal grid is drawn by extending the sides of the pyramid, and a 52-degree diagonal line is drawn heading south-west from the south-east corner of the Great Pyramid it will define the south-east corners of the other two pyramids. So the pyramids are spatially – geometrically – related and, evidently, to their builders this angle had special significance. To explain this to myself I scratch a little diagram on the ground. Three squares of different sizes – the ground plans of the pyramids – set within an irregularly spaced right-angular grid through which a diagonal line snakes – connecting all. Its like a chessboard with a streak of lightning passing along it. The clever diagonal line is what makes sense of it all, gives meaning, connection and cohesion to the plodding, self-contained squares. But what is the meaning? I stare at my curious diagram, my enigmatic hieroglyphs in the sand. Then I scratch in the long straight causeways, which ran to the east connecting each pyramid with the life-giving waters of the Nile. Water, stone, pyramid, a Greek name like pyre, implying fire I wonder? Is all of this to do with the four elements? I can't be sure. If there's a message written here I can't understand it – not yet anyway. I climb up the broken surface of the Great Pyramid – the time has come to enter its bowels, for my treasure lies deep inside.

I pass into a tunnel that was excavated into the side of the pyramid in the 9th century AD by Khaliph al-Mamun who took this

The Avenue of Sphinxes at Luxor. On the bottom left, in front of the entrance pylons, is the statue of Ramesses II with its tiny statue of Nefertari below his knee.

drastic action when he was unable to discern any sign of a door in the then still intact outer casing of the structure. This rough-hewn passage curves through the body of the building and quickly joins the real entrance which had been outflanked, made redundant, by this 9th-century cutting. Here the entrance passage descends from the original entrance opening, and then continues to descend to a deep underground chamber that is now said to be the first, and unfinished, burial chamber. But I clamber up the Ascending Passage, a steep passage into the body of the pyramid. It brings me to what is, in many ways, the most startling moment in any exploration or investigation of the Great Pyramid – the Grand Gallery. It leads upwards, into the gloom. The fact that the Grand Gallery is here at all is astounding but even more astounding is its form. It is tall and narrow, and gets progressively narrower still as it rises for the walls corbel-in, forming seven horizontal bands as they reach the ceiling. There is a structural reason for this queer arrangement: the lower area of the gallery needs to be as wide as possible for practical reasons, while the top needs to be as narrow as possible so that the gallery can be spanned successfully and safely by one slab of stone. The gloom, the shadows in the Grand Gallery seem as real, more real, than the walls.

As I get to the upper end I begin to see, in the darkness, the narrow end wall in front of me. I get a strange vision, the light plays tricks. Rather than being the end wall of a room with its upper portions stepping in towards me I see it as a pyramidal building with its upper portions stepping out – it's a steep, step pyramid – this place is getting to me! I now stoop again and virtually crawl – as if in an attitude of prayer – through a small vestibule. And what was in the chamber beyond? In all honesty nobody knows. I enter it. This is where all has been leading – I'm at the heart of the pyramid. The chamber is tall and broad, familiar and comfortable in proportion. The walls are formed by huge blocks of granite, perfectly plain with no sign of painting. At one end is the massive stone sarcophagus. There is no record of a body having been found in it but it stands at the west end of the chamber – the west, where the sun sets, was for Egyptians the realm of the dead. I examine the walls of the chamber – they are magnificent, some of these stone blocks must weigh around 40 tonnes, those forming the ceiling perhaps 80 tonnes each; their edges are razor sharp and straight and their surfaces absolutely smooth and flat. Could this precision have been achieved using stone pounders and soft bronze chisels?

And then there are the two so-called air shafts – the two small channels that run straight and upwards from the chamber to the outside world, one facing south and the other north, oriented it is said towards the positions that certain stars in the constellation of Orion would have occupied 4500 years ago – to the northern sky which the Egyptians believed was the realm of the gods. Strangely, I have seen such a shaft before – in the burial chamber of King Pakal within his 7th-century AD step-pyramid at Palenque, Mexico. Although these channels in the Great Pyramid are small they are amazing pieces of engineered construction, cut diagonally through the horizontal stone courses of the pyramid and made of stones shaped and sized to withstand the hundreds of thousands of tonnes of weight pressing down on them. Whatever job these small shafts were intended to do – to let the soul of the dead leave the tomb or to let light or the elemental wind in – it must have been considered essential, for these shafts would have been incredibly difficult to construct.

My affection for this superb structure increases the more I look at it – I can't keep my hands off it but, as I run my fingers over the vast stones, marvelling at their tight joints, we are suddenly plunged into utter darkness. We stand alone in blackness that's tangible, in the heart of the pyramid – in a stillness that is beyond silence. When no one speaks nothing can be heard, nothing – we are insulated from the world by thousands of tonnes of granite and limestone. A voice breaks the silence – a message is shouted from afar, it's a power cut in Cairo, we could be in the blackness for some time. We decide to stay, and as we chat I notice the extraordinary echo in the chamber. I sit on the floor, in the black, rich atmosphere, my back to the granite wall, facing the sarcophagus. Is this what it was like, I wonder, thousands of years ago, sitting in this womb-like room waiting for something to happen, waiting for some kind of rebirth?

The light returns. I look again at the chamber. I consider its shape. It rises about 6 metres in height, and I pace its width, six strides and a bit, so about 6 metres wide, and then I pass its length, a little over 12 strides, so nearly 12 metres – of course the room is a double cube, the proportion that has haunted my travels – the proportion found in sacred buildings, from all ages, from all over the world. It's a proportion promoted by Renaissance architects in the 16th century, followed rigorously by Classical architects in the 18th century. Incredible, it's a proportion that seems to possess innate beauty, reflect immutable laws of harmony, to carry something about it that is both human and divine. Perhaps it all started here – the chamber is the temple, the sarcophagus is the inspiration for the Ark of the Covenant, an altar containing a spiritual treasure rather than a corpse. I look afresh at the sarcophagus, I measure it – yes, of course, it too is a double cube in proportion. As I bow to leave I look back – it's incredible, being in this chamber is like being present at the birth of architecture.

63 QUEEN NEFERTARI'S TOMB PAINTINGS, LUXOR

Thursday 14 October
We take a night train to Luxor. As it gets light I lift the blinds and look through the carriage window. All night the train has been following the course of the Nile and now I see the mighty river at dawn. Before me is a wide sheet of water – still, placid – and on its banks all is fertile – grasses and crops grow, people and animals thrive. Occasionally I get a glimpse of the world beyond the river and its verdant banks. And often the glimpse reveals desert, very nearby, and reminds that the Nile and its water were, and remain, the life blood of the country – a sliver of paradise snaking through this hot and inhospitable land.

Then off to Luxor Temple to meet my next treasure. As I near the temple the sun is still low and bright, casting long shadows. I walk between the entrance pylons, through the first courtyard to the great colonnade formed by a parallel row of huge columns. I want to see these first, for this colonnade was completed by the young Tutankhamen to demonstrate to all that he had returned to the old gods and to the old temples. I look for the name of Tutankhamen on this work – his cartouche – but all save one have long ago been obliterated. Removal of a name was a serious business in ancient Egypt. The name was one of the key aspects of a person's existence, indeed if a person's name was not preserved, if it was not read, said and remembered, then their very afterlife was in question. To obliterate a name was to obliterate – to kill – a soul. Why on earth would his successors want to do this to Tutankhamen?

The statue of Nefertari below the knee of Ramesses II at Luxor is exquisite, even though her face has been vandalised.

Pondering this I return to the first courtyard. This was built by a later Pharaoh about 3230 years ago, one of the greatest and most powerful of them all – Ramesses II. This court is lined with statues of Ramesses, but there is one in particular that I find fascinating, a colossal image of the Pharaoh, seated, and next to him, reaching to just below his knee, is a statue of his Great Wife Nefertari. Her name means 'Lovely one' and her statue is exquisite, with the fabric of her dress tight across her beautiful body. But her face is gone – smashed in some frenzied attack. There are many other sculptures of the pair in the adjoining courtyard but all are damaged and not of a quality to compare to this. I am in quest of Nefertari for she is my next treasure. Her tomb is one of the most beautiful and best-preserved ever discovered in Egypt. In it I can see the resting place of her body and the domain of her spirit and soul, and discover more about the Egyptian approach to death and the afterlife. The tomb, now closed to the public in an attempt to preserve it for posterity, lies buried in the Valley of the Queens on the west bank of the Nile – in the land of the dead, the Kingdom of Osiris, the lord of the underworld.

Before looking at Nefertari's tomb in detail I have to remind myself of the rudiments of Egyptian religion and sacred art. It's generally agreed that the central theme of Egyptian theology was the preservation of the body after death as a means to ensuring the well-being of the dead in the afterlife. The human had eight parts – the body, life force, soul, heart, spirit, power, shadow and name. These may be reduced to the essential three – body, soul and spirit. Most of these aspects of the dead were believed to require a home and worldly nourishment to ensure a satisfactory rebirth in the Other World. Egyptians viewed the preservation of the corpse as a means to an end. The simple analogy is the root of a plant. Like the corpse, the root may look dead and withered. But in the right conditions, treated in the right way, life can flow from it. Similarly, from a mummified corpse can grow a beautiful spiritual body. Within the Egyptian Book of the Dead, a text containing spells and rituals to help the dead survive in the underworld, the deceased says: 'I exist, I exist; I live, I live; I germinate, I germinate' and 'I germinate like the plants'.

Nourishment for the dead was an all-embracing term. It included the provision of food, tools and utensils used in life, the supplying of essential information about the rituals followed after death, and – very important – the preservation of the life-history of the dead and their name. In addition there was protection, invoked from the gods by means of prayers, spells and amulets. This nourishment and protection included the creation of a world in which the dead could reside. This world was the tomb – perhaps envisaged as an everlasting dwelling for an aspect of the dead, perhaps only a temporary but vital stage on the path to everlasting light. And crucial to the tomb were the wall paintings. They followed a code, showing the world in a characteristic, informed and informative manner – creating images that played a part in, and were relevant to, the process of achieving afterlife. The drawing and colouring of animals and objects of daily life show that Egyptian artists were capable of naturalistic drawing. But for sacred art, for art that was to act as a guide or inspiration for humans entering the afterworld, they chose not to follow nature. They were aiming at an art beyond reality – a higher, spiritual rendering of the human form. The Golden Age of Egyptian art was the 500 years of the New Kingdom – from about 1550 to 1080 BC – and the paintings in Queen Nefertari's tomb are among the best created during this time.

Friday 15–Saturday 16 October

We breakfast early and, as the sun rises, cross the Nile by ferry. It has occurred to me that the best way to approach the Valley of the Queens is the old way. So I hire a bicycle and, in relative peace and quiet, with time for reflection and anticipation, I ride towards Nefertari – I am going to see the face of the 'lovely one' in intimate circumstances, in a room that, if she didn't inhabit in life, she occupied for centuries in death.

It is a strange lunar place, this realm of the dead. Arid, hot, with small valleys cut through rugged cliffs and hills. And everywhere limestone chippings, a pale ivory colour, the ancient spoil from tomb cutting – and tomb robbing. I arrive at Nefertari's tomb. The entrance is merely a hole in the ground sheltered by a semi-circular roof. This hole leads to a steep flight of steps at the bottom of which stands a door – once sealed and protected by magic spells to keep out thieves and evil.

To cross over the threshold of this tomb is not just to enter the Egyptian world of the dead – it is to see it in startling, living colour, seemingly as fresh, bright and vivid as the day it was applied. It is utterly breathtaking. The door opens into an anteroom, which has a square floor plan. Standing with my back to the door there are, on my right, two smaller rooms and, in front of me, a staircase that leads down to the burial chamber, off which are three very small rooms. The wall surfaces and most of the ceilings in all these rooms were painted, and the paintings survive, generally in excellent condition. I look around at this story of Nefertari's afterlife, her judgement and rebirth, told in bright images and arranged like strip cartoons in a comic. I must try and read these images to understand what was meant to happen to Nefertari after death – to follow the spiritual voyage of her soul to the kingdom of the dead and beyond.

It is clear that the story starts to my right, to the east, suggesting that with her death Nefertari is re-entering the world of the living, fast-tracked to rebirth. First I see

From left
The paintings in Queen Nefertari's tomb are from the Golden Age of Egyptian art – 1550–1080 BC. The colours are bright and varied, the figures light, elegant, bodies elongated, garments ethereal. I start by looking (from left) at two images of Nefertari and (right) Re-Harakhty, to whom Nefertari is being introduced on her journey to the underworld.

Nefertari herself – in the splendour of her vibrant death – making an offering to the gods Osiris, lord of the underworld that she is now entering and Anubis, the jackal-headed son of Osiris, who presided over the abode of the dead and was the patron of embalmers. But this painting of Nefertari is badly damaged so I can hardly see her face. I walk into the next small room to the east and now I see Nefertari for the first time, perfectly preserved and beautiful. She is wearing a long white robe and on her head is a hat in the form of a vulture sprouting two tall, feathered plumes. The vulture was the emblem of the great goddess Mut – wife of Amen and one of the Theban Trinity. Nefertari must be appealing to Mut for protection during the ordeal to come, seeking her as a champion. Nefertari is being led by the falcon-headed god Horus towards her judgement. In front of her – waiting to receive her – are the sun god Re-Harakhty and the goddess Hathor-Imentet, another protecting and nurturing goddess.

It's clear what is happening. Nefertari is to meet the gods, to appeal to and appease them, for she will soon be judged – and in this room she meets those powerful gods who are to protect her and support her during her ordeal. The view of these protector gods about the outcome of Nefertari's judgement is made clear, for hieroglyphs in the vestibule declare that they will endow Nefertari with 'eternity', the form of 'Re in the heavens', and life eternal, strength and endurance. Endurance – yes she will need it. I now walk east into the next chamber. This is a breathtaking room – it is virtually a double cube in form and with walls loaded with information. It seems that in here Nefertari is being instructed in her best course of action, how to prepare for judgement. She consecrates two large tables of offerings, in front of her main judges, Osiris and Atum, a powerful creator-god identified with Re. Here is Nefertari using all the powers at her disposal, at the disposal of her magicians and priests, to save her soul – she's even bribing her judges. Nefertari is audacious, but a lot is at stake – eternal life. I pass back into the main antechamber and now I see it all. Nefertari's fighting for her existence, she's done her best to win support, and now has to descend into the underworld. I go down with her, into her burial chamber.

I descend slowly. To my right, at the top of the wall, a huge winged serpent protects Nefertari's cartouche – fending off all who might want to destroy her name and so consign her to oblivion. Below is an image that takes me aback. It's a beautiful portrait of Isis, bare-breasted and kneeling, and above her head is her name, written as a hieroglyph. It's a rectangle standing on one of its short sides with one of its long sides and one of its short sides extended outwards. The image that's created is three steps – much like those I saw on ancient tombs in Iran and Petra. I wondered what this abstract image could mean – a stairway to heaven perhaps – and now I see it could be an

From left
The typical Egytian portrait was profile face but with eyes, shoulder and chest as seen from the front. Here Anubis, son of Osiris and patron of embalmers, welcomes Nefertari to his kingdom and her new abode, she meets the scorpion goddess on her journey, and Osiris (right), in front of whom she faces judgement.

invocation to Isis. Certainly Isis was worshipped in Petra. Golly, I'm amazed. Travelling around the world at this speed – the dramatic juxtapositions between different cultures, countries and histories – makes it possible to gain an overview, makes it possible to see the connections, to piece the jigsaw together.

I reach the end of the staircase and above my head is a painting of Maat, the winged goddess of truth, cosmic order and justice. This could be the place – the moment – of Nefertari's judgement. The scene is not shown but is implied. Here she would start to present her case to be let into the next world. Chapter 125 of the Book of the Dead tells Nefertari what to say. Having made her opening statement, a willing confession of her faults, she would then enter the underworld and face judgement in front of Osiris. Now the soul of the queen is weighed on a scale of justice, balanced against the feather of truth. If the scales balanced Nefertari would have been justified, declared to be 'True of Voice' and admitted to the next world. If the scales did not balance her soul would have been thrown to the beast – the 'Devourer of the unjustified', part crocodile, hyena and hippopotamus – and she would have gone out of existence.

So what happened to Nefertari? The paintings in the centre of the burial chamber provide the answer. The roof is supported by four square piers, the sides of which show her being congratulated – feted – by the gods. It seems that Nefertari made it, was justified and permitted to enter the underworld, the essential step to rebirth.

In between these piers is the space in which Nefertari's sarcophagus and body would lave been placed. I lie there, to get the queen's perspective on the room, or rather the view her soul would have had as it hovered over her body. Above me is the cosmos, for the ceiling of the tomb is painted with thousands of small stars set against a dark blue background – these stars are the queen's ultimate destination. On the inner faces of the piers I see images of Osiris – so the lord of this realm is standing in attendance on the queen, welcoming her, declaring 'I grant you eternity, like Re my father'. But for the Egyptians the tomb was not a cold and sterile place of death, it was a place of god-like fertility, of new life that grows from old – it was a womb. And from this womb Nefertari would, she at least believed, be reborn. What do the paintings in the tomb tell me about this final phase? I rush back up the stairs, to the anteroom, and it's all there – painted on the west and south-west walls.

Now I read from right to left, from the burial chamber and towards the sunlight – life – flooding in through the door of the tomb. On the south wall – the wall containing the entrance door – are images of Nefertari kneeling in prayer, and of her soul in the form of a human-headed bird. She is about to fly from the tomb – from the realm of death. The final image is extraordinary. Nefertari is shown playing Senet with an invisible adversary, death I presume. This was a board game in which players traversed 30 squares – perhaps representing the days of the month – trying to avoid various pitfalls and make it home. It was a game of luck as much as of skill because moves were determined by the fall of dice-like sticks. So a game of chance, set within the constraints of time, in which luck as well as experience plays a part. Can this be Nefertari's comment on the process she has just been through, is this an image of her celebrating her victory over oblivion in which she wins the prize of eternity? And then she's gone – transformed, she returns to the daylight and, as a higher being, is reunited with the sun god Re and continues on her journey.

Nefertari's soul has gone – but what of her body? When her tomb was discovered in 1904 it was empty. It is assumed her internment had taken place because fragments of a sarcophagus and scraps of a mummy were found. Was the tomb brutally plundered down to the last item, or were its contents, including the mummy, systematically removed – for reasons now unknown – for re-internment elsewhere? We simply don't know. It's yet one more of the mysteries of Egypt.

64 THE TEMPLE OF HORUS, EDFU

We drive from Luxor to the temple at Edfu that lies about 100 kilometres to the south. This is one of the largest, best-preserved temples in Egypt – although also one of the last to be constructed, for the existing building was started in 237 BC by Ptolemy III and completed only in 57 BC. So it's from that strange Graeco-Roman Ptolemaic period when Egyptian theological traditions were sustained, seemingly little altered by these foreign powers, largely for political reasons. But, although late, the temple follows ancient principles in its planning, forms and embellishment so I should be able to walk in the footsteps of an ancient Egyptian – to confront the true scale of its architecture, to sense the masses of masonry, to experience its sequence of spaces and to read its details in a coherent manner. I can reconstruct temple life and worship – incredible.

Edfu is the traditional site of the epic battle between Horus and Seth, between good and evil, life and death. Seth was the brother of Osiris, a fallen god, the spirit of chaos and storms, the patron of violence and prototype for Satan. Horus, the god of the sky and son of Isis and Osiris, battled with Seth because this dark god had killed Osiris – who later underwent a Christ-like resurrection thanks to the prayers and magic of Isis. So, naturally, this temple is dedicated to Horus and, within, its stones tell the story of this clash of the gods.

I enter the first court, passing between two statues of Horus in the form of a giant, crowned falcon. This large, light and open court is as near as most worshippers could get to the inner shrine – the Holy of Holies ahead of me that was the powerhouse of the temple in which the most charged image of Horus was kept. From here on the temple becomes increasingly exclusive and intimate as its buildings gradually take the worshipper from the world of the profane to that of the sacred. In several distinct stages the spaces ahead become smaller and darker with different types of worshippers excluded, so that finally there were only two men in the land who could enter the inner shrine. So, in this court, ordinary people gathered, looking at the images incised on the columns and on the walls shaded by the columns. The common worshippers could follow a narrow open passage, next to the temple's perimeter wall, that leads from the outer court and wraps itself around the inner sacred spaces. I will pursue this route of

It took 180 years to complete the temple at Edfu but it only functioned as intended for 30 years because in 30 BC the Emperor Augustus eliminated Ptolemaic culture and brought Egypt fully under the rule of Rome. After nearly 3000 years, independent dynastic rule in Egypt ended and with it came, gradually but remorselessly, the end of a remarkable period of cultural, religious and artistic continuity. The walls of the pylons depict the Pharaoh Ptolemy XII smiting his enemies.

pilgrimage before entering the halls of the temple. Entry to this passage is not obvious but I see an opening on the east side of the outer court and walk through it to find myself between two high walls. I'm in the ambulatory. The walls are covered with incised images and hieroglyphs. It's extraordinary – these stones really do speak. In a country ruled by foreigners – Macedonian Greeks – the priests of temples such as this at Edfu clearly feared that foreign kings could decide to suppress, even obliterate, the ancient gods, religious customs and rituals of Egypt. So, in temples constructed during this uncertain period, history and tradition were literally built onto the fabric by being carved into the walls – but in a script so complex and obscure that it can only be read with great difficulty. The messages are coded – the priests wanted their secrets preserved.

I return to the outer court and become an Egyptian grandee. I leave the milling masses, and journey on, to the dark heart of the temple. First I enter a rectangular hall in which stand 12 tall columns, set in four groups of three, which help support the heavy stone roof above. This is the first of the three main spaces within the shrine, which culminate in the Holy of Holies or sanctuary. Entering this hall gives a good impression of what entering the Temple of Solomon must have been like, for his temple was divided into three portions and was clearly inspired by ancient Egyptians of the sort that provided the prototype for this temple at Edfu. I look at my small plan of the temple – yes its outer walls, excluding the pylons, are of 3 to 1 proportion. It's as if I'm in the Temple of Solomon – at last – and making my way to the Holy of Holies. In Solomon's Temple I would have found the Ark of the Covenant there, guarded by angels. What, I fear, will I find here? I walk, north, through a small door. More of the band of worshippers would have fallen away because where I'm going would have been open only to the elite of the land – the royal family and nobility, and priests. This hall is smaller and of familiar proportion. I check, yes, its floor plan is a double square and the hall looks as high as it is wide, so, again a double cube – that sacred form that men have, through the ages, believed to be in harmony with the works of the gods. And here, as in the previous hall, 12 columns grouped in four sets of three. Are the individual columns marking the months of the year and the groups of columns marking the four seasons? Time, cycles and eternity – the essential issues for a religion focused on death, rebirth and the desire to escape the endless repetition of earthly existence. The Egyptians believed in the power of the representation of things. As long as the cartouche of your name remained, carved in stone, you lived in memory and so your soul survived. So I suppose a physical representation of time – the diagram formed by these columns – allowed the priests to, in a way, own or control time.

Now, in front of me, there is yet another narrow entrance. It leads into a thin sliver of a room – in the short, west wall of which is a small recess. In this strange space offerings would have been made and beyond it is a corridor that runs entirely around the shrine. Off this corridor are a number of small cells, each of which would have been a private chapel dedicated to one of the favoured gods of the region – Re, Osiris. I have a look in these chapels. Most have incised images on the walls, once painted and now mostly damaged – faces scratched away by early Christians or Islamic fundamentalists. I enter the first temple on my left. I look at the carvings on the wall – many mutilated – but the mutilations form a strange pattern. I look more closely and suddenly realise that it is a chapel to Min, the protector of fertility, who is shown in ithyphallic form – bandaged as a mummy, holding a lash and with a huge erect penis. He confirms the cycle of existence, that from death comes new life, and was the patron of harvests of all kinds. But what has been chiselled away, on most of the images

One of the statues of Horus as a giant, crowned falcom which stand at the gate to the first court at Edfu.

near ground level, is the god's member. Who on earth would have done this, I wonder? Exactly when did fertility and the means by which humans undertake the divine act of procreation become a thing of which to be ashamed, something dirty, lewd and embarrassing? Shame and guilt certainly lurk in the Old Testament where any sexual activity that is purely pleasurable and not strictly related to procreation is frowned upon. The same is true of the Koran, so I suppose this vandalism could be the work of early iconoclasts. But I can't rid myself of the image of 19th-century Grand Tourists having a phallus knocked off for fun. Can one of Min's members, I wonder, be standing erect on a mantelpiece in the Home Counties – a much loved family heirloom? It's just possible.

Having walked around this corridor I arrive back at the front of the sanctuary. As I cross over the threshold into this shrine I am doing what only two men on earth were permitted to do when this temple was consecrated and working. Only the high priest of the temple and the Pharaoh in his capacity of supreme high

The first hall, with the stone slabs of its ceiling supported by twelve stout columns, arranged in four groups of three. Perhaps these columns, carved with images of gods and Pharaohs, symbolise the months of the years and the seasons – are a calendar, suggesting that the priests of the temple had time under their control.

priest could enter this windowless, cubical, stone-built sanctuary. I go inside. It reminds me of the chamber in the heart of the Great Pyramid and the shrine in front of me seems to correspond with the altar-like sarcophagus. It stands 4 metres high, is constructed from a single block of grey granite and is far more ancient than this temple in which it rests. In it would have stood the image of Horus, the religious focus of the entire temple. Texts on the wall describe the rituals that took place here, the morning service when the high priest exposed, washed, fed and dressed the image of Horus, burning incense and reciting spells – prayers – of praise and purification, and the distribution to the priests of the 'daily bread' – the sanctified bread that had been offered to the gods in the various chapels around the sanctuary. It seems clear where many Christian rituals come from.

I leave the temple. It is, despite its near complete condition, one of the most melancholy places in Egypt. The priests were right to worry. It took 180 years to complete this temple but it only functioned as intended for 30 years because in 30 BC the Emperor Augustus eliminated Ptolemaic culture and brought Egypt fully under the rule of Rome. After nearly 3000 years, independent dynastic rule in Egypt ended and with it came, gradually but remorselessly, the end of a remarkable period of cultural, religious and artistic continuity. In Edfu you can see – sense – this end coming. The stones here are far from mute – to look at the frantic carvings that cover them is to see the death spasms of a doomed civilisation – a civilisation that, in many ways, is the greatest the world has ever known.

The old religion died – but the temple builders did achieve a form of immortality. The names of the gods and of the great of Egypt live on in the stones – and while their names are still spoken they are, in part at least, still alive.

MAN AND NATURE

Sunday 17 October
For the first time, after four months away, we are about to return to Europe. We are flying to Istanbul – the threshold of the continent – and then we will thrust into western Russia. In this chapter of our travels we plan to look at the way man has worked with nature, often in a dramatic manner, to create a series of cultural treasures – many of them underground, deep below the surface of the earth. We shall see how landscapes have been traversed or manipulated, and how little islands of spiritual and artistic beauty have been created in remote and inhospitable regions. We will also see how those dreams can go bitterly – hellishly – wrong.

Tonight we dine with our local fixers to plan tomorrow's shoot. There is scaffold in Hagia Sophia – which is bad for us – but this problem could be turned to advantage if I can get a close view of the structure. Getting this consent is proving difficult. We have to plot – and a bottle of wine helps the concentration. We go to a restaurant in the Beyoglu district, take a table outside and examine the menu. Ah! Lambs' brains. This should help. I order a portion and wolf them down. Delicious – sweet and fine, the best such thing since the ram's testicles I devoured at Petra.

65 HAGIA SOPHIA, ISTANBUL, TURKEY

Monday 18 – Tuesday 19 October
Hagia Sophia, or Ayasofia as it is called in Istanbul, is only a few minutes' walk from our hotel, so we get up early, see the sun rise over the Golden Horn – the water of which turns a deep, red-flecked gold – and then go on to our treasure.

Hagia Sophia – 'Holy Wisdom' – was commissioned by Emperor Justinian I in 532 and when completed five years later was regarded as not only the greatest church in the Eastern Roman Empire – Byzantium – but as the greatest church in the world. In both scale and architectural ingenuity it outstripped the Holy Sepulchre in Jerusalem and St Peter's Basilica in Rome and was heralded as one of the new wonders of the world. Its architects – Anthemius of Tralles and Isidorus of Miletus – seem to have been determined to eclipse the domed and massively constructed Pantheon in Rome, that was completed in about AD 128 as a pagan temple to all the gods. Hagia Sophia achieves its stupendous scale with an elegance, refined minimalism and scientific ingenuity that puts the Pantheon in the shade. Indeed its lofty dome seemed, when first completed, to be an almost supernatural incarnation of God's creation, to be a celestial hemisphere that hovered – virtually unsupported – between heaven and earth. It was pioneering – nothing quite like it had ever been created before. When Justinian saw the completed interior for the first time in 537, he revealed another inspiration for the building: 'Solomon,' he exclaimed, 'I have surpassed thee.'

My first view of the Hagia Sophia is shocking – it's a sacred mountain of a building, vast and elemental, rising out of humdrum urban surroundings. It's like seeing the pyramids rising above the banal suburbs of Cairo – giant works of genius, almost not of this world, set among the dross of man's daily life. The violence of the visual juxtaposition is almost like a bodily assault – I blink to take it in. The huge dome, with its dark covering, is now framed by much later minarets – added in the late 15th and 16th centuries after the church was converted to a mosque when the Turks seized

Constantinople in 1453. The exterior is complex, but what is clear is that the building is really all to do with the interior space created. It's the inside that's important, that is a simulation of God's creation – and, of course, the most important part of the interior is the celestial dome.

I enter the building through a door in its south-west corner, which leads below a wonderful early mosaic that reveals the source of the Holy Wisdom after which the church is named. In its centre is the Virgin Mary – the new Christian personification of Mother Earth, female power and wisdom that had been earlier represented by great goddesses such as Isis, Ishtar and Minerva. The Virgin is flanked, and being bowed to, by Emperor Constantine who holds a model of his city of Constantinople and by Justinian who holds a model of Hagia Sophia. They are offering, dedicating, their creations to the Virgin, asking her protection.

Little can prepare you for the experience of the main interior. It's like entering a new, ideal world, over which the dome of heaven presides. That, of course, is just the point. It's a magical harmony of square and circle – the symbols of the material and the sacred worlds. I imagine all who have walked here before me, the English crusaders who came here in the 12th century – men from the fogs and damps of northern Europe where architecture was massive and ponderous. What on earth would they have made of this? A tall, airy structure, light flooding in, a huge dome – like a flying saucer – high above their heads. It must have been beyond comprehension. Although the great central dome dominates, this is far more than just a spectacular domed interior. The space created is complex, in both its form and its meaning. Early churches in Europe generally took the traditional form of the Roman basilica – a rectangular hall with a central nave divided by columns or piers from flanking aisles that, usually, had lower ceiling heights than the nave. This form, with the addition of short transepts to create a cruciform ground plan, suited Christian liturgy – its parades, processions and festivals – and it is this that inspires the plan of Hagia Sophia. The main body of the building is rectangular with the nave forming a double square in plan. In the centre of this nave floats, high up, the dome.

The way in which the rectilinear basilica transforms, as it rises, so that it sustains – in a sense becomes – the curvaceous series of domes and semi-domes is miraculous. The four main piers of the basilica sprout four huge semi-circular arches that leap from one pier to the other. These are linked by four concave triangular forms – called pendentives – that join to form the circular ring on which the base of the drum sits. This structure, that subtly squares the circle, is doing much to support the weight of the dome. But this is only the obvious part of the support system. Because this structure appears so minimal and elegant the dome appears to float – especially since its lower portion is pierced by a closely set row of windows to let light pour in, making the junction between dome and supports look transparent, almost non-existent.

The brilliant and brave science comes with the way in which the outward – lateral – thrust of the central dome is handled. Domes are immensely strong structures capable of supporting great weights and spanning wide spaces – but they are difficult to construct and difficult to keep standing. The curved form, although strong by design like an eggshell, means that much of its weight exerts a horizontal thrust so the dome –

When complete Hagia Sophia proved to be one of the great inspirations for the design of sacred buildings. Circular and domed, it is of such a scale and elegance of construction that it appears to defy the laws of nature. Much of what I see outside – the buttresses and terrace-like blocks of structure – only make sense when it is realised that they keep the great dome in place.

The interior of Hagia Sophia. It's like looking at a prayer floating up to heaven. This apparent lightness is the genius of the design for it is achieved by sleight of hand, by clever structural tricks grounded on a thorough understanding of the science of construction. It's brilliant.

by its nature – wants to spread, to flatten itself. This outward thrust can be reduced depending on the materials or methods of construction and can be resisted in an ugly or elegant fashion. At Hagia Sophia the solution is breathtaking. The lateral thrust of the huge central dome is balanced by the opposite and roughly equal counter thrusts exerted by two half-domes opening to the east and west and by the small domes at the four corners of the nave. Sturdy buttresses to north and south transfer much of the horizontal thrust of the dome into the rest of the structure and carry it down to the ground. All is in equilibrium, poised, the laws of science, of nature, are used to keep the structure standing. This was an unprecedented structure but its designers never lost their nerve.

I have received permission to climb the scaffold that rises below the central dome so, now, up I go. It is a high climb but I can see wonderful things. When Islam first took over the building the Christian decoration – showing figures like Mary and Christ who are venerated in the Koran – was tolerated. But in the 16th century a harder attitude was taken and all images showing living beings were painted over in case God might think them idols. As I climb higher I get a close view of the consequences. The pendentives below the dome contain curious things – within each is a huge, swirling being that seems to have no head – just feathery wings, and lots of them. I assume they are meant to be angels. Now, as I get level with them, I can see what happened. In the midst of each swirl of feathers is a star on a disc, a detail that has always struck me as odd – now I can see that this star covers a face. They were angels but, by the simple device of covering their faces with stars, these abstract celestial beings were made acceptable to the Islamic iconoclasts. However, as I climb higher and look down into the galleries, I'm reminded these 16th-century Muslim fundamentalists were not the first to rob this place of some of its beauty and meaning. In the 8th century the Byzantine church resolved to stop the production of icons because it was feared that congregations were worshipping the image itself rather than the divinity it portrayed – in short, Christians were becoming worshippers of idols. This, said the church, was in direct opposition to the word of God, with only the cross, an admirably abstract object, being an acceptable focus of prayer. The spiritual and artistic consequences were massive, and existing icons were destroyed or obliterated. In the galleries I can see the remains of marvellous mosaics plastered over in the 8th century, and only revealed relatively recently. I catch a glimpse of the original magnificence and glory of this interior.

From the top of the scaffold I can reach the narrow timber gallery that runs around the bottom of the dome. This is a very precarious place to be – its floor slopes, the ancient timber rail is decayed and I must be about 40 metres above ground level. It's thrilling. If I fell, what a place to die! I can see the brick with which the dome is built – suddenly I see the structure afresh and comprehend the achievement, a huge brick dome. Imagine the difficulty of creating this vast structure, so high above ground level – a structure that would, as it rose and its inward lean increased, have become more and more awkward and would only have been stabilised when the final key bricks were in place. Heroic indeed.

I stand in the nave once more, below the dome, and look up at this epic construction – an elemental work that has withstood the violence of nature and of man. It's been rocked by earthquakes, ransacked by invaders (notably crusaders who attacked Constantinople in 1204) and repainted by fundamentalist iconoclasts. But here it is, a mighty prayer in brick and stone rising up to heaven. A vast building that, paradoxically perhaps, achieves spiritual power through the supreme understanding of the material world. Here, the forces of nature have been harnessed to realise a structure that makes God's wonder and wisdom manifest.

66 UNDERGROUND CITY OF GOREME

Wednesday 20 – Thursday 21 October

We fly to Goreme, in the central Turkish region of Cappadocia in Anatolia. This was the heartland of an ancient civilisation – the Hittites who, 3000 years ago, were one of the great powers on earth and in constant contention with Egypt for domination of the region between these two great nations and empires. By the 6th century the Hittites had come under the control of the Achaemenid Persian Empire and I saw bas-reliefs of Cappadocian tribute-bearers making their way up the staircase in Persepolis. Now I'm going to see part of their land, in fact a place that seems to come straight out of a fairy tale. We take a balloon ride to best see this strange landscape – a landscape from the world of the imagination, from the world of pure fantasy. We rise, packed into a basket and suspended below a vast, multicoloured envelope into which our pilot is repeatedly sending gushes of hot air from a flame just above my head. I can smell burning – I hope it's only me. We drift where the wind blows us, across these playful works of nature. I can see that some of the towering rock chimneys have been burrowed into – as have the rocks and cliff faces below and around them. They imply that much is going on beneath the surface of the earth – that it's inhabited! I want to find out more – but landing is a problem in this rocky terrain. At last we come to a halt. The pilot looks immensely relieved. Perhaps landing was trickier than I realised.

Our vehicles soon arrive and we are off to look below the surface of things. We drive to Derinkuyu, a small and ancient town – but it's what lies beneath that is my treasure. The promise of the fairy chimneys is here fulfilled – there is a city below the ground. Quite when or exactly why this city was built is unknown. It stretches 55 metres below ground and consists of at least eight levels – although there could be more, for only about a quarter of this subterranean world has been excavated. Consequently estimates about its potential population vary wildly – from 5000 to 30,000, if nearby enclaves are included. But most agree that it was not inhabited permanently – perhaps during special seasons or rituals, almost certainly during times of war and invasion. As to its age, well that is complex. The first excavations may date from the Hittite period and so be, perhaps, over 3500 years old. The first recorded mention of such subterranean cities in the area is a description from about 400 BC by the Greek historian Xenophon, who

Previous page
*Goreme sits
within one of the
most fantastic
landscapes on
earth. For miles
around the
volcanic terrain
undulates with
small mountains,
steep cliffs,
plateaus and
gorges and –
most bizarre –
eruptions of tall
slivers of rock
that are known
locally as fairy
chimneys.*

wrote that the entrances to the houses were like wells and that families lived with their animals, with food and drink stored in great bowls. Whatever its origin, this city changed, evolved and grew over the centuries so that what now exists is the product of different ages, even of different cultures and peoples. Some portions may date from the earliest times with others excavated after AD 17 when the Romans occupied the region, or from the period of Byzantine control, from around AD 400.

I walk towards the entry, which lies at the base of a rocky outcrop that, I notice, contains the blocked remains of other doors – perhaps escape routes. Then down even deeper, by means of narrow, winding passages cut from the soft tufaceous rock, off which run innumerable multi-roomed cells. I wind down, the route splits, passages, narrower still, lead down in different directions, and I catch glimpses as I walk of floors yet lower down. The noise down here must have been fantastic when full of thousands of people – every movement produces a ringing echo – and what of the smell? Then I come to a small opening, waist-high, that helps answer the question about ventilation. I thrust my head inside the opening and get a shock. It's a mighty shaft that runs from the surface right down and deep into the city's bottom levels, although I can't see exactly where it terminates because the base of the shaft disappears into darkness, into the as yet unexcavated portions of this troglodyte megalopolis. But even with the gloom I can see, I estimate, at least 85 metres of shaft. It's truly huge, and beautifully wrought and regular in form. This is clearly part of a once complex ventilation system in which fresh air was sucked in and circulated around different levels as stale air rose and was expelled.

I keep on going down and find other spaces, large landings that are crossroads where passages meet, and halls that had communal uses. One is said to be a church – and certainly it must have been so at one time, for a sanctuary and altar stand at one end, the base of a font in the middle and ancient crosses are carved on one wall. I sit on the wall-benches carved from the rock. The Christian congregation would have sat here, perhaps in the late 1st century AD, escaping Roman persecution, or in the 7th century sheltering from Islamic marauders. This church may even have been a refuge in the 8th and 9th centuries for renegade clerics escaping the official church anathema against icons and, as religious rebels, bringing their sacred icons here for safety. What a thought. This cave-like hall could once have been packed with sacred images, glowing with gold.

I pursue my journey through the labyrinth, moving along passages and galleries that seem to get ever smaller as I plunge deeper and deeper. When occupied, this city must have been quite a community. To survive here, to make life bearable, all had to work together – to allow the air to flow, water and food to be brought in and stored, and for waste to be removed. What an amazing organism this city must have been, with people pumping through its passages like blood, the communal halls, church, water cistern, wine vaults and kitchen functioning like its vital organs.

I make my way upwards and, near the surface, enter a strangely narrow passage that opens into a low hall. To one side of the threshold is a huge and heavy stone – round and thick like a mill wheel, sitting on a slight ramp that slopes down to the threshold. This is a block stone, for use in emergencies to stop invaders entering by means of a sneak attack. By just removing a wedge one man could let the heavy stone roll down through gravity to block the door – the work of a moment, but it would take many men much time to roll the heavy stone back up again. Then I realise why the passages leading to this hall are narrow and its ceiling shallow – it's to prevent attackers wielding their swords with ease. Whoever created this subterranean barbican certainly knew what they were doing.

I finally make it back to the surface and, looking back, there is nothing to be seen of this city – as populous a thousand years ago as many surface cities. It's a heroic manipulation of the landscape, an extraordinary example of man working with nature and, a few yards away from the exit, you don't even know it's there.

This evening we are to see a sacred dance performed by dervishes. The dance is taking place in a far from ideal place – in a tourist restaurant. It seems to me rather like going to see the entertaining ritual of Holy Communion celebrated in a cocktail bar. Anyway, I keep my thoughts to myself and off we go. The restaurant turns out to be a horrendous and soulless hall and the event is clearly organised by some hapless local entrepreneur. I'm plunged into gloom – until the dervishes appear, clad in white jackets and trousers, with garments like a skirt hanging from their waists and all wearing tall felt hats. Slowly, as the rhythmic music starts, they begin, one by one, to turn, to whirl. Dervishes have danced since at least the 13th century. They are part of mystic Islam, Sufism, which believes that dancing, singing and chanting are a route to the divine. For dervishes dance is an act of prayer. They believe themselves a channel through which energy passes from above to below, from heaven to earth. It's an incredible thought – each man a little temple, doing his bit to bring stability to a rocky world.

The next day we look at Goreme from the ground. We go to a small place called Yanalak and I'm enticed into one shopping emporium that displays an intriguing sign outside: Hair Museum. The enterprising owner has come up with a clever ploy to make his shop – selling the usual tourist trinkets – different from his neighbours' trinket-touting shops. He attempts to cut a sliver of hair from every female who enters – and over the years he seems to have been surprisingly successful in this endeavour, for the two upper rooms of his shop – his 'museum' – are a true monument to what a determined fellow can get away with. There is hair everywhere, hanging from the walls, in drapes from the ceiling, of all colours and textures, thousands upon thousands of specimens, each labelled with the name and address of the donor. It's like walking into Bluebeard's parlour – the husband who, in the fairy tale, murdered his many wives and kept them in his castle. The hair floats in my face as I walk down the room. Strange sensation – I look up, half expecting to see a grinning skull attached to the end of each dangling bunch of hair. After all, this is fairyland.

The subterranean world at Goreme in Turkey dates from the time of the Hittites – around 3500 years ago. These are houses – complete with living rooms, bedrooms with bed alcoves and basement storage areas – and the spiralling passages are streets. This is extraordinary – it's like being a termite in a mound, an ant in a nest. The room on the left was transformed into a church.

Friday 22 October – Moscow

We spend the night in Istanbul and make an early start for Moscow. We enter the city at dusk. As we get near the centre the roads are fearsomely wide, many seemingly cut with wild abandon through the fabric of the city. Twenty years ago these roads were great and largely empty symbols of modernity and power, their use the privilege of the few party members and officials who had cars. But that, with the Soviet Union, is a thing of the past. Now in the new thrusting, ambitious Russia all have cars, and most of these seem to be on the section of road we are trying to use. We are stuck in a frightful traffic jam. Eventually we arrive at our hotel – and inside I experience the full, and not unpleasant, force of the Moscow character. You could call it rude and brutal, but I think that would be unfair. Honest and direct is probably nearer the mark. The young and not unattractive girl behind the reception desk shows no interest at all in us or our arrival. As far as she is concerned it would be perfectly alright if we simply picked up our bags and went off to another hotel. I fully understand – in fact I feel just the same way. After looking through us for a bit, she manages a grimace and we plod through the paperwork and eventually get our keys. This is a precious little backwater of the old USSR – no one here has heard of customer choice or practises the sad, hypocritical niceties that go with service culture. The message is direct and clear – if you don't like it, go elsewhere. Right, there's nothing to do but go out and have a very stiff drink indeed – probably vodka.

Our Moscow fixer – a young lady called Dasha – arranges a table at a nearby and, she says, very popular restaurant. Now I meet the new Muscovites – and it's an experience never to forget. If the men are suave and worldly, the women are absolute killers. Many look amazing. Not because of their looks so much, but because of their tribal clothes that scream wealth, success, style, and all manner of materialistic values. Virtually all wear shoes with long and very pointed toes and high, slender heels. Dresses are, naturally, brief and black, make-up heavy and hair – well, the hair is almost the best of all. To have a natural colour seems to be a disgrace – peroxide blonde is popular but the favourite, the colour of the moment, seems to be a red of a most unlikely hue. I wonder what on earth will happen to this emerging world which, tonight, looks particularly godless, materialistic and selfish. There's a darkness about it all. It's like watching the French Ancien Régime in its last days. Will the new freedoms in Russia – of which all this is an expression – suffer the same sudden end; will the guillotine fall here once again?

67   THE MOSCOW METRO, RUSSIA

Saturday 23–Sunday 24 October
The new anti-terrorist precautions being taken in Russia mean that anything that is in or near a government building is now out of bounds to us. But today our treasure is confirmed as the Moscow Metro – not the oldest, but certainly the most handsome and politically inspired underground service in the world and, I hear, one of the best. The story of the Moscow Metro is a fantastic tale. An underground railway system for the city was discussed first in 1901 but it was not until 1931 that it came to be seen as a project that could act as a showcase for Soviet technical and artistic excellence and construction was approved. In the early years of the new regime the arts were characterised by revolutionary avant-garde creations – abstract, radical, just the thing, you might think, for a nation born out of revolution and with a vision for a new, egalitarian social order. But for reasons that are still debated the ruling elite reacted against such revolutionary art – by the early 1930s the Soviet Union's experiment with radical Modernism was over. Official art and architecture were now to be based on tradition, paintings were to be figurative, heroic, showing the people of the nation – healthy, dedicated, unified and strong – marching into the bright new future. Architecture was to be based on the Classical tradition, and so speak in a language that most could understand. And so Socialist Realism was born. This could result in the soulless, mechanical and over-scaled Classical constructions that arose in both the USSR and Nazi Germany during the 1930s. Or it could mean the fantastic utopia that was created below the streets of Moscow.

I make my way to one of the early stations, Mayakovskaya, where I begin my descent into this peculiar underworld. It's immediately clear that mass public transport was intended to be a thing of delight – to inspire, to evoke national pride and to inform the people – by means of mosaic and sculpture – of the Soviet version of history. I walk down the platform and look up at the domes – in the centre of each is an oval opening, an oculus, which contains a mosaic showing a view of the world above. It's a socialist dream. The platform suddenly becomes an elegant arcade, threading through an ideal city, glimpses of which I see when I look up through the openings in the vault – towering, beautiful, modern buildings, aircraft flying in stately ranks, happy workers toiling, a balloon drifting serenely through the sky. These are windows into the new socialist world, vignettes – dreams – of things to come. I begin to read the message embedded in the Metro – 'If we can't yet build the future above ground we can build it below'. It was to be a parallel world, a world formed by a distinctly Soviet architectural vision, offering warmth, safety, cleanliness, beauty – and political instruction – to the people of the city, to all who used it. It was, and remains, propaganda of the highest order.

I jump on a train and move on to my next stop, Komsomol'skaya. This large station was opened in 1952, but incorporates work from 1935 and is one of the most extraordinary creations on the entire Metro system. Early Metro stations tended to be built by the cut-and-cover system, which means that they were excavated, while later stations were deeper and created by tunnelling. It's easy to tell which are which because the cut-and-cover stations have platforms with high, flat ceilings supported on columns while the tunnelled stations have lower, semi-circular ceilings. Komsomol'skaya combines both types of space to amazing effect. I walk along a wide, barrel-vaulted tunnel, reach a corner – dominated by a massive chandelier – turn and suddenly find myself contemplating a Baroque hall of great grandeur. I walk along it. Above me is a fine, decorated Classical ceiling containing a series of coloured mosaics that have a distinctly bellicose tone, revealing that the grandeur of this station is, at least in part, a cry of triumph for the hard-won victory of 1945. I see an image of Lenin, standing below the walls of the Kremlin and addressing the crowds in Red Square, and an image of Victory, holding aloft a hammer, sickle and palm fronds while trampling on Nazi banners. This, indeed, is a train station with attitude.

I walk through Komsomol'skaya Metro station in Moscow. A row of sparkling chandeliers hangs from the barrel-vaulted ceiling supported by squat octagonal columns. The walls are clad in marble and the vault enlivened with erudite and powerful Baroque detail. This is the corridor between platforms.

It's an amazing vision – this beautiful bronze figure, one of a pair, adorns the corridors of Revolution Square station. The Moscow Metro is a wonderful and efficient public service – catering for 7 million journeys a day. Not only are the stations well looked after but so are the trains, many of them original. It makes underground travel a positive pleasure.

I arrive at Revolution Square station – Plosschad Revolyutsii – that was opened in 1938. It is the most powerful yet – the barrel-vaulted central corridor is connected to the platforms on each side by a series of round, arched openings, on the corners of which are squat, slightly larger than life-size bronze figures. The figures are organised in pairs on each side of the opening and the story they tell is that of the October Revolution and the realisation of the new socialist society. There is a kneeling sailor, armed with a revolver and hand grenade; a bearded peasant and a young city girl – both clutching rifles; young male and female scholars lost in learning, idyllic; a buxom female athlete, still the picture of health after nearly 70 years of loitering on this platform. As I contemplate these works I also watch the inheritors of that world thread their way – un-looking – between the heroic statues. An intent man of business scurries by, a couple of drunken youths – clutching the ubiquitous bottle of beer – lurch past, a young girl in short tartan skirt and impossibly pointed high heels lingers below the ever alert sailor with his pistol cocked for posterity. This really is a most amazing place – a functioning station with a powerful political message.

I make the journey back to Tverskaya, the stop near my hotel. This has been a strange journey indeed – into the heart and soul of the Revolution, into its dreams and imagination, a trip through a vast and dream-like underground city where all the travellers are, if they wish, princes and princesses inhabiting fairy palaces. It may all seem a mighty paradox – a Party of the proletariat people creating these palatial interiors, inspired by the Tsarist era that had been forcibly overthrown. But there is wisdom and method in this apparent madness. The Party gave the people what the people wanted – it gave happiness to all who entered these subterranean halls. I walk through the white marble passages of the station – yes, the Metro is used by everyone and everyone seems to love it – and not just because of its physical beauty; it speaks, in a way, of freedom – the freedom to imagine, to fantasise, it makes the humdrum business of travel a fine exercise in escapism. I feel it as I walk.

In the evening we go to another restaurant that Dasha tells us is popular and amusing. It has an intriguing theme. It's the Cold War. We soon find ourselves in a dark courtyard looking down at a firmly closed basement door. The door pushes open, and a steep staircase lies before us with, fixed to an arch halfway down, a large insignia showing the hammer and sickle and emblazoned CCCP. Incredibly, this image, less than 20 years ago, struck fear into half the world, was a thing of awe. Now here it is, an amusing bit of popular art, an image that seems from an ancient world. We knock at the door – a couple of suited heavies open it and, without a smile, let us in. I assume they are part of the show, but when I see a uniformed fellow lounging in a back room, his AK-47 by his side, I'm not so sure. We are seated in a room redolent with the spirit of the 1950s and given a menu in the guise of a KGB file. Oh dear – that the great adventure of the Communist Revolution should have come to this, a thing to be mocked and scorned. It was an egalitarian vision that deserved a better fate. The fact that greedy and wicked leaders like Stalin ultimately betrayed the heady ideals of the revolution, the fact that the utopian vision failed utterly and miserably, became corrupt, evil and spawned murderous institutions such as the Gulags, really is no laughing matter. And now these Muscovites sit here, smirking wryly at their own past, while protected by armed guards. I suppose it's one way to come to terms with such grim recent history, one way to rob it of its sting. It's all so sad, I suppose, that you've just got to laugh.

68 SOLOVKI MONASTERY, ARCHANGEL

Monday 25–Tuesday 26 October

This morning we leave Moscow by air and head north towards Archangel, a great port on the White Sea. We are lucky, today there happens to be a scheduled flight to our next destination – which lies yet further north – although there will not be one to bring us back. To return to Archangel we have to charter a helicopter – that's something to look forward to. We are flying to Solovki, a place that haunts the memory of all Russians. It is part of the Solovetsky archipelago, consisting of six large islands, that represent the history of Russia in miniature, that enshrine its heart and soul – its flights of spiritual glory and its descents into darkness. Solovki has been a place of pilgrimage and one of the most sacred places in Russia, a monastery, frontier fortress and provincial capital supported by Ivan the Terrible and Peter the Great, a scene of siege and battle, a Tsarist prison and the location of the first Gulag – those Soviet concentration camps in which millions died in such beastly circumstances. To choose Solovki as a treasure may seem strange, but only if evil is allowed to eclipse goodness and beauty. It's a treasure because it's a place of redemption, of optimism, it shows that darkness does pass, that evil does not, in the end, prevail.

We load our gear and bump into town. We are just 160 kilometres south of the Arctic Circle and it's getting cold. The landscape is bleak. We pass by a small group of timber buildings, then the pitted earth road swerves to one side and I see onion dome-topped towers ahead. An amazing sight unfolds. The towers are growing from a bulky white building and this rises from the centre of a walled citadel – the kremlin of Solovki. This incredibly romantic image packs an enormous emotional and visual punch – it has the quality of a dream. With its cathedrals and domed and conical-roofed towers, this monastic city is both a spiritual beacon in a threatening landscape and a deeply sinister

The Solovki Monastery, a heaven and a hell. It's a beautiful site. The walls glow momentarily in the sun turning it into a shimmering golden city, but Solovki was also home to one of Russia's most notorious Gulags.

Left *The
'Quarantine'
barracks at
Solovki – all
male prisoners
spent their first
three months here
where they were
introduced to the
terrifying regime
of the camp.*
Right *A spiral
labyrinth on one
of the Solovki
islands. It is made
of small stones
which stand on
high land and by
the water's edge.
Spirals are a
powerful symbol
of pilgrimage.*

spectre – because this place was the very heart of the darkness that overtook these islands in the 1920s and 1930s, when the monks were expelled and the kremlin became the brutal epicentre of the Gulag.

We drive past the silent and brooding walls and towers. The wind is now blowing hard, it's almost as if the stones are howling. On one side is a sheet of water, stagnant and quietly filling the wind with the stench of rot. On the other side are tall, decaying wooden structures. These, the driver confirms, are barracks from the Gulag days. He points to one and informs me that it is where some of the women prisoners were lodged. The building looks derelict now, but it's not. Lights glimmer in some of its broken windows. It's used by seasonal workers and by pilgrims, for the monks and holy icons are now back in the monastery. Prayers are now again being said in places that were once filled with tears and groans of despair.

When we stop I walk around the kremlin, between the walls and the water, contemplating each of the gloomy towers. The monastery was founded in unusual circumstances. In 1429 two monks, called Savvatii and German, arrived in a small boat seeking refuge and solitude from the world. They built themselves cells, a small chapel and gradually they, and Solovki, acquired a reputation for holiness. Savvatii died in 1435 and German, who was joined by a young disciple called Zosima, dreamed of a great church on Solovki – and so the monastery was constructed. Once inhabited it became obvious that Solovki had great political, military and commercial potential. It was the frontier that Russia shared with the Swedes and Poles, a potential trade outlet for merchants coming from the West, and a growing spiritual centre. Tsar Ivan the Terrible grasped the importance of the place and appointed a Father Superior of the monastery. From 1548 were built the walls, towers and churches I now walk around.

It was Peter the Great, that most problematic figure who was undoubtedly one of the most successful of all Russian rulers, who cast a sinister shadow over Solovki, and set the precedent for using the monastery as a place of imprisonment. Peter first saw Solovki in June 1694, after being almost shipwrecked in the White Sea. A shaken man, he spent three days praying at the tombs of Savvatii and Zosima, thanking God for his deliverance. Although this was Peter's first visit to Solovki he had been sending political and religious prisoners there since 1691. It had become a place of terrible exile, its remote location making escape or rescue very difficult. Peter returned once more to Solovki, in August 1702, as the great and powerful Tsar. He ordered his soldiers to build a church on the nearby Zayatsky Island. This small structure, made out of timber logs, was soon completed and – despite 300 years of storm and neglect – still stands. We hire a little boat to make the journey across the smooth, but freezing and often lethal waters of the White Sea. The island is now uninhabited, but once it must have been home to a fishing community for among its rocks and lichen-covered banks are numerous spiral labyrinths, dating back perhaps 4000 years. Such creations – among the earliest of man's manipulation of the natural landscape – are found all over the world.

Monastic life in Solovki survived the turmoil of the 1917 Bolshevik Revolution – at least at first. But everything changed dramatically in 1923 when the monastery suffered a dreadful fire that did much damage to one of its cathedrals. The government – now the owner of the buildings – decided that this accident made Solovki the ideal place in which to conduct a pressing social experiment. The monks were moved out, political prisoners moved in and the buildings in the kremlin adapted to their brutal new full-time use as a prison, with other barracks and compounds built on Solovki and neighbouring islands. The experiment was the political re-education of those many Soviet citizens who were un-enamoured with Bolshevism, and with unsympathetic foreigners who fell into the hands of this new regime. Whatever the original intention, this re-education rapidly consisted of nothing other than sheer terror, given force by displays of mind-numbing brutality aimed at breaking the will of prisoners.

There is one room I must see here – perhaps the most infamous room in Soviet history. It was constructed in the mid-19th century as the Cathedral of the Holy Trinity but in 1923 became Company 13 – or the 'Quarantine' barracks – of the Gulag. The room is now an empty shell, a ruinous brick hulk, but in the early 1930s – when the Solovki Gulag held around 50,000 prisoners – as many as 850 men at any one time were crammed into the room. Lice and bed-bugs hung on the walls like curtains, planks of wood served as bunks that rose in tiers to the ceiling, and a colony of children cowered below the bunks – unregistered and unfed. It was psychological warfare. Latrines had been placed in the sanctuary at the east end with the image of Christ replaced by an image of Lenin. All was mockery. Those here were utterly alone, lost souls in a hell of despair. As Alexander Solzhenitsyn wrote in *Gulag Archipelago*: 'This was the basic idea behind Solovki. It was a place with no connection to the rest of the world…a scream from here would never be heard.'

When released from Company 13, prisoners were catagorised according to attitude and usefulness but, essentially, all were slaves of the state. No matter how minor or evidently non-existent their alleged crimes, most prisoners were in the Gulag system for perpetuity, with many being, quite literally, worked to death – and at Solovki the most brutal and murderous of work regimes was logging. In freezing conditions, with little food and no medical care, men were worked until they dropped. It's been estimated that between 1918 and 1956 at least 15 million and perhaps as many as 30 million people died in the Soviet Gulag – many of them at Solovki.

The Gulag at Solovki was closed in 1939 and the prisoners shipped elsewhere. The fighting with the Finns made the Soviets feel uneasy – the Solovki Gulag was too near potential enemies and its secret might be found out. The buildings were used by the navy during the war and then left to rot. But salvation came with the collapse of the USSR and in 1992 it seemed that history had come full circle. The bodies of Saints Savvatii, German and Zosima – that had been carted away by the Bolsheviks to a museum of religion in Leningrad – were brought home. Tonight I go to a service, in the church in the monastery, at which the saints are to be celebrated. In the dark, I make my way into the kremlin and ascend to the church above the gate. It is small, lined with icons, the curtain is open so I can see the Holy of Holies beyond the screen. In the middle of the church are the tombs of the saints, surrounded by monks and townspeople. The monks are chanting, the people praying and crossing themselves. It's a heartbreaking scene – the horrors are being buried, the old values are being reasserted. For a moment it's as if the nightmare had never been – but all in the church know that raw evil had washed over this place, and all the centuries of piety had been unable to stop it. Will things ever be the same here, in this strange and haunted place; will the ghosts ever be laid to rest?

69 PETER THE GREAT'S CABIN, ST PETERSBURG

Wednesday 27–Thursday 28 October

St Petersburg is, indeed, another world. Not only remote from the Arctic wastes and grim history of Solovki but also from the grime and high-pitched pace of Moscow. It is one of the great European cities – sedate, majestic, it speaks the familiar language of Classicism, it vies with Paris, Rome and Vienna. And this, of course, is just the point. Peter the Great founded St Petersburg in May 1703 to show his subjects – and the world – his vision for the nation, the direction in which he was determined his ever-growing empire was to develop. As Pushkin was to later write, St Petersburg was to be the Tsar's 'window through to Europe', the place from which he could contemplate the world and assure himself that Russia was now also a member of the community of great, powerful and progressive nations. Peter established the city through a combination of sheer will power, threats and the use of forced labour – as early as 1704 he was referring to it as his capital, his 'paradise'. During the next decades he laid out the basic network of the city's main streets on a hostile terrain of swamp and desolate islands, collected a population and initiated the construction of a number of major buildings. But, by the time Peter died in 1725, the great city – although the Russian capital since 1712 – was still more dream than reality. His successor and the court immediately took themselves back to Moscow. All could have been over – the vision unfulfilled, the place a ruin and a monument to mad ambition. But Peter's daughter Elizabeth, when she became Empress in 1741, returned the court to St Petersburg, which once again became the Russian capital. This fresh display of royal faith and commitment was to have extraordinary consequences – within little more than a hundred years Peter's fantasy was fact, his vision vindicated.

What has been produced is, arguably, the greatest Classical city in the world. The scale and breadth of the achievement is breathtaking, the quality of many of the individual buildings superb. Although created over a period of more than a hundred years, by different individuals and institutions using different architects, St Petersburg has incredible artistic coherence. The heroic and elemental nature of the site – the broad river Neva, the flat marshland stretching to infinity – seems to have inspired the makers of the city. All was conceived on the majestic and monumental scale, with diverse buildings, united by the erudite use of the Classical language and by the powerful use of a limited number of colours. Yes, the St Petersburg that was eventually realised is a city that cannot disappoint. To walk its streets, to scan the wide Neva, is to experience the exquisite marriage of man-made and natural beauty. But there is one very precise route that I want to take through the city, a route that will take me through its heart, to the very place of its origin – of its conception.

To extract the best from this journey I must undertake it in an open carriage so that I can experience the city in the way its creators intended – at a slow pace, and with my eyes raised to its splendours. Finding an open carriage in St Petersburg proves difficult but, just as I despair, an open carriage appears. It is painted white and driven by two jolly young girls. I hail it, we rapidly agree terms, and off we go, the horse puffing clouds of fiery steam. I feel that I've been picked up by two good angels and am trotting into a fantasy. Quickly they take me to my destination, the eastern end of the city's great and fashionable boulevard – Nevsky Prospect.

I start by the Anichkov Bridge. It crosses the Fontanka, one of the waterways that loop around the centre of the city to give it a sense of Amsterdam – a city Peter much admired. The view from this bridge is deeply impressive. Nevsky Prospect runs wide and true, with only one slight bend in its route, for nearly 5 kilometres from the Alexander Nevsky Monastery to the very heart of the city. The portion I'm about to parade down in my carriage runs for nearly 2 kilometres, as straight as a die. It's heroic stuff – and

shows Peter's determination to make nature submit to his will, to bend forest and field under the lash of rational geometry. This main route into the new city was key. Swedish prisoners of war were set to work to construct the long carriageway, but very little else happened before Peter's death. So, like much else in St Petersburg, the vision for the prospect is Peter's – he could see its noble vista in his mind's eye when all was still marsh – but the realisation of the vision was left to later generations. What I love, as I clatter down the road, is the architectural diversity within the discipline of the long, straight street – the unexpected architectural episodes, spaces and vistas that suddenly reveal themselves, evolve and, as suddenly, disappear. A square reveals itself with, in its centre, a dominating statue of Catherine the Great and, at its far end, the Aleksandrinsky Drama Theatre, designed by Carlo Rossi in the mid 1820s. This, architecturally, is what St Petersburg is all about – or rather what it came to be all about after 1812. The theatre is painted a beautiful ochre stone colour with white trim and is embellished with a noble colonnade topped by a statue of Apollo in a chariot. This big, bold and brave neo-Classicism – large in scale and in spirit – is absolutely right for Peter the Great's larger-than-life conception, for this giant of a city made by a giant of a man.

The tower of the Admiralty – standing on the Neva – draws me gradually forward. But now, without warning, the most dramatic of the Prospect's buildings erupts in front of me. First the dome and then the sweeping, curved wings of Kazan Cathedral come into view. As I move past, the wings open, embrace and then withdraw. It's amazing mobile geometry. Designed in 1801, the cathedral is modelled on St Peter's in Rome and so the message is clear. As St Peter's and Rome are the spiritual centre of the Catholic church so Kazan Cathedral and St Petersburg are the heart of the Russian Orthodox faith. Beyond the cathedral is the best of the palaces in the Prospect, in fact one of the best in the city – it is painted pink, while its luscious Baroque details are picked out in white.

The Winter Palace designed in 1754 by Rastrelli for the Empress Elizabeth is now part of the Hermitage Museum.

It's the Stroganov of the 1750s, an amazing vision – the exotic, brightly coloured and playful Baroque of southern Italy set beneath these brooding and icy northern skies.

Now, just across the Moyka, my carriage turns suddenly to the right. The main act is about to begin. As the turn continues it brings me in front of a huge stone-coloured arch, loaded with neo-Classical detail. The curving street has kept me in suspense, promised great things and then has brought me into, and the arch has framed, one of the greatest urban squares and 18th-century buildings in the world. Before me is the vast Palace Square with, on its far side, the Winter Palace, now part of the Hermitage Museum. I pass through this arch, from enclosed space and shade into the broad sweep of the square and the sharp, bright sunshine.

I stop and get out of the carriage. This place is not only a supreme example of the theatre of architecture, in which buildings evoke mood and tell stories, but also one of the crucibles of modern history. I try to imagine the events that were played out here – the most famous events were to do with the overthrow of monarchy and Tsarist military might. In January 1905, 150,000 striking workers and their families gathered in protest in the square to hand a petition to the Tsar requesting amnesty for political prisoners and basic civil rights including an eight-hour working day. But as the crowd marched through the city it was fired on by the Imperial Guard, with over several hundred demonstrators killed or wounded, many in the square itself. And then in October 1917 the square and the Winter Palace were once more the focus of protest and the scene of a key moment in the Bolshevik Revolution when the Winter Palace was stormed. So this great square, despite its imperial origin, associations and architecture is – paradoxically – a shrine of proletariat revolution. I sense the dead of 'Bloody Sunday' 1905 haunt this place, not the dead monarchy.

I board my carriage and move on. Finally I arrive at a small, late 19th-century brick building and go inside. I'm confronted by an extraordinary sight – within the brick building is another building, this one built of large, squared logs. I'm looking at the smallest palace in Russia, the first house in St Petersburg. Put together in three days by Russian soldiers in 1703, on the marshy banks of the Neva, within ancient forests, this is where Peter conceived his great city, this is where he dreamed of the things that were to come. I walk around the cabin, long protected from the elements and now with an interior furnished as it may have been in Peter's time. The place is miniscule. There's a study, a dining room and a tiny lobby that, apparently, served as Peter's bedroom. He, a giant of a man, stood over 2.5 metres tall, and would barely have fitted inside – let alone lived within it comfortably. What is all of this about?

I puzzle, look at some objects from Peter's time – including a cock-fighting chair he made himself – read some contemporary accounts, and gradually it dawns on me. Peter was a shrewd man, a man who saw the political potential of myth-making, of

architectural imagery – the whole of his vision for St Petersburg confirms this. In 1723 – two years before his death – Peter ordered that this little cabin should be protected and preserved for posterity. Of course – he saw the power of the image, and this building – so simple it seems absurd – is one of the most important and revealing structures in Russia. Just as St Petersburg opened a window on Europe, so this little cabin opens a window into the soul, the mind, of one of Russia's greatest rulers. This primitive hut, that Peter was determined should outlive him, carries his message from the grave. It was a piece of inspired propaganda that promoted, for popular consumption, the almost fabulous origin of Peter's empire and the myth of Peter's self-effacing modesty. It asks the same rhetorical question now as when first built. How can a man who preferred to live in a humble hut rather than a palace not be a good man? I suppose that in 1723, five years after Peter had organised the torture and execution of his own son, and with death stalking him, he must have been deeply troubled in mind – seeking to justify and vindicate his dark deeds, to present himself and his actions in the best possible light. So the cabin is like a holy icon – a casket to contain the Tsar's troubled soul. It proclaims that Peter wanted to build one of the greatest cities in the world not for his own glorification but for that of holy mother Russia, just as he had executed the son and heir he regarded as useless not because of impious fury but to save Russia from misrule by a weak and incompetent Tsar.

I take a last look at this strange dwelling feeling deeply troubled. Like the witch's sugar plum cottage in the tale of Hansel and Gretel, the cabin looks quaint and appealing but concealed a sinister intention. In this primordial construction sat Peter – dreaming of a celestial city – yet willing to achieve it and his empire through any means necessary. I imagine his huge bulk lurking in the shadows of these small rooms, his powerful and fiery personality – himself like one of the elements, a primordial being. I tear myself away and, in the evening light, walk along the bank of the Neva, looking at the city – Peter's vision. He did indeed create one of the most beautiful cities in the world – but at a price.

Friday 29 October – Poland

As a child I lived in Poland for a number of years and have never returned. Just the thought of going back stirs deep and pleasant memories. I lived in Warsaw, where we shall, sadly, not be going – but once visited Krakow, where we are filming. Although young when I walked its streets I have powerful memories of the city. Its ancient houses, towering churches and the squares of its Old Town had a strange and potent effect on me – inflamed my imagination, opened my eyes to architectural beauty. I realise that returning to Krakow is a very personal pilgrimage – a return to my roots in a way. I'm looking forward greatly to going back. We fly via Munich and don't arrive at our hotel until 3.00 am. We have to leave for our location at 7.30 am. It's been another long day.

Left *Peter the Great lived in this tiny log cabin in 1703 when he started building St Petersburg.* Right *The interior looks like a dwelling from a fairytale and is furnished much as it would have been when he lived there.*

70 WIELICZKA SALT MINE, POLAND

Saturday 30 October

I drag myself up, pump myself with coffee, and we're off, with just a quick glimpse of the spires of Krakow as we drive past. We are travelling only 17 kilometres but it is a journey that will take us into the very heart of the Polish nation. We are going to a mine from which salt has been extracted since the Middle Ages and which now, strange as it may seem, has become a place of national pride and identity. In the past salt was wealth and power, and so helped to sustain independence in an ever hostile and predatory world. It was literally as good as gold.

Salt provided the economic foundation of the state and was a means of payment and currency. It was difficult and expensive to obtain in the quantities required, so those nations or institutions that had abundant supplies were able to make fortunes through trade. The monks at Solovki, Russia, became wealthy by processing salt on their islands and so did the people of Krakow. By the 14th century the mine at Wieliczka created 30 per cent of the nation's income, and by the 16th century it was one of the largest business enterprises in Europe. The body needs salt, it has medicinal qualities, many foods are improved in taste by its addition and – most important – it can preserve certain foods. Preservation and storage of food in time of plenty allows an escape from hand-to-mouth existence and grants man time to think, to create, for his imagination to blossom. So salt and civilisation go hand in hand. We arrive at the mine where, after more than eight centuries of production, the commercial mining of salt finally ceased in the mid-1990s – salt can now, it seems, be won more economically by other means in other places. So this mine is now a museum. I was last here nearly 50 years ago but, not surprisingly, I recognise little of the above-ground buildings – my vivid memories are of what happens underground.

The mine is on nine levels, which reach 327 metres deep and, counting all chambers and passages, it stretches for over 300 kilometres. It was a world in itself. As well as miners at the salt face the mine employed many other trades – carpenters, barrel-makers, smiths and stable boys, and contained chapels, kitchens and an infirmary. It's the vast and dramatic remains of this world that I am about to see again, after so many years. But our first destination is an extraordinary work of nature found by man's burrowing deep below the surface of the earth. We descend to one of the very deepest parts of the mine and then head off along galleries – many sustained by aged pit props, some of which, I notice with mild alarm, have been splintered by recent movements of the earth. We trudge on and, after a couple of kilometres, I'm in a grotto formed by clear, solid salt crystals. This is most un-organic nature – amazingly, these small, crystalline constructions possess the planar, geometrical perfection that the

The Chapel of St Anthony at the Wieliczka salt mine near Krakow has life-size sculptures of saints carved in salt and is lit by rock crystal chandeliers.

pyramid builders were aiming at. It seems obvious – the Great Pyramid is nature's architecture rendered by man on a gigantic scale, the chamber within a Euclidian grotto. The local guides with me are tremendously proud of the grotto, this wonder of nature formed by their national mineral. Poles are generally devout Catholics – certainly in this part of the country – and it is obvious, from the numerous shrines we've passed, that the deep mine, its life-giving salt and crystalline beauty, had a deep spiritual significance for the miners. They were trespassing in the underworld, it was a dangerous business. All they could do was to ask

Decorated graves at the cemetery in Krakow on All Souls' Day.

God's forgiveness and protection. The men with me – all former miners – seem to retain these values and exude veneration and awe for the hidden world around them.

We make our way back through the galleries and return to the surface so that we can, through a different route, approach the now more accessible portions of the mine. We pass along winding galleries, peer into huge shafts and enter vast grottoes with pools of still water forming their floors. I discover the rock-cut Chapel of St Anthony, peopled with life-sized figures of gnarled salt saints illuminated by rock crystal chandeliers, and then enter the largest hall – an amazing place, a salt-cut cathedral with carved religious tableaux enlivening all the walls. It's a fantastical marriage of man's work and nature that I've seen many times in my dreams, in my mind – it's the place that, when I saw it first as a very young child, confirmed that fairyland did indeed exist. This, with the other caverns and galleries, is the mine I remember – but it has been strangely transformed. The great hall and chapel remain moving but elsewhere are grotesque dummies of medieval miners toiling and even humorous gnomes lurking in grottoes. The place is being over-presented, turned into a theme museum – things that kill the magic of the place and paralyse the imagination. I scurry off, not wanting the spell to be broken.

Sunday 31 October – Krakow

Today is All Souls' Day in Poland – a most important occasion in Catholic countries, for it is a time when the living remember the dead, when families go to the graves of their ancestors to pray, place flowers and light candles. I will go to the cemetery this evening to see this sombre spectacle but first I want to find the old Jewish quarter. I want to see what's left of the Ghetto, this once thriving part of the city. The fabric has not been utterly destroyed – like the rest of Krakow this quarter survived the war and the Nazi occupation of the city. But what of the people? A memorial in the square provides the answer. It tells me that 65,000 Jews from Krakow and the region were killed during the Second World War. As I suspected, these charming streets have seen horrors.

With heavier step, I walk back to the Stare Miasto, the old town, and enter the narrow streets, full of life and lined with an amazing array of ancient buildings – some medieval, many Renaissance in manner, but the majority 18th-century, painted in gay colours and with frivolous Baroque decorations. It's astonishing how southern European it all feels. The strong Catholic belief of the people has, over the centuries, meant that Krakow was built as a sort of miniature Rome. It reminds me of King Lalibela building his capital in Ethiopia as the New Jerusalem. I see a Jesuit church, St Peter and St Paul of 1596 to 1616, modelled on Vignola's mighty Gesu in Rome, and a powerful provincial version of one of my favourite Roman churches – Santa Maria della Pace. This essay on the exquisite prototype – called the Church of the Conversion of St Paul and completed in 1728 – is, like the other churches I've looked at, packed. There can be little doubt that

Polish Catholicism survived the spiritually arid and hostile years of communist rule.

Finally I arrive in the central square, framed by tall buildings, few later than the 18th century and many of outstanding quality. As the hour strikes a trumpet call sounds from one of the towers. It's mournful and stops mid note – a memorial to a brave sentinel who stuck to his post during a Tatar raid on the city in the 13th century and was rewarded with an arrow through the throat.

The trumpet calls, the rich and diverse details in the square, bring back deep memories – it all looks and sounds so familiar, evokes emotions. It was here, I suppose, that when a child, I fell in love with architecture. To return now to this place is to journey into my own past, into my memory, to begin to discover the origin and roots of passion. Most odd, and not a little disturbing. To cheer myself I go to the cemetery. It's dusk when I arrive and, to my amazement, this realm of the dead is full of life. Candles, in their thousands, burn everywhere, flowers are strewn on graves, music echoes from a chapel. The families of Krakow are visiting their dead. I stroll among the graves – there's a festive atmosphere. It makes me think of other rituals of death and burial that I have discovered on this journey – the prolonged funerals in Sulawesi, the Great Necropolis of Petra. Coming to terms with death, making sense of the loss of a human life, is a concern that unites all people through the ages.

71 VOLKSWAGEN BEETLE, MUNICH, GERMANY

Monday 1 – Tuesday 2 November
We fly to Berlin and I find myself again at Munich airport. It's quite a shock. After nearly five months out of western Europe, in generally run-down and dusty countries, I'm now back in a very familiar world. Everything around me is thoroughly designed, all is bright, clean, state-of-the-art, monitored and controlled. I can suddenly see my world for what it is – it's more than a little alarming. But this is about the best place on earth to confront the demon of design, because design in Germany is not only of high quality but has, in recent history, carried a massive political as well as an artistic punch. And the period that I'm going to confront in Germany – the 1920s and 1930s – is the most problematic of all. This is an epic epoch in world history that saw the clash of conflicting ideologies – Marxism and National Socialism – both of which used design to promote and express their very different world views. I'm going first to look at a car – one of the most successful ever produced – and then at a building which launched an entirely new way of seeing – of living in – the modern world.

Our hotel is in the very centre of Berlin, on Friedrichstrasse just off the Unter den Linden. This was east Berlin before the wall came down, but you'd never know that now. In the old days east Berlin was wonderfully dowdy, its buildings still pocked with bullet holes from the 1945 battle for the city. But all that is gone. And only on Unter den Linden do the great imperial dreams linger – here are mighty Classical buildings worthy of a world empire.

Into this setting there arrives a vehicle that is both of its time and strangely out of time. It's my treasure and transport of the day – a Volkswagen Beetle. This car was in production for 65 years; by 1981, 20 million had been made, and still they rolled off the assembly line. It's one of the most familiar and best-loved design objects on the roads around the world – I took great pleasure to see it in large numbers in Mexico City, where the Beetle is still used as the standard taxi. But the model before me now is curious. It's painted a dark grey-green, there is no chrome anywhere, and there are some unexpected details. I talk to the chap who has driven the car to the hotel and, to my surprise, I discover that this particular VW was made in 1943 – it's a wartime Beetle!

The VW Beetle has an extraordinary history that goes back to the early years of the 20th century when Henry Ford demonstrated that pioneering mass-production and assembly-line techniques could be applied to the manufacture of cars to create a cheap and reliable automobile. The Model T was born in 1908 and with it the possibility that the ordinary working man could own a car and so gain freedom of movement – individual mobility. The scale of the dire environmental and ecological consequences of mass mobility – roads destroying the very beauty travellers sought, cities wrecked by congestion, fumes and vast pollution – were not foreseen. People wanted cars – politicians who could realise this dream would win votes, and manufacturers who could deliver cheap and reliable cars would make a fortune. To succeed in the manufacture of readily available automobiles was, it seemed, to become master of the machine age.

Adolf Hitler, when in prison in 1923, read Henry Ford's biography and found it inspirational – here was, indeed, a master of the modern age. Ford's methods and achievement must have haunted Hitler for, in 1933, just after he had become Chancellor, Hitler gave his full backing to the creation of a people's car – a Volkswagen. By creating a true Volkswagen he would win popularity while also helping to increase the military power of Germany. A generation of young men who had learned the skill of driving would make useful soldiers, while the mass-production techniques developed for the manufacture of a Volkswagen could be applied to arms production. It would be the creation of panzer divisions by stealth – and the world would not even know what was happening. So the creation of a Volkswagen became a key Nazi project. Hitler commissioned a design from Ferdinand Porsche (then currently working for Daimler Benz and who later designed heavy tanks for the German army), who was supplied with a very specific brief. The car was to carry two adults and three children, at a maximum speed of 60 miles per hour and consume a minimal amount of fuel, and have a robust suspension to cope with Germany's rough roads – but that was another problem the Führer was soon to deal with. By the time the Beetle was in full production it could hurtle along the new military roads that Hitler created to unite the country and to act as routes to help German forces invade neighbouring countries – the Autobahns. Porsche got to work, came up with a lightweight 984 cc air-cooled engine that supplied the required speed and achieved 33 miles per gallon of fuel. To save money, the engine was mounted immediately above the rear driving wheels. Porsche also did his best to make the modest family vehicle as comfortable as possible with hot air heating.

The first prototype was tested in 1937, faults were rapidly ironed out, an assembly-line factory – modelled on Ford's works in Detroit – was built and the first Type 60 Beetle rolled into the world in August 1938. This relatively speedy transformation of a dream into a fully engineered and mass-produced reality was made possible through the manipulation of the national economy.

Essentially, when the creation of a people's car became a political

The KdF-wagen, the 'Strength-through-Joy vehicle', represented the aspirations of the 1930s. It was the child of new technology and new methods of mass production. Twenty thousand cars were produced in the first year. This is a 1943 model.

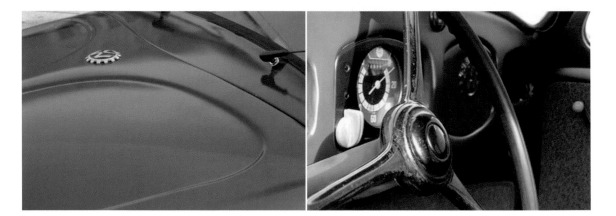

Left *Hitler's close
involvement with
the design of the
Beetle is revealed
by his instructions
to Ferdinand
Porsche: 'It
should look like
a beetle,' he said.
'You've only to
look to nature to
find out what
streamlining is.'
Right *The
instruments are
minimal and easy
to see and read.
The dashboard
is perfectly
symmetrical so
it can be used
for left or right
hand drive.*

issue, the project was subsidised through various Nazi Party organisations. The Nazi Kraft durch Freude – the 'Strength-through-Joy' organisation – that aimed to politicise workers' leisure time also became involved since the Beetle was, ostensibly, a machine of leisure. Indeed so close was the involvement of the KdF that Hitler decreed that the Type 60 VW be called the KdF-wagen, the 'Strength-through-Joy vehicle'. Porsche's opinion of the extraordinary name bestowed upon his creation by the Führer is not recorded. In just over a year after the commercial production of the KdF-wagen had started, Germany invaded Poland and launched the Second World War. By this time the 'Strength-through-Joy vehicle' had already been appropriated by the military – just as Hitler had planned back in 1933 – and many German officers rode to war in the military version of the KdF-wagen that was turned out in huge numbers from the factory.

The Beetle I climb into is immaculate, having been restored to its original condition. The interior is sparse but comfortable and I have no problem fitting my rather long legs into the driver's seat. I start the Beetle by turning the ignition key and pushing the start button. All goes well – the engine purrs happily. Then into gear, no worry there – the gear box, organised as in modern cars, is oily smooth. Hand brake off, and away I go. The drive is smooth, but now I get a shock. The foot brake 60 years ago is not what a foot brake is today. Alarmingly, this car, like all cars of its generation, only glides to a gradual halt and for a modern driver – as I almost discover to my bitter cost – this can have painful consequences. But I survive – and learn to master the brake's slower reaction time. I must say my slightly troubled state of mind is not helped by the fact that I can see little through the rear window, and wing mirrors were not a feature of the early Beetle. But I'm lucky to see anything at all, for in the original design rear windows were omitted to save money and only added – by some sensible fellow – when the Beetle went into mass production.

Despite its rather military-looking colour scheme, the KdF-wagen I'm driving was made for the civilian market. But, as I discover from its current owner, this is no standard KdF-wagen. Its first owner was Alfred Rosenberg, an early and close associate of Hitler who is said to have helped the Führer write *Mein Kampf*, went on to be Reich Minister for the Eastern Territories and in 1946 was executed for crimes against humanity. And it's this fellow's car I'm driving. It's so strange – even monsters like Rosenberg can be absorbed within the hazy glow of nostalgia. The VW Beetle does, indeed, have a dark history and – like all cars feeding off oil and belching pollution – is responsible for many of our planet's current ailments. But seen simply as a machine, as a designed object, it must be acknowledged as one of the greatest automobiles ever made. The Beetle has risen above its unsavoury origins and, as long as humanity demands the right of individual mobility, the VW Beetle is about the best 'people's car' you can hope to get.

72 BAUHAUS CHAIR, DESSAU

Wednesday 3 November

In the morning I drive my VW Beetle to a building that expresses artistic and political aspirations very different to those of the Nazi Party. The building I've come to see was completed in 1926 and is the nucleus of the Bauhaus school of design. The vision it promoted was of an egalitarian socialist state in which good design was seen as essential for mankind's well-being. Not only were better – healthier – homes and cities for workers to be created, but all the objects needed in the home and in the city were to be rethought from first principles. Beauty was to come from fitness for purpose, from the honest expression of materials and means of construction. The Bauhaus may not have achieved its aim as initially intended – within a few years it was closed by the Nazis – but the design principles that it promoted did ultimately play a significant role in the creation of the world we now inhabit.

In the first decade of the 20th century history remained the key inspiration – the touchstone – for most artists, be they painters, sculptors, architects or decorators. This had, in the West, been the case for well over 2000 years. Then came 1914 and the four years of bitter war that rocked – and forever changed – the world. Old certainties, old values and beliefs were challenged and, in many cases, overturned. Little was the same after 1918 – certainly not in the world of the arts and crafts.

It was in this atmosphere of change that the Bauhaus emerged in Germany. It had been founded in 1906 as the Staatliches Bauhaus Weimer to promote the ideals of the Arts and Crafts movement, but when Walter Gropius was made Director in 1919 the school rapidly moved away from its original ideals. Gropius had served during the war and was well aware of the evils that result when pioneering technology is misused by man. This sombre lesson – the loss of innocence of the new machine age – had a great influence on him. The Bauhaus was not simply to preach the virtues of the machine and raw technology. It was to accept the machine, extract its lessons and virtues, and synthesise these with the older arts and crafts traditions. All was to be driven by a social purpose – to create a better world for the common man.

At the Bauhaus the slavish and unthinking reference to history, to past styles, was

Home of the Bauhaus school of design in Dessau, Germany. Built in 1926 this building used modern design and modern materials to create a realisation of the Bauhaus manifesto and aspirations.

over. Style should, instead, be derived from the materials and techniques of construction and from the function the object – be it a building or a chair – was to fulfil. And if form was to follow function, and the objective and practical laws that governed the machine were to be applied to architecture and the crafts, then art had to become more scientific and well-organised research was essential. It became necessary to consider the practical demands of the brief in great detail, to consider the most economic and efficient way to achieve the optimum. For four years the Bauhaus (the name means literally 'build house') flourished as a craft-based school and developed a bias towards communal art that was, essentially, an expression of communist philosophy. But by the mid-1920s it was becoming apparent that technology needed to be harnessed to create functional, beautiful and well-designed objects that could be mass produced and so – in theory – be cheap and available to the mass of ordinary people.

In 1924 funding for the Bauhaus was cut drastically by the conservative and increasingly nationalist authorities in Weimer. They considered it – the staff and students – too 'cosmopolitan'. It had to seek a new home and in 1925 the Bauhaus re-opened in the industrial and socialist-sympathetic town of Dessau. Within a year of moving the Bauhaus occupied a building purpose-designed by Gropius – and this is the building that now rises in front of me.

It's a powerful architectural statement – a tangible demonstration of the design principles of the Bauhaus and a glimpse into the future of architecture. All overt reference to history is gone – all ornament is an expression of function, utility – everything is doing a practical job. This interior, which has recently been carefully restored, still has the power to shock. It's nearly 80 years old, an historic building, but it's still avant-garde – still utterly modern – still futuristic.

The building remains the core of a school of design and – of great interest to me – contains an archive that is a treasure-trove of pioneering and inspirational 20th-century design. I gain access to this archive to choose one item – one treasure – that captures the spirit of the Bauhaus. There are racks and racks of objects – and many chairs. Yes, it must be a chair. Many of the leading designers who passed through here attempted to design the ideal chair, which is not surprising since chairs are complex and demanding objects, in many ways architecture in miniature. They have to be designed to carry – to house – the human form with comfort, they have to be engineered to support the weight of the body and survive the rough and tumble of daily use – and all this means the use of materials made strong through design, the conception and sound construction of joints, of struts and stretchers – of all manner of structures. The chair I select is formed by a chrome-plated tubular steel frame that curves to form base, legs, arms and back. The tube looks continuous because its two ends are welded together and the join is invisible. Slabs of leather are placed between the frame to form seat and back – and that's it. Minimal, elegant and – I sit on it – strong and comfortable. But to achieve such a simple solution – to make a strong and comfortable chair with so little structure – much work had to be done, much had to be stripped away. The basic structural principle is the cantilever, for the seat projects from the pair of front legs and there are no rear legs. The more I look at this chair the more I see in it. The simple-looking design demanded research into metallurgy, a thorough understanding of the principles and possibilities of the material used and the skilful application of a structural principle – the cantilever – so that the weight of the person sitting on the chair

I finally select an object from the Bauhaus archive that, for me, captures the spirit of the place. It is deceptively simple in appearance but ingenious. It's the Brno Chair designed by Mies van der Rohe in 1929. Almost 30 years later he completed the design of the Seagram Building in New York, another one of my treasures.

actually makes the chair work – it keeps it stable. It's a brilliant piece of design in which the function of the chair determines its form, and the chair's sinuous precision-made form is its greatest ornament. It's the Brno Chair of 1929, designed by Mies van der Rohe, who became director of the Bauhaus in 1930.

Anyone who has sat on a tubular steel chair has been sitting on a bit of the Bauhaus's legacy. But there is an irony about all this. The social aim of the Bauhaus was to utilise mass production to make good design cheap and available to all. But most of the chairs I'm surrounded by have never been cheap, with many soon becoming exclusive art objects available only to rich collectors. And here they stand, not in a worker's home but in a design museum.

The Bauhaus lasted only 14 years before being closed by the Nazis in 1933 but its influence was – and remains – massive. It has become part of the culture – artistic, social, political – of our time. It played a major part in forging the physical world in which we now live. Many of those aspects of the world we take for granted – like tubular steel chairs – have their roots in the Bauhaus. Ironically it was the Nazis' objection to the ideas of the Bauhaus that helped spread those ideas. To support the Bauhaus and its artistic philosophy, practice and product was to make a stand against the Nazis.

I drive away from the Bauhaus in my little VW Beetle. Although the totalitarian and artistically reactionary Nazis and the socialist and avant-garde Bauhaus were at different ends of the political and artistic spectrum, these two worlds do meet in this car. It is, I suppose, about the best example of an object made in accordance with Bauhaus principles to have gone into mass production in Germany during the Bauhaus era. Paradoxically, the VW Beetle – Hitler's 'Strength-through-Joy vehicle' – is the greatest object the Bauhaus never made.

73 MOSTAR BRIDGE, BOSNIA

Thursday 4–Friday 5 November
We fly to Vienna and then to Sarajevo, in Bosnia-Herzegovina, from where we journey to Mostar. The structure I have come to see tells the story of the centuries of struggle in this region – a home to people of different ethnic origin and religions – and specifically of the recent fighting. It's a structure that also suggests redemption is possible, that communities long locked in bitter fighting can be reconciled and that – against all the odds – peace and prosperity are returning to this beautiful but much troubled land. I have come to see Mostar's famous historic bridge – one of the most beautiful in the world and a symbol of great national pride – that was villainously destroyed during fighting in 1993. Work of reconstruction has just been completed and I am fascinated to discover if the rebuilding of this monument will have helped to right some of the great wrongs that happened here, will have helped to reunite and heal the community.

We drive to the small historic centre of the town and pass dramatic evidence of the vicious fighting that took place in and around Mostar. As the state of Yugoslavia fragmented so did its population and the battle for Mostar became a microcosm of the wider struggle. It was a complex three-way conflict between Orthodox Christian Bosnian Serbs, Slavic Muslims and Roman Catholic Croats. People from all three groups lived in Mostar and its region yet were divided by deep, historical grievances.

The road I'm in, lined with gutted and bullet-riddled buildings, is startling. They have simply been sprayed with machine-gun fire. There is real hatred in this. As I walk through these modern ruins I can reconstruct the events that took place here. It's only too clear to see that, ten years ago, this was one of the most dangerous places on earth as the various factions locked in bloody battle to gain or retain control of the city, to stay alive. Clearly elemental passions had been unleashed, there was savagery – insanity – in the air.

As I walk past the ruins and get near the heart of the city things change, they get better. There is now little sign of fighting. Old Mostar is a delightful place, with the winding river Neretva cutting through a gorge above which terraces of buildings rise in picturesque irregularity. To my surprise life seems much as normal.

The narrow road rises and turns and then I get my first view of the bridge, a single, minimal and elegant arch leaping across the gorge. It looks splendid – much as it did before its tragic demolition. The Mostar bridge, when completed in 1566 after nine years of construction, was a wonder of the age. It rose 19 metres above the water and, with an arch 29 metres in length, was then the largest single-span bridge in the world. Its construction was of the finest quality and very ingenious. It was made of squared limestone blocks joined by wrought-iron pins called cramps that gave the joints greatly increased strength. The cramps were coated in lead to protect them from water which would cause the iron to rust, expand and crack the stone.

The bridge was a masterpiece of well-calculated scientific design and a great testimony to the engineering skills of the architects of the Muslim Ottoman Empire. By the mid-16th century this was one of the greatest and most powerful civilisations of modern times, in which trade, military prowess, a deep concern for art and beauty and the pleasures of life combined in a most memorable manner. The Ottomans ranged deep into western Europe, taking Islam nearly to the heart of the continent. They established Islamic traditions and culture that survive to this day, with the Muslims in Bosnia being the direct descendants of their presence.

The bridge was a fitting symbol for the empire and of the land in which it stood. Bosnia and Herzegovina had – historically – been the bridge between the Eastern and Western portions of the Roman Empire. For centuries people of different religions and races lived and worked together and the world's great trade routes threaded their way through the area, bringing wealth and civilisation. Christians, both Roman Catholic and Orthodox, lived here, and after the fall of Constantinople to the Turks in 1453 Islam entered the region. Tensions between these different peoples were inevitable – the long-established Christians having to make way for – or at least accommodate – the newly arrived, and conquering, Muslims.

Violence engulfed Mostar and its people in early 1992. After the siege of the Bosnian Muslim government in Sarajevo – 70 kilometres to the north-east of Mostar – the Bosnian Serb military pursued a policy of terror and ethnic cleansing in the region. During May and June the city was overwhelmed by Bosnian Serb military units and shelled from the surrounding hills. And then, during their bid in November 1993 to seize all Mostar and expel the Islamic Slav community, Croat troops deliberately and savagely destroyed the bridge by shellfire. It could be argued that the bridge was a military target of strategic significance. But no one – not even the Croats – really believes this. Quite simply, as old hatreds and barbarism were given free reign, this old and apparently intolerable symbol of Ottoman power and sophistication, of Muslim Slav pride and national identity, was obliterated. History and beauty were at the very heart of modern conflict, directly in the firing line – and taking a savage beating.

But a great wrong was to be put right. In the late 1990s it was resolved that the bridge was to be rebuilt – to symbolise the end of war in the region and the birth of new hope. The people of Mostar decided that they wanted their old bridge back, to heal the wounds and remove painful memories.

A German engineer, Gregor Stolarski, was appointed by UNESCO, and research was started to discover how the old bridge had been calculated and constructed. Meanwhile original building stones were salvaged and new cut from a nearby quarry. As research progressed, the design team became increasing puzzled by the Ottoman architect's pioneering and ingenious construction methods. How had he managed to construct the largest free-standing stone arch of the time without steel and concrete, and how had he kept the wide arch standing – poised 19 metres above a river – during construction, before it was locked together by the keystones? The answers to these questions were not found, but it is thought likely that the iron cramps played a vital role.

The rebuilding of the bridge was completed in July 2004, utilising as many of the old stones as possible and employing traditional materials and techniques of construction. So, as much as it is humanly possible, Mostar again has its sublime arched bridge. The reconstruction is just about as good as it could be. As I walk along a street, lively with shops and cafes and overlooking the bridge, I see a stone block set up against a wall. Two words have been written on it – and recently: 'Don't forget'. I look at the beautiful arch of the bridge, completing this pretty scene which suggests that Mostar has returned to normality. But, I wonder, is it nothing other than a comely mask hiding a bitter and distorted grimace, a scarred visage, a scream of rage? You can rebuild a bridge, but you can't, I fear, so easily repair a shattered soul or a broken heart.

The newly restored Mostar Bridge in Bosnia. Begun in 1557 on the orders of Suleiman the Magnificent, it became an object of local and national pride. The work restoration has been done with love and care. The spirit of the bridge lives.

THE OLD WORLD

Sunday 7 November
Today we fly to Athens to see a building that the Western world over the last 400 years or so has regarded as the apogee of architecture – the Parthenon.

The cultural significance of Athens is clear and, generally, unquestioned. But now I have to question it. During the next couple of weeks I will see what are acknowledged to be some of the greatest achievements of European, indeed of world, culture – buildings, cities, sculpture and painting. But how will these measure up when compared with some of the wonders of the world that I have seen in recent months? I know most of my European treasures well but will – I'm sure – now see them in a fresh and critical light.

74 THE PARTHENON, ATHENS, GREECE

Monday 8 November
I walk up the sloping path towards the sacred plateau on top of the Acropolis – the high abode of the Athenian gods, the enclave where the people kept their most precious treasures. The Greek gods dwelled on mountain tops and the Acropolis is Athens's own holy and magic mountain. And then I see a sight that has reduced grown men to tears, made them fall to their knees as if in prayer. It is the Parthenon. Since the Parthenon was completed in 436 BC it has been regarded as a model of artistic perfection in which sculpture and architecture work perfectly together – each giving added meaning and purpose to the other – and where all is governed by number, ratios and proportion. The Parthenon was lost in obscurity during the centuries when the Ottomans ruled Greece, and it was not until the mid-18th century that it was fully surveyed, documented and published – and when that happened it caused an artistic sensation. It, and its companion buildings, inspired an entire artistic movement – the Greek Revival. This passion was given new force when Lord Elgin displayed the marbles from the Parthenon that he had acquired from the Ottoman authorities in Athens.

But, as I approach, I see that something very odd is going on. The Parthenon is now a building site with a huge crane rising from its bowels, scaffolding all around, piles of dismantled building components and – most alarming – stacks of new and freshly carved

The new and heavily restored drums strike a discordant note within the balanced harmony of the Parthenon's composition.

blocks of marble. The Parthenon is being rebuilt! The problem goes back to 1687 when, during a Venetian attack on the Turkish garrison in Athens, a gunpowder magazine inside the Parthenon exploded. It was this that dislodged and scattered most of the marbles that Elgin was later to acquire. In the 1920s the Greek authorities made an attempt to make good some of the damage and a number of columns were re-erected, and it is this work that has been dismantled. As I near the works entrance at the east end of the building – the original main entrance containing the long-lost, huge golden image of Athena – I am amazed. The tall Doric columns of the peristyle are made from a number of solid marble drums, one standing on top of another, and have been damaged. The damage has now been repaired – but the new marble is white, sharp and shiny while the old is pale yellow, mellow, weathered and textured. The contrast between the old and new material is visually painful.

I meet an archaeologist – a smart young woman – who tells me the work in the 1920s was not good. They want to put this right, using only authentic materials. What she says makes sense and the new work is of high quality, but there is such a lot of it. Much of the magic of the ruined Parthenon came from the fact that it was a ruin – and honest and authentic ruins are always visually thrilling, emotionally stimulating. They speak of things lost, of ancient beauty, of continuity, they proclaim mortality and are salutary reminders that all civilisations – no matter how high and mighty – do eventually fall. I know the Parthenon had been thoroughly repaired before, but somehow its magic and visual beauty survived. I wonder if it will survive this more authentic yet also more thorough overhaul.

Putting the conundrums of the present time aside I explore the building – what is now left of it – to try and discover its meaning and the nature of its beauty. The strange thing about the Parthenon is that no one is really sure what it was for. It wasn't a temple in the conventional sense – it wasn't served by a corps of priests or priestesses, nor were regular rituals or services held in or around it. But without doubt it was the domain of the virgin goddess Athena, and the focus of the Panathenaic procession held in Athens every four years in her honour. So it was, at least in part, a sacred building. However, early inventories also show that the Parthenon served as a treasury, packed with the treasures and heirlooms of the city. I suppose, in the end, it was simply a great public building, created by Pericles to express and commemorate the glory and triumphs of Athens.

I walk into the columned pronaos that forms the west front of the Parthenon. It's a moving space, with its wide-girthed and fluted Doric columns – here I get the sense of number and ratio that governs and relates all. But structurally the building is relatively primitive. The Greeks had not developed the arch or dome and so could not span wide spaces. Their building technology was essentially that of Egypt a thousand years or so earlier, although somewhat refined. Marble, like all stone, is strong in compression so the blocks of the columns can carry vast loads. But the flat horizontal marble lintels supported by the columns are operating in tension, and marble has little tensile, or elastic, strength. So the spaces between the columns are necessarily narrow, limited to the

The Parthenon has been a reference point for Western civilisation since the end of the Renaissance. I admire the proportions and the visual harmony and refinements of the building but I wonder if it's not over-rated.

distance that can be spanned by one block before it cracks. As far as structural principles go, the Parthenon is only a little more sophisticated than Stonehenge.

I move outside to contemplate the Parthenon from a distance, to see its famous and almost complete west facade. This is where the power of proportion is most apparent. It was generally believed in the early 19th century – when the direct influence of the Parthenon was at its most potent – that the Greeks had discovered and applied the immutable universal laws that govern the construction of the natural world. It was argued that these laws – essentially a series of ratios, geometrical forms and proportions – are what give beauty to God's creation.

I study the mighty building before me. Its architects – Ictinus and Callicrates – certainly achieved visual harmony and repose, and by the use of a system of geometrical proportions created a structure in which plan, elevations and details are plainly and pleasingly related. The geometry seems to have been inspired by Egypt and, as with pyramids and Egyptian temples, is organised around the circle and the square. Yes, the Parthenon is a wonderful creation – the fountainhead of much Western architecture and a continuing inspiration. But does it move me – inflame my imagination – more than anything else I have seen on this journey, is it truly the world's greatest building? It's tricky to be objective – I'm now used to raw beauty, to crawling over and through long-neglected or forgotten buildings, to experiencing an exhilarating sense of discovery. The Parthenon is now too over-presented for my tastes, too over-restored. It seems that it's being turned into a national symbol, even a political gesture. So the answer must be no. It's not the building that has moved me most during this journey, and seeing it afresh I wonder if the Parthenon has, due to the romantic notions of the early 19th century, basked in a glory and prominence it doesn't quite merit.

75 THE PANTHEON, ROME, ITALY

Tuesday 9 – Thursday 11 November
Today we plunge into the heart of Europe, into the country with the greatest quantity of the highest quality art treasures on earth – Italy.

Since I first confronted the Pantheon 30 years ago it has been, for me, one of the great human creations. It's not so much its majestic scale as the fact that it is such an elegant and precise summary of a set of artistic beliefs that stretch back, through the Parthenon, to at least as far as ancient Egypt. It uses proportion with a sureness that seems to confirm the designer's certain belief that he was dealing with immutable natural laws and artistic truths.

The building is the creative marriage of three primary forms – the essential and cosmic virtues of which were extolled by Plato. The triangular form of the great portico – with its series of massive monolithic columns from north Africa – sits in front of a huge drum that rises from a circular plan, while the interior volume of the building – from the ground to the top of its vast domed roof – fits within a cube. And then there are the materials and astonishing techniques of construction used in this 1900-year-old masterpiece. All is so pioneering, experimental and bold. The mighty coffered dome, with a span of 43 metres, is made of mass concrete that had to be carefully mixed and cast to prevent it cracking and collapsing as it dried. Its original function had a profound influence on its appearance. It was built between AD 118 and 128, during the reign of the Emperor Hadrian, and – as its name implies – was to be a temple to all the gods. Since it was a home to all the gods, each god had to have its own home within the temple. This meant the construction of a series of niches, ultimately seven in number, with the main door occupying the place of an eighth niche.

The Pantheon is a sublime building. Nothing quite like it had been built before, in form or in scale. Here the histories of Egypt and Greece combine with the contemporary powers and building skills of Rome to make a truly modern and distinctly Roman architecture. The concrete dome and the play of light through the oculus are magnificent.

I arrive in the piazza in front of the Pantheon just as the sun rises. The portico of the temple – eight columns wide and three columns deep – faces north, so sits brooding in the shadows, like a great beast, like the Sphinx. The clash of cultures seems to be one of the themes of this extraordinary composition, and as I look it occurs to me that this temple front is making a bold statement. There are clear references to Egyptian and Greek architecture in a composition dominated by a mighty, crowning Roman dome. It is proclaiming boldly that the Rome of Hadrian now dominates these two great earlier empires – has absorbed them – and is taking civilisation to new heights. No earlier civilisation could have made the Pantheon, with its huge internal space, covered by a dome that floats above the ground without the need of any support other than the wall on which it sits.

I walk through the portico, past the gnarled columns and the niches that once contained images of Augusta and Agrippa. But now these niches contain the images of sleeping men. The scene is fantastic – like an allegory of the fall of empires, for ragged fellows now sleep within the places once occupied by deified emperors, cook their breakfasts and loll between the lofty columns, within the portico of the home of all the ancient Roman gods – a building that once marked the centre of the civilised world.

I enter the Pantheon. It is, as always, overwhelming. A lofty space which proclaims the power of simple geometry. The whole of the cylinder and dome would fit within a mighty cube, so the diameter of the round floor is the same as the distance from floor level to the top of the dome. And the heights of the cylinder and the dome are equal. It's all so straightforward, so deeply pleasing – and the meaning is clear. In here, I'm in the world of the gods of Rome. I look up at the dome – the great wonder of the place. Concrete had been used by Roman architects in the construction of large, open-plan buildings for a couple of centuries before the dome of the Pantheon was cast – it wasn't a pioneering material, but it had never been used quite like this. Usually the weight of a dome exerts a powerful lateral thrust and so demands complex buttressing, but a homogeneous concrete dome has minimal external thrust, with most of its weight being transferred directly to the vertical supports or wall below it. The strength of concrete came through design, it came with the shape into which it was cast, and when cast into the naturally strong shape of a dome concrete could, in theory, be immensely strong.

The portico of the Pantheon is distinctly Greek in its architectural style. The columns however are from Egypt and in their scale and material are reminiscent of obelisks.

However, theory was one thing, practice another, and the successful casting of complex forms needed great craft skill. To cast the dome of the Pantheon a gigantic timber mould had to be made – essentially the inner surface of the dome in negative – and suspended at the correct position on timber scaffolding. Then a vast amount of concrete would have to be mixed to an exact formula, carried and poured very precisely, all the time making sure the mix was not too dry and not to wet. There have been cracks in the dome over the centuries, but no major problems – which is a tribute to the fantastic skills of these sadly anonymous Roman builders and engineers.

My aim now is to walk within the walls of the cylinder for, although they are the support for the 5000-tonne weight of the dome, they are not simply solid walls. They can't be because, as well as providing maximum support, they had to have the large niches scooped out of them which were deemed essential if the Pantheon was to fulfil the purpose for which it was built. So the builders had to use their ingenuity – they had to give the walls of the cylinder strength through engineering. They are made of concrete poured between two skins of brickwork. There are eight large, semi-circular relieving arches set within the wall, which correspond to the eight large internal niches, and these transfer the weight of the dome away from the areas weakened by the excavation of the niches onto areas of solid wall.

Prolonged negotiations with the authorities currently running the Pantheon – it's now a Roman Catholic church – finally result in my being allowed to penetrate the structure. I enter a small external door in the east niche in the portico and wind up a dark and near-derelict staircase. The wall on my right curves – it's the wall of the cylinder – and then there is a small opening – a door. I squeeze through it, and enter the wall. Amazing – it's about 6 metres thick. I climb a small staircase set behind the niche that now holds the main altar. Here I get a spectacular view of the massive, square, slab-like bricks used in the construction of the Pantheon. Many are stamped with the name of the consuls in power and of the works where the bricks were made – a sudden glimpse into the world of the men who made this place, a moment of intimacy.

Before I leave, as I contemplate the concrete dome, the sun comes out and casts, through the oculus, a distinct and bright circle of light onto the coffers. Of course, the sun god illuminates the interior of the temple, brings light, life, animation. As the circle of sunlight, the sun itself in miniature, moves perceptibly across the coffers, it confirms the symbolism of the dome as the heavens, as the cosmos – and as an image of the canopy of the Roman Empire that embraced the known world. Michelangelo, who was overwhelmed by the Pantheon, observed that it was 'of Angelic not human design'. He was right. The Pantheon is no disappointment. It's the grandfather of all massive domed structures – the Hagia Sophia in Istanbul, the Duomo in Florence, Michelangelo's St Peter's in Rome and Wren's St Paul's in London. Although much copied, the Pantheon has never been bettered. Its simple form and geometry give it an elemental power and grandeur.

76 THE MEDICI CHAPEL, FLORENCE

Friday 12 November
Michelangelo's admiration for the Pantheon influenced not only his design for the dome of St Peter's but also inspired the building I have come to see in Florence – the Medici Chapel or Sacristy at San Lorenzo. This chapel is, for me, the most fascinating of Michelangelo's creations. It's the only place in which to see sculpture, conceived and partly carved by Michelangelo, in the architectural setting he designed for it. So, from the art historical point of view, the chapel is undoubtedly one of the masterpieces of the Renaissance. But there is more here than art and history. There are politics, a complex web of human relationships and passion. It was in this chapel, a receptacle for tombs of members of the Medici family, one of the most powerful in the land, that Michelangelo confronted the reality of death – his own death.

The chapel was commissioned in 1519 by one of the most formidable men in Rome and Florence, Cardinal Giulio de' Medici. The cardinal wanted a monument to his family's greatness located in San Lorenzo, the great Florence church that was virtually a family chapel, and the most seemly way of expressing worldly power in a sacred setting was to cast it in the form of a mausoleum. I arrive in front of San Lorenzo, an ancient church that was rebuilt in the 1420s by the pioneering Renaissance architect Filippo Brunelleschi. I enter and am confronted by one of the great architectural sights of the world. Brunelleschi was intent on rediscovering and re-creating the Classical past. In San Lorenzo he created an idealised version of a Roman basilica adapted to Christian worship. It's a bold and incredibly moving antique interior – the light flooding in from high-level windows, the semi-circular arches springing from the tops of the columns, the beautiful blue-grey of the *pietra serena* from which the columns and architectural details are carved. It is, indeed, a house of God.

I walk through this space to the east end and enter one of the most powerful architectural spaces in the world – the realm of the noble dead as perceived and created by Michelangelo. The room is square in plan – a cube – upon which sits a dome rising from pendentives. It's based on Brunelleschi's earlier chapel – an act, on Michelangelo's part, of both respect and Classical propriety. But this form is also related to a far older tradition – I've seen it throughout the world. The cube represents the world of man, the spherical dome the world of God – this design speaks of the soul ascending. This sense of apotheosis is reinforced by the architectural treatment of the four walls of the chapel. Each is like the elevation of a Roman triumphal arch with powerful architectural elements. This implies the heroic status of the Medici entombed in the chapel – but the composition also says something else. It is divided, visually, into three horizontal portions, and these each get less busy, contain fewer details, as they rise from floor to dome. All of this is a prelude to the dome that contains, in its centre, an oculus topped by a glazed lantern through which light – the light of God – can enter. The material world is gradually left behind until the abstract spiritual world is finally encountered. Michelangelo viewed the human body as the *carcer terreno* – the earthly prison that confines the soul – and he must surely have imagined the liberated souls of the dead Medici flying to heaven via the oculus.

The dome, sitting on a high drum, is a miniature version of the dome of the Pantheon. It's all, emotionally, incredibly effective – sombre and grave. Michelangelo is refining – almost inventing – the neo-Classical language of death and, in so doing, providing inspiration for generations of Classical architects. This building trembles, in an incredibly exciting and tense way, between two different approaches to the past – re-creation versus informed but radical reinterpretation – and they are colour-coded. The Brunelleschian Roman Classical architecture is wrought in the blue-grey *pietra serena* while Michelangelo's radical and inventive Classicism is made in white marble – like the sculpted figures and the sarcophagi. The sculpture is extraordinary and its meaning, even its authorship, is still hotly debated.

Two of the Medici to be honoured in the chapel were Giuliano, Duke of Nemours, and Lorenzo, Duke of Urbino. Statues of the dukes were duly finished – imposing seated figures, clad in Roman armour and costume, that sit brooding. But more compelling – and mysterious – are the four figures that Michelangelo created to lie at the feet of these two men, to drape across the tops of their sarcophagi. Below the Duke of Urbino are a male figure representing Evening and a female figure representing Dawn. The female figure wears a strange expression. Languid, exhausted – an unusual representation of dawn, more the image of death, of evening. The actual image of Evening is a naked man whose face, turned to the spectator, is rough, textured stone, apparently unfinished. Set below the Duke of Nemours are also a male and a female figure. The male represents Day and, as with Evening, his face seems to have been only roughed-out. The faces of these two bearded men are thrilling. Their incompleteness gives them an almost abstract, ruthless, power and immediacy. I can't read their expressions for they have no mouths, they barely have eyes. They communicate by other means, they speak of the essence of things, they are elemental beings.

The female represents Night. She is the most complex of the chapel's four emblematic figures and is generally agreed to be entirely the work of Michelangelo – not least because she leans on a

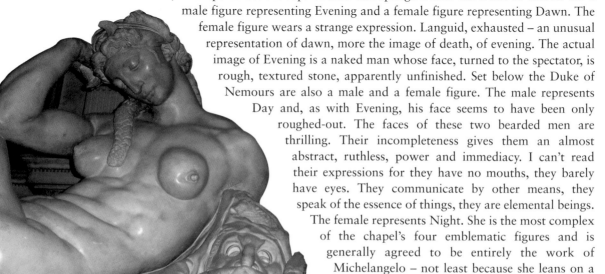

The female figure representing Night is one of four figures created by Michelangelo at the Medici Chapel in Florence. The mask upon which she is leaning is a self-portrait of the artist.

mask which is clearly a portrait of the artist, presumably a self-portrait. Night bows her head. She is, appropriately, falling asleep, while below her raised knee perches an owl. All these images have to do with time – that enemy of mortal man that marks remorselessly the path from birth to death.

Death was greatly on Michelangelo's mind while he worked on these sculptures – and not merely because they are for a mausoleum. By about 1524 the construction of the chapel was complete and Michelangelo had turned his attention to the sculpture. But in the late 1520s and early 1530s politics in Florence took a dramatic turn. In 1527 a Republican government was re-established in Florence and Michelangelo – while completing the chapel celebrating Medici greatness – gave his active support to the Medici's enemy. However in August 1530 the Medici were once more restored to power – and this time they hung on to it with an iron grasp.

Michelangelo was in an intolerable position. He had few contacts with the younger, thrusting and no doubt vengeful generation of the Medici and believed that his life was in danger – as no doubt it was. He went into hiding – perhaps even taking refuge in the chapel of San Lorenzo. A secret subterranean room has been found in recent years, its walls covered by sketches that could be the work of Michelangelo – bizarrely entombed within the tomb of the family for whom he was working and from whom he was hiding. Michelangelo resumed work, but must have dreaded the sound of a footfall behind him as he waited for the arrival of a Medici assassin. It's little wonder, in these unsettling circumstances, that he couldn't bring himself to put the finishing touches to the figures of Evening or Day. But Michelangelo survived. In 1534 Giulio de' Medici, by now Pope Clement VII, died and, in the same year, Michelangelo fled from Florence to Rome.

As I leave the chapel I look once more at the carved self-portrait, with its vacant and hollow eyes, upon which Night reposes. Now I see it for what it is – a death mask carved by Michelangelo while still alive. He must have feared Night had come upon him. In this chapel, one of his greatest creations and a monument to the dead, Michelangelo faced his own mortality, stood fearing for his life – it is, in a way, a monument to his own death.

77 THE GRAND CANAL, VENICE

Saturday 13–Sunday 14 November

In the morning we take a train to Venice – always a fine experience. Trains in Italy are comfortable and generally punctual, the stations of splendid functional and streamlined 1930s design – all, I suppose, a legacy of Mussolini's obsession with the railway. Arrival by rail at Venice never fails to delight. The train passes depressing industrial outskirts of the city and then rolls into Santa Lucia Station – so far Venice has concealed its delights, with only tracts of oily water on display. But when the doors of the station swing open the world erupts – right in front is the Grand Canal, lined with a dizzyingly wonderful array of architecture. Arriving in Venice by train is one of the greatest pieces of architectural theatre to be enjoyed anywhere in the world.

We jump into water taxis and make our way along the Grand Canal to our hotel, that lies just beyond the Rialto Bridge. On the canal – framed by glorious buildings – Venetians are living life. There are water buses, craft delivering all manner of goods and merchandise, heavy-laden, workhorse-like boats collecting garbage, pleasure boats plying to and fro and – of course – fleets of gondoliers. It is a beautiful scene, and this is my treasure – the Grand Canal.

The Grand Canal is a natural waterway that has, over the last thousand years or so, been improved by man. It is the shape of a reversed S and divides the two main islands

The 13th-century Byzantine style Ca' da Mosto at high tide on the Grand Canal in Venice.

on which the city of Venice is built. At its north-west end the canal is relatively narrow and modest but, by the time it has snaked to the south-east – and opens into the Giudecca – it is one of the greatest, indeed grandest, thoroughfares in the world, offering spectacular views and vistas of some of the most appealing architecture on earth.

I board a small craft in the Rio di Noale, north of the Grand Canal, and just a little above the Ponte di Rialto. The Rio di Noale is in the shade, quiet, enclosed and then, as we swing out into the Grand Canal, I'm in a world of light, of sun – the water is alive, reflecting sky and colour – I see the city as a living thing. It's an amazing moment. The *acqua alta* or flood tide has come in – so buildings appear to be floating on the water, rising from the deep. The quays and landing stages are awash, lost below the sparkling blue flood waters that ripple around the bases of loggias. Venice was the final destination of many of the great trade routes coming from the East, bringing spices and silk. It was the centre of a maritime empire that, by the early 16th century, was one of the most powerful forces in the world, and the Grand Canal was where the merchant princes stored – and displayed – their wealth. These mighty palaces, jockeying for position along the greatest trade highway in medieval Europe, were also warehouses and places of trade. By the early Renaissance a happy formula had been evolved that allowed them to function both as grand palatial homes and as places of commerce. A formal entrance would be contrived to face onto the Grand Canal with a tradesman's entrance on a side canal, and on this lower level goods would be stored, with offices and minor accommo-dation on a mezzanine floor above. From here a grand staircase would lead up to the first floor, and this was another world – a world of immense grandeur. It was the *piano nobile* – the floor of nobility – with apartments comprising grand reception rooms and closets. This arrangement would be reproduced on the floor above – the second *piano nobile* – where the family would live with a little more intimacy and comfort.

The great palaces on the canal not only display the wealth of the city but also, in their exotic design, reveal Venice's valuable trade connections. The palace that looms before me, the Ca' d'Oro, is one of the most exquisite palaces in Venice. It was completed in the mid-1430s for the procurator of San Marco and originally – as its name implies – it had a facade that glittered with gold leaf. It has an open loggia at canal level, but also two above, and the columns and tracery decorating these upper pair of loggia are fantastic – they are Gothic, with cusps and ogee arches, but also distinctly Islamic. Along the trade routes from the East came not just goods but cultural ideas and influences.

And now the Ponte di Rialto, completed in 1588, and until the 19th century the only bridge across the Grand Canal. The bridge is located at one of the canal's two sharp turns so a trip beneath it is a most theatrical experience. First I see nothing but the outside of the arch, then its underside, and suddenly I see a framed view of the middle portion of the canal, the vista widening rapidly as I move forward. Ahead is architectural variety and beauty – a vision in which relatively little has changed since the late 17th century. A journey along the canal is a trip back through time, returning to an idyllic past. The canal's also a highway through history, a cross-section, for on each side are prime examples of architecture from different cultural epochs – Byzantine, Gothic, Renaissance. Now I'm nearing the south-east end of the Grand Canal and major architectural works are coming thick and fast – the journey is reaching a spectacular climax. There is the church of Santa Maria della Salute, with its bulging dome apparently anchored down by a series of massive scrolls that majestically uncoil themselves around its drum. Completed in 1687 the church is, indeed, a sight to see. Now the canal opens like a funnel and I'm almost at the Piazza San Marco – one of the greatest urban spaces in the world – that will open up on my left while, to my right, in the distance is one of the greatest Classical churches in the world – San Giorgio Maggiore, designed by Andrea Palladio and completed in 1580. The church, with its pale stone and facade of interlocking pediments, looks magnificent and distant – a bold Classical dream seen across time, shimmering in the sunshine.

My journey along this curvaceous sliver of water ends. My boat sidles up to a quay and I come ashore. It's true, the process of travelling through this city is its greatest delight – to move along the Grand Canal is to experience the extraordinary and creative collaboration of man and nature. In the end, it's the light that amazes – flashing across the water, on the buildings, bringing life to the fiery earth colours, the brick and the stone. It's a city of the elements that seems not to belong to this world, but to hover between heaven and earth, on the brink.

The flood tide has subsided and I walk back to my hotel, along alleys, across bridges and canals and through small and perfect campos. No, even after all I've seen, Venice does not disappoint.

A view of the Grand Canal from the Rialto Bridge showing the variety of architectural styles. The tall building is the 16th-century Palazzo Papadopoli.

78 PICASSO'S 'GUERNICA', MADRID, SPAIN

Monday 15 – Tuesday 16 November

I have come to the Museo Nacional Centro de Arte Reina Sofia in Madrid to see one of the most famous paintings of the 20th century, painted by – arguably – its greatest painter. The painting is 'Guernica', the artist Pablo Picasso. I turn into a stark white gallery, pass various sketches by Picasso – and then I see the long canvas, the angular figures rendered in a rich monotone that, as I get closer, resolve themselves into the familiar figures of the domineering bull, the rearing, agonised horse and the wailing women. I stand and stare at these images, savage, elemental, executed with energy, in anger – and at speed, to judge by the trickles of paint almost hurled onto the surface of the canvas. People have been moved to tears by this vivid declaration of war on war makers, this visually violent protest against violence. Well, I don't cry – but it's an almost physical shock to stand before it. What is clear is that not only does this painting say much about Picasso as an artist and as a man, but also much about 20th-century history.

'Guernica' documents a specific tragedy – but it also rapidly became an image of the tragedy that was engulfing the world in the late 1930s when vast armies were massing, different, incompatible totalitarian ideologies competed for power and when war – on an unprecedented scale – seemed certain to soon engulf the world.

In February 1936 in Spain the People's Front – a coalition of republicans, socialists and communists – won a free election. This was intolerable to reactionary and conservative forces – particularly the military – and on 18 July a group of generals, led by General Francisco Franco, launched a coup d'état. Fighting broke out and Spain fragmented as it slid into civil war. The world watched in horror and wonder. There were huge issues at stake – democratic freedom, the rights of elected governments – and Spain became, by proxy, the battleground in the mounting struggle between fascism and communism. The international community fretted and talked frantically, pleaded and advised and, in the end, decided to do – nothing. In August 1936 a non-intervention pact was signed by France, Great Britain, Italy, Germany and the Soviet Union. The US had already passed its Neutrality Act. But Germany and Italy side-stepped the agreement and flooded 'advisers' – strangely, heavily armed – into Spain to assist Franco, while the USSR sold arms to the government. A sorry and tragic tale – the people of Spain were essentially abandoned to their fate by the Western democracies and preyed upon by the totalitarian states.

In January 1937 Picasso was asked by the Republican government to paint a mural for the Spanish pavilion at the international fair in Paris – but, although a declared supporter of the Republic, he was reluctant to take the commission. He believed that artists should not work for governments, and that art and politics do not mix. But on 26 April 1937 an event took place that changed Picasso's mind – and which changed his art, and the art of the 20th century, forever. Bombers from the German Condor Legion attacked the Basque city of Guernica. The planes were loaded with a mixture of heavy explosives to shatter walls and blow in windows and incendiaries to consume the city by fire. Low-flying bombers machine-gunned people as they fled. The aim of the raid had been to inflict maximum destruction and loss of life – to visit the city with terror and to break the will of the Basques to resist Franco. Over 1650 people were killed and 890 wounded in this surprise attack on the undefended city, and 70 per cent of its buildings were destroyed or seriously damaged.

Picasso was – like most of the world – horrified and outraged by this attack. His immediate response was to accept the government commission for the Paris pavilion. The difficulty Picasso faced artistically was how to respond to such a massacre. He was the first to acknowledge that art can suffer if used in the service of politics and that art with an obvious and direct message – no matter how moral that message – does become

propaganda. Was he falling into a trap, attempting the impossible – the creation of a work that would respond to a specific event and carry a clear and direct message, but which would also become timeless, a work that retained power after the events that led to its conception were long past, even forgotten?

With great bravery and determination, Picasso rose to this challenge and plunged into the creation of the mural. He worked hard for nearly a month, transforming reports of the event – photographs, written and verbal descriptions – into painted forms. He also delved into his own repertoire of images – the weeping woman, the bull, the horse – but imbued with direct rather than ambiguous meaning. There were to be no half measures, no cowardice here, no subtle or weaselly symbolism behind which to hide. The meaning of this mural had to be clear for all to see. It had to speak for the people of Guernica who suffered and speak against what Picasso loathed most – what he called the 'military caste' that was capable of inflicting such suffering.

The process of creating the large work – the canvas measures 7.75 metres by 3.5 metres – was experimental. All the time he was stripping away – making it simpler, more stark, more elemental. On 6 June the work was complete and Picasso unveiled it to a group of friends, including Giacometti, Max Ernst, André Breton and Henry Moore. The mural still had some colour, including slivers of bright-red paper forming tears from the eyes of the bull. As the group of artists watched in reverential silence Picasso time and again approached the canvas, each time removing one of the coloured attachments until none were left. No, there was to be no colour to relieve this image of hell. The tears of blood flowing from the bull's eyes implied that it was suffering, a victim of the onslaught, but with the tears removed it assumed a very different role, that of the aggressor. This was a bold move on Picasso's part for the image of the bull in Spain is never neutral. Picasso later fully explained the images he used in 'Guernica' – they were not, and were never meant to be, ambiguous. The bull represented the brutality of Franco and his forces, the dying horse suffering.

Picasso personally delivered the mural to Paris where it went on display on 12 July. Next door to the Spanish pavilion was the huge pavilion designed by Albert Speer for Germany – an amazing juxtaposition, those responsible for the deaths at Guernica next to the painting bemoaning the massacre.

Pablo Picasso's 'Guernica' is the greatest anti-violence painting ever made – its images have the same impact now as when painted nearly 70 years ago.

Without doubt Picasso avoided the pitfall of producing a piece of propaganda that dates painfully. He did not make direct visual references to the specific event – there are no bombers shown, no bombs falling and only a subtle implication of a burning building. Instead there are crying women, their features tortured in utter anguish, a dead baby and dismembered body, and the horse – like a picador's dying horse from the bullring, the picture of innocent, non-comprehending suffering. So Picasso has gone for the image of universal – elemental – suffering that makes the work continually relevant, applicable to all pain, a protest against all acts of violence.

In the end 'Guernica' is a masterpiece because it gets the balance between art and political imagery absolutely right. The painting is almost like a living thing, an object with a voice and power of its own that makes it leap out of the museum and into the wider world. But the story is not yet over – all the wounds of the civil war are not yet healed, its horrors not yet remote and painless history. Just a few minutes' drive from 'Guernica' is a large bronze and heroic equestrian statue. It's Franco. Almost within sight of the great painting mourning the death and destruction that took place at Guernica is a statue of the man ultimately responsible for the massacre. No wonder Picasso's painting remains provocative, controversial – a living work of art.

79 THE ALHAMBRA, GRANADA

Wednesday 17 – Thursday 18 November

We fly to Granada, in the south of Spain, to see the greatest remains of one of the most sophisticated cultures to ever flourish in Europe. In AD 711 Muslims from north Africa – the Moors – invaded Spain, then divided among weak and often warring Christian states, and in the south established the land of al-Andalus. Over the following centuries al-Andalus was to become one of the richest, most fabulous and cultured places on earth – the promised land of Islam, the jewel of the Muslim world. Under Muslim control, but with the active and welcome participation of Christians and Jews, al-Andalus became a paradise of learning. The treasure I seek is one of the most magnificent and well-preserved Muslim palaces in the world – the Alhambra.

I walk from the centre of Granada, up towards the mighty gate in the outer walls of the Alhambra. I leave behind narrow and winding streets and alleys – like a north African kasbah – which reveal the origin of this city and of many of southern Spain's cultural traditions. I am here to see one of the most historically important rooms in the world and, in a sense, to go back to the place in which this journey – my quest – started. This walk is, for me, like a walk back in time.

I find a small gate that takes me into a narrow court. This is the gentle entrance to a magic world, the complex of palaces, paradise gardens and celestial domes that the Nasrid Dynasty created during the 14th century. I progress to the Patio del Cuarto Dorado, where the world of the common man met the exalted world of the prince of the land. At the far end, between the two doors, sat the sultan on his throne. Here he would give audience, dispense justice. The doors behind the sultan opened into two routes – both of which were only to be trod by the select, the elite, of the land. The door to the sultan's left led to his private apartments, that to his right led into the heart of his palace. To be invited to pass through this door was to enter a paradise created when al-Andalus was the cultural centre of the world.

I go through and am in the Court of the Myrtles, a place of heartbreaking beauty – a great reception room, open to the sky, the

The 14th-century colonnade at the Court of the Fountain of the Lions at Alhambra, one of the most beautiful examples of Islamic architecture in the world.

heart of the palace. I blink in the sunlight. This is a court, of double square proportion, in which the work of man complements – sits between and below – the work of God. Plants – including myrtles after which the court is named – line the walks. To Islam, nature was sacred, a gift and sign of God and his greatness. To reinforce this connection between God and nature there sits, in the centre of the court, a large rectangular sheet of water. Glassy, still and clear, this water reflects the sky above and the buildings on each side and at night the stars and the moon.

Further on is the Court of the Fountain of the Lions. I recognise its arrangement from the Taj Mahal in India, from the Koran. It has four channels of water running through it and joining the central fountain, each channel marking a cardinal point on the compass. The Garden of Eden was said to have been watered by four rivers. Yes, this is an Islamic vision of Paradise. And there's more – the circular basin of the fountain is supported by 12 lions. This is a familiar number – the Old Testament states that the fountain or 'sea of bronze' set at the entrance to Solomon's Temple in Jerusalem was supported by 12 bulls, thought to represent the 12 tribes of Israel. So this palace, though a place of beauty, was also an evocation of that temple in Jerusalem, believed to be of divine origin, which was sacred to both Jews and Muslims.

From here I make my way back to the Court of the Myrtles, to a long, thin room that occupies one entire end of the court. I am now getting near the palace's epicentre of power. This room carried ambassadors and eminent visitors from the bright and light world of the court into the dark and sombre room beyond and into the presence of the sultan. This was the throne room, and this is my particular treasure within the Alhambra.

I enter the hall, now called the Hall of the Ambassadors. Hardly to my surprise it is a huge cube in form topped by a dome – the familiar symbolism of the world of the material topped by the world of the spirit. I walk into the centre of the room and stand next to a section of tile floor that looks like a Persian carpet and is decorated with the name of God. Here ambassadors would have stood, blinking in the darkness, straining to see the sultan in front of them. They couldn't see him because of a cunning piece of design. Three of the walls of the room each contain three deep, arched recesses through which light filters in via small windows and screens. Other windows are small and set at

The Court of the Myrtles at Alhambra. Through the main door lies the domed and cubical Hall of the Ambassadors where the Sultan conducted his business. In Muslim houses such courts reflected the economic and social status of the people who occupied them, and those who visited them as well. It would have been a rare privilege indeed.

The Court of the Fountain of the Lions at Alhambra is an Islamic vision of Paradise.

a high level, so the room is dark, cave-like, a hard place in which to see things. But that's not the real trick. The sultan sat in the central bay, framed by light entering through the screen behind him. He appeared simply as a silhouette, framed by a halo of light. The sultan could see but not be seen. This was psychological warfare of the subtlest sort – the ambassadors hardly stood a chance.

I contemplate the room and think of the two events that took place here, both to do with conquest, both within the space of a year, that changed the world – whether for better or worse is still hard to say. It was in this room, on 2 January 1492, that the last Muslim ruler in Spain, the Nasrid sultan Muhammed XII, known as Boabdil, finally accepted defeat and agreed to go into exile in north Africa – turning Granada, the solitary surviving Moorish enclave in Spain, over to the Catholic monarchs Ferdinand and Isabella. The Christian reconquest of Spain from Islam had a long history but in the mid-15th century it became fanatical and utterly intolerant. The Catholic monarchs' theory of 'purity of blood' for Spain – a sort of genocidal Christian fundamentalism – declared that only those of the Roman Catholic faith could live there. The centuries of rich cultural mix were over – Muslims and Jews had to convert or, preferably, get out. Their failure to do either of these would, naturally, result in execution. In place of this paradise that had practised religious and racial toleration came persecution and control. By the 1570s the Arab language, costumes and customs were banned and by 1610 the last colonies of Moors – Christian converts as well as pockets of Muslims – had all been exiled. Spain now had 'purity of blood' and one religion.

The other great event that took place in this room is intimately connected with the humiliation of Boabdil. In the same month – January 1492 – Christopher Columbus stood in the Hall of the Ambassadors before the new rulers of the Alhambra – Ferdinand and Isabella – and asked them to support him in his quest for a new trade route to 'the regions of India' – a quest that would, eventually, lead to Columbus setting foot in the New World. As well as finding a better sea route to India and wealth for Spain he could perhaps further their religious aims, and take Roman Catholicism to foreign idolaters, heretics and heathens. So, on 17 April 1492, this Italian adventurer was dubbed an admiral, viceroy and governor-general of lands and regions not yet discovered.

In the Hall of the Ambassadors one great epoch in world history ended and another began. Here one event took place that marked the end of an 800-year-old civilisation while the other led, by chance, to the centuries of rich trade, exploitation and ruthless conquest that have resulted in the utter ruination of all the native civilisations in south, central and north America. It was among what remains of these civilisations that I started my world journey five months ago so it is, I suppose, appropriate if depressing that, at my journey's end, I see the place that was the beginning of the end for the Inca, the Aztecs, the Maya and the other great but fragile civilisations of the New World.

80 CHARTRES CATHEDRAL, FRANCE

Friday 19–Saturday 20 November

I am now going to see one of the greatest of Europe's Gothic cathedrals – I'm going to Chartres. The cathedral sits on an ancient sacred site far older than Christianity, rising high above the town. I see it at sunrise, silhouetted against a fierce red morning sky, and it looks just what it is – an elemental material structure that makes manifest man's deepest beliefs in the immaterial world, the world of the spirit.

Sunrise at Chartres Cathedral in France with the sharp spires of its two unequal western towers pointing to heaven. Where the money and skills came from to realise this marvellous building is shrouded in mystery.

Chartres, with its powerful proportions, its geometry and its very distinct sculptural decoration, is almost as mysterious as the Great Pyramid, to which its geometry appears to be related. Indeed, the very construction of Chartres seems as miraculous. A church was erected here, over an ancient sacred grotto, soon after Christianity came to the region. This was replaced from 1020 by a mighty cathedral that was engulfed by fire in June 1194. Rebuilding started immediately and by 1220 was virtually complete. In 25 brief years the art of Gothic construction – still pioneering and tentative in 1194 – reached speedy and marvellous maturity. In the nave and aisles of Chartres the structural potential of the Gothic pointed arch is utilised to gain high vaults and wide bays, and the Gothic structural system of ribs, buttresses and flying buttresses is fully developed. This system is used to create an elegant structure – a house fit for God – in which the outward thrust of the high vaults and arches is carried to the ground via external structures – thus leaving the interior light and open – and is neutralised in the most elegant manner imaginable by being met by the opposite and equal counter thrust exerted by flying buttresses. This skeletal structure – with loads carried on arches, stone ribs and buttresses – relieved the walls of much of their structural role and so allowed them to be pierced by large windows through which God's light – manipulated by emblematic stained glass – could illuminate the interior of the church and the minds of the worshippers gathered within. When virtually complete in 1220 Chartres became one of the wonders of the world. Pilgrims flocked here to worship at the shrine of the ancient great goddess – who took the form at Chartres of a Black Virgin – and to see a great relic, the Veil of the Virgin. They must also have come to see the wonder of the architecture – an earthbound image of the celestial city, a building that was the Bible built in stone and a reconstruction of God's house in Jerusalem, the Temple of Solomon.

I walk the pilgrim's route, wind my way up and though the remains of the medieval town and arrive in front of the wide and ornate porch attached to the north transept. It is alive with sculpted images – saints, apostles and images from the Bible, along with other images, familiar and not exclusively Christian. There is Solomon sitting in judgement and, strangely, the signs of the zodiac. So the creators of Chartres were invoking the powers of earlier systems of religion. I walk around to the west front of the cathedral and see the mighty royal portal that is believed to have been completed in about 1155 and survived the fire. It consists of three doors, each flanked and topped by sculpture that is utterly mesmerising. The north door is the Gate of the Ages, presided over by a panel showing the Ascension of Christ – charmingly, he is being carried on a cloud upheld by two angels. In the surrounding arches are more signs of the zodiac, alternating with images showing the works of man. Some of these carvings are very odd indeed, especially that of what appears to be a huge beetle – perhaps a scorpion – that has a human head. Can this be a weird medieval marriage of ancient sacred images – including an Egyptian scarab? The south door is the gate of birth – presided over by the Virgin Mary. And I see two men sheltering behind a shield. This could be another zodiac sign – Gemini – or an image representing the Knights Templar, the religious military order based on the Temple Mount in Jerusalem, who were almost certainly involved in this inspired re-creation of Solomon's Temple in the flat fields of northern France.

Finally I look at the central door. This shows Christ sitting in judgement within a pointed oval – the vesica piscis. In the Middle Ages this geometrical form was perceived to possess deep power and meaning, being employed on the design of churches, painting and sculpture. Possibly, as in ancient cults of fertility, it was seen as a representation of the vulva, like the yoni in Hindu sacred art – the shape of Meenakshi's eyes in Madurai. In that case this striking image shows Christ sitting within the passage through which he was born, through which the Virgin gave mankind its redeemer. Around Christ in the vesica sit the Beasts of the Apocalypse as described in the biblical Book of Revelation. This door is to do with judgement, the end of this world and the coming of the New Jerusalem.

I go inside, where light is all-important. Chartres is virtually designed around its windows, with their richly coloured stained glass – the best collection of early stained glass in the world – that bathes the interior in a beautiful, mystic and fiery light. On all four cardinal points of the compass are vast, circular rose windows that contain geometric patterns imbued with powerful symbolic and mystic meaning. The rose is one of the symbols of the Virgin – so these could be dedicated to her – and each is organised around the number 12. Can they also – as I've seen in ancient Egyptian and Roman temples and in mosques – be to do with time, the hours of the day or months of the year?

Left One of the rose stained-glass windows at Chartres Cathedral – they are all are organised around the number 12. Right The stone labyrinth at Chartres – a destination of pilgrims since the Middle Ages.

I walk through the aisles, around the curved east end and towards the south transept. As the Bible makes clear it is not the seen, but the unseen world that is most important, that possesses sacred powers, and so it is in a cathedral. It's not the walls that are important, no matter how glorious their stones might be, but the space they define. God lives in space, in light and colour. Yes, it all gets back to light, and the source of all physical light – the Sun, that most ancient deity that I have found worshipped around the world. Christ has been seen as a Christian manifestation of ancient Sun gods – as Apollo – and this connection seems to have been in the minds of the creators of these great cathedrals. Like all Christian churches in Europe, Chartres is oriented towards the east. When worshippers stand in the nave and look towards the High Altar they are looking towards Jerusalem, the Holy Land, but also – like worshippers from long before

the Christian age – they are gazing towards the rising Sun, towards the symbol of life, of resurrection, of fruitful cycles of nature, towards the old universal god. And on the floor of the south transept is extraordinary evidence of this continuing veneration for the Sun within the medieval Christian church. Below my feet there is a rectangular flagstone, set aslant to the others, and in it is set a shining, lightly gilded metal tenon. Every year, at midday on the summer solstice of 21 June, when the sun is at its highest, brightest and most powerful, a ray strikes this stone – a ray that comes through a specially made space in the stained-glass window above.

I go back to the nave and stand on one of the greatest mysteries of the cathedral. It is a huge circular labyrinth, wrought in stone, that marks a long and winding journey from its point of entry, to its centre and then back again. It is placed over the sacred grotto, the crypt, and so holy is this site that in the Middle Ages it was believed that to make a pilgrimage through this labyrinth, on bended knees, was the equivalent of going to Jerusalem. Pilgrims still walk this labyrinth – when it is clear of chairs – and I walk it now. It's like walking the 4000-year-old labyrinth on Solovki, like the ancient spiral patterns I have seen at sacred sites throughout the world.

I know this cathedral well, but now I see it in a fresh light illuminated by my recent travels. Like all great buildings it speaks an international language, deals with the great ideas that have obsessed all men through the ages – life, death, morality, eternity, where we come from and where we are going to. There is a universal religion – that rises far above petty issues of ritual and forms of worship – and that is a mighty quest for truths, for the essence of life. This church – like the Great Pyramid – is an expression of that universal religion and universal culture. This rapid journey around the world has allowed me to see unlikely connections across time and space that offer a thrilling view of this planet and its civilisations Everything does, indeed, seem to be connected to everything else and during this journey many more mysteries have been revealed than mysteries solved, many more questions raised than answered. But that's the only way to end a journey like this – teetering on the edge of your seat, gripped by expectation and hoping for more. This journey is now over – but the next will soon begin.

First published in Great Britain in 2005
by Weidenfeld & Nicolson

10 9 8 7 6 5 4 3

Text copyright © Dan Cruickshank 2005
Design and layout © Weidenfeld & Nicolson 2005

By arrangement with the BBC
The BBC logo is a trade mark of the British Broadcasting
Corporation and is used under licence.
BBC logo © BBC 1996
Around the World in 80 Treasures logo © BBC 2005

Photographs copyright © Basil Pao endpapers, 11, 48,
56–7, 61, 63, 71, 89, 90–1, 99, 100–1, 125, 126, 129,
181, 182 (right), 189, 190 (left), 198–9, 214–5, 241; AA
Travel Library 57 (top); Acestock.com 52-3; AKG Images
233 (Erik Bohr); Art Archive 20, 37, 38, 212 (left)
(photos Dagli Orti); Bridgeman Art Library–British
Museum 9; Corbis 14 (Nathan Benn), 4 and 16 below
(Ed Kashi), 77 below (Michael Freeman); Angelo Hornak
51; Robert Harding/Travel Library 115; Katz Pictures 15
(Carlos Angel); Museo Nacional Reina Sophia, Madrid ©
DACS 2005 249; Peter Newark's American Pictures 45;
V&A Images 78–9.

All other photographs were taken on the road by Dan
Cruickshank, Andrea Illescas, Lee Curran, Mike Garner,
Tim Dunn, Tim Sutton and Nicholas Reeks.

A CIP catalogue record for this book
is available from the British Library.

ISBN 0 297 84399 0

Design director David Rowley
Editorial director Susan Haynes
Designed by Clive Hayball
Edited by Jennie Condell
Cartography by Maps Ink
Title logo designed by Nick Robertson, Wordsalad
Additional picture research by Tom Graves

Printed in Italy

Weidenfeld & Nicolson
The Orion Publishing Group Ltd
Orion House
5 Upper Saint Martin's Lane
London WC2H 9EA

www.orionbooks.co.uk

Above *Dan within sight of home.*

Acknowledgements

I would like to thank Jane Root, former Controller
of BBC2 and Roly Keating, Controller of BBC2,
for commissioning and supporting the 80 Treasures
project; Mark Harrison, Creative Director of Arts,
and Franny Moyle, Controller of Commissioning
Arts, for their commitment to the series and Basil
Comely, Executive Producer, for his major creative
contribution and tireless energy; Tim Dunn and
Jonty Claypole for inspirational conversation
during filming; John Holdsworth for his initial edit
of the early material and John Mullen, Andrea
Illescas, Jan Cholawo, Joanna Crickmay and
Andrea Carnevali for their skill and great energy in
the edit suite; Matthew Hill, Phil Cairney, Laura
Martin-Robinson, Rocio Cano and Seren Beckett
for help with research and organisation; Paul
Ralph, Production Manager, and Simon Larkins,
Production Co-ordinator, for their logistical
support; Nick Ray, Chako Bellamy, Paul Cripps,
Toby Sinclair, Samson Mekonnen, Ruthy Lustig-
Dassa and Ousmane Diallo for help in their
respective countries. At the publishers, Michael
Dover for commissioning this book, Susan Haynes,
Editorial Director, and editor Jennie Condell for
working at speed with a very long manuscript
appearing in irregular – and often rather infrequent
– instalments, and David Rowley, Design Director,
and designer Clive Hayball for making a fine
looking book in a such a very short period of time.